It's My Retirement Money
Take Good Care of It
The TIAA-CREF Story

Other publications of the
PENSION RESEARCH COUNCIL

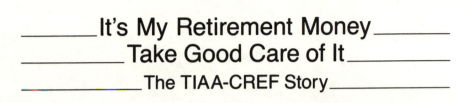

It's My Retirement Money
Take Good Care of It
The TIAA-CREF Story

WILLIAM C. GREENOUGH, PH.D.

Published for the
Pension Research Council
Wharton School
University of Pennsylvania

by

IRWIN

Homewood, IL 60430
Boston, MA 02116

© 1990 by Pension Research Council of the Wharton School
University of Pennsylvania

Sponsoring editor: Michael W. Junior
Project editor: Paula M. Buschman
Production manager: Diane Palmer
Compositor: BookMasters, Inc.
Typeface: 10/12 Melior
Printer: R. R. Donnelley & Sons Company

Library of Congress Cataloging-in-Publication Data

Greenough, William C.
   It's my retirement money—take good care of
it: the TIAA-CREF story by William C. Greenough.
     p.   cm.
  ISBN 0-256-08657-5
   1. Teachers—Pensions—United States. 2. College teachers—
Pensions—United States. 3. Teachers Insurance and Annuity
Association. 4. College Retirement Equities Fund. 5. Pension
trusts—United States—Investments. 6. Retirement income—United
States. I. Title.
LB2842.2.G74 1990
331.25'2913711'00973—dc20   89–26898
                                              CIP

Printed in the United States of America
1 2 3 4 5 6 7 8 9 0 D O 7 6 5 4 3 2 1 0

PENSION RESEARCH COUNCIL

STRUCTURE AND ROLE OF THE COUNCIL

Founded in 1952, the Pension Research Council is one of several research organizations within the Wharton School of the University of Pennsylvania. As part of the nation's first school of business, the Council functions in a bracing environment of academic freedom and objectivity. The basic purpose of the Council is to undertake research that will strengthen those arrangements designed to provide the financial resources needed for a secure and dignified old age. It seeks to broaden public understanding of these complex arrangements through basic research into their social, economic, legal, actuarial, and financial foundations. Although geared to the long view of the pension institution, projects undertaken by the Council are always relevant to real world concerns and frequently focus on issues under current debate.

The Council is composed of individuals from large corporate plan sponsors, organized labor, actuarial consulting firms, the accounting profession, the legal profession, investment counselors, banks, insurance companies, not-for-profit organizations, and several academic disciplines. The Council does not speak with one voice and espouses no particular point of view. The members do share a general desire to encourage and strengthen private sector approaches to old age economic security, while recognizing the essential role of Social Security and other income maintenance programs in the public sector.

The members of the Council are appointed by the dean of the Wharton School and serve indeterminate terms. The Council reviews the findings of current research projects, acts to generate new research proposals, and reviews external proposals. In performing these functions, the members identify areas in which additional research is needed, consider the general form the research should take, then evaluate the qualification of persons deemed capable of carrying out the approved projects.

The research projects are carried out by persons commissioned under individually designed ad hoc arrangements. The researchers are normally academic scholars, but non-academic experts with special qualifications for the tasks involved may be used. The research findings are reviewed by members of the Council, who may offer criticism as to both the substance of the report and the inferences drawn from the studies. The author of any manuscript is free to accept or reject the criticisms of the Council members, but the latter have the privilege of recording in the published document their dissent from any interpretative statements or points of view expressed by the author. Whether or not written dissents are included, publication should not be interpreted to indicate either agreement or disagreement by the Council or its individual members with the substance of the document or its inferences.

Preface

This volume is a history of the largest private sector retirement system in the world, a trailblazing organization that helped shape the private pension movement from its earliest days. The history has been told by someone who observed the organization for almost a half century and played a major role in its affairs for 38 years. The author, Dr. William C. Greenough, joined the organization in 1941 as assistant to the president and remained with it until 1979, the last 22 years as president and then chairman and chief executive officer. Because of TIAA-CREF's pioneering role, Dr. Greenough's chronicle sheds important light on the evolution of pension philosophy, policy, and practice in the United States, a longtime interest of the Pension Research Council.

It's My Retirement Money—Take Good Care of It is an admonition frequently heard by TIAA-CREF representatives in their contacts with TIAA-CREF participants. It seemed fitting, therefore, to use that title for a book that traces the origins and early tribulations of TIAA-CREF and describes the operating philosophy and practices of an organization that holds in trust the retirement hopes of more than one million college professors and supporting staff.

This is not an "official" history of TIAA-CREF. Rather, it is a history of the organization as witnessed, interpreted, and, to a substantial degree, *made* by Dr. Greenough. It is a *sanctioned* history, receiving the full cooperation of the company. Dr. Greenough had unlimited access to the company's files, archives, oral history, and staff. The completed manuscript was reviewed by appropriate company executives for factual accuracy as to all events and developments.

This is a story of the successes, failures, enthusiasms, controversies, and stunning growth of TIAA-CREF. Dr. Greenough vigorously and, for the most part, persuasively defends TIAA-CREF policies and practices, many of which he was instrumental in implementing. He does not presume to be detached or objective in his assessments of the organization's contribution to the academic world, social welfare, the economy, or the sound development of the private pension universe. In contemporary jargon, Dr. Greenough puts his own, inimitable "spin" on events and policies.

The book is written in the forceful and arresting style that those who have known Dr. Greenough over the years have come to expect— and savor. It is spiced with wry humor and interesting anecdotes, usually in the first person singular. It should be of special interest to the more than a million individuals affiliated with TIAA-CREF: the trustees, officers, and employees of the organization; participants in the system and their beneficiaries; and sponsoring colleges, universities, and scientific bodies. Competing financial institutions— insurance companies, banks, mutual funds, and investment advisors—would be well advised to read it. The rich detail of the book should make it especially appealing to the serious student of private pensions.

Dr. Greenough passed away suddenly only weeks before this book went to press. The book is at once a monument to the unique organization that he served for 38 years and a testament to his own managerial skills, grasp of broad economic forces, creativity, political acumen, social sensitivity, and dedication to a financially secure retirement for those who labor in the vineyards of academe.

The Pension Research Council is proud to publish this authoritative account of the life and times of a truly distinctive, innovative, social-minded pension institution. Needless to say, the views and opinions expressed in the book are not to be attributed to the Council or any of its members.

January 1990   Dan M. McGill

                                                     Chairman and Director
                                                     Pension Research Council

Foreword

I first became a TIAA-CREF policyholder in 1957 when I was a young foundation officer. Not long after that, the name "William C. Greenough" began to appear on my pension fund materials. Later, as I moved to Michigan State University and then to the State University of New York, taking my TIAA-CREF policies with me, that name seemed to be following me. It was practically synonymous with TIAA-CREF.

In time, I came to know Bill Greenough personally. And I came to the realization that in his 16 years as TIAA-CREF chairman, the distinction between Bill and TIAA-CREF's reputation for excellence was practically invisible. Bill's remarkable tenure of 38 years with the company covers more than half of TIAA-CREF's total corporate history!

Thus, when it came time to write "the book" on TIAA-CREF, there was only one person who could give the inside story. And that is what Bill has done.

This is not an official history sponsored and published by TIAA-CREF. It is an individual project undertaken by Bill Greenough several years after his retirement. In doing so, he had the full cooperation of TIAA-CREF in his extensive research to assure the accuracy of the material.

The book tells how he saw events from his unique perspective. It describes the significant happenings that occurred over nearly three quarters of a century to shape a remarkable nonprofit organization that was to become the largest private pension plan in the world. Perhaps most importantly, it relates the philosophy behind the pioneering efforts to establish a portable pension system that would provide a dignified and secure retirement for those employed in colleges, universities, independent schools, and other educational institutions identified in our charter.

Along the way, Bill Greenough became *the* recognized expert on pensions and public policy and the application of retirement systems to American higher education. He has written books on the subject and has spoken extensively here and abroad.

It's My Retirement Money—Take Good Care of It, by William C. Greenough, then, is more than just a book about a company. It is the story of a movement that has transformed the way we think about, and plan for, retirement. My only regret is that Bill is not with us to witness the culmination of his tremendous efforts. We are indebted to Bill Greenough for telling that story and for his contributions to it.

Dr. Clifton R. Wharton, Jr.

Chairman and CEO
TIAA-CREF

Author's Acknowledgments

The name of this study, *It's My Retirement Money—Take Good Care of It*, is a direct quote or near quote from thousands of our friends, acquaintances, or newly met academics over the years. It reflects their deep interest in TIAA-CREF and its importance to their financial security.

What a pleasure it would be if I could include in the text all of the names of the college presidents, professors, business and personnel officers, officers of the educational associations in Washington, and the trustees, officers, and staff of TIAA-CREF over the last 70 years who helped build the college world's pension plan, extend its services to college people, and administer its actuarial, legal, investment, benefit payment, and other operations. It was especially difficult to omit the names of so many people with whom I had worked closely; I thank them all.

In doing this study I have enjoyed the full support and cooperation of TIAA-CREF, including access to voluminous files, correspondence, oral histories, and talks and communications with many people. Dr. Clifton R. Wharton's encouragement was crucial. Three officers, Peter C. Clapman, Francis P. King, and Robert Perrin, read entire drafts and made helpful suggestions. I must mention just a few TIAA-CREF names as proxies for the rest: Bruce L. Boyd, J. Daniel Lee, Jr., James S. Martin, John J. McCormack, James M. Mulanaphy, Claire M. Sheahan, William T. Slater, John A. Somers, Thomas G. Walsh, and Steven N. Weisbart. Alan Pifer and James A. Perkins, former officers of our parent Carnegie organizations, made useful suggestions as to Carnegie support of pensions. A number of knowledgeable outside people, including TIAA-CREF trustees, responded to drafts of chapters or sections.

Carolyn Kopp, my research assistant on the project, is responsible for the quality of the references, organization, and research. I appreciated her ability to return my word processor to human control whenever I lost it.

I accept full responsibility for the inadequacies, the errors of omission and commission, and the views and conclusions expressed.

New York   William C. Greenough
December 1989

Contents

PART ONE

Carnegie Parentage— TIAA's First 35 Years

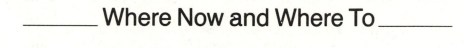

CHAPTER 1

Where Now and Where To

One million college staff members and their 4,300 employing educational institutions have built, over the last 70 years, the largest private pension system in the United States and in the world. This is the story of that system. It is the story of the successes, the failures, the enthusiasms, the controversies, and the stunning growth of the system and the implications for financial security throughout life.

This system is an unexpected twosome with a full paragraph for a name: Teachers Insurance and Annuity Association of America and College Retirement Equities Fund. I will save several pages in this book and some of your time by referring to it as TIAA-CREF.

It is the only large, multi-employer, immediately vested, portable, fully funded pension system anywhere in the world. In a number of ways, it is a model toward which U.S. private pension plans, encouraged by federal legislation, are moving.

Unique it is. But the story of TIAA-CREF and its predecessor free pension system for college professors is intertwined with America's steps toward retirement security for all its people; therefore, it has broad interest. The Carnegie free pensions established in 1905 for college teachers were among the early organized pensions in this country; the portable TIAA system in 1918 preceded by 20 years portable pensions through Social Security for employed Americans. The invention of CREF in 1952 marked an exciting attempt to attack the financial distress caused for retired people by inflation. Crucial to these events were many educators, economists, governmental and financial leaders and also frequent interactions with government, most pleasant and positive, some less so.

Andrew Carnegie's free pension scheme for college professors might not have been proposed if he had not been elected a trustee of

Cornell University in 1890. He "was shocked to discover that college teachers were paid only about as much as office clerks."[1] So in 1905, he established a free pension fund, the Carnegie Foundation, with the hope that "this Fund may do much for the cause of higher education and to remove a source of deep and constant anxiety to the poorest paid and yet one of the highest of all professions."[2] When the college world outgrew the Carnegie plan 10 years later, a new organization, TIAA, was set up to fund and make permanent a system of college pensions for institutions in the United States, Canada, and Newfoundland. TIAA, in turn, invented the variable annuity based on equity investments in 1952 to help professors cope with the growing economic problems of inflation.

EARLY PENSIONS

Individuals and societies have had to cope with the presence and problems of the aged for a long time. Almost all of the coping was through family efforts, tribal and community support, or charity. Bismarck introduced the first national social security scheme in Germany in 1883 and 1889, preceding Social Security in the United States by half a century.

The first formal pension plan in the United States, that of the American Express Company, was established in 1875. The plan originally applied only to "permanently incapacitated" workers, that is, disabled elderly employees.[3]

Before 1890, such few pension plans as there were in the United States were scarcely more than announcements that the employer hoped to pay stated benefits to those who fulfilled certain requirements.

College pension planning was no further advanced than industrial planning.[4] During the 19th century, most colleges were small, intimate groups of professors and students. When a professor reached the point where he could no longer continue in service, he might have been given a pension out of the institution's current income in recognition of his service and accomplishments. As was true in other walks of life, no responsibility for planning ahead on a group basis was recognized in the colleges. Problems of retirement were thought

---

[1]Robert M. Lester, *Forty Years of Carnegie Giving* (New York: Charles Scribner's Sons, 1941), p. 45.

[2]Ibid., p. 153.

[3]Murray Webb Latimer, *Industrial Pension Systems in the United States and Canada*, 2 vols. (New York: Industrial Relations Counselors, Inc., 1932), vol. 1, p. 21.

[4]William C. Greenough (hereafter WCG), *College Retirement and Insurance Plans* (New York: Columbia University Press, 1948), pp. 7–8.

of as individual and were handled individually. In 1763, for instance, Samuel Johnson, the first president of King's College, later Columbia University, was retired on a pension of 50 pounds per annum. During the next 129 years, a number of Columbia faculty members were retired on university-paid stipends. In 1892, the university started providing a pension of half salary at the option of the professors or the trustees for any professors at age 65 who had completed 15 or more years of service.

By the turn of the 20th century, Yale, Harvard, Cornell, the University of California, and, in Canada, McGill and the University of Toronto all had established more or less, usually less, formal plans for retirement of faculty members.

OLD AGE SECURITY, THEN AND NOW

For workers and their families in America, real progress toward retirement security came with the introduction of Social Security half a century ago. It continues to be the main reliance for income in old age. In 1986, it provided over 40 percent of all income for persons aged 70 or older.[5] It now covers nearly all working Americans and their dependents. It pays out over $300 billion in retirement, disability, survivor, and medical benefits each year.[6] Social Security benefits are supplemented by a broad range of federal, state, and local welfare payments based on needs. A large and rapidly growing element of old age security is employer pensions, private and public, now amounting to almost $200 billion a year.[7] Additional old age financial security comes from private savings and other sources.

The proportion of old people who are poor is now slightly smaller than the proportion of younger people who are poor in America. Most of the old who are poor are women, and recent changes in public and private pensions should gradually reduce this problem. What a contrast with 50 years ago when 90 percent of older people were in poverty or only escaped it through charity, poorhouses, or family support. Social Security, private pensions, and personal savings have transformed our society since the Great Depression.

Social Security came late to the college world—on a voluntary basis in 1951 for employees of private institutions and 1955 for public institutions. Its retirement and survivor benefits, and later disability and medical benefits, proved to be a welcome foundation for the pri-

---

[5]U.S. Department of Health and Human Services, Social Security Administration, *Social Security Bulletin, Annual Statistical Supplement, 1988*, p. 6.

[6]Ibid., pp. 2–3.

[7]Employee Benefit Research Institute (EBRI), *Employee Benefit Notes* 9 (November 1988), p. 9.

vate pension plans that had come early to the colleges. TIAA-CREF has paid out $24 billion in benefits and dividends credited since 1918. The rapidly increasing benefits including dividends now exceed $3.5 billion a year. Two hundred thousand people are receiving TIAA-CREF retirement income.

TIAA benefit plans also protect against other risks. Long-term disability benefits are provided for 400,000 individuals employed at 1,500 institutions; group survivor benefits are provided for 174,000 employees. Some of this has been developed with the encouragement of the Ford Foundation and other foundation grants, some in working directly with the college world. As a result, the tenured college professor continues to have among the broadest lifetime security arrangements of all professions, even though many claim with good reason that the profession is persistently and chronically underpaid when considering the educational attainment of its practitioners.

The story of TIAA-CREF is deeply intertwined with the story of financial security in America and of higher education in America. And because of their impressive size, TIAA and CREF are major factors in the investment world, providing capital for America's growth.

But on with the story. First, a visit with Andrew Carnegie, who started it all.

ANDREW CARNEGIE, FANTASTIC SCOTSMAN

His Philanthropic Impulses

I never saw Andrew Carnegie. I was five when he died. But I am sure I know him. I have a clear picture of him in my mind. Diminutive (5 feet 2 inches), a natural Santa Claus, handing out from his half-a-billion-dollar philanthropic sack more than 2,500 libraries in the United States, Great Britain, and the Commonwealth; a great museum in Pittsburgh; a grand concert hall in New York; 7,600 church organs; vast research, scientific, and learning institutions from Pittsburgh to Washington to Edinburgh, Scotland; and a hope-inspired Peace Palace in the Hague.[8]

Nor did Carnegie suffer from an edifice complex; he was also a humane people person. He applauded individual attainments—for example, a die caster who sustained serious injury in rescuing a man

---

[8]On Andrew Carnegie's life and philanthropic activities, see: *Andrew Carnegie's Own Story* (Edinburgh: The Carnegie Dunfermline Trust by permission of Houghton Mifflin Company, Boston and New York, 1984); Simon Goodenough, *The Greatest Good Fortune: Andrew Carnegie's Gift for Today* (Edinburgh: Macdonald Publishers, 1985); Burton J. Hendrick, *Andrew Carnegie* (Garden City, N.Y.: Doubleday, Doran and Company, Inc., 1932); Lester, *Forty Years of Carnegie Giving*; Joseph Frazier Wall, *Andrew Carnegie* (New York: Oxford University Press, 1970).

whose clothing caught fire in a foundry; a pregnant woman who jumped into fast-flowing water and saved a small boy and just four days later gave birth; and a mine superintendent who lost his life leading a rescue party back into the mine. His various Carnegie Hero Fund Scrolls of Honor contain over 13,000 names of peacetime heroes, each of whom received a Carnegie award and usually financial help. Over the decades a changing society is reflected in the hero awards: rescues from drowning have remained high, but incidents involving trains have declined sharply and rescues from runaway horses have almost vanished.

Carnegie also glowed with personal concern when it came to the field of pensions, the objective of this study. He was deeply worried about the financial plight of productive persons when they became too old to work. Nineteenth century America had seen the start of only a few industrial pension plans, often with questionable financial and contractual soundness.[9] Carnegie was a leader in starting pension services. One of his first gifts after selling his steel interests in 1901 was a pension fund of $4 million for his Carnegie steel employees, which in 1910 became the United States Steel and Carnegie Pensions Fund.

He set up the Home Trust Company also in 1901 to handle his financial interests after his retirement and to assure that the pensions he had promised would continue. These pension promises included, in addition to his Carnegie steel workers, provisions for his former co-workers on the Pennsylvania Railroad, fellow telegraphers from the Civil War, and scores of others. Carnegie wrote in his autobiography:

> Of all my work of a philanthropic character, my private pension fund gives me the highest and noblest return. No satisfaction equals that of feeling you have been permitted to place in comfortable circumstances, in their old age, people whom you have long known to be kind and good and in every way deserving, but who, from no fault of their own, have not sufficient means to live respectably, free from solicitude as to their mere maintenance. Modest sums insure this freedom.[10]

One of his humane, but politically disastrous, impulses was to propose an annual pension of $25,000 for each ex-president of the United States and his unmarried widow because the government "failed to uphold their dignity by providing such pensions." He ran

---

[9]Rainard B. Robbins, *Pension Planning in the United States*, ed. WCG (New York: unpublished manuscript distributed by Teachers Insurance and Annuity Association of America, 1952), pp. 2–3.

[10]*Andrew Carnegie's Own Story*, pp. 143–44.

into a cacophony of editorial and political criticism from Maine to California for trying to use his wealth to influence the presidency of the United States. As a result, his free pensions for all presidents were never implemented. But under Mr. Carnegie's will, pensions were paid to Mrs. Grover Cleveland, Mrs. Theodore Roosevelt, and William Howard Taft.

In 1905, Carnegie established the free pension system for college professors, which led directly to the development of TIAA and then CREF. It is interesting to contemplate why the editorial writers and public became so exercised over the "dangers" of great wealth influencing the presidents of the United States by providing some financial security in old age, but worried far less over the possible influence on thousands of professors and their succeeding generations of students through the same provision of free pensions.

All of Carnegie's concern was in character. In 1889, when his wealth was piling up, Carnegie's famous essay on wealth appeared in the *North American Review*; it was reprinted in Britain under the better-known title *Gospel of Wealth* and published in book form in 1900. Carnegie's proposals for a scientific philanthropy rested on his belief that the millionaire should "sell all that he hath and give it in the highest and best form to the poor by administering his estate himself for the good of his fellows."[11]

Carnegie's *Gospel of Wealth* also contained high-flown and descriptive elements of his philosophy: "Not until the dollars are transmuted into service for others, in one of the many forms best calculated to appeal to and develop the higher things of the moral, intellectual, and esthetic life, has wealth completely justified its existence."[12]

A Bit about His Life

Andrew Carnegie was born in Dunfermline, Scotland, on November 25, 1835. The town's most important industry was linen weaving. With a population of 11,500, there was about one hand loom for every three people. But the importation of "cheap cotton" from the European mainland and the development of mechanized looms in factories that "exploited women and children" spelled doom for the linen industry in Dunfermline. When riots and strikes broke out in Scotland, Carnegie wrote that Dunfermline was "long renowned as the most radical town in this kingdom." Carnegie wrote that he "developed into a violent young republican whose motto was 'death to priv-

---

[11]Quoted in Goodenough, *Greatest Good Fortune*, p. 4.
[12]Ibid., p. 45.

ilege.' " It is perhaps not surprising that the laird of Pittencrieff Park and Glen excluded the Carnegies from his private park. Years later, Carnegie bought the park and opened it to the public.

In 1848, the Carnegie family joined the flood of 2 million people who crowded between decks of small sailing vessels to come to America. Andrew, then age 12, his parents, William and Margaret, and his brother, 5-year-old Thomas, landed in New York and set out for Pittsburgh, where Margaret's sisters lived. It does not now sound sensible to go to Pittsburgh via Albany and Cleveland, as they did, but there were no railroads, let alone autos, buses, or airplanes, from the East Coast to Pittsburgh in 1848.

Young Carnegie was a hustler. By age 33, he had an income of over $50,000 a year and concluded, "Beyond this never earn—make no effort to increase fortune, but spend the surplus each year for benevolent purposes. Cast aside business forever except for others."[13] Carnegie then decided to retire at age 35 and study; he missed his retirement date by 30 years and several hundred million dollars. But he did turn over active management of his companies to his brother and to others after 1868, and spent much of his time in Scotland and traveling in Europe. He was probably history's most successful "part-time" employee (a hands-off executive).

Carnegie was a builder in the age of America's empire builders and financial wizards. He built the Carnegie steel works, he invested in oil, sleeping cars, and the telegraph. When Carnegie learned trains were often delayed coming into Pittsburgh because sparks ignited the wooden bridges, he joined forces with a Pennsylvania mechanic-inventor, and their venture became the Keystone Bridge Company. Carnegie built companies to build things Americans needed. He was not free of controversy—the notorious Homestead Strike in July 1892 hurt his reputation as a conscientious employer. At the time of the strike, Carnegie was in a remote area of Scotland when Pinkerton guards, hired by Carnegie's manager, Henry Clay Frick, were used to forcibly break the strike. Carnegie acquiesced to Frick's tactics, though he had originally instructed Frick to simply close the plant in order to break the union. He paid dearly for his silence in the scathing articles and editorials that appeared in newspapers on both sides of the Atlantic.

A few years earlier, Carnegie had strongly stated in his *Gospel of Wealth*, "A person who dies rich dies disgraced," advice of limited practical use to most people. When he reached 65, in 1900, Carnegie did retire. He sold his Carnegie Steel Company to J. Pierpont Morgan for $480 million as part of by far the largest leveraged buyout up to

---

[13]Ibid., p. 25.

that time. Some say Carnegie could have gotten another $100 million, that he did not drive a hard enough bargain, but that would have made his job of not dying "disgraced" that much harder.

Carnegie not only did not die disgraced, but his great charitable tradition is alive and strong 150 years later. I was privileged to represent TIAA and CREF as well as the Carnegie Institution of Washington at a 1985 gathering of his philanthropic clan at Skibo Castle, Carnegie's summer home in Dunfermline, Scotland. The weeklong affair was resplendent, academic, nostalgic, and a great honor to the fantastic Scotsman. Interestingly, his daughter almost attended but was too frail—think about it, he was born in 1835! Margaret Carnegie Miller was born in 1897 to Carnegie's late marriage; she is an honorary member of the board of Carnegie Corporation of New York.

CHAPTER 2

_____ A Stunning Announcement— _____
_____ Carnegie Free College Pensions _____

Into the embryonic pension world of the early 20th century came the stunning announcement of Andrew Carnegie's magnificent gift of $10 million to pension all present and future college professors at a number of prestigious American colleges and universities.

When Carnegie became a trustee of Cornell University in 1890 he was appalled to find how small were the salaries of the professors.[1] He concluded it was almost impossible for a professor to save for his old age. The problem made a deep impression on him, and he frequently discussed the matter with prominent educators of the time.

In 1904, Carnegie found a kindred spirit in Henry S. Pritchett, then president of the Massachusetts Institute of Technology. Pritchett, an astronomer, had served with distinction as director of Washington University's Observatory and as head of the Coast and Geodetic Survey. At MIT, however, his tenure as president since 1900 had been controversial. Pritchett's proposal that MIT strengthen its financial and educational position by a collaboration with Harvard University's Lawrence Scientific School had met with vocal opposition from the institute's alumni and faculty.

Fortunately, Dr. Pritchett's broad interests included the Carnegie Institution of Washington. In the spring of 1904, Mr. Carnegie and Dr. Pritchett met at a White House luncheon given by Theodore Roosevelt (the president was an ex-officio member of the Carnegie Institution's board of trustees). The Pritchetts and Carnegies shared adjacent train seats from Washington, and during that summer, Dr. and Mrs. Pritchett visited the Carnegies' summer home, Skibo Castle, in

---

[1]Lester, *Forty Years of Carnegie Giving*, p. 45.

1905–1930
FROM FREE TO FUNDED

Andrew Carnegie

*Henry S. Pritchett, President,
Carnegie Foundation, 1905–30;
President, TIAA, 1918–30.*

Scotland. Asked by Carnegie about his mission in Europe, Pritchett replied, "I am trying to get a $25,000 professor for a $7,500 salary."[2] (Pritchett was aiming high or perhaps memories were a bit fuzzy; full professors' salaries at that time averaged $1,800 a year.)

The two men talked about ways to improve the economic standing of college teaching and of the importance to teachers and to higher education of old age provisions. Carnegie knew all his millions could not greatly raise teachers' salaries, but he believed he might help education by providing retirement allowances for professors in leading colleges and universities. Having decided on this, he announced his gift on April 16, 1905, in a letter to the 25 educators who were to become trustees of the administering organization:[3]

> Gentlemen:
>
> I have reached the conclusion that the least rewarded of all the professions is that of the teacher in our higher educational institutions. . . .
>
> I have, therefore, transferred to you and your successors, as Trustees, $10,000,000 . . . the revenue from which is to provide retiring pensions for the teachers of Universities, Colleges, and Technical Schools in our country, Canada and Newfoundland under such conditions as you may adopt from time to time. Expert calculation shows that the revenue will be ample for the purpose. . . .
>
> I hope this Fund may do much for the cause of higher education and to remove a source of deep and constant anxiety to the poorest paid and yet one of the highest of all professions. Gratefully yours,
>
> (Signed) Andrew Carnegie

THE CARNEGIE FOUNDATION

The trustees at once established the Carnegie Foundation, incorporated in the state of New York. During the summer of 1905, a special committee of trustees composed of Dr. Pritchett and Frank A. Vanderlip, a financier, sought information from institutions of higher education throughout the United States and Canada that would lead to an assessment of the number of institutions eligible to participate in the pension system and of the number of pensions required.

The first formal meeting of the newly incorporated foundation was held at Carnegie's residence, 2 East 91st Street in New York City, November 15, 1905. The meeting was attended by the heads of the top

---

[2]This incident was related to Abraham Flexner by Henry Pritchett; see Abraham Flexner, *Henry S. Pritchett: A Biography* (New York: Columbia University Press, 1943), p. 87. See also, Henry S. Pritchett, "Beginnings of the Carnegie Foundation," in The Carnegie Foundation for the Advancement of Teaching (hereafter cited as CFAT), *30th Annual Report*, 1935, pp. 29–35.

[3]CFAT, *1st Annual Report*, 1906, pp. 7–8.

private institutions in America, including Nicholas Murray Butler of Columbia University, Charles W. Eliot of Harvard, Arthur T. Hadley of Yale, Charles C. Harrison of the University of Pennsylvania, David Starr Jordan of Stanford University, Henry C. King of Oberlin College, Henry S. Pritchett of MIT, Jacob Gould Schurman of Cornell, and Woodrow Wilson of Princeton. At this meeting, Dr. Pritchett was elected the first president of the Foundation.[4]

SURVEY OF HIGHER EDUCATION—FIRST OF MANY

The initial step of the trustees was to make perhaps the first national survey of higher education. The free pension system was limited to private, nonsectarian colleges and universities. So the trustees had to determine which colleges imposed "any theological test" and which were really preparatory schools. Because state universities were not included until Carnegie added $5 million a year later, the degree of public association had to be determined. From these studies emerged a new interest in the character and quality of educational institutions. The Carnegie Foundation has continued through the decades and under exceptional leadership—Henry Pritchett, Henry Suzzallo, Walter A. Jessup, Oliver C. Carmichael, John W. Gardner, Alan Pifer, Ernest L. Boyer—to be a voice of conscience and leadership in education.

In 1906, the Carnegie Foundation was reincorporated under a federal charter with a new name, The Carnegie Foundation for the Advancement of Teaching. The new charter accomplished two major purposes: it provided for a self-perpetuating and permanent board of trustees, and it broadened the foundation's mandate to reflect Carnegie's and the trustees' objective of "the upbuilding and the strengthening of the calling of the teacher."[5]

Meanwhile, Dr. Pritchett was getting the free pension system under way.[6] Originally, the foundation had concluded 112 institutions were tentatively eligible for the provisions of the gift. Among these institutions were 2,653 teachers of professorial rank, averaging $1,800 in annual salary. Assessing potential liabilities, it was estimated that pensions of 50 percent of active pay might be payable to about 300 retired teachers, at an annual cost of $300,000. After adding a plan for disability pensions for "those who break down in health and are compelled to give up active work," the total estimated annual expenditures of the foundation, including administrative costs, were

---

[4]CFAT, *1st Annual Report*, 1906, p. 10.

[5]CFAT, *1st Annual Report*, 1906, p. 18.

[6]See the Carnegie Foundation's Annual Reports and, for a general history, Howard J. Savage, *Fruit of an Impulse: Forty-Five Years of The Carnegie Foundation, 1905–1950* (New York: Harcourt, Brace and Company, Inc., 1953).

$410,000. The sum was deemed to be well within the income-generating capacity of the foundation's $10 million endowment.

The foundation refined its first list of eligible institutions by adopting rules for academic acceptance. New York State laws were used for the definition of a *college*, and entrance requirements followed closely those set by the College Entrance Examination Board, founded in 1900. The definition of *professors* included those of rank of "presidents, deans, professors, associate professors, and assistant professors," with at least 15 years of service. Provisions were also made for widows if they had been married for at least 10 years of the professor's service (widowers were not specifically provided for). Also eligible were "librarians, registrars, recorders, and administrative officers of long tenure."

By June 1906, 52 institutions had been placed on the accepted list for free pensions for their staff members. Retiring allowances had been granted to 33 professors and 4 widows. By 1915, 73 colleges and universities were admitted to the associated institutions. The final number was 96.

OVERCOMMITMENT

The original system was for a somewhat open-ended group of eligible individuals. Gradually recognizing the financial implications, the foundation tried to restrict its rules for allowances after 1909. Not even these measures sufficed, however, and in November 1915, the foundation took steps toward closing its list of eligibles. This difficult and thankless task was not completed until 1931, when the foundation adopted its final list, by name, of professors, wives, and widows. (There was an occasional woman professor, but no widower recipient.)

Another serious financial problem arose from the standard benefit formula. In 1909, the retiring allowance given to a professor in an accepted institution after attaining age 65 and after completing 15 years of service as a professor was computed at $400 more than one half of active pay—averaged from age 60 to age 65—with a maximum of $4,000.

This formula had an unintended result. College trustees apparently concluded full professors suddenly became worthy of a higher salary from age 60 on than they ever had before. When this halo effect was added to the inflationary rise of all salaries, including those of college professors, and when college staffs began to increase rapidly, the foundation found itself going broke.

This free pension scheme was essentially a defined benefit "final average salary" pension plan. It initially provided "$400 plus half salary"—open-ended benefits to an originally open-ended number of people—supported by a limited fixed fund. This arrangement was not likely to achieve financial success any more in the early 1900s than at present.

It became clear that the foundation would run out of money long before it ran out of eager, eligible professors. Facing serious financial problems, the foundation inaugurated a comprehensive review in 1915. Rapid growth of faculties coupled with rising salaries after World War I made it necessary to limit the number of persons who could benefit and the generosity of the benefits originally announced. Beginning in 1923, the half-salary plus $400 pension at age 65 was scaled down for new retirees, with a reduced maximum benefit available later. By May 1, 1931, the Carnegie Foundation had established a "Closed List of Pensionables." No names could be added to the list; deletions occurred because of deaths and withdrawals from service at specified institutions.

For the succeeding years, only those whose names were on the closed list and who remained in the service of specified institutions until retirement received allowances. The new normal allowance to begin at age 70 was $1,000 a year, plus a $500 a year additional single life annuity purchased by Carnegie Corporation from TIAA for the professors. Under a 1938 rule, an eligible professor could take a smaller benefit for retirement between age 65 and 70. A widow's benefit equal to half the professor's benefit was paid to widows married at the time of his retirement and married for 10 years at the time of his death.

These cutbacks, however, were not sufficient to solve the foundation's financial problems. The rescue came from another Carnegie philanthropy, Carnegie Corporation of New York. The corporation, created in November 1911 when Carnegie was 76, was endowed as a permanent philanthropic corporation with the bulk of his remaining fortune, $125 million.[7] Over the years, Carnegie Corporation gave the foundation $12 million and lent it interest-free an additional $15 million to support the free pensions. It also purchased $6.9 million in supplemental annuities for Carnegie pensioners from TIAA.

From its establishment in 1905 to June 30, 1989, the CFAT paid a total of $86,967,822 in free retiring allowances, disability allowances, and widow's pensions. On that date, 68 persons were still receiving free Carnegie pensions: one professor, Orlan W. Boston, and 67 widows. This remarkable disparity resulted not only from the greater longevity of women, but also because CFAT placed no restrictions on the age of wives at marriage. The dollar figures compare startlingly with the $15 million given by Andrew Carnegie for free pensions.

---

[7]Goodenough, *Greatest Good Fortune*, pp. 151–71; Wall, *Andrew Carnegie*, pp. 882–83.

Carnegie's letter of gift in 1905 had said of the original endowment gift: "Expert calculation shows that the revenue will be ample for the purpose. . . ." The free college pensions ended up with a cost overrun worthy even of the Pentagon!

OTHER PENSION LESSONS LEARNED

The pioneering free college pension system was rich in learning experiences for the entire pension world. Not all of its lessons have yet been well learned.

The lessons were not solely economic. As the foundation discovered, the administration of the free pension system had many problems.[8] For one thing, it had become increasingly difficult to justify the selection of a small group of "associated" institutions to the exclusion of others. In a given state or province, two colleges might both be doing useful work, but only one of them might be included in the free pension scheme, to the substantial detriment of the other.

Moreover, a system for a limited number of institutions, although seemingly sound at its formation, had led to the creation of an educational tariff barrier favoring a small group, excluding a larger group, and, as the foundation put it, tending "to restrict the healthy migration of teachers from one college to another."[9] The system tended to strengthen the strong colleges and weaken the weak. It introduced a nonrelated economic factor into professorial job choices. In considering this aspect of the problem, the foundation's Commission on Insurance and Annuities, discussed in full in the next chapter, underlined in its 1917 report the importance of providing pensions broadly and on a contractual basis: the successor system should be able to

> furnish to the teacher the security of a contract, so that the man who enters upon the accumulation of an annuity at 30 may have a contract for its fulfillment . . . [and] to afford these forms of protection in such a manner as to leave to the teacher the utmost freedom of action, and to make his migration from one institution to another easy.[10]

The lesson of security and mobility was especially relevant in the early years of the 20th century when most employer pensions were considered gratuities that could be withheld at the whim of the employer.

---

[8]Henry S. Pritchett, "A Comprehensive Plan of Insurance and Annuities for College Teachers," CFAT, Bulletin no. 9, 1916, pp. 52–58.

[9]CFAT, *11th Annual Report*, 1916, p. 22.

[10]"A Report to the Trustees of the Carnegie Foundation by the Commission Chosen to Consider a Plan of Insurance and Annuities," in CFAT, *12th Annual Report*, 1917, pp. 73–74.

Another problem was that free pensions, in the foundation's view, did not seem to bring out the best in recipients. It was perhaps inevitable that the early liberal eligibility and benefit rules, followed by retrenchments, would cause some vigorous differences of opinion. The so-called service pensions proved especially troublesome. These pensions, granted after 25 years of service completed before age 65, were originally intended for exceptional cases such as disability. But in the foundation's first three years, the majority of 25-year service pensions were granted to professors who were relatively young, at a cost to the foundation far higher than anticipated. "It seems that this rule offers too large a temptation to certain qualities of universal human nature," the foundation concluded.[11] In changing the rules, however, the foundation put itself in the uncomfortable position of disappointing the expectations of a group characterized by Carnegie as "one of the least rewarded of all professions."

One case was especially noteworthy, involving a former professor at Princeton and future president of the United States, who was not happy when he lost his Carnegie free pension because of a career change. As president of Princeton University, Woodrow Wilson was an early board member of the Carnegie Foundation. During his tenure on the board, an ambiguous revision to the service pension rule was made, providing that a free pension might be granted "after the years of service [25] . . . to the executive head of an institution who has displayed distinguished ability as a teacher and educational administrator."[12]

When Dr. Wilson resigned from the Princeton presidency, in order to run for governor of New Jersey, he had to drop off the board of the foundation. But he also lost his free pension under the interpretation of the rules by Dr. Pritchett and the board.[13] Wilson's correspondence with the foundation at the time included such comments as, "I would never have gone into public life with all its risks and uncertainties had I not believed myself entitled . . . to a full retiring allowance. . . . It chagrins me very much . . . to feel that I have been asking for a favor. . . . "[14]

Nonetheless, Dr. Pritchett and the board did not want to be in the position of appearing to give preference to one of their own trustees, especially one only 53 years old, and the allowance was not granted.

---

[11]CFAT, *4th Annual Report*, 1909, p. 72.

[12]Ibid., p. 189.

[13]See Savage, *Fruit of an Impulse*, pp. 85–89; see also Arthur S. Link, ed., *The Papers of Woodrow Wilson*, vol. 22, 1910-1911 (Princeton, N.J.: Princeton University Press, 1976), editor's footnote on pp. 24–25.

[14]Quoted in Savage, *Fruit of an Impulse*, pp. 87–88. This letter is not included in the Princeton edition of Wilson's *Papers* and is apparently not extant.

Apparently Dr. Pritchett personally returned Governor Wilson's application for a free pension, calling it "very injudicious" and worrying that it might be used against him politically. This was undoubtedly good advice, in view of the controversy that ensued when Andrew Carnegie made his offer of free pensions to presidents of the United States and their wives.

Woodrow Wilson's case was by no means an isolated one. The foundation's trustees had originally expected that free pensions would dignify the individual teacher's calling and that the system would exert, as Dr. Pritchett expressed it in 1911, a "moral influence."[15] It was a great disappointment to the foundation to find that a goodly number of college teachers and presidents did not necessarily wish to devote their entire active professional years to college teaching and administration. Dr. Pritchett was bitter in his disillusionment, writing in 1918:

> It would astonish the public, as indeed it astonished the trustees of the Foundation, to discover year by year how many university presidents and teachers, men in the early 50s and in sound health, persuaded themselves that for one reason and another the cause of education or of the public good would be advanced if they were endowed with a pension under some special ruling. The effect of the so-called free pension system is demoralizing to any group in the body politic. Perhaps no other social device goes farther to confuse the sense of responsibility and of personal independence among good men. It is the most prolific breeder of human selfishness. This is the fundamental objection to it.[16]

"So called free pension system!" "Prolific breeder of human selfishness." "Endowed with a pension under some special ruling." "Demoralizing to any group in the body politic." Strong words, these! Do these words, from the start of the century, have any relevance at the end of it?

The reductions in benefits and eligibility for the Carnegie pensions caused some dismay in the educational world and occasioned discussions of moral obligations and rights. The American Association of University Professors took vigorous exception to the reductions in benefits and the limiting of the eligibility lists (see Chapter 3). Professor Harlan Fiske Stone, later Supreme Court Justice, chaired an AAUP committee (formed at Dr. Pritchett's request) that issued two harshly critical reports on the foundation. Some professors even opposed establishment of the successor plan, TIAA, on the grounds that it represented an evasion by the Carnegie Foundation and Corporation of their responsibilities.

---

[15]CFAT, *6th Annual Report*, 1911, p. 22ff.
[16]CFAT, *13th Annual Report*, 1918, p. 21.

MAJOR ADVANCE IN PENSIONS

The most direct benefit of the Carnegie scheme was that by July 1, 1989, it had paid out $87 million in pensions to professors and widows to help them achieve financial security in their old age.

Unquestionably the greatest single contribution to pension philosophy made by the Carnegie free pension system was the concept of portability. To qualify for a retiring allowance under the foundation's original rules, it was not necessary that a teacher spend any specified length of time in any one of the associated institutions. In 1918, this concept of mobility was carried over to the much broader TIAA plan, operating within the entire college world. Then in 1935, 30 years after the foundation was organized, the Federal Social Security Act established transferable old-age retirement benefits for most of the American working force. Thus, Carnegie had an enduring influence on pensions.

BRITISH UNIVERSITIES SUPERANNUATION SCHEME

Midway between the establishment of the free pensions in the United States and the setting up of its permanent successor, TIAA, there was a comparable development in Great Britain. The Federated Superannuation System for Universities, a name almost as unmanageable as Teachers Insurance and Annuity Association of America, was inaugurated to provide portable pensions for teachers in British universities. Two of the basic pension philosophies of the FSSU were parallel to the later conclusions of the Carnegie Foundation, namely, that pensions should be portable and that they should be guaranteed by a third party.[17]

There were two major differences between the FSSU and TIAA. The number of university teachers in Britain was too small to warrant establishment of a new company. So it was decided to contract out the actual provision of annuities. Six British life insurance companies were originally selected to underwrite the plan. The other difference, a significant one and one that had much to do with the eventual demise and restructuring of the FSSU decades later, was the allowance of a lump sum cash amount as an alternative for an annuity upon retirement. In this respect, the FSSU was acting as a deferred savings plan and was not meeting the retirement income objectives either of the British universities or their professors. The allowance of cash values proved to be a fatal flaw.

---

[17]Sir Douglas Logan, *The Birth of a Pension Scheme. A History of the Universities Superannuation Scheme* (Liverpool: Liverpool University Press, 1985).

As early as 1913, the president of the Carnegie Foundation for the Advancement of Teaching, Henry Pritchett, had criticized the cash payment feature of the FSSU:

> The fact that this insurance may be received in a cash payment instead of purchasing an annuity raises a serious question. One of the great benefits of a pension system is the guarantee of support in old age, when, through lack of connection with business affairs, people are peculiarly liable to the danger of bad investments, and susceptible to the influence of designing persons. Whether the security of an annuity should be sacrificed in order to give to the individual great freedom of choice is questionable. In any such system cases are bound to occur, sooner or later, in which a retired beneficiary who had converted his contributions into cash will have lost the money and be in real need.[18]

The most serious defects in the original scheme related to too many uncontrolled choices and the availability of cash. There also were problems with new requirements, in 1947, by the British tax authorities. The old FSSU was replaced April 1, 1975, by a new system, the Universities Superannuation Scheme Limited, which, among other improvements, eliminated the 100 percent lump sum option. This scheme grew painfully out of the remains of the FSSU and was designed to correct its defects. As of March 31, 1988, this new scheme had 236 member institutions, 61,988 active members, and 10,884 retired members.[19]

---

[18]CFAT, *8th Annual Report*, 1913, pp. 45–46.

[19]Universities Superannuation Scheme and Universities Supplementary Dependants (and Ill-Health Retirement) Pension Scheme, Report and Accounts for the Year Ended 31st March 1988, pp. 4, 21.

CHAPTER 3

Getting Ready for TIAA

During its first years, from 1905 to 1918, the Carnegie Foundation conducted pension studies that were the most exhaustive and definitive—epoch making, the foundation called them—of any up to that time. The federal government, states considering public pension plans, and private industry all used the Carnegie studies as important sources of information on pension philosophy and practice. They remain pension classics.

The results of the studies were published in the foundation's annual reports and in special issues of its bulletins. By the mid-1920s, nearly 500 pages in 20 annual reports had been given over to discussion of pension developments, "touching not only teachers, whether in public or endowed institutions, but also workers in industry, military and naval veterans, governmental, state and municipal employees, and even citizens at large, and covering North and South America, Europe, and Australia." Three foundation bulletins discussed pensions for public school teachers, with special reference to plans for the states of Vermont, Virginia, and Colorado.[1]

The studies proved to be crucial to the administration of the foundation's own trust. By 1917, the foundation had reached the broad conclusion that, for college teachers, "a contributory system of annuities is the only one which society can permanently support, and under which the teacher shall be sure of his protection."[2]

---

[1]CFAT, *21st Annual Report*, 1926, pp. 48–49.
[2]CFAT, *12th Annual Report*, 1917, p. 20.

FREE PENSIONS FAIL, CONTRIBUTORY PENSIONS SUCCEED

The foundation's endorsement of a contributory system, and its philosophical abandonment of a free pension system for future plans, was reached after much study and discussion. In a special 1915 report, the foundation's president, Dr. Pritchett, outlined in general terms a new "comprehensive plan of insurance and annuities for college teachers," based on the concept of an individual contract with teacher or employee contributions.[3] Dr. Pritchett suggested the new system be administered through a subagency of the foundation, which "might be called the Teachers' Insurance and Annuity Association."[4] At the same time, the foundation needed to maintain the present system of free pensions long enough to satisfy "the just expectations" of teachers in the associated institutions.[5]

The foundation's trustees proceeded cautiously. Without formally adopting the proposed plan, they approved confidential distribution of the president's report to teachers and trustees of the foundation's associated institutions. And in 1916, at the trustees' annual meeting in November, the foundation appointed a special Commission on Insurance and Annuities to further study and report on the new pension system.

CARNEGIE COMMISSION ON INSURANCE AND ANNUITIES

The 1916 commission included six Carnegie Foundation trustees and five members representing four national associations for higher education. The Carnegie Foundation members were: President Slocum of Colorado College; Foundation President Pritchett; President Crawford of Allegheny College; Chancellor McCormick of the University of Pittsburgh; Sir William Peterson, principal of McGill University; and President Van Hise of the University of Wisconsin. The other commission members were Professor Cook of Yale University and Professor Rietz of the University of Illinois for the American Association of University Professors; President Goodnow of Johns Hopkins University for the Association of American Universities; President Duniway of the University of Wyoming for the National Association of State Universities; and President Cowling of Carleton College for the Association of American Colleges.[6]

The commission held three meetings in New York in December 1916, one in Chicago in February 1917, and another one in New York

---

[3]Pritchett, "Comprehensive Plan."
[4]Ibid., p. 50.
[5]Ibid., p. 49.
[6]Report of the Commission on Insurance and Annuities.

in April 1917. President Slocum acted as chairman, and Samuel S. Hall, associate actuary of the Mutual Life Insurance Company, provided actuarial information. On April 27, 1917, the commission unanimously agreed on a comprehensive plan of insurance and annuities and recommended it to the trustees of the Carnegie Foundation.

The recommendations of the commission were remarkable for the time. Seventy years ago, when the commission was meeting, most pensions were payable only as gratuities, and group life insurance was scarcely available. The idea of providing individually owned, contractual, contributory, fully funded annuities under an employer-sponsored pension plan was revolutionary. The commission emphasized the individual's responsibilities: joint responsibility with his employer for his own old age independence and full responsibility for his family members.

The conclusions of the Commission on Insurance and Annuities, as summarized in the foundation's 1917 *Annual Report*, are crucial in the history of TIAA, of higher education, and of pensions in general:[7]

THE FUNDAMENTALS OF INSURANCE AND ANNUITIES

... The commision set forth ... that both insurance systems and pension systems were devised to protect the participants against dependence. ...

The obligation to provide a certain measure of protection for those depending upon him is solely an obligation of the individual. An employer, whether a corporation or an individual, cannot concern himself as to the dependents whom an individual employed by him may support. The obligation to secure protection from dependence in old age likewise rests first upon the individual, but the employer has a direct interest in providing a system under which employees may retire upon an equitable basis when their working capacity diminishes. The payment for insurance is therefore an individual obligation; the payment of the cost of old age annuities is a joint obligation of employer and employee, and the cost should be borne jointly.

Certain actuarial and financial principles must be observed in order that any plan offering insurance and annuities shall be sound. ... Whether the individual participates in insurance or in a deferred annuity, he can be secure only when the relation is contractual. ...

To attain its full purpose, participation in an annuity system to the extent of an agreed minimum should form a condition of entering the service or employment whose members are cooperating in an insurance or annuity plan.

A definite form of organization called The Teachers Insurance and Annuity Association of America, to be organized under the laws

---

[7]Ibid., pp. 22–23.

of the State of New York, was recommended by this commission as fulfilling the conditions with respect to security, permanence, and economy under which men upon modest salary may secure the highest returns. The commission expressed its conviction that society does its best for the individual when it provides the machinery by which he may obtain needed protection for himself and his dependents at a cost within his reasonable ability to pay.

Acting on these recommendations, in May 1917, foundation trustees unanimously voted to "approve the fundamental principles of the teachers' pension system as defined in the report of the Commission on the Plan of Insurance and Annuities." The trustees also recommended to Carnegie Corporation of New York that it provide the initial capital of $1 million to establish Teachers Insurance and Annuity Association, and it did so.

The thinking had been done; the old college pension scheme was being wound down; an endowment was in hand to start a new plan; and nearly everyone wanted it.

CHOOSING GOVERNMENT REGULATION

The first policy decision had to do with the structure of the new plan. A firm decision had been made to provide contractual annuities and insurance through a third-party funding agency, to protect all the rights of the participants and the employing institutions. This decision led directly, in 1918, to an insurance company formed under state regulation of insurance. To accomplish these objectives in 1918, there was no alternative to state regulation of insurance. Bank trust agreements offered practically none of the assurances sought and did not provide for guaranteed annuities with lifetime incomes. The Securities and Exchange Commission did not appear until 15 years later. It was another 40 years before the federal government began directly to regulate pensions. Even in the life insurance industry, group annuities were not introduced until 1921, three years after TIAA was established.

The next question was, which state? In 1918, state regulation of insurance was exceedingly uneven. New York, Massachusetts, and a few other states had strong laws and competent regulation and examination procedures. But many states required no real financial protection for policyholders. So the tough New York domicile was chosen.

The decision to place the new pension plan and insurance system under insurance regulation also determined the corporate form. TIAA is a legal reserve life insurance company. But it is sui generis in its limited eligibility and nonprofit form of stock company. Its charter contains unique provisions:

ARTICLE EIGHT

The purpose of the corporation is to aid and strengthen nonproprietary and nonprofit-making colleges, universities and other institutions engaged primarily in education or research by providing
annuities, life insurance, and sickness and accident benefits suited to
the needs of such institutions and of the teachers and the other persons employed by them on terms as advantageous to the holders and
beneficiaries of such contracts and policies as shall be practicable,
and by counseling such institutions and their employees concerning
pension plans or other measures of security, all without profit to the
corporation or its stockholders. The corporation may receive gifts
and bequests to aid it in performing such services.[8]

The insurance company form under state regulation has, over the
years, achieved the objectives sought. But it was not without serious
problems from time to time. Those problems probably could not have
been solved without the charter provision limiting eligibility and de-
claring nonprofit status.

Insurance companies usually start in one state and eventually operate in several states, but relatively few operate in all states. TIAA,
to serve its purpose, had to be nationwide from the start. It had to
serve the College of Idaho as well as New York University, Knox College as well as the University of Michigan. It needed to provide annuity contracts that were uniform and transferable throughout the
country and not modified by varying restrictions and provisions of 50
separate state laws and regulations. Significantly, it was to operate
without soliciting agents. All of this could be achieved through operating by mail from one state of domicile.

Thus, the original decision was to incorporate only in the strictest
regulatory state, New York. This worked well for more than 40 years
until the courts changed their interpretations of mail order operations, as discussed in Chapter 20.

ARMSTRONG INVESTIGATION

Some New York State investment limitations that TIAA found burden-
some from time to time were the result of excesses in the insurance
world in the late 19th and early 20th centuries. At one especially glo-
rious party, James Hazen Hyde, vice president of the Equitable Life
Assurance Society, invited New York society to a "Louis XIV" ball at

---

[8]Charter of Teachers Insurance and Annuity Association of America. Originally filed
March 4, 1918; as Amended November 24, 1987.

Sherry's at 522 Fifth Avenue, at a cost of $100,000.[9] The party gained such notoriety that it helped to goad public authorities to "do something."

The result of the extravagance and other similar excesses was the famous Armstrong investigation in 1905. Senator Armstrong was the chairman of the committee, and Charles Evans Hughes, later chief justice of the U.S. Supreme Court, was the examining counsel. Testimony covered three broad problem areas: government and control, investments, and expenses and costs of insurance.[10] The resulting report led to constructive strengthening of New York insurance law and regulation but also to limitations on investments that proved too confining.

Purely by chance, TIAA's home office ended up in the same building in which Hyde's "Louis XIV" party had occurred. The Sherry Hotel was converted to an office building in 1919, and Carnegie Corporation and the Carnegie Foundation moved into it in early 1920, bringing with them the newly created TIAA to occupy one small office at the rear of the corporation's headquarters. TIAA remained at 522 Fifth Avenue until 1959, when its own office building was constructed on Third Avenue.

STOCK OR MUTUAL?

Much thought was given as to whether the new insurance company should be stock or mutual. The AAUP in a 1916 committee report, discussed below, called for a mutual company. The New York State Insurance Department, on the other hand, had recommended nonparticipating policies (i.e., a stock company).[11] There was apparently some misunderstanding between the Insurance Department, the AAUP, and the foundation as to legal aspects, but eventually it became clear that there were "very real difficulties in mutualizing such a company."[12] Objections to the stock company structure were removed by the nonprofit provision of the charter and the selection of policyholder representatives on the board. So the company was organized in the stock form.

[9]Abram T. Collier, *A Capital Ship: New England Life. A History of America's First Chartered Mutual Life Insurance Company, 1835–1985* (Boston: New England Mutual Life Insurance Company, 1985), p. 74.

[10]Joseph B. Maclean, *Life Insurance*, 5th ed. (New York: McGraw-Hill Book Company, Inc., 1939), pp. 532–33.

[11]Robbins, "Comments on TIAA's Genesis and Development," April 1950, TIAA-CREF Corporate Secretary Files.

[12]CFAT, *12th Annual Report*, 1917, p. 43.

INNOVATIVE APPROACH TO PENSIONS

There are fundamental philosophical differences between higher education's approach to pensions and that of other employments. Both the Carnegie free pensions and the new TIAA embraced innovations in pension structure and philosophy. Since 1905, and especially since 1918, they became a testing ground for these developments:

1. *Full funding*: Enough funds accumulated for each individual and under his or her ownership as annuities to provide appropriate retirement income.
2. *Contractual rights*: Standard arrangements for each participant without any kind of favoritism or ability to achieve special pension status or differential treatment.
3. *Third-party supervision*: Under governmentally established law and regulatory authorities, guaranteeing "fair and impartial treatment among policyholders."
4. *Multi-employer*: Currently more than 4,200 colleges, universities, educational associations, research and scientific organizations and their staff members participating in a nationwide pooling of portable benefits. This makes mobility of talent within the academic world widespread and available without loss of pension rights.
5. *Full and immediate vesting*: Complete ownership by the individual in benefits arising from the first, last, and all intermediate contributions made by the individual and all employers on his or her behalf.
6. *No cash values*: This gave assurance to both the college and the individual that the money saved for retirement would not be dissipated for other purposes or forfeited when an individual left a college or for any other reason.
7. *Contributory*: Unlike in industry, the great majority of college retirement plans accumulate funds from contributions of both the participant and the employer. Requiring or allowing individual contributions helps to achieve an adequate level of benefits and a flexible system in which the pensioner is an active, interested partner.
8. *Nonagency, low cost*: The Carnegie Foundation selected a nonagency form for TIAA, believing colleges and their staff members could choose good pensions themselves with access to effective written material and other forms of communication prepared by full-time staff.

IT WAS NOT ALL EASY

The new college pension system was welcomed mainly with enthusiasm. But some potholes made the early trip uncomfortable. The distinguished parentage and the endowment helped, but the closing of the free pension scheme left a number of disappointed, articulate people. The American Association of University Professors demanded the Carnegie Foundation "honor its commitments" before starting a new organization.

Opposition of AAUP

When Dr. Pritchett distributed copies of his proposed "Comprehensive Plan of Insurance and Annuities," the AAUP, at his request, appointed a committee to study the new plan and the principles on which it rested.[13] The AAUP Committee on Pensions and Insurance (Committee P) was chaired by Harlan Fiske Stone, who at that time was dean of the Columbia University Law School (he was appointed to the U.S. Supreme Court in 1925 and was made chief justice in 1941). Committee P took strong exception to Dr. Pritchett's argument that the free pension system had rested on a "defective social philosophy." If financial problems necessitated a change in the system, the AAUP argued, the foundation first had a moral obligation to meet the pension expectations of individuals in the associated institutions.

The AAUP's Committee P continued its discussions for more than three years, with extensive correspondence and a number of interviews of individual committee members with Dr. Pritchett.[14] The committee remained critical of the Carnegie Foundation's change in policy for free pensions, and its reaction to the new contributory system through TIAA was guarded. The AAUP had its own ideas as to how the new insurance plan should be organized and managed. It wanted cash surrender values in the annuities and a contractual disability policy. Most importantly, the AAUP favored a mutual company form, objecting to the role of the Carnegie Foundation in the management of TIAA.

---

[13]The AAUP reports are collected in: J. McKeen Cattell, *Carnegie Pensions* (New York and Garrison, N.Y.: The Science Press, 1919), pp. 184–253. See also Savage, *Fruit of an Impulse*, pp. 138–40.

[14]Pritchett to Stone, December 19, 1918, and Stone's reply, December 24, 1918, TIAA-CREF Archives, Columbia University file. As noted in this correspondence, and in the committee's second report, two committee members, Chairman Stone and Professor H. L. Rietz of the University of Iowa, were invited to be on the first TIAA Board of Trustees, but they believed they could not accept the appointment while the committee's second report was pending. Professor Rietz was subsequently elected to the TIAA Board as a policyholder-selected trustee in 1933.

Along the same lines, the AAUP Committee strongly opposed what it regarded as certain compulsory features of the plan. It believed, to use a contemporary expression, the foundation was "overselling" the new insurance company.

At times, criticism of the suggested new plan, both from a few individual AAUP members and from such outspoken opponents as the well-known science editor James McKeen Cattell, had the mark of a personal attack on Dr. Pritchett. Cattell, for instance, nicknamed the president of the Carnegie Foundation "Mr. Pecksniff," after the character in Dickens's *Martin Chuzzlewit*.[15] In the foundation's 1919 report, Dr. Pritchett took the detractors to task:

> The policies of the Teachers Insurance and Annuity Association have had to encounter not only the natural prejudices that confront any new form of insurance machinery. They have had to encounter as well an unexpected amount of misrepresentation and active hostility. . . .
>
> The policies of the Insurance Association have met a bitter attack from a small group of college professors. The words dividend, mutual, and participating have been discussed with much heat by gentlemen who were scarcely familiar with these terms a few months ago.[16]

While some of the rhetoric that accompanied these discussions might be regretted, the fledgling TIAA no doubt benefited from the AAUP's intense scrutiny. The foundation held fast to certain basic features for the new company. TIAA was organized as a nonprofit stock, not a mutual, insurance company. The principle of noncashability was established for the basic retirement plan. However, most colleges and universities joining TIAA made participation in the plan optional, and the foundation did not press further the question of obligatory participation.

TIAA also redoubled its efforts to provide clear and readily available information about its policies. A "Handbook of Life Insurance and Annuity Policies for Teachers" was first issued in 1918, and questions from college and university officers received detailed replies.[17] These efforts soon bore fruit. By 1920, Dr. Pritchett could favorably report on an "increase in understanding" between TIAA and the AAUP.[18] And a Columbia University professor, in thanking the association for information about its policies, commented:

---

[15]Cattell, *Carnegie Pensions*, pp. 41–42.

[16]CFAT, *14th Annual Report*, 1919, p. 25.

[17]For example, TIAA's correspondence with Colorado College and with Columbia University, 1918-1920, TIAA-CREF Archives.

[18]Minutes of the Meeting of the Executive Committee, TIAA, April 23, 1920.

My impression is that any early feeling adverse to these policies growing out of disappointment in reference to the original Carnegie pensions has almost disappeared and that among my colleagues at Columbia there is now a general realization that the insurance protection you offer is both cheaper and better adapted to our needs than that of any of the commercial companies.[19]

Actuarial Adversities

A serious problem for the new company was that actuaries in 1918 did not know how long people were going to live in the 1920s, 1930s, and 1980s. Yet the fledgling association issued guarantees reaching that far ahead. It is hard to believe annuities were in their infancy in 1918 when TIAA started. President Pritchett selected, with the help of staff, the McClintock Annuity Mortality Table, 4 percent interest, and no provision for expenses, as the long-term actuarial assumption to calculate annuity rates on which to base guaranteed lifetime income payments.

McClintock's table was the only major annuity mortality table available. Published in 1899, it was based on the annuity experience of 15 American companies before 1892. This table was retrospective in that it was not adjusted to reflect improved mortality rates for each succeeding generation. Actuaries had not yet begun to adjust mortality tables to project how long people were going to live decades in the future, as longevity increased because of such things as medical advances and improving sanitary conditions. And TIAA used the McClintock table from 1918 to 1928, 30 to 40 years after the experience on which it was based.

The second factor of major financial importance was the guaranteed interest rate. TIAA's founders chose 4 percent because prevailing interest rates had always been above that level. And nothing had to be added to the rates for expenses; the Carnegie Foundation would pay all operating expenses.

Pritchett then asked both existing actuarial societies to give advice as to the appropriateness of the new rates.[20] The American Institute of Actuaries said the rates provided "ample financial security." The Actuarial Society of America suggested the "mortality among college professors may be lower than the McClintock table, thereby creating a loss," but investment interest earnings above 4 percent would easily take care of any deficiency in mortality rates.

---

[19]Henry R. Seager, faculty of Political Science, Columbia University, to R. L. Mattocks, November 18, 1920, TIAA-CREF Archives, Columbia University file.

[20]The reports of the actuarial societies are reprinted in CFAT, *13th Annual Report*, 1918, pp. 57–73.

Were they ever wrong! Each of the actuarial factors chosen caused trouble, not immediately but within 20 to 30 years. Errors in annuities show up very slowly. The annuitants lived a good deal longer than the table said they would; interest rates fell to below 3 percent; and TIAA grew so rapidly the Carnegie Foundation could not forever pay all of its expenses.

The final result of the choice of inadequate annuity rates for the start of TIAA was unintended but not all that bad. What transpired was a gradual transition from wholly free to wholly financed pensions for the colleges, instead of the intended rapid change. As mentioned, Carnegie Corporation provided the initial capital of $1 million. In 1938, when TIAA and Carnegie Corporation separated, the corporation made additional grants of $6.7 million. And finally, from 1948 to 1958, Carnegie Corporation provided an additional $8.75 million to strengthen the longevity, interest, and expense provisions underlying the original contracts. Exit the free, enter the funded, but oh so slowly!

This will be discussed further in Chapters 5 and 6, but it deserves some attention here because the Carnegie grants did provide a gradual transition between the free and the fully paid-for annuity.

CHAPTER 4

Getting TIAA Started

PEACE AND TIAA

Peace and TIAA arrived together in 1918.

Barbara Tuchman's *Guns of August* dramatically tells of the falling apart of the world. Yet it was during the cataclysmic days of America's participation in World War I that the Carnegie Commission was studying college pensions and arriving at its recommendations regarding establishment of a new pension system. And it was during the postwar adjustment and then the roaring 20s that the infant took its first steps.

INCORPORATION

April 23, 1918, was the date of the first meeting of "The Incorporators of Teachers Insurance and Annuity Association of America." All the preliminary certificates of incorporation, various public notices, and other rigmarole had been completed.

On May 17, the Board of Trustees of TIAA held its first meeting at the office of the Carnegie Foundation for the Advancement of Teaching, 576 Fifth Avenue, New York City. Henry S. Pritchett was elected the first president of TIAA.

On May 22, Carnegie Corporation of New York deposited in the Guaranty Trust Company of New York $1 million to the account of TIAA. This amount continues to be carried on TIAA's balance sheet.

GOVERNANCE—THE FIRST BOARD

Four college staff members, three Carnegie Foundation officers, the treasurer of Carnegie Corporation, and five corporate executives, in-

IN, AND OUT, FAST

TIAA's original ledger was a simple bank book. The first entry was the $1 million endowment received from Carnegie Corporation, deposited May 22, 1918. Check No. 1 against the account, for $895,063.33 "for purchase of bonds," was endorsed by Henry S. Pritchett the previous day, May 21. TIAA's enviable reputation for being fully invested at all times started early.

The first annuity check of $10 was issued to Charles Guerard.

cluding an actuary, attended the organizational board meeting of
TIAA. From the colleges were Frederick C. Ferry, president of Hamilton College; Frederick A. Goetze, treasurer of Columbia University;
Michael A. Mackenzie, professor of mathematics at the University of
Toronto; and Frank W. Nicolson, dean of Wesleyan University. Corporate executives included Thomas W. Lamont of J. P. Morgan & Co.;
George J. Baldwin, vice president, and Frank A. Vanderlip, chairman,
of American International Corporation; Charles V. Rich, vice president, National City Bank; and Samuel S. Hall, associate actuary, Mutual Life Insurance Company.

From the start, TIAA was able to draw trustees "from the top of
the establishment." The original board members were succeeded over
the years by an ambassador to the Court of St. James, eminent university professors and presidents, top bankers and business executives,
including Elihu Root, Jr.; George Whitney; Charles Mitchell; Ada
Comstock; Pierre Jay; John W. Davis; Lewis W. Douglas; and Henry M.
Wriston, all of whom answered the call of the tiny pension plan.

POLICYHOLDER PARTICIPATION IN GOVERNANCE

An extraordinary step was taken in 1921. Six years earlier, when
TIAA was just being proposed, Dr. Pritchett had suggested a contributory system should involve "some form of oversight" by the colleges
and teachers directly involved.[1] One of Carnegie Corporation's most
important contributions to the new association, as the original owner
of its stock, was achieving this aim.

Carnegie Corporation had intended from the start "to provide machinery by which the policyholders, through representatives selected
by them, shall participate in the election of the trustees who manage
the association."[2] Two years after TIAA was founded, the number of
policyholders had grown to 1,000 distributed among 200 colleges in
the United States and Canada. To put the machinery in motion, TIAA
proposed in a March 1921 letter to policyholders that the Carnegie
Corporation appoint a committee of policyholders to formulate a
practical plan for achieving policyholder representation. Of the almost 500 responses, 460 gave their unconditional approval to the proposed plan. The president of Carnegie Corporation, James R. Angell,
subsequently appointed a 20-member committee of policyholders,
which met in New York on the morning of May 13, 1921, and made its
report to an open meeting of policyholders that afternoon, with unanimous approval. The method chosen was the election of a five-person
nominating committee.

---

[1]Pritchett, "Comprehensive Plan," p. 52.
[2]TIAA, *2nd Annual Report*, 1920, p. 6.

The first candidates designated by the nominating committee and voted on by policyholders in October 1921 were Thomas Scott Fiske, professor of mathematics, Columbia University; Guy Stanton Ford, professor of history and dean of the Graduate School, University of Minnesota; Christian Gauss, professor of modern languages, Princeton University; William Herbert Kenerson, professor of mechanical engineering, Brown University; and Samuel McCune Lindsay, professor of social legislation, Columbia University. Ballots were returned by 426 of 1,400 policyholders, recommending Professors Lindsay, Fiske, and Ford, in that order. Professor Lindsay was formally elected the first policyholder-selected TIAA trustee by the stockholders representing the Carnegie Corporation on November 15, 1921.

The original nominating committee in turn named its successor. The procedure was repeated annually from 1922 through 1988, providing for, the *Third Annual Report* stated, "the selection of one trustee each year on the direct nomination of the policyholders, an advantage not enjoyed, so far as we are aware, by the policyholders of any other life insurance company."[3] This unique and democratic system was also used for selection of CREF trustees after its establishment in 1952.

The first ten policyholder-selected trustees, each chosen for four-year terms by balloting among five candidates, were:

Samuel McCune Lindsay, professor of social legislation, Columbia University, 1921–1925.

Thomas Sewall Adams, professor of political economy, Yale University, 1922–1926.

Frank Aydelotte, president of Swarthmore College, 1923–1927.

James W. Glover, professor of mathematics and insurance, University of Michigan, 1924–1928.

Henry Rogers Seager, professor of political economy, Columbia University, 1925–1929.

Roland George Dwight Richardson, dean, Graduate School, and professor of mathematics, Brown University, 1926–1930.

William O. Miller, comptroller, University of Pennsylvania, 1927–1931.

James W. Glover, for a second term, 1928–1930 (president of TIAA, 1930–1932).

Christian Gauss, dean of the College and professor of modern languages, Princeton University, 1929–1933.

Gilbert Ames Bliss, professor of mathematics, University of Chicago, 1930–1934.

---

[3]TIAA, *3rd Annual Report*, 1921, p. 7.

A typical announcement of policyholder trustees balloting was that for Frank Aydelotte in 1923:

> In accordance with the plan of having one-fourth of the Trustees of the Association elected upon direct nomination by the policyholders, Frank Aydelotte, President of Swarthmore' College, was elected ... he having received the largest number of recommendations from the 898 votes sent to the policyholders committee. His familiarity with middle western as well as eastern institutions, through his professorships at Indiana University and the Massachusetts Institute of Technology, his connection with the War Department Committee on Education, and his position as American member of the Rhodes Scholarship Trust will be of particular value to the Association.[4]

The report also noted that all trustees of the association served "without any financial reward and as a public service ... putting their great knowledge of investment matters at the service of an agency which itself made no profits but offered to teachers a service at cost ... against the hazards of life."

THE REAL PURPOSE—SERVICE

Thirty institutions joined the new contributory retirement system during its first year. The list included large state universities, small and large private colleges and universities, and research organizations. The list was:

Alfred University	McGill University
Allegheny College	New York University
Alma College	Packer Collegiate Institute
Bryn Mawr College	Polytechnic Institute of Brooklyn
Carleton College	Queen's University
Carnegie Institution	Ripon College
of Washington	Rose Polytechnic Institute
Case School of Applied	Stevens Institute of Technology
Science	Swarthmore College
Centre College	University of Michigan
Coe College	University of Pennsylvania
Colorado College	University of Pittsburgh
Columbia University	University of Toronto
Dickinson College	Vanderbilt University
Hamilton College	Wells College
Lawrence College	Yale University

---

[4]TIAA, *5th Annual Report*, 1923, pp. 6–7.

"WHO'S ON FIRST?"

After all the preparation and all the study, who stepped up first to join the college pension system? It does not really matter now, but the question did lead to a bit of disputation. I remember on TIAA's 30th anniversary in 1948 debating with McAllister Lloyd, then chairman of TIAA, about whether Colorado College or the University of Michigan was the first cooperating institution. Some at TIAA were holding out for Michigan because TIAA received the first "Retirement Resolution" of a board of trustees establishing a retirement plan for its faculty. Mac Lloyd, having come to TIAA from the Bank of New York, presented what he believed was an overwhelming argument in favor of Colorado College—it was the first to send money! The banker's perspective!

Now, 70 years later, Colorado College, the University of Michigan, and the rest of the original 30 cooperating institutions except for Canadian ones, are still participating institutions, and all of them now have more than one TIAA plan, plus CREF.

TIAA's first life insurance policyholder was a man who knew a good thing when he saw it: Professor Louis Charles Karpinski, at the time associate professor of mathematics at the University of Michigan. He applied for Life Insurance Policy No. 1 in late December 1918. He followed that with eight additional TIAA life insurance policies. Professor Karpinski retired in 1947 after an eminent career at Michigan and received a Carnegie free pension as well as his TIAA annuity.

Dr. Charles Wesley Flint, then president of Cornell College in Iowa, owned Annuity Policy No. 1, applied for on January 8, 1919. In 1948, on the occasion of TIAA's 30th birthday, TIAA wrote to Dr. Flint for his permission to mention his name as its first annuity owner, and he answered with a good illustration of the peripatetic academic world: he wrote that he was proud of the fact that as president of Cornell College and later as chancellor of Syracuse University he established TIAA plans at both institutions, and as a trustee, he moved the adoption of TIAA plans at American University and Western Maryland College.

How quickly did TIAA start to fulfill its ultimate purpose of providing benefits? Very quickly, and more dramatically than one would guess! The first death among insurance policyholders was that of President Winthrop E. Stone of Purdue University, who lost his life while mountain climbing in July. The only other death that first year, occurring 10 days later, was that of Professor Alfred M. Kenyon of the same university. I do not know whether they fell down the same mountain. Both benefits, which were paid within three days after receipt of proof of death, were for $2,500. President Stone's contract, of term insurance to age 60, had been in force for 17 months, and he had paid premiums of $116. Professor Kenyon had paid one premium of $93 on his whole life contract, which had been in force for less than two months. Also during the first year, two annuity owners died, and the accumulated premiums and interest earnings were paid to their survivors.

The little new company settled unobtrusively into a back office of its parent's abode at 576 Fifth Avenue, New York City. When Carnegie Corporation and the foundation moved to 522 Fifth Avenue in 1920, TIAA toddled along. This seems sensible, because it was getting free rent; all of its expenses were being paid by its parents; its president, chairman of the board, vice president, secretary, and treasurer were either not paid at all or were paid by the foundation, and it had only two full-time officers. It was still Andrew Carnegie's "little insurance company."

For the next few decades, 522 Fifth Avenue, at 44th Street in New York, was a gathering place for college presidents and other educators throughout America to visit and seek funds from Carnegie Corporation for their institution's projects. As a side stop, the educators would drop in at TIAA to talk about establishing a new retirement plan for the college or to take out individual life insurance.

They could meet with Henry Pritchett, the former president of MIT who had first talked with Carnegie about free pensions for college professors, who was then president of both the foundation and TIAA. Clyde Furst as TIAA secretary and Robert A. Franks as treasurer filled the same positions at the Carnegie Foundation. Frank A. Vanderlip, chairman of the American International Corporation, was the unpaid chairman of the TIAA board; Eugene F. Russell was the part-time medical director. Raymond L. Mattocks as actuary and Samuel S. Hall, Jr., as assistant treasurer were the first paid TIAA officers. Two of the original employees knew Carnegie well. Jean Morrison Shirley was distantly related to him. She later became TIAA's first woman officer. And Franklin Slater, of the same diminutive size as Carnegie, was an assistant secretary to him in his final years and then joined the TIAA staff.

TAX STATUS CONFIRMED

The federal government had only one significant decision to make with respect to the new pension plan for the colleges—its tax status. TIAA was to operate under the jurisdiction of New York State insurance law and supervision, but otherwise was sui generis among insurance companies. It limited eligibility for its services strictly to the nonprofit sector, and within that sector only to certain categories of educational and scientific institutions. All the pension and other premium contributions from educational sources were nonprofit in origin.

Application for tax exemption to the Internal Revenue Service was approved in July 1920 when the Treasury Department rendered its decision that TIAA "is exempt from income taxes under the provisions of Subdivision 6, Section 231, of the Revenue Act of 1918."[5] Subsequent rulings over the decades by the Treasury and the IRS confirmed that TIAA was tax exempt under Section 101(6) and its successor provision, Section 501(c)(3).

During its first nearly seven decades, TIAA's tax exemption was based on Treasury and IRS rulings. The Tax Act of 1986 specifically provided for the tax exemption of TIAA's pension arrangements. Its group medical, disability, and life insurance plans and individual life insurance became taxable under that act, starting in 1987. Chapter 20 will discuss challenges to and defense of these tax rulings and statutes over the years.

CONSERVATISM

An early annual report carried a discussion of "conservatism" that in hindsight is more intriguing than in foresight. The report said: "At the beginning of its work a policy of sound conservatism caused the Association to limit its assumption of insurance upon a single life to $10,000."[6] In December 1919, this maximum was increased to $15,000 and then to $20,000 in 1921. Not a word was said about annuities, which later were to incur losses in the millions of dollars. Two years later, TIAA's annual report mentioned that three insurance policies had terminated through death of the professors, resulting in total claims of $18,000, "considerably less than that expected according to the American Experience Table of Mortality."[7] Thus, from the start, life insurance proved easy to write conservatively and annuities difficult.

TIAA did avoid issuing certain forms of coverage—these included double indemnity and health insurance. In 1921, the association surveyed policyholders about their interest in disability income insurance, with little positive response. The decision was made not to issue such coverage, but TIAA continued to study the need for disability protection and referred policyholders to the availability

---

[5]TIAA, *2nd Annual Report*, 1920, p. 5.
[6]TIAA, *3rd Annual Report*, 1921, p. 7.
[7]TIAA, *5th Annual Report*, 1923, p. 5.

of contracts from various commercial companies.[8] It eventually designed and issued its own form of group total disability income insurance and major medical in 1956 with the help of a Ford Foundation grant.

STEADY, SOLID GROWTH

Each year during the 1920s, additional colleges joined the growing system. The number just missed 100 by 1925; 99 colleges and universities were participating plus scientific and educational organizations and endowed schools to bring the total to 140. All six Carnegie and all four Rockefeller scientific, educational, and research organizations were in. The large Canadian universities were participating.

By the 10th year, 134 colleges and universities and 65 research and other institutions, a total of 199, were participating. These covered all aspects of higher education, from the fast-growing state universities like Alabama, Arkansas, Colorado, and Michigan; to Ivy League institutions like Yale, Brown, and Columbia; and to private and denominational colleges like Antioch, Berea, Brigham Young, the University of Chicago, Colby, Oberlin, Trinity, and many others.

The number of policyholders was surprisingly small, in comparison with the explosive growth of the post-World War II period. In 1928, the 10th year, 6,956 annuities and 5,021 life insurance policies were in force. For all its illustrious parentage and intensively researched beginnings, TIAA now settled into a period of comfortable but unspectacular financial growth. By that time, it was clear that pension plans and not life insurance would be the great growth area for TIAA. This was just the opposite from the commercial insurance companies, where life insurance overwhelmingly dominated the business until the 1970s.

Having started out with the $1 million Carnegie seed corn, TIAA's assets reached $5 million by 1924, $19 million by 1929, and nearly $47 million by 1934. Substantial surplus funds had accumulated, and TIAA was in strong financial condition to weather the economic stresses of the Great Depression. But comfort depends on where one is sitting. In the next office was Carnegie Corporation of New York, watching nervously as TIAA grew faster than the corporation had expected; it was rapidly obligating the corporation for growing but necessary operating expenses.

---

[8]TIAA, *4th Annual Report*, 1922, pp. 8–9.

INVESTMENTS

TIAA's first investment portfolio has a quaint ring to it. Of assets of just more than $1 million in 1919, $200,000 was invested in United States of America Third Liberty Loan 4¼s due 1928. Next was New York City Gold 4½s due 1967 for $100,000. Then came two small holdover U.S. Steel Company Fifty Year 5s. And all the rest, $700,000, was invested in railroad bonds: Atchison, Topeka and Santa Fe, Baltimore and Ohio, Central of New Jersey, Chicago, Burlington and Quincy, Illinois Central, New York Central, and Pennsylvania Railroad. The last of these had a good strong feel to it—Pennsylvania Railroad General Mortgage Gold 4½s, due 1965. The Atchisons were due in 1962 and 1995; the New York Centrals in 1997. By the way, these first investments are not being held to maturity!

During the mid-1920s, the growing portfolio was diversified primarily into telephone and electric utility bonds. By 1929, some municipal bonds appeared plus a number of industrials—Armour, Gulf Oil, GMAC, International Paper, Du Pont, Associated Dry Goods, and several others. But main reliance continued to be on transportation and power obligations.

Annuities for Canadian colleges were roughly balanced by Canadian investments.

TIAA could not have been more conventional in its investment policy than it was during the 1920s.

PRITCHETT RETIRES: GLOVER, THEN JAMES SUCCEED

Henry S. Pritchett, the organizer of TIAA in 1918 and its president for the first dozen years, retired at age 65 on September 1, 1930, continuing as trustee until 1934. Dr. Pritchett had worked with Andrew Carnegie in setting up the original free pension systems, and he had served as president of both the Carnegie Foundation, from 1906 to 1930, and of TIAA since its founding in 1918. In 1934, the board of trustees of TIAA resolved: "The Association will never outlive its debt to Dr. Pritchett's devotion, foresight and wisdom; and what the Association has already been able to do and may still do for the colleges of the United States and Canada and their teachers will always be in great measure attributable to his initiative."

Though Dr. Pritchett continued actively to advise TIAA as a trustee, his retirement marked the end of an era in college pensions. For TIAA it marked a turning point: for the association's internal relations with the Carnegie Foundation and Carnegie Corporation, and its position in the larger economy during the tumultous economic, social, and political changes caused by the Great Depression and then World War II.

1930–1945
DEPRESSION, TIAA WEANED, WAR

James W. Glover
President, 1930–32

Henry James
President and Chairman, 1932–43
Chairman, 1943–47

Devereux C. Josephs
President, 1943–45

There had been several changes in the association's leadership during the 15-year period. Dr. James W. Glover succeeded Dr. Pritchett as president in 1930. Dr. Glover was professor of actuarial science at the University of Michigan and serving his second term as a policyholder-selected member of the TIAA board. He did not last long as president, not nearly as long as the elaborate solid oak furniture with which he adorned his office.

The foundation and, by 1930, also the Carnegie Corporation were paying all of TIAA's expenses, and they expected the same kind of dignified austerity generally found in the academic and foundation world. The corporation expected more progress than was forthcoming toward freeing Carnegie from meeting the growing expenses of an expanding pension plan. Dr. Glover returned in 1932, much earlier than expected, to his professorship at the University of Michigan.

The trustees elected Henry James chairman and acting president of TIAA in the late spring of 1932. He was at the time treasurer of the Rockefeller Foundation and a member of the board of Carnegie Corporation of New York. James was elected TIAA president in 1934. He was the first of the seven TIAA presidents I have known; I missed only Pritchett and Glover. James was a Pulitzer-prizewinner for his biography of Charles W. Eliot and editor of the letters of his father, the Harvard philosopher and great pragmatist, William James. His Uncle Henry early moved to England from whence he wrote his, as Dorothy Parker characterized them, "not too deuced lucid," novels. TIAA's Henry James's second wife was Dorothea Draper Blagden, sister of the famous actress Ruth Draper and granddaughter of Charles A. Dana, early editor of *The New York Sun*.

My first encounter with James was when he asked me to write the announcement of my appointment as assistant to the president of TIAA in September 1941. He telephoned me long distance, calculated to make an impression in 1941, at Indiana University to inform me that nobody starts out a news article with the word *the*. The next was when he told me he vigorously disliked the word *special*, and would I consider changing the title of the first pamphlet I ever wrote for TIAA, titled, "A Special Company for a Special Clientele."[9]

Mr. James (it was always either that or H. J.) was a board member of the New England Telephone and Telegraph Company and other establishment entities. The one that brought him the most pleasure was member of the Harvard Corporation. He helped to bring Harvard into TIAA in 1936; it partially escaped in 1950 but reentered in 1970.

Henry James was elegant, with a dapper mustache. He was quite short, but had a remarkable way of looking down at people a good bit

---

[9] I didn't change it; it was part of my coming of age.

taller than he was. James was a chain-smoker who never started for the ashtray with less than an inch of ashes at the end of his cigarette, and he rarely arrived with any. This was his way of saying that fastidiousness can be carried too far.

James and his second in command, the actuary Rainard Robbins, became an excellent team. James had breadth of vision; Robbins had depth of mathematical and actuarial knowledge. James had capacity to work with the board and educators; Robbins had administrative ability. Both were good writers, but it was Robbins who constructed TIAA's booklets and reports and usually testified and spoke on pension matters. Together they led TIAA through the Depression years, the spin-off from Carnegie Corporation, and the early years of World War II. Working with Devereux Colt Josephs as head of investments, they assembled a strong staff that brought TIAA to the postwar period ready to go under new leadership. James served as president or chairman until 1947, with Josephs as president from June 1943 to October 1945.

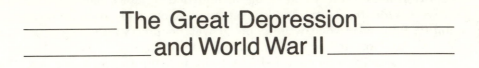

CHAPTER 5

The Great Depression and World War II

THE GENERAL ENVIRONMENT

It is hard, half a century later, to comprehend the Great Depression. None of it seems reasonable.

One out of four American workers was unemployed! The unemployment rate at its zenith was 24.9 percent,[1] and nearly all without jobs were heads of families. Now, when the rate rises much above one out of 14, or 7.1 percent, everyone is nervous. And many of the unemployed now are in two-earner families, or are not heads of households.

The gross national product (GNP) plummeted by almost half—from $104 billion in 1929 to $59 billion in 1932.[2] That represents hundreds of thousands of cars and houses and toasters that did not get built; vast acreages of grain that were not harvested; and thousands of farmers who went broke.

The cost of living declined rapidly, believe it or not. From the post-World War I high of 65.4 in 1920, prices declined to 39.3 in 1933 on the old base, representing an increase in value of the dollar of more than one third. The other long period of decline in the American price level was an almost steady drop from 1869 to 1897, but that was a long time ago.

The financial world suffered monstrous losses. The closing of every bank in America when President Franklin D. Roosevelt took office

---

[1]U.S. Department of Commerce, Bureau of the Census, *Historical Statistics of the United States. Colonial Times to 1970,* Bicentennial Edition, 2 parts (Washington, D.C.: Government Printing Office, 1975), part 1, p. 135.

[2]U.S. Department of Commerce, Bureau of Economic Analysis, *The National Income and Product Accounts of the United States, 1929–82. Statistical tables* (Washington, D.C.: Government Printing Office, 1986), p. 1.

March 4, 1933, left Americans for a few days without their major medium of exchange. The pleasant phrase chosen for the collapse, Bank Holiday, added a bizarre twist to the affair.

The 1930s inflicted an intensely personal impact on most people who went through the decade. The economic and social realities have influenced a remarkable amount of America's thinking since—thinking as to Social Security, inflation, guarantee of bank deposits, unemployment, deficits, and on and on. And it includes a complete change in attitude toward financial dependency, individual responsibilities, and the governmental role in personal financial security.

When my daughter was a teenager in the mid-1960s, she said something about Calvin Coolidge and the 1930s. I said, "Martha, that happened in the 1920s, not the 1930s." "Big difference," said Martha.

Well, it was a *big difference* to our emerging generation. The decade of the 20s, with the Charleston and President Coolidge and "the business of business is business," was utterly different from the 1930 depression years and the war and aftermath years of the 1940s. Each of the ensuing decades have also left their indelible mark on our consciousness.

In my case, rather than turning me into an unreconstructed conservative, the events of the 1930s led me to two conclusions:

1. The Great Depression taught more people more lessons that weren't so than any other period in our economic history.
2. Frequently, the riskiest course you can choose is to try to avoid all risk.

Those conclusions have helped me through the gestation days of CREF and in developing investment policy ever since.

My father was a poet and journalist turned banker. The 1930s were not vintage years for those endeavors, so he got me a job as Indiana University correspondent for Indiana's biggest newspaper, *The Indianapolis News*, a job I held for four years while in college. It was interesting work, enriching my college education. During the summer, like many of my colleagues, I worked for alphabetical agencies—the National Youth Administration, the Civilian Conservation Corps, and as an assistant bank examiner.

From 1935 to 1937, I attended the Harvard Graduate School of Arts and Sciences, majoring in economics, primarily, I suppose, because it seemed it was the economic life of America and the world that was mixed up. It was a period when students and faculty could challenge the established order. I had the great good luck of being there at a high point of Harvard economics—Professors Joseph Schumpeter, John Williams, Sumner Slichter, Alvin Hanson, Seymour Harris, Gottfried von Haberler, Abbott Payson Usher, Kenneth Galbraith. And the students were just as good—Paul Samuelson and I roomed together one year, to my great but humbling advantage. (Samuelson later became a policyholder-selected trustee of CREF, serving with distinction from 1974 to 1985.) In February 1936, "Shumpy," John Williams, Paul Samuelson, and I and other students went to Boston Harbor to pick up the first shipment of a new book whose fame was already germinating, John Maynard Keynes' *General Theory of Employment, Interest, and Money.* Faculty and students literally studied it together.

Recently, I got out my beat-up copy of Keynes and was intrigued to note how little attention was given to inflation in the mid-Depression. Investment received 15 inches in the index; employment, 12 inches; money, 8 inches; inflation, one inch.

After Harvard, I returned to Indiana University for four years of teaching and administration as assistant to the president before joining TIAA in 1941. All of this education and experience was helpful and relevant to my later employment at TIAA.

POLITICAL AND SOCIAL ENVIRONMENT

The Great Depression was a period of recognition by America of its social and economic problems. Before that time, nobody worried much about the poor, the unemployed, the minorities, the widowed, or the immigrants. President Herbert Hoover, a fine public servant, was doing his job in his own way when in 1929 his head was chopped off by the guillotine of a free-falling Dow Jones Industrial index. Franklin Roosevelt succeeded in 1933, with his jaunty cigarette and his reassurance to America that "the only thing we have to fear is fear itself."

But there was no way to overlook the closed banks, the lengthening bread lines, the Hoovertowns, "the Okies" and other migrations of the poor and unemployed. Roosevelt mightily extended the service of the federal government by setting up many emergency agencies for agriculture, conservation, housing, business, public works, and economic recovery.

Three of these agencies were durable institutions that have affected TIAA-CREF and college benefit plans over the years in important ways: the Federal Deposit Insurance Corporation, the Securities and Exchange Commission, and Social Security.

Federal Deposit Insurance Corporation

The FDIC insured bank deposits for the "little guy," re-establishing confidence throughout the country after the banking crisis of 1933. My father was chairman of a Bank Study Commission in Indiana at the time. Herman B Wells, later president of Indiana University, my first boss, and an original CREF trustee, was its executive director. They wrote and guided through the Indiana state legislature a set of laws that became models across the country.

Built on top of stronger state and federal regulation of banks, the Federal Deposit Insurance Corporation was one of the most economical things ever done—assuring individuals they could get their money out of the banks at any time and thereby making general runs on the banking system a matter of historical interest only. No financial panic has occurred since.

The half-century absence of financial panics has meant that TIAA and CREF could operate normally during the entire period without the trauma and large investment losses suffered by many investors during the Great Depression. It has meant the continuance of banking services for the colleges and for TIAA-CREF participants, and the confidence this brings, especially to annuitants. I wonder, if there were no deposit insurance, whether the more than half of TIAA-CREF annuitants who have their checks deposited electronically would do so? With the current deep troubles of the savings institutions and a few commercial banks, the danger for the economy would be far greater without the federal insurance funds.

Securities and Exchange Commission

In the early 1900s, manipulation and skulduggery were widespread on the New York and other stock exchanges. The 1929 crash widely destroyed faith in the equity markets. In the middle 1930s, the Securities and Exchange Commission, seeking honest and dependable securities markets, came in with regulation based mostly on disclosure and availability of reliable facts. This restored some confidence in the equities markets. The existence of the SEC and its function of assuring more efficient and honest securities markets has aided materially in the effective investment of CREF's funds for its participants and in its ability to rely on the accuracy of published information.

Social Security

The Social Security system is by far the most important of all legacies of the Great Depression. It has changed Americans' outlook on the financial exigencies of life more fundamentally than any other program, private or public. Its influence on retirement and other financial security programs such as those discussed in this study is profound.

Social security came late to America. The Iron Chancellor, Otto von Bismarck, established the first state social security program in Germany in 1889. Bismarck's scheme gained him great political credit in Germany and renown as a farsighted public servant, yet it cost very little. It was based on benefits starting at age 70, and not many people then lived beyond age 70. Most other European countries also set up plans well before the United States.

The United States acted only under duress of financial calamity. In 1935, President Franklin D. Roosevelt appointed a special committee of cabinet members, including Secretary of Labor Frances Perkins, Secretary of the Treasury Henry Morgenthau, and others, to recommend a new social insurance system. They immediately called upon the academic world for ideas. Dean Edwin Witte of the University of Wisconsin and Dean Douglas Brown of Princeton were two of the principal designers.

After a false start of imitating private-funded insurance in 1935, Social Security was redesigned into the Old Age and Survivors Insurance system (OASI). Benefits were accelerated to start in 1940 at a level presuming longtime participation. Workers nearing or over age 65 were made eligible for benefits after the briefest participation. Survivor benefits were quickly added to protect widows and children of workers. Social Security then became a true income transfer system, depending on a social contract between the generations.

Social Security had a secondary objective in the late 1930s, that of getting older workers out of the labor force and out of competition with younger workers and heads of young families. The initial retirement age of 65 was chosen to help meet this objective without rendering the plan too costly. The retirement age was later lowered to 62 with reduced benefits.

The new design minimally met the immediate needs of American workers. Congress has increased the level of benefits many times, added disability and medical benefits, and increased wage taxes to support the enhanced benefits.

No program has been more durable, and more capable of maintaining the broad support of the American public, than Social Security. During the last half century, it has made the major contribution to the economic security of Americans, to a compassionate society, to eradication of poverty, to maintenance of human dignity at all ages. It truly represents a crucial social contract between generations.

SOCIAL SECURITY AS ECONOMIC STABILIZER

Social Security was one of the important economic stabilizers put in place during the Depression. The illustrious British economist, John Maynard Keynes, in his *General Theory*, considered the development of purchasing power as a major antidote to depression. Francis Townsend, in California, gained nationwide attention by demanding free pensions of $200 a month for all people over age 65. Governor and then Senator Huey Long of Louisiana promoted his "Share the Wealth" populist program.

Many people supported the idea of getting the old folks out of the labor force and out of the way by retiring them. Quite predictably, the professors and politicans considered these pressures in the design of Social Security. There were no benefits unless a person effectively retired from covered employment; benefits were to commence quickly instead of waiting until funds had accumulated; and the benefit amounts were to take into account family composition, larger benefits for married people, still larger if they had children; benefits were heavily weighted in favor of lower wage earners.

The system has led to a higher level of retirement during recessions; it has led to an automatic release of purchasing power during slack business conditions; and it has acted as a contracyclical factor of some importance.

CONNECTIVE TISSUE

The philosophical companionship between Social Security and TIAA-CREF is very real. The theoreticians and philosophers of Social Security in America—Edwin Witte, J. Douglas Brown, Wilbur Cohen, Robert Ball, Arthur Altmeyer, Robert Myers—all were college professors or became ones. They were familiar with the basic objectives incorporated into TIAA. They believed there should be flexibility as to when benefits start. They believed in portable pensions, ones that credited benefits to individuals regardless of whether they stayed with one employer or moved during their working years. They believed in pensions as a matter of right; in the case of TIAA, rights established by each dollar of premium as paid; in the case of Social Security, rights established by a social contract between generations.

One vast improvement has occurred in private pension plans. Thirty and more years ago, most workers received no benefits except from their last employer, and then only if they stayed until retirement age, and there were usually no benefits for wives (it was wives, not spouses, then) before or after retirement. There was little vesting; a change of jobs could mean complete forfeiture of all credited retirement benefits. Successive federal laws have reduced the delayed vesting period to five years of participation.

Social Security, based on generational transfers of funds, builds only minimal reserves[3] and does not contribute to the capital base of the economy. Now, most private pension plans are well funded. This

---

[3]This has been the case, but the current FICA tax schedule, if it is not modified, will produce gigantic reserves in the early years of the 21st century, in preparation for the retirement of the "baby boom" generation.

in turn means workers in our society, through their own and their employers' pension savings, are funding their own retirement benefits by providing the capital to finance productive enterprise. This diversity between public and private sources of financing the huge resources needed for pensions has worked and is working well.

THE COLLEGES WERE LEFT OUT

The original Social Security Act was not all-inclusive; it left many employment groups uncovered. Colleges were not excluded as a class, but as members of three distinct categories. Public institutions were excluded because of constitutional concern over federal taxation of states; denominational colleges over separation of church and state; and private colleges over concerns about taxation of nonprofit institutions. All of these categories, and therefore all of the colleges, were made eligible in the early 1950s, after substantial effort led by TIAA. This is discussed in Part Four.

CORPORATE INDEPENDENCE FOR TIAA

Circumstances Leading to Severance from Carnegie

The most important corporate event of the 1930s for TIAA was the declaration of independence from the Carnegie parentage. Unlike the 1776 event, the baby, TIAA, was shoved out of the crib because it was getting too big. And TIAA was eager to stand on its own feet, if possible, and to be in charge of its own destiny. But it did not quite make it; it had to come back to daddy twice more for money in the 1950s.

In establishing TIAA, Carnegie Corporation endowed it with $1 million, and the Carnegie Foundation agreed to pay any additional expenses for overhead not covered by income from the endowment. At TIAA's inception in 1918, Carnegie Corporation desired in principle to keep its obligations for solving the problems of teachers' pensions definite both as to amount and duration. "The present trustees of the Corporation are not justified in mortgaging the future," the corporation told the foundation.[4]

When TIAA was starting, the endowment income and overhead provided by the Carnegie Foundation seemed ample. But by the mid-1920s, it appeared that the expenses would, within the next decade, exceed the sums available from TIAA endowment income and the foundation. At the suggestion of the New York State superintendent of

---

[4]James Bertram, secretary, Carnegie Corporation of New York, to Charles F. Thwing, secretary, CFAT, November 20, 1917, Carnegie Corporation Archives, TIAA file.

insurance, Carnegie Corporation in 1924 adopted a resolution stating it would make further grants to TIAA through the foundation "as may be necessary from time to time" in order to enable it to meet all of its operating expenses.[5] The corporation, as holders of TIAA's stock, reserved the option to limit the number of new policies written in order to keep the overhead expenses to a sum that could be "guaranteed by the Corporation without embarrassment to its other responsibilities."[6]

By 1930, Carnegie Corporation was faced with a complex set of funding obligations for college pensions. The Carnegie free pensions were still having their troubles, while the TIAA plan was a gratifying, but also somewhat expensive, success. To offset the disappointment caused by the reduced Carnegie free pensions in 1929, the corporation had agreed to purchase supplemental annuities from TIAA. This entailed setting up a special fund, costing the corporation at the outset $600,000 annually for nine years.

Moreover, TIAA's growth was proceeding at an impressive rate, raising the cost of its overhead expenses. Between 1925 and 1929, TIAA more than doubled in size: assets rose from $7 million to $19 million; the number of policyholders from 5,200 in 1925 to 10,600 in 1929; and gross overhead expenses from $59,000 for 1925 to $144,000 for 1929.[7]

The Carnegie Foundation was drawing on its emergency reserve fund to make annual grants to TIAA to cover the increases in overhead; from a grant of $15,000 for 1926, this rose to $85,000 for 1929.[8] A year later, the foundation's grant had increased to $115,000, and Carnegie Corporation had supplemented this with $25,000. The foundation's emergency reserve fund was dwindling, and Carnegie Corporation's 1924 resolution committed the corporation to responsibility for TIAA's operating expenses in the event that the foundation could no longer meet them.

By September 1930, TIAA and the Carnegie Foundation were under new leadership following Henry Pritchett's retirement from his dual presidencies. The Carnegie Foundation's new president, Henry Suzzallo, anticipated a complete administrative separation of the foundation and TIAA.[9] From the standpoint of Carnegie Corporation,

---

[5][Frederick P. Keppel] to R. L. Mattocks, October 24, 1924, and enclosed trustee resolution, October 23, 1924, Carnegie Corporation Archives, TIAA file.

[6]Carnegie Corporation, *Annual Report*, 1925, p. 24.

[7]TIAA annual reports and, for overhead expenses, Henry James, "Memorandum as to the T.I.A.A.," May 10, 1933, appended table of Annual Statistics, Carnegie Corporation Archives, TIAA file.

[8]Savage, *Fruit of an Impulse*, pp. 201–3; "TIAA History of Carnegie Grants," TIAA-CREF Actuarial Files.

[9]Savage, ibid., p. 196.

the transition provided a natural opportunity to bring up for review the terms of its financial commitment to TIAA.

Dr. James W. Glover of the University of Michigan was elected the second president of TIAA. Dr. Glover had distinguished credentials as an actuary, and it was Carnegie Corporation's hope that with his help, the corporation and TIAA could "come to some equitable agreement which could be so recorded and which would look forward to the ultimate independence of the Association."[10] Glover began planning for an expansion of TIAA's business, especially into the area of disability insurance.[11] This was not what the corporation had in mind by "independence"; from the corporation's view, such expansion meant an even larger overhead and a still more indefinite financial obligation.

By 1933, the corporation had already supplemented the endowment and CFAT income to the extent of $210,000 to cover TIAA's expenses.[12] If the trend continued, Andrew Carnegie's "little insurance company" was soon going to outgrow its parent, Carnegie Corporation, and consume it in the process. As one corporation trustee privately put it, "This teachers' pension business may yet do to us what it did to the [Carnegie] Foundation."[13] One of TIAA's founding trustees used a child-and-parent simile that would be echoed more than once:

> Can we not approach the matter in a spirit of mutual helpfulness? The Association is the child of the Foundation and the Corporation, and the parents have properly looked after this child during its infancy. Now the child is growing up and promises to be a very big boy indeed. It is time to think about his coming capacity to stand upon his own feet and take his proper share of the cost of his maintenance. He will never do the best of which he is capable so long as he is spoon-fed. He must learn to face the fact of an expense ratio as a check upon extravagance.[14]

The corporation's efforts to come to a mutual understanding with Glover were unsuccessful, and around December 1931, he was informed the corporation desired his resignation. As mentioned earlier, Glover returned to the University of Michigan, from which he had taken a leave of absence, and resumed his professorship. Henry James, a Carnegie Corporation trustee, was elected chairman of the board of trustees of TIAA and subsequently, acting president and then president in 1934.

---

[10]Keppel to Glover, June 9, 1930, Carnegie Corporation Archives, TIAA file.

[11]The plans for disability insurance are discussed in the minutes of the meetings during 1931 of the TIAA Board of Trustees and Executive Committee.

[12]Carnegie Corporation, *Annual Report,* 1933, p. 23.

[13]Russell Leffingwell to Keppel, May 20, 1931, Carnegie Corporation Archives, TIAA file.

[14]Michael A. Mackenzie to Keppel, July 8, 1931, Carnegie Corporation Archives, TIAA file.

James led TIAA through the many months of complex negotiations between the association and the corporation that followed.
Various possibilities were considered for defining the corporation's
financial responsibilities toward TIAA. A special committee even
briefly raised the possibility that the association wind up its business,
perhaps by having it reinsured or taken over by an existing insurance
company, but this was believed to be premature and the association
should first carefully study the alternatives.[15]

The idea of setting up a separate reserve for TIAA gradually took
hold. The TIAA board appointed a committee of trustees to make a
formal report and recommendations. This committee recommended
that steps be taken toward a friendly separation of TIAA and Carnegie
Corporation. Carnegie Corporation would endow the association with
funds to cover all future expenses of contracts already on the books,
and the association would be on its own for contracts written from
then on.

TIAA's 1935 *Annual Report* announced a new endowment grant
from the corporation in these words:

To summarize briefly,

1. The Association will receive from the Carnegie Corporation an endowment grant of $6,700,000. . . . This grant, made without imposing any
   restriction upon the Association's freedom to apply the money, principal and income, to any of its corporate needs, replaces the prior
   understanding [i.e., under which the corporation paid TIAA's ex-
   penses]. . . .
2. The Carnegie Corporation has agreed to release its stock ownership
   [of the association's non-profit stock]. . . .
3. A charge sufficient to cover the expense of servicing new policies has
   been introduced into the premium.

The TIAA report concluded, "It would be ungracious to the Carnegie Corporation not to express, at this time and in this place, grate-
ful recognition of the fact that this grant of $6,700,000 makes effective
a very liberal, and for the policyholders of the Association a very advantageous arrangement."[16]

At the time, the arrangement looked liberal; by 1948, as discussed
later, it was necessary to go back to the corporation for additional
grants, equaling $8.75 million, for a total Carnegie subvention of $17
million.

---

[15]"Committee to Study the History of the Relation between the Corporation and the
Association," June 16, 1932, Carnegie Corporation Archives, TIAA file.

[16] TIAA, *17th Annual Report*, 1935, p. 4.

Trustees of T.I.A.A. Stock

Carnegie Corporation and TIAA completed the transfer of payments in September 1938. Meanwhile, possible legal forms of ownership of the association's nonprofit stock were studied. One question was whether to mutualize TIAA, or to incorporate a board of trustees to hold and vote the stock, through a special New York State charter.[17]

For a number of reasons, the stock company form was chosen. It was reported that neither teachers—the major group of policyholders—nor institutional officers favored vesting ultimate control of the company in its policyholders. And there were legal advantages for the association as a stock company organized for philanthropic purposes. There were also differences in the regulations for mutual and stock companies in the handling of reserves, free surplus, and dividends, with somewhat greater latitude for stock companies. And TIAA was exempt from certain federal income taxes to which mutual companies were liable.

A special charter was drawn, providing for a board of trustees, under the name of "Trustees of T.I.A.A. Stock," to accept and hold the stock of the association. The charter confirmed in Section 2 that all activities were to be accomplished "without profit to the corporation or to its stockholders." Trustees of T.I.A.A. Stock receive no fees. And the charter provided in Section 5 that "no Trustee, officer, member or employee of the Corporation shall receive any pecuniary profit from the operation thereof, other than reasonable compensation for services rendered, reimbursement of expenses incurred in its service, or benefits received as a proper beneficiary of its strictly charitable purposes."

The Special Act to incorporate Trustees of T.I.A.A. Stock became a law June 3, 1937, with the approval of the legislature and governor of New York.

All of this makes TIAA, in the fine old legal phrase, sui generis. In 1952, CREF was also set up as a Special Act New York corporation. Its Members are the same persons who are Trustees of T.I.A.A. Stock. (Chapter 19 discusses governance in detail.)

At the first meeting of the Trustees of T.I.A.A. Stock on June 15, 1938, Frederick P. Keppel, president of Carnegie Corporation of New York, turned over the stock of TIAA to the new board, along with an endowment of $100,000, the income from which was to pay the board's expenses, and $6.6 million of new funding. In its 20th report, the association announced to its policyholders that

---

[17]H. J. [Henry James], "As to Disposition of T.I.A.A. Stock," December 29, 1936, Carnegie Corporation Archives, TIAA file.

the incorporated Board of Trustees, which holds and votes the stock[18] of the operating Association, is, and henceforth will be, an important body in the affairs of the Association. It elects the trustees who do run the Association, even though it has no power to interfere in the details of management. One of its first acts was to affirm its intention to continue the practice of electing four trustees of the operating Association on the basis of policyholder balloting.[19]

OTHER DEVELOPMENTS IN THE 1930s AND 40s

Collective Decreasing Insurance

TIAA did not, in the early years, provide group life insurance coverage for the colleges. As written by the commercial companies, traditional group life insurance was not transferable among employers. When insureds left an employer, they either dropped the insurance or converted it to high premium permanent insurance, the only option. Group life usually provided large amounts of insurance at the higher, expensive ages because it typically related the amount of insurance to salary and position, not family needs. And it took no notice of the accumulating death benefits in fully vested defined contribution annuities. The colleges needed an alternative designed to meet the needs of their staff members.

In 1936, Dr. Rainard B. Robbins, coming to this problem from his background as an actuary, invented an intriguing new form of (group) life insurance coverage, which TIAA named Collective Decreasing Insurance. The insurance would be issued through college employers to groups of college employees, without medical examination. Individuals would have their own policy, not merely a certificate. The amount of insurance provided would be expressed in units, each costing $1 of premium a month. This provided a level *premium* at all ages and a decreasing *amount of insurance* as age increased.

This met the objective: high initial amounts of life insurance coverage that would reduce over the years as individuals and their spouses grew older, raised their children, sent them through school, and achieved an ever-growing annuity death benefit. Because the coverage was provided through an individual policy, the employee could simply keep the coverage in force on his or her own following termination of employment. The growth of Collective Life Insurance, how-

---

[18]I decided, when I became chairman and president of TIAA in 1963, that I should see if an actual stock certificate exists, or if it is just a "book entry." Sure enough, an appropriate certificate was resting in its solitary glory in the Bankers Trust Company in a small safe deposit box with rusty hinges.

[19]TIAA, *20th Annual Report,* 1938, p. 4.

ever, was slow, and during the last two decades, it has largely been supplanted by standard group life insurance. This will be discussed in Part Four.

Investments

The early 1930s were a strenuous proving ground for investment policies of financial institutions. The insurance industry itself came off well during the 1930s. Compared with the widespread failings of commercial banks, no insurance company failed with a loss of policyholder money in the state of New York and very few across the country. Instances of catastrophic losses were rare. While this was all true, the investment experience of insurance companies was dull and unrewarding. The reward-risk ratio was low. The 1930s were, however, an excellent time to have a portfolio with a low-risk element to it.

TIAA was affected, but not unduly so. Most of its investments were in railroad bonds, United States Steel and other heavy industry bonds, telephone and electric utilities, state, local, and federal obligations. TIAA invested in almost no mortgages and only a few other industrial bonds.

During the 1930s, TIAA ran for cover by moving from railroad and equipment bonds and utilities to U.S. government obligations.[20] In 1933, 2.5 percent of TIAA's assets were in U.S. government obligations, and this had grown to 19 percent in 1937. Interestingly, the obligations of subdivisions had declined from 16 percent to 10.5 percent. Meanwhile, railroads and equipments had declined from 24 percent in 1933 to 20 percent in 1937, and utilities had dropped from 38 percent to 27 percent in the same period.

The crisis of the early 1930s caused financial institutions to move toward shorter maturities in their bond portfolios. In the TIAA case, the major shift was made from June 1935 to December 1937. Maturities from zero to five years changed from 3 percent of portfolio to 20 percent, while 30 years and over changed from 27 percent to 14 percent. The 1937 report comments, "A preference for short maturities cannot be exercised without accepting a lower rate of return than might be obtained from long-term investments." The result of these investment policies in the 1930s was that losses were minimal, interest earnings also were low, and capital gains were sizable.

In explaining its dividend policy for the year 1937, TIAA said:

> Everybody knows that the interest return obtainable on sound investments has declined markedly in recent years and that it still remains very low.

---

[20]TIAA, *19th Annual Report*, 1937, pp. 10–12.

The total income actually collected during 1937 . . . amounted to a return of 3.82 percent on the main ledger value of all stocks, bonds, and mortgages compared with 4.14 percent for the year 1936. [This] will be found to compare not unfavorably with income percentages that are being reported by other insurance companies.

The trouble was, however, that TIAA was guaranteeing 4 percent on most of its annuity contracts.

Harvard, Yale, Princeton, and Others

By 1939, all but 4 of the original 96 institutions eligible for Carnegie free pensions had set up TIAA contributory retirement systems. Two of the six colleges that had established retirement plans even before the advent of Carnegie pensions in 1906, Columbia and Toronto, dropped their own plans and joined TIAA in 1919. The only institutions with Carnegie free pensions and without TIAA plans were the University of Minnesota, Vassar, University of California at Berkeley, and MIT.

Princeton, Yale, and Harvard were slow to come into the new system.[21] They all had large endowments and, to some extent, self-funded their initial supplements to the Carnegie pensions.

Yale had established a pension plan in 1897, providing half salary as a retirement benefit at age 65 for assistant professors or higher rank who had served for 25 years. In 1920, Yale established a voluntary contributory plan, using TIAA contracts or, "if the treasurer of the university was satisfied with the reasons for such different choice," a different form of contract or with a different company. In 1930, the university decided to accumulate the funds itself. In 1938, Yale eliminated its lump-sum payment provision and its self-funding arrangement in order to establish a TIAA contributory plan.

Princeton did not have an early plan. It established a contributory plan in 1934 using either TIAA or Prudential Insurance Company contracts. Prudential was later dropped.

Harvard was one of the six educational institutions that had established somewhat formal plans before the Carnegie pensions. In 1899, the president and Fellows of Harvard established a noncontributory retirement plan for "officers of instruction and administration," under which persons aged 60 or more who had served at least 20 years in the rank of assistant professor or higher could retire with an allowance not to exceed two thirds of salary. The university could

---

[21]See Rainard B. Robbins, *College Plans for Retirement Income* (New York: Columbia University Press, 1940) for descriptions of plans at these and other colleges and universities in the late 1930s.

require retirement at age 66. In 1915, Harvard closed this plan to new entrants, depending thereafter on the Carnegie Foundation free pensions. After the Carnegie Foundation was started in 1906, Harvard added no new funds to its own plan, which consequently became entirely inadequate to furnish retirement benefits.

In 1920, Harvard established a contributory plan with full cash values upon withdrawal or death before retirement. In the early 30s, this plan also became inadequately funded because of the poor investment experience of common stocks. Harvard was funding fixed-dollar pension obligations with volatile equity investments. So this plan was also closed in 1936. At that time, Harvard decided the provision of a lump sum upon withdrawal from service was a feature of questionable value and eliminated it insofar as future contracts were concerned. Harvard then established a TIAA retirement system for officers of instruction and administration.

A major breakthrough with a statewide system of public higher education happened in 1937 when all of the public institutions in the state of Indiana—Indiana and Purdue Universities and Ball State and Indiana State Teachers Colleges—were brought into the TIAA retirement system by act of the legislature. These and the private universities mentioned above are examples of the extensions of service made during the 1930s.

Taxation of Annuity Premiums

In 1935, the Bureau of Internal Revenue (now IRS) ruled that contributions made by Columbia University toward deferred annuity contracts did not constitute taxable income to its employees.[22] TIAA's report for 1934 concluded:

> Accordingly it would appear that such contributions need not be included by college and university authorities in making information returns to the Internal Revenue Bureau concerning salaries and wages paid to employees, and that the employees themselves need not include the college's contribution to annuity premiums in their individual returns.[23]

The IRS decision followed the stand initially taken by TIAA, the AAUP, and other organizations and subsequently confirmed by explicit legislation.

Of Little Note, But to Me

There appeared in the 1941 TIAA *Annual Report* the following item:

---

[22]I.T.-2874, XIV-1 Cum. Bull. 49 (1935).

[23]TIAA, *16th Annual Report,* 1934, pp. 8–9.

Mr. William Croan Greenough, recently Assistant to the President and Personnel Director of Indiana University, joined the staff of the Association in 1941.

Mr. Greenough's present title is 'Assistant to the President,' but it is expected that he will devote himself particularly to relations with the colleges and to what, within the office, is sometimes referred to as the work of the New Business Department.

This may not seem to be an earthshaking event to the reader, but it was to Doris and me. It started a relationship that has continued to 1989, when I am writing this book.

Abruptly, in June of 1943, I joined millions of other Americans in a temporary career change. I became a Navy Air Combat Intelligence officer. By great good fortune, my assignment was to help organize U.S. air-sea rescue forces for the B-29s in the Pacific. Air-sea rescue is the positive side of war, emphasizing long life. I became impressed with the substantial advantages of living a long time, an essential ingredient for maximum enjoyment of a pension, which I am currently trying to achieve.

TIAA during Wartime

In July 1943, Devereux Colt Josephs became president of TIAA, succeeding Henry James, who continued as chairman of the board until shortly before his death in December 1947. Josephs had been a partner of Graham, Parsons & Co., an investment organization in Philadelphia, from 1923 until 1939, when he joined the Carnegie-Teachers Investment Office in New York. This cooperative office handled all investments for a number of Carnegie trusts and for TIAA. He was financial vice president of TIAA from 1939 to 1943 and president from 1943 to 1945. From 1945 to 1948, Josephs was president of Carnegie Corporation of New York, whose offices were just down the hall from TIAA at 522 Fifth Avenue. He then became president, and later chairman, of the New York Life Insurance Company, serving until his retirement in 1959. During these years, he served many pro bono causes—trustee of the Metropolitan Museum of Art, the Johns Hopkins University, the New York Public Library, and a number of corporate boards of directors.

Josephs' talents were underutilized during World War II because TIAA's investment policy shifted strongly toward U.S. government investments, about the only security that was being generated in large quantity. Partly as a result of this, the net interest earnings of the association continued to decline. Josephs also conducted a program of sales of investments, taking capital gains that could then be added to reserves. This helped the current and short-term balance sheet but created longer range problems with annuity guarantees.

World War II was a holding operation. Richard Hurd, top mortgage officer, and I went off to service, as did a number of other staff members; Rainard Robbins went to Washington part-time to work on Social Security; Henry James was a part-time chairman with other eleemosynary interests, and Devereux Josephs was limited in what he could do with investments during the war.

The war had an enormous effect on people and on companies that produced and distributed materials and commodities. But it had little effect on life insurance and pension plans, except that government bonds became the preponderant investments. TIAA had to cut back on the clerical services it provided for colleges and individuals because typewriters, calculators, and workers were in scarce supply. And it paid for five extra life insurance claims in 1942 because of the war—all from aviation. (I remember picking up a newspaper one noon to read about a crash of two blimps over Lakehurst, New Jersey; later, insurance claims revealed that a TIAA policyholder was on each blimp, engaged in lighter-than-air research.) The 1945 *Annual Report* captured the essence of the situation well: "The year 1945 was undoubtedly one of the most dramatic in the history of the world. Dictators came to ignominious ends. . . . These events did not in themselves create any unusual problems for TIAA."

I was finally free to return to TIAA at the end of 1945, to face a new and to me unknown president, R. McAllister Lloyd, who had succeeded Devereux Josephs in October 1945 when Josephs became president of Carnegie Corporation.

R. McAllister Lloyd Takes Charge

On October 1, 1945, R. McAllister Lloyd assumed the presidency of TIAA for what was to be more than 17 years of extraordinary times for the heretofore little college pension system. Lloyd, a Harvard graduate with family and business roots in the Northeast, took on the job of guiding TIAA through the challenging and opportunity-filled postwar years with vigor and style.

The choice of Mac Lloyd as president of TIAA was a fortunate one. His experience in banking as a vice president of the Bank of New York, his leadership of the investment side of TIAA and later CREF, and his organizing ability all served the policyholders superbly.

When Mac Lloyd was asked in an oral history interview why he became president of TIAA, he mentioned his banking experience, but almost all of the rest of his answer had to do with people. He was well and widely known among lawyers, brokers, members of boards of charitable and educational institutions, and bankers through his Bank of New York vice presidency. He was a member of prestigious clubs, the Union Club, the Harvard Club, the Lunch Club, the Cen-

1945–1980
CREF, OTHER SERVICES, EXPANSION

R. McAllister Lloyd
President, 1945–57
Chairman and CEO, 1947–63
Service, 1945–63
(Bachrach)

William C. Greenough
President, 1957–67
Chairman and CEO, 1963–79
Service, 1941–79
(Bachrach)

tury Association, and the Down Town Association. His wife's social and charitable activities, as he said, widened his circle of friendships.

Lloyd served as chairman and president of TIAA until 1957 and as chairman until his retirement in 1963. At its annual meeting in January 1963, the Association of American Colleges paid tribute to Lloyd's long service to higher education:

> This is too early for him to retire—but not too early to honor him. For he has been a clear headed leader in American education, a considerate human being who cared about the welfare of each of us and each of our institutions, and a personal friend of many of us. We take this opportunity of expressing our gratitude to him.

GREENOUGH BECOMES PRESIDENT, THEN CHAIRMAN

It was my privilege to succeed Lloyd as president, from 1957 to 1967, and as chairman and CEO from 1963 to my own "graduation" from TIAA-CREF in 1979 at age 65. I continued on the board to 1984.

I had worked closely with Lloyd, the trustees, the educational world, and the staff, throughout all his years of leadership, and then through my own more than a quarter-century of presidency, chairmanship, and board membership. Thus, my contact with the people, events, philosophies, and innovations reported on in this book are firsthand and intimate during the entire period of extraordinary change since just before World War II to the mid-1980s.

CHAPTER 6

Postwar, Pre-CREF Period

SHIFT TO PEACE

Peacetime brought dire predictions as to what would happen to the post-World War II economy of the United states. Eleven million returning servicemen, eager to restart their interrupted careers, their education, their family life, clambered back onto American's shores and to its cities and towns. Wartime industries were closing; inflation was gaining momentum. Prospects for employment for the returning servicemen looked dim. Interest rates were at historic lows; common stocks had been in the doldrums during the war. Many economists predicted a period of painful economic readjustment. Henry Wallace, vice president of the United States from 1941 to 1945, was criticized because he called for a national goal of 60 million jobs in America by 1950.[1]

What did happen? With only a momentary stumble, industries began to fill the consumer goods voids caused by the Great Depression and war years. In 1943 and 1944 combined, only 700 American automobiles were produced (somebody forgot to turn off a production switch at a big plant). By 1946, production was back up to 2.15 million passenger cars, and by 1950 reached 6.666 million.[2]

A vast pentup demand for housing had resulted from the Great Depression followed by a long war. This meant no or inadequate housing for millions of returning servicemen and for those ready to start families or upgrade their housing after the 16 years of scarcity. Again, there was a rush to fill the void. The federal government's ex-

---

[1]Henry A. Wallace, *Sixty Million Jobs* (New York: Simon and Schuster, 1945).
[2]*Historical Statistics,* Part 2, p. 716

periments with guaranteed mortgages under the pre-war FHA program were extended to GI and VA mortgages, and housing starts doubled and then tripled. Hundreds and then thousands of identical houses sprouted on Long Island's vast moraine. Levittowns were called towns although they did not initially have school buildings, town halls, or other civic necessities.

Somebody had to make the cars and build the houses. Rosie the Riveter could not continue to do it all. This activity caused civilian employment to jump from 53 million in 1945 to 59 million in 1950, confirming Henry Wallace's prediction.[3]

Students overwhelmed the colleges. Here again the doomsayers were wrong. There was a general expectation that worldly students back from Paris, London, Hawaii, and Australia would demoralize innocent college campuses and coeds. What campuses received was an overwhelming number of diligent, in-a-hurry, highly motivated service men and women and others who had been drawn into the war effort, eager to finish their education and catch up with their lives. The number of bachelor's degrees had dwindled during the war, dropping to 126,000 in 1944, the fewest since 1930. By 1950, the number had increased more than threefold to 432,000, a figure that was not topped until 1963.[4] These serious students were superimposed on the normal number of 18- to 22-year-olds arriving on schedule at the colleges.

TIAA AT FOCUS OF TWO POWERFUL TRENDS: PENSIONS AND HIGHER EDUCATION

Private pensions in America first came to prominence during World War II for several reasons. The first and major one was that wage and price controls during the war set a ceiling on the ability of war industries to attract a requisite number of workers. But benefit plans were not controlled. Therefore, war industries established pension plans at a rapid rate throughout World War II. The powerful force of labor unions was added to the already strong economic impetus toward pensions when, in 1948, the National Labor Relations Board ruled that companies were required to bargain on pension plans.[5] This Inland Steel case, when added to organized labor's clout and the employers' own economic drives toward pensions, formed irresistible power, and pension growth became an important part of American economic life.

---

[3]Ibid., Part 1, pp. 126–27.

[4]Ibid., Part 1, pp. 385–86.

[5]Inland Steel Co., 77 NLRB (April 1948); Inland Steel v. NLRB, affirmed 170 F. 2nd 247 (C.C.A. 7, 1948), cert. den. as to the welfare fund issue, April 25, 1949, 336 U.S. 960.

Pensions established in industry at that time were far different from those in the colleges. As shown in the studies by Robbins and by Latimer, the original pension plans were largely gratuities on the part of benevolent employers, given to employees after long periods of faithful, and perhaps subservient, employment.

The new wave of pensions were a considerable improvement over the benevolent but retractable charitable pensions of the earlier days. However, most companies continued to use pensions as a method of tying one's employees to the company—a golden handcuff. Most of the early pensions provided no retirement benefits for persons who changed employers before retirement. There was no vesting of benefits and no protection from widespread firing shortly before retirement. Frequently, there were no death or disability or widow's benefits. The current widespread use of life annuity options protecting either widows or widowers with monthly lifetime incomes was not much in evidence. And most of the plans were vastly underfunded, if funded at all, and depended on the continued financial well-being of the donor company.

Pensions in the college world, which had generally preceded those in industry by 40 years, also enjoyed rapid growth after World War II. To the 190 TIAA college and university annuity plans existing in 1939, for example, 70 had been added by 1945, and in the next five years, coverage expanded to 374 colleges and universities.

The growth for other educational institutions such as junior colleges, scientific and research institutions, and independent secondary schools was even more striking. In 1939, the statistics for the noncollege group were not even given in TIAA's annual report, but by 1945, the association announced that 135 such institutions were cooperating with their staff members in the purchase of TIAA annuities. By 1950, this figure had risen to 217, and their names were given for the first time in TIAA's list of cooperating institutions. This growth also was accomplished by a vast expansion in the employment characteristics of colleges.

The numbers of students and, therefore, the number of faculty members that needed to be attracted grew at remarkable rates. Most of the growth was in the public sector of higher education, where state universities, state teacher colleges, and then junior colleges accepted much of the challenge of providing education for very large numbers of people. Faculty members in most of the public institutions of higher education were at the time covered by the state teacher or public employee retirement systems of the various states and municipalities. Many of these plans did provide portability and vesting of pension benefits *within a given state*. But this improved feature did not meet the needs of higher education, where job transfers generally cross state lines. The Kokomo high school teacher may well end up in

Fort Wayne or Indianapolis, but the Purdue professor is more likely to go to MIT or Caltech than Indiana University or Notre Dame. Indiana University and Notre Dame bring in new staff members from across state lines, not from Depauw or Purdue.

TIAA came out of the war lean and ready for growth along with the colleges.

IT IS TOUGH WRITING ANNUITIES

The history of life insurance coverage has been, in a sense, easy. Health improvements, industrial safety, and public health advances have resulted in steady improvements in mortality rates. At the turn of the century, American males from birth had a life expectancy of 48 years; females, 51 years. By 1950, longevity had increased to 65 and 71 years, respectively. By 1987, it had reached 71 and 78.[6] This has meant that retrospective life insurance mortality tables overstated realized death rates from the start, and their use in calculating prices for life insurance policies was conservative. This provided room for increased dividends to policyholders from mutual companies or profits, plus dividends for participating policies, for stock companies.

Annuities are the reverse of this, and frequently with reverse effects. At the turn of the century, American males who had avoided the vicissitudes of life—runaway horses, railroad accidents, infectious diseases—and reached age 65 had on the average another 11 years to live; women had 12 years. By 1950, for those who had dodged horseless carriages, trolleys, and airplanes to age 65, this had become 13 for men and 15 for women. And by 1987, 15 and 19 years, respectively.[7]

Thus, from 1900 to the present, longevity from birth has increased 23 years for men and 27 years for women; and longevity from age 65 has increased 4 years for men and 7 years for women.

For annuities, these improvements mean substantial increases in annuity payouts over the lifetimes of recipients. In reaction to the challenges, most insurance companies were not interested in offering annuities; real effort on the part of agency companies, with perhaps the exception of the Equitable Life Assurance Society, did not start until the 1950s.

TIAA was thrust into this arena early, before refined methods of writing annuities had been developed. During its first 20 years when its stock was owned by Carnegie Corporation, it used the standard approach of the time for calculating annuity rates, which unfortu-

---

[6]*Statistical Bulletin*, July–September 1988.
[7]Ibid.

nately was not nearly conservative enough. Then it set to work to solve the problems of how to write annuities and developed significant and creative solutions.

In choosing annuity rates—that is, how much annuity income to guarantee for a certain premium level—the first major factor is longevity. One might ask why Pritchett, with his intimations of mortality from recollections of early Carnegie free pensions, did not choose more conservative rates than he did. Good data on annuitant mortality rates were not available or, if available, were retrospective and, therefore, not appropriate for annuity purposes because annuity mortality rates should be reflective of the future and not the past. Medical advances were accelerating. Most of the advances in the early decades of the century were in the control of communicable diseases and problems of childbirth, having little to do with annuitant mortality. But general health prospered, antibiotics conquered lung problems and infections for older people, and longevity continued to improve.

In 1918, President Pritchett, the original actuaries, and the board chose the McClintock annuity table for TIAA's first mortality rates. This table was a retrospective table 30 years old at the time TIAA was established. But it was in standard use. Starting in 1941 and the following decades, TIAA pioneered in "look-ahead" annuity rates, and now all annuity providers try to project mortality rates 30 to 60 years into the future, not a rear-view mirror image of 30 years into the past, in estimating how long people will live for annuity purposes.

The second powerful influence on annuity rates is the interest rate that will be guaranteed on policyholder funds for the future. Four percent was initially chosen for TIAA. Prevailing life insurance company guaranteed interest rates were less than this at the time, usually 3 percent. Looking backward from 1918, the lowest net yield on life insurance company assets was 4.33 percent in 1900. The rate had been above 5 percent before 1893. It had climbed from 4.33 percent in 1900 to 4.81 percent in 1917 at the time Pritchett and the others were choosing 4 percent as the initial TIAA guaranteed interest rate.

Six years later, a secular downtrend in interest rates commenced and was exacerbated by the economic strains of the 1930s. Such trends can be distressing or exhilarating, regardless of whether economists give them exotic names like Kondratieff cycles. Interest earnings hit a high point for life insurance companies of 5.18 percent in 1923 (TIAA's earnings for 1923 were 5.78 percent; TIAA's high point was the following year, 1924, at 6.12 percent). From there, earnings declined steadily, dropping below 4 percent for the first time in the history of life insurance companies to 3.92 percent in 1934. TIAA's rate remained well above the industry rate—4.87 percent in 1934. The decline continued. Rates dropped steadily to a low in 1947 of 2.88 percent for the industry and 2.90 percent for TIAA.

There was to be no expense loading on the TIAA contracts, because Carnegie Foundation and Corporation were to pay all of the new company's expenses and did until the mid-1930s.

As indicated in Chapter 3, both actuarial societies were asked to advise on the original TIAA rates, and they generally approved.

The original TIAA contracts had additional features that later added to the financial problems. The contracts allowed participants to increase their premiums at the original guaranteed rates by enough to purchase an annuity of $500 a month above whatever the initial premium rate purchased. That is, if a college professor started out purchasing, say, a $250 a month annuity (remember, this was a very good income in 1918), he could add enough additional premium over the years as his salary increased to purchase another $500 of month annuity at the original guaranteed annuity rates. Such purchases frequently occurred decades later, after major changes in interest rates and longevity.

TOWARD MORE CONSERVATIVE RATES

Uneasiness developed early as to whether TIAA, or anybody, should attempt to guarantee minimum interest and mortality rates for many decades into the future.

Annuity contracts are about the longest lived of any in the entire system of contract law. A young instructor may start purchasing an annuity when he is in his 20s or early 30s. He or she may retire 40 years later and live to 80 or 90 or more and leave a life annuity to continue to the surviving spouse.

The question was: how much lifetime annuity income should be *guaranteed* no matter what happened—war, peace, inflation, depression, low interest rates or high, medical advances leading to longer life spans. It was important to guarantee amounts that could be paid under a variety of conditions. It would not serve the interests of either the colleges, their staff members, the system of higher education, or the country to guarantee too much. The question of guarantees has less to do with the actual dollar amount of annuities that would be *paid* to retired people by TIAA than it would with other insurance companies, since TIAA annuities are participating. TIAA, as a nonprofit pension fund, had to pay out to its annuitants in the form of additional annuity amounts any earnings over the guaranteed amounts and proper levels of contingency funds.

TIAA made its first changes toward greater conservatism in annuity rates in 1927 and 1928, a decade after its establishment. It adopted a new and more up-to-date mortality basis, Hunter's American Annuitants Select Tables. This basis assumed a longer lifetime for annuitants, and the table matched well with TIAA's own investigation of mortality rates among Carnegie Foundation pensioners.[8]

The 1927 change was to use the new mortality table and an interest rate of 4 percent for annuities commencing at once. The 1928 change was to use the new mortality table and 3½ percent interest for deferred annuities, with one especially long-term option based on 3 percent interest.

This marked the first time a different interest rate was used for long-term guarantees than for shorter periods. When guarantees may stretch 50 to 70 years into the future, it seemed the part of prudence to guarantee lower rates of interest over that period. This system of using lower interest guarantees for long-term annuities than for short-term annuities was used in most TIAA rates from then on.

The 1932 Annuity Contract

In 1932, TIAA made a different type of change in its annuity guarantees. The 1932 contract provided for layering of annuity rates. That is, the original premium rate would continue to purchase annuity income under the original guarantees right through retirement. But any additional annuity amounts representing salary increases or lump-sum amounts paid in the future would purchase at the annuity rates in effect at the time of the first of the changes.

The 1936 and 1938 Rates

In 1936, small reductions were made in the guaranteed interest rate and mortality assumptions, and this was also true in 1938. Also, in 1936, an expense charge was inserted. This reflected TIAA's rapid growth; Carnegie Corporation could no longer defray TIAA's total expenses without hobbling its other eleemosynary programs.

At Last, a Sound Approach to Annuities: The 1941 Annuity Contract

TIAA in 1941 made the most important changes ever made in the structure for making guarantees under individual annuity contracts. Under the new arrangement, all premiums received from colleges and their participants up to a given date would purchase annuity income at a given guaranteed rate based on specific interest and mortal-

---

[8]R. L. Mattocks, "Mortality Investigation among Men Pensioners of the Carnegie Foundation," July 13, 1923, TIAA-CREF Corporate Secretary files.

ity factors. But all premiums received after that date on participants' contracts would purchase annuity income at the rate then in effect for the most recently issued contracts. That is, TIAA would make lifetime guarantees for each annuity contribution when received, but it would no longer guarantee a specified rate for a premium that might not even be received until 20 or 30 years in the future, under very different economic conditions. For example, mortality rates were changed, usually only slightly, in the 1941 contract, 1948, 1958, 1969, 1977, 1984, and 1985. New interest rates were incorporated in some of these vintages.

This change was accomplished by placing in each annuity contract issued after 1941 a provision that upon 90 days' notification, the annuity rates guaranteed for all future premiums could be changed. No change could be made in other provisions of the contract or in guarantees for premiums paid to the date of change.

Dr. Robbins and Wilmer A. Jenkins, associate actuary of TIAA, developed the new contract. Both of them were major influences in pension developments. Robbins has already been mentioned; Jenkins later was elected president of the Society of Actuaries, and in 1948, in collaboration with Edward Lew of the Metropolitan Life Insurance Company, he developed the first annuity mortality table that built in projections for expected future mortality improvements. He retired as executive vice president of TIAA in 1966.

The original TIAA annuities had guaranteed a specified monthly annuity amount for all premiums paid over a lifetime of work. The system put into effect by 1941 guaranteed the monthly annuity amount from each premium as paid, but reserved the right to change annuity amounts for future premiums paid. Thus ended a long and successful search for a satisfactory way of providing very long-term annuities with guaranteed incomes that cannot be outlived, but ones that can be soundly written during widely varying conditions. These changes allowed TIAA to continue writing annuities, although a number of commercial companies either had dropped out or were questioning the viability of annuity business. And the changes assured the continued financial strength of the college world's pension system.

The TIAA trustees, President James, Dr. Robbins, and Mr. Jenkins believed the 1941 contract should be explained in detail to the college world so there would be no misunderstanding as to what was guaranteed and what was not. Several articles were written and printed in educational journals. The American Association of University Professors was actively involved in this effort, especially through Mark H. Ingraham, professor and then dean of the College of Letters and Science at the University of Wisconsin and at one time president of the national AAUP. Dr. Ingraham also headed a visiting AAUP committee to report on the general condition of the association.

All other major features of the original TIAA annuity contracts have stood the test of time and experience. Many improvements have been made over the years. But the design of the contract turned out to be durable, socially and economically advantageous for college staff members, their spouses, and the colleges, and a significant breakthrough from all then existing annuity contracts.

FINAL CARNEGIE GRANT

Carnegie Corporation and TIAA had one more grand cooperative venture, from 1948 to 1958. The annuity contract and rate changes described above solved the problem of writing annuities after 1936 in a sound financial manner, while assuring college professors that their annuities during retirement could not be outlived.

It was another story with the annuities written before 1936. As mentioned before, the deferred annuities based on the McClintock mortality table at 4 percent interest assumption before 1928 caused particularly ominous losses. Interest rates were in a longtime secular decline, and the earnings of institutional investors dropped below 3 percent by the late 1940s, well below the 4 percent guaranteed in the old TIAA contracts. Annuitants were living substantially longer than the mortality table predicted. The losses had reduced TIAA contingency funds to about 3 percent of liabilities by 1947, and the erosion was continuing.

Something vigorous needed to be done. Devereux Josephs was president of Carnegie Corporation at the time. Since he had been president of TIAA before going "down the hall" (up?) of the 10th floor of 522 Fifth Avenue, New York, to become Carnegie's president, he was both knowledgeable about TIAA's financial needs and also in a position where favoritism, or the opposite, could be charged. Therefore, Carnegie Corporation and the Trustees of T.I.A.A. Stock agreed that a highly regarded independent expert should be chosen to make recommendations. The Trustees of T.I.A.A. Stock commissioned Louis Pink, former superintendent of insurance of New York, to head the study.

The Pink study found that the TIAA insurance and annuity contracts written since 1936 were on a sound basis; undoubtedly no further assistance from Carnegie Corporation would be needed for this part of TIAA's business. The danger, in Pink's view, was that "sound as are the policies and contracts since 1936, it must be admitted that they are affected to some extent because the pre-1936 business is not soundly reserved." Pink suggested "serious consideration be given to the possibility of securing adequate reserves for pre-1936 business from the Carnegie Corporation . . . for the protection of TIAA against the losses of the early business."[9]

The initial request from TIAA was for a $20 million lump-sum amount to fund all future expected losses from the old contracts. Carnegie decided, as an acceptable alternative, to award $1 million a year, from 1948 to 1953, and then consider the needs. This made sense. If economic trends continued to be adverse, the $20 million might not meet the needs, but if they reversed, it might prove redundant. After payment of the first $5 million the matter was revisited in 1953. By then, Charles Dollard had succeeded Devereux Josephs as president of the corporation. The contact with Carnegie Corporation became my interesting assignment. Together with Robert M. Duncan, TIAA's actuary, we worked in great detail with Dr. James A. Perkins, vice president of the Carnegie Corporation, to produce many financial and mortality projections and their effects on TIAA's future. Dr. Perkins later became a member of the TIAA board and then president of Cornell University.

The final result was that Carnegie Corporation from 1948 to 1958 gave TIAA an additional $8.75 million to apply toward losses on the old contract vintages. This did the trick and finally allowed the corporation to get out of the annuity business.

It is reasonable to ask what the Carnegie Foundation and Corporation thought of all this largess, some of it unintended and unplanned for. Was it worthwhile? It certainly directed substantial corporation and foundation funds into pension plans for college teachers.

Dr. Perkins, in his oral history given to Columbia University in 1978 concerning TIAA and CREF, stated with respect to the Carnegie Corporation grants:

> I think that the Corporation has been properly pleased with this; I mean, not only was it good, but the Corporation is pleased. I think, as a matter of fact, the relationship between the Corporation and the TIAA, and then TIAA-CREF, has been almost a model of the foundation relationship with an institution it helped to create. It's been supportive, but not directive. It's been interested and concerned, but has not tried to dominate, nor has it tried to second-guess decisions of management. It's been a creative model, if that's the proper word, of professional relationship between people who were interested in the same thing.[10]

Robert M. Lester, the longtime secretary of Carnegie Corporation, sent us in 1961 his views based on his close observation of TIAA for

---

[9]Louis H. Pink, "Report to the Trustees of T.I.A.A. Stock on the Teachers Insurance and Annuity Association of America," March 3, 1950, TIAA-CREF Corporate Secretary Files.

[10]Interview of James A. Perkins by Margaret Everett, April 13, 1978, TIAA-CREF Oral History Project, Columbia University Oral History Research Office.

some 44 years: "It seems to me that the Carnegie funds devoted to the initiation and development of the Association could not have been spent for a better purpose. The Association has more than justified the hopes of its founders."[11]

Alan Pifer, president of Carnegie Corporation, writing as acting president of the Carnegie Foundation on its 60th anniversary in 1966, gave an impressive history of the trials, tribulations, and successes of the free pension system and the efforts to finance it and the development of its successor arrangement, TIAA.[12] He outlined all of the foundation contributions to both efforts. And, regarding TIAA and CREF, he wrote:

> The fifth area of Foundation activity, establishment of the Teachers Insurance and Annuity Association, stands out clearly today as the most important of the Foundation's accomplishments. The Association started its life essentially as a division of the Foundation and owes its very existence to the parent organization. As the development of TIAA, and its partner the College Retirement Equities Fund (CREF), into a $2 billion pension system is one of the great success stories of American education, it seems only right that the parent should enjoy some of the reflected glory of its illustrious child.

And Pifer said, giving appropriate credit to Henry Pritchett: "But most importantly he conceived the idea of TIAA and brought it to fruition. This feat must surely rank among the finest achievements of modern American philanthropy."

And thirdly, Pifer said:

> CREF was the first experiment in variable annuities and as such was a bold innovation requiring considerable determination and courage to launch. Its experience thus far has been successful beyond the highest expectations of its originators.

END AND START

The transition from wholly free to wholly self-supporting annuities for college staff members was finally completed in 1957. Not that the Carnegie free pensions had become history: in 1956–57, 37 newly retired eligible professors began their Carnegie free pensions, bringing the total then retired to 1,109 professors and 873 widows receiving pensions or disability allowances, at a cost for the year of more than

---

[11]Robert M. Lester to WCG, November 3, 1961.

[12]Alan Pifer, "A Notable Year," in CFAT, *61st Annual Report,* for the year ended June 30, 1966, pp. 7–18.

$1.5 million.[13] All annuities of TIAA participants had been fully strengthened by 1957. There were only 4,833 participants from the first 17 years of TIAA who had not yet started their annuity income (by 1980, this had dwindled to 34). The reserve and solvency crisis for TIAA was over.

During the ensuing third of a century, TIAA has grown to huge size. No reserve or solvency problems have come close to developing, and none is likely. The methods of writing annuities developed over the decades continue to serve well. All TIAA annuities are written on a conservative basis, under careful procedures established by the trustees, supervised by the New York State Insurance Department for solvency and fair treatment of policyholders and by various federal agencies for fiduciary standards and fairness. The key philosophy for TIAA is one of using conservative mortality and interest guarantees, with appropriate buildup of contingency funds and reserves during the annuity purchase period, and each year returning any unneeded funds (earnings in excess of the mortality and interest rate guarantees) in the form of additional dividend credits both before and during the retirement years.

INFLATION

One large economic cloud darkened the picture for all annuitants— inflation. World War II brought the usual inflation associated with massive diversion of national effort to production of war equipment. As inflation was starting to wear off (the cost of living actually declined slightly in 1949), war again exploded. Wages could go up during inflation; corporate earnings and interest rates could go up, but all people living on fixed incomes including annuities were in trouble. Could anything be done? It was time for something star- tling—the invention of CREF.

---

[13]CFAT, *52nd Annual Report,* June 30, 1957, p. 45. The last eligible person to retire was Professor Arthur J. Knight of Worcester Polytechnic Institute, in 1965; see CFAT, *61st Annual Report,* June 30, 1966, p. 11.

PART TWO

CREF—The First Variable Annuity

CHAPTER 7

Genesis

A GENERATION OF GREATER SECURITY

The variable annuity, a new approach to pensions, was born a working lifetime ago, in the early 1950s. Basing lifetime pension income for the first time directly on common stock investments, the College Retirement Equities Fund was established to provide the new pensions for colleges and their staff members.

CREF commenced operations July 1, 1952, by issuing CREF Certificate No. 1 to Henry M. Wriston, then president of Brown University. A year and a half later, CREF's assets passed the $1 million mark; a month after that, half of TIAA's then 609 participating institutions had made CREF participation available to their staff, and a month after that, CREF participants passed the 10,000 mark.

Now, a generation later, the vast majority of those first 10,000 participants in CREF have retired. They were the first to receive the announcements of CREF, *Should TIAA Establish CREF* and *A New Approach to Retirement Income.* They have had a full career covered by Social Security, TIAA, and CREF. It is a good time to take stock.

Why was CREF started and how? Was it easy or hard; was there opposition; were there rough spots along the way? Has it served the college world well? Has CREF worked as expected? This part, devoted to CREF, will address all of these questions.

First, a word on "Has it worked as expected?"

If "has it worked as expected," means has it added significantly to security in retirement for college staff members and has it helped to adjust for the large swings in economic security and activity for more than a third of a century, the answer is yes. Has it, working with TIAA and Social Security, helped college staff members achieve a quite remarkable level of retirement security, despite inflation, well beyond what would have been dreamed possible in 1952, the answer is again yes!

If "has it worked as expected," means has it met the expectations of those of us who worked on it in the early 1950s, I must admit that never in our wildest dreams did we imagine that, by the end of 1989, CREF would have become a $35 billion common stock fund with 900,000 participants investing in it for their retirement security and 120,000 individuals receiving retirement income from it. If you mean, did we expect to have more than 4,000 participating educational institutions by 1989, we did not. Did we imagine a Dow Index reaching a level, at least briefly, of more than 10 times its level when we started CREF? Well, we could dream, couldn't we? And the cost of living? Yes, we would have bemoaned but accepted the possibility that it would rise 4½-fold from 1952 to 1988.

Did we expect some complaints when individuals' CREF accounts suddenly went down sharply in 1972–74 after generally rising for many years? Yes. We had been warned it was ever thus, and we went ahead and established CREF anyway. Did we expect complaints from some people when CREF went up 30 percent in a year because it "should have gone up 31 percent that year"? Yes, that too.

Dr. Henry M. Wriston, Chairman of Trustees of T.I.A.A. Stock and President of Brown University, was issued Participation Certificate No. 1 in CREF, July 1, 1952.
(Brown University Archives)

The speed and volatility of economic change and the huge size of CREF would have astounded us. But except for speed and size, things have worked out much as expected. This retrospective, current, and prospective view of CREF will consider those factors. Such a view can be of use both for those who are retired or who are now completing their careers as the first full-career participants in CREF and for those who are participating or considering doing so.

Certainly one of the useful things that has occurred is the improvement in the total financial security of college staff members in retirement, compared with 1950. College staff members were not then eligible for Social Security. This came to the private institutions, on a voluntary basis, in 1951, and voluntarily, after a vote, for the public institutions in 1955. And in 1952, between the extension of Social Security to the private and public institutions, TIAA established a third leg to the financial stool, in the form of CREF, to achieve still greater diversification of investments and a partial hedge against inflation for retirement benefits.

ECONOMIC CLIMATE BEFORE CREF

It is useful to review some of the economic history, the post-World War II years, the challenges they posed for retirement savings plans, why CREF was established, and how it was done. People still ask how the idea of CREF arose, why TIAA (out of 1,800 then existing life insurance companies and thousands of pensions plans) was the place of its invention, whether there was anything unique about the college world or its existing pension plan that caused its implementation there, and whether there was any opposition.

There have been a few spectacular inflationary blowoffs in history—for instance, the Holland Tulip Bulb inflation and John Law's clever schemes in France. But until recently, inflations were almost always creatures of wars and the aftermaths of wars. This was true of the Revolutionary War, the Civil War, World War I, World War II, Korea, and Vietnam.

As one looks backward during this century, the sharp war-caused inflation of 1916 and 1920 leveled off and then turned downward to the Depression. The cost of living *declined* one third between 1920 and 1933.

The Depression years were ones of low, stable or declining faculty salaries, little development of benefit plans, low individual savings, and little progress toward financial security in retirement. The World War II years were even more unfavorable so far as progress toward financial security was concerned. To the above problems were added interruption of careers, continued low interest rates on savings, and growing inflation, all of which hurt pensioners. In 1941, the cost of living index stood at its 1918 level, but it increased 80 percent by 1951. By 1950, the post-World War II transition, from winding down the military economy to winding up prosperity, had been accomplished. Eleven million servicemen had been reabsorbed into the domestic economy. But then came Korea, and more inflation.

By the early 1950s, TIAA was a working lifetime old. Some professors then retiring had been covered by TIAA throughout their working years. By 1952, it covered over 80,000 policyholders at more than 600 cooperating institutions. The college world's pension plan was working well, providing fully vested, portable, contractual, fully funded pensions, a far better arrangement for higher education than the forfeitable benefits in industry. But it shared with other pension plans one overriding problem—inflation—and the damage inflation does under any fixed-income savings plan.[1]

TIAA, with its benefits based on fixed-dollar investments, was paying out every dollar it had guaranteed to annuitants and more with dividends, but many annuitants did not have enough money to live on after inflation. Social Security had not yet been indexed to cost of living changes, and it covered less than half of the college world. TIAA's investments, like those of other pension plans, were traditional fixed-dollar bonds and mortgages, with little chance of hedging effectively against inflation. Prevailing interest rates were distressingly low for all savers—less than 3 percent per annum. In many years, savers were receiving a negative real rate of return on bonds. Common stocks had acquired a bad reputation among American investors during the Great Depression. The press, government officials, pension executives, and the public blamed inflation for the situation, and they were right to do so. But that did not solve the problem. A few suggestions came to TIAA, mainly from policyholders, that it should be investing their pension savings in gold, diamonds, artworks, indexed government bonds, and other impractical or unavailable assets.

GENESIS OF THE IDEA

TIAA turned out to be a natural and, after some early discomfort, a congenial place for the variable annuity to originate. I was especially lucky to be a trained economist, part of whose job at TIAA was to improve its services to higher education. The problem of inflation was bothering some of the executive staff. The invention of CREF was a direct response to the inflation of World War II, rekindled soon after in Korea.

---

[1]Defined benefit pension plans tying benefits to final average salary give some protection against inflation that occurs far enough in advance of retirement to be reflected in the final average salary but do not protect against inflation occurring during retirement.

In late 1949, I started seriously to ponder doing something drastic about annuities and inflation. But a piece or two was missing. Would a pension plan funded only by equities do the job? But such a plan probably would go broke sooner or later in a sharp market drop, unless there was a way to avoid using dollar valuation of assets and liabilities. How could you do that, in the annuity business? Furthermore, how do you give participants a stake in the good experience when stocks are doing well, but protect them when they are not? Or— aha!—*should* you attempt that? All annuities then were guaranteed to provide a fixed number of dollars; was that necessary?

One day in late 1949, I had a chance to chat with some of my colleagues about my developing ideas. A half dozen of us met near Wall Street for a luncheon at Mazzalotti's restaurant. Dr. Roger Murray, vice president and economist of the Bankers Trust Company, Walter Mahlstedt and Disque Deane of TIAA's investment office, and two others were in the group. That was the first time I ever talked outside about the idea.

In his recent oral history, Dr. Roger Murray brought up that luncheon.[2] He indicated he remembered it very well after 40 years because of the intriguing idea presented. He said:

> When you invited me and a couple of others to lunch to discuss the very general outline of what you had in mind, what you had been thinking about, it was not that you gave us a specific blueprint. . . . Here you were talking about an annuity that didn't have a "guarantee" or a prescribed rate of anything; you're going to pay them in funny money, as compared with the standard so many dollars a month for life.

Dr. Murray emphasized the intriguing nature of the idea, but he was worried:

> My concern was that it would be extremely difficult to get a bunch of academics to understand, sit down, and listen in the first place. . . . People had been indoctrinated from childhood to the certainty of an annuity. . . . You came into this world of annuity income with an expectation that it was going to be precisely the same amount to the penny for your life and for the life of your spouse.

As to accepting the idea of common stocks for pension investments, that was no problem for Dr. Murray; his expertise on investing in equities was why he was invited to the lunch. He had been instrumental in getting a portion of corporate pension funds to try common stock investing at Bankers Trust.

---

[2]Interview with Dr. Roger Murray by WCG, March 10, 1988.

In the interview, I asked Dr. Murray about inflation, my main worry in 1950. He said inflation "was not in the range of our real concerns at the time." He was interested in the investment opportunities of the idea: "The state of the capital markets was so compelling, as you [WCG] were talking about . . . you could double your current income by owning stocks instead of bonds."

In the spring of 1950, on a trip to my alma mater, Indiana University, I visited a number of my former economics and business school faculty colleagues. On the top of our minds were the economic challenges. We discussed pensions, inflation, college endowments, investments, and the TIAA retirement system. We worried because interest earnings then of less than 3 percent on fixed dollar investments with an inflation rate of 3 percent to 4 percent meant a negative rate of real return. This did not treat savers very well. And it made saving adequately for retirement income nearly impossible.

My early teaching colleague, Finance Professor Edward E. Edwards, had his "acadermic" needle out for me: "Croan (my Indiana family name), what is TIAA doing about inflation, and why isn't it?" I then went next door to see Dr. Harry Sauvain, finance professor and later a CREF policyholder-selected trustee. We talked for some time and discussed an idea of his for investing the cash values of life insurance in equities. From my different perspective, I was thinking about annuities.

It was that specific conversation that dropped into place the final missing piece for the variable annuity.

I can still remember how neatly it all suddenly arranged itself in my mind. A lifetime annuity free to move up or down in direct proportion to the value of a portfolio of common stocks. The "aha" idea was "express everything in units, not dollars." Go ahead and make guarantees, but express them as units not dollars. And let the unit values flow freely, up and down, precisely in tune with the immediate values of the common stocks in the fund.

This fit perfectly with my conviction that a pension based on equity investments should have no reserves, no solvency tests. It should be constructed exactly backward from usual annuities. In conventional annuities, the life insurance company, or pension fund, added up its liabilities first, then its assets. If the assets exceeded the liabilities, great. It not, bankruptcy or shovel in more money.

The new fund would do it the other way. Add up the assets and then by definition have the liabilities equal—be defined by, as it were—the amount of the assets. And express it in units. When stock prices were high, the unit values would be large, and assets and liabilities would both be large. When the market was depressed, unit values would be low, and assets and liabilities would both be low. Liabilities would equal assets by definition. There could never come a time of forced liquidation of stocks at the worst moment, at the bottom (or any time).

The Indiana University group continued its interest in and helpfulness toward the variable annuity. The group included Sauvain and Edwards; Herman B Wells, then president of Indiana University; Arthur M. Weimer, dean of the School of Business; and Professors John Mee and Edward Hedges.[3] Some time later, it became the first outside group to discuss the concept in depth. Professors Sauvain, Edwards, Mee, and Weimer and President Wells all recounted in their oral histories the excitement generated by the discussion of the idea of "TERF" (CREF's early working name, Teachers Equity Retirement Fund) and their pleasure at being present at the creation.[4]

The idea had been developed, but a vast amount of work by many people lay ahead. There were many chances for failure and a good bit of opposition. Professor Sauvain, writing later to a third party, commented, "The road from having the idea to implementing it in the form of CREF on July 1, 1952, was a long, difficult, and chancy one. You deserve to know what the pioneers at TIAA accomplished on behalf of the college world." But *Business Week's* issue of June 6, 1959, put it somewhat differently: "Credit—or blame, depending on your point of view—for the variable annuity concept belongs to William C. Greenough. . . . "

My initial attempts at TIAA to suggest a lifetime annuity based on common stock investments were not welcomed; in fact, they elicited a "How could anybody be so stupid" response. The psychological climate in 1950 and 1951 for use of equity investments to support annuity payments was not good. As an example, the TIAA Financial Report for 1949, published in the spring of 1950, stated the traditional approach against investing pension funds in common stocks:

> Safety of principal must of necessity be the primary criterion when investing funds of this type. . . . Retirement and life insurance reserves should be invested in relatively risk-free obligations. . . . Securities of a fluctuating or speculative nature, such as common stocks, have little justified use for such purposes. Pension funds which have been invested partially in common stocks with sincere intent to provide some hedge against inflation will undoubtedly be "under water" in the future as they have been at times in the past.

---

[3]Sauvain was selected by the policyholders for the TIAA board in 1966 and served on the board until 1976 and on the Finance Committee from 1969 to 1976; Wells was an original CREF trustee, serving from 1952 to age 70 in 1972.

[4]TIAA-CREF Oral History Interviews with Professor Harry Sauvain, October 6, 1980; Professor Edward E. Edwards, October 7, 1980; Professor John F. Mee, October 6, 1980; Professor Arthur M. Weimer, October 7, 1980; and Dr. Herman B Wells, November 6, 1980; Robert Lord, interviewer.

A breakthrough in selling the CREF idea occurred at the American Economic Association meeting in Chicago in December 1950. Dr. Harold Torgerson, finance professor at Northwestern University, sought me out to tell me that Northwestern was very much in favor of TIAA, thought it did an excellent job, but that some people were so worried about inflation and its effects on pensions that they were studying alternative ways of handling their pension funds. They had looked at the New York insurance law and found it so restrictive that TIAA could not meet their needs.

I told Dr. Torgerson something about my thoughts on annuities based on common stock investments and suggested they wait awhile and give TIAA a chance. Meanwhile, similar pressures had built up at the University of Chicago, Columbia, and Harvard—no answer to the problem, but a questioning as to whether New York insurance law was too restrictive on the investment side.

Armed with this additional pressure, I returned to TIAA, asked for a meeting of the management committee, and at that meeting opened it by saying, "Unless we do something, within the next year I believe we will lose three of our six most important institutions, and not from dissatisfaction with TIAA, but with dissatisfaction over the limits in the New York insurance law on investments for life insurance companies."

This approach improved the acoustics. I then presented my ideas for an annuity based on common stock investments. The management committee discussed the ideas for about 2 ½ hours. From that day in early January 1951, none of the top five officers of TIAA got much rest or relaxation until CREF was in operation July 1, 1952.

INITIAL BARRIERS

Had it not been for unusual factors, TIAA might not have been successful in establishing CREF. The obstacles were great. All of the state laws regarding insurance and annuities and the federal tax laws were based on the assumption of fixed-dollar investments standing behind guaranteed insurance and annuities. Equity investments were sharply limited or forbidden. Solvency tests were provided in the laws and regulations. There was no provision for a variable annuity based solely on equity investments because none had ever been proposed. And there was the formidable barrier in the early 1950s of fear of common stocks, stemming from the Great Depression.

The idea of common stocks as a basis for pension plan savings was radical. As Dr. Murray in his oral history interview said concerning the late 1940s and early 50s, "The idea of owning significant quantities of equities [in any pension plan] was still very strange and unreal."

Too many people had lost too much money during the Great Depression. They had bought stocks at the height of the enthusiasm in 1929, not in 1924, and by 1932, stock prices were back to their 1924 levels. They bet on the nose of one stock, having literally heard a tip in an elevator or from a supposedly knowledgeable shoeshine boy (insider information?). And they bought on margin. It was not common stocks that were bad; it was the methods of investing and speculating in them that were. But few were ready to accept the idea of common stock investments for anything depending on "safety of principal."

The first full-scale memorandum I distributed to TIAA's top management was titled "How Can TIAA Best Serve Higher Education."[5] In the January 10, 1951, memorandum, I tried to present a fair and systematic appraisal of all TIAA contracts, identifying the many provisions that accomplished our goals, but also pointing to clear weaknesses, especially as to the purchasing power of annuities. The memorandum concluded:

> The major weaknesses [of TIAA] have to do with the investment side of the program, statistically with yield and inflation. These weaknesses, of course, are not unique with TIAA; they are inherent at the present time in all dollar savings plans, for instance, government, corporate, utility or other bonds, other life insurance companies, savings banks, and the sock in the mattress. Consideration should be given to alternative methods of investment which might ameliorate some of the problems.

CREF'S FORTUNATE PARENTAGE

Variable annuities could not have had a more congenial birthplace than within the college retirement system. CREF was lucky to have as its parent the extraordinarily designed TIAA retirement system for colleges and universities. TIAA was unique in providing full and immediate vesting. And it was the only large defined contribution plan with individually owned contracts. All of these aspects fit with the new suggestion of broadening the investment base for pensions, with participants sharing fully in the investment performance.

In the case of TIAA, participants receive full title to all contributions and earnings thereon paid on their behalf by themselves and by their employing institutions. They receive the full investment performance from dividends, interest, and net capital gains. Nothing is siphoned off to profits. Surplus or contingency reserves not needed to meet losses are returned, actuarially, to annuitants both before and

---

[5]WCG, "How Can TIAA Best Serve Higher Education," January 10, 1951, TIAA-CREF Archives, Law Department Files.

during their retirement. Policyholders accept the risk of investment performance less favorable than expected and receive as a reward all of the gains on their investment funds over their lifetimes.

When CREF was established, it was easy philosophically and practically to carry the same principles over from TIAA to CREF, with even more current precision. TIAA was a fully participating annuity in practice; CREF was specifically so designed but with equities as its investment base. TIAA's benefits were immediately and fully vested in the participant; so it would be with CREF. TIAA's benefits were portable, and contractual; so it would be with CREF. This permitted the establishment of long-range common stock investment fund participation that would give the individual an opportunity for investment across business cycles, in the ups and downs of the market, a pattern that always, over any reasonable length of time, had performed well.

In 1952, most conventional retirement plans were based on defined benefit formulas. Under such plans, whether for industry, business, or government, the investment fund is, in a sense, just a convenience to the employer in meeting future obligations. Under a defined benefit plan, the employer takes the risk of investment performance poorer than expected and receives the benefit of investment gains. The employee looks to his or her employer to pay the promised benefits, not to the pension investments, which are a means of carrying out the employer's promises. So the variable annuity concept is not applicable to defined benefit plans.

The college world's defined contribution approach to retirement income also was more compatible than defined benefit plans with the inflow of investment money to pension funds. Defined contributions in the college world were based almost always on the same percentage of salary at all ages being used to purchase annuities. This assured the individual participant that he or she would be purchasing common stocks through CREF with a reasonably even flow of funds at all levels of the market, thereby minimizing the risk of large fluctuations. It also assured full participation in the long-term gains of common stocks and the development of the American economy.

All of these aspects of the operating TIAA college retirement system were incorporated in CREF. This permitted the retirement system built up by the colleges over the years to remain stable while changing the investment options through adding CREF.

COMMON STOCK INVESTMENTS FAMILIAR

There were other reasons the college world was a friendly place for the variable annuity innovation. A number of farsighted colleges in America had invested part of their endowments in common stocks as early as the 1920s. Even a casual look backward at common stock investments during the first years of the 20th century encouraged the conclusion that this could be a good source for college endowment investments. A survey by Morgan Stanley in July 1950 showed that at 14 major colleges, an average of 43 percent of endowment college funds were invested in common stocks.[6]

The insurance industry had taken just the opposite tack. As mentioned, common stocks were not legal investments for life insurance companies in New York from 1906 to 1950. By an accident of history, TIAA was the only insurance company domiciled in New York whose investment staff had been investing in common stocks for many years. TIAA shared in the Carnegie Teachers Co-operative Investment Office, a central office handling the investments for TIAA, the Carnegie Foundation for the Advancement of Teaching, the Carnegie Institution of Washington, the Carnegie Endowment for International Peace, and other Carnegie trusts.[7]

The Carnegie trusts had no legal restrictions on their investments. Therefore, the Co-operative Investment Office, operating since 1927, had experts in equity investments as well as in bonds and mortgages. The Carnegie Foundation discontinued its participation in the office in 1948, and when CREF was established, TIAA took over the entire office, including its common stock experts; the other Carnegie endowments went to other investment managers.

---

[6]"Pension Plans and Common Stocks," Morgan Stanley and Co., July 1950, p. 49.

[7]Savage, *Fruit of an Impulse*, pp. 132–133, 324. Savage relates that the idea of a cooperative office was proposed in a 1923 memorandum by Samuel S. Hall, Jr., of TIAA, apparently prompted by President Henry Pritchett.

CHAPTER 8

New Approaches, New Decisions, New Designs

Selling the idea internally was an interesting challenge, but, once accomplished, all TIAA turned to development of the new variable annuity with enthusiasm, support, great technical ability, and imagination.

Development of the variable annuity quickly involved all aspects of pensions and annuities and, therefore, the time of TIAA's then small staff of actuaries, lawyers, the economist, investment people, and management. A challenge for TIAA was how to keep everything going well, while directing the time and energies of several top officers to the new venture. New concepts of actuarial valuations and structuring, very long-term investment approach to common stock ownership, operational matters, public explanations, and complicated and at times exasperating efforts to change laws, regulations, and supervision at the federal and state levels were all necessary.

In the winter and early spring of 1951, TIAA sought the opinions and advice of people especially familiar with TIAA: the trustees, officers from the Carnegie Foundation and Carnegie Corporation, and a few representatives from college business offices. Management also wanted to know the response of TIAA's longtime actuary and a member of the TIAA board, Rainard Robbins, then living in retirement in Charlottesville, Virginia.

Robbins was skeptical of the plan for a variable annuity. In a long memorandum, he presented many questions and objections; he was especially concerned as to the reactions of participants in a down market. He also emphasized difficulties in the administration of an open-end trust.[1] It says much for the strength of McAllister Lloyd's

---

[1] Robbins, "Pension Payments from an Open End Trust," January 30, 1951, TIAA-CREF Archives, Law Department Files.

acceptance of the variable annuity idea that Robbins' strong criticisms did not shake Lloyd's dedication to the proposal.[2] Although TIAA's chairman and president was by no means convinced that the efforts would be successful, he would do everything possible to achieve success. Robbins died shortly afterward; I believe he ultimately would have been in favor of CREF.

We heard many doubts, reservations, and questions, but the overriding reaction to the idea of an equity fund was favorable. The results of the early conferences and meetings with TIAA's trustees, officers of the Carnegie organizations, and college business officers encouraged management to proceed.

TERF

As reported earlier, the working name for CREF during the early months was TERF, Teachers Equity Retirement Fund. The pronunciation of the working name conjured up visions we were not enthusiastic about, so we acceded gracefully when the New York Insurance Department refused to allow the use of "Teachers" in the name of the new fund for fear of implications that a New York insurance company would be financially responsible if something went wrong.

TASK FORCES

In organizing the work to be done, McAllister Lloyd appointed task forces to attack the massive and complicated problems:

- *Economic task force* to study whether the idea as presented would help provide better economic security for college staff members during varying economic conditions, how the proposal for common stock investments would have worked in the past, and what investment approach would be appropriate.
- *Actuarial task force* to work out the pioneering new formulas for the variable annuity and the many basic departures from conventional insurance practices.
- *Legal task force* to draft new contracts and legislation, to meet and overcome any political opposition, and to spearhead the effort to achieve all approvals necessary.
- *Organization task force* to design corporate governance for the new pension plan and attract the level of board and officer talent needed for its success.

There followed 18 months of 80-hour weeks in which everyone was exhausted, but no one felt tired. The effort was much too exciting

---

[2]Lloyd to Robbins, February 5, 1951, TIAA-CREF Archives, Law Department Files.

and potentially worthwhile for that. But it takes much work to make a fundamental change in a 200-year-old publicly regulated industry steeped in conservatism and legal restraints.

This chapter describes the economic and actuarial task forces. Chapter 9 will report on the opposition and support for the new idea and the sometimes delicate, sometimes exasperating, but ultimately successful efforts to achieve legislative and regulatory approval. Chapter 9 will also report on the organization and implementation of CREF.

Economic Task Force

The first job was to see whether the proposed variable annuity had a reasonable chance of working in practice. It seemed appropriate to test whether a variable annuity would have worked well in the past. Such a study would be no guarantee it would work well in the future, but it was the only real test of experience available.

The economic studies were under my direction. To accumulate and analyze a vast amount of data was a challenge in the pre-computer age. Each request to the TIAA Actuarial Department to study the data in some different pattern resulted in a two-week additional burden. In the 1980s, all of the data would be in a central processing unit, and someone could sit at a console studying a dozen different configurations in only a few minutes. But not then.

I was unprepared for the knowledge gap that existed. I had assumed there would be many reliable studies of the relationship between the cost of living, common stock prices, and dividends. At a minimum, I expected reliable studies of accumulating common stock investments. I found there were none. We commissioned TIAA's top investment officer, Parker Monroe, and two outside economists to find valid studies, and they came up empty-handed.

There were many studies of a single-sum payment to purchase common stocks on a given date, accumulated with dividends, and then sold later. These showed extreme volatility according to whether the single sum was invested at a low in 1921 or a high in 1929 and taken out at a high in 1929 or a low in 1933. Slightly better were a few illustrations of the dollar cost averaging principle applied to buying a single stock. One studied the consequences of investing $1,000 each year in Atchison, Topeka & Santa Fe Railroad beginning in 1927 and ending in 1946. Ten other prominent single stocks were similarly studied for the limited period.[3]

---

[3]C. R. Sanderson's July 1947 *Exchange* article is summarized in Benjamin Graham and David L. Dodd, *Security Analysis,* 3rd ed. (New York: McGraw-Hill Book Co., Inc., 1951), pp. 58–59.

All of the then current studies of common stock investing were based on methods that led to great glee or to disappointments and catastrophes, according to the timing of purchases or choice of a particular stock. And this was, in general, the pre-CREF approach to common stock investing. It was a major reason common stock investing had such a bad name.

We designed CREF to use an utterly different approach to common stock investing, namely, monthly contributions over the entire working careers of educators would be invested in an accumulating fund during all levels of business conditions and then withdrawn as an annuity over a number of years, not in a single sum. This method of accumulating and "decumulating" over time was shown by the economic study to have great promise of success, and it has so worked in the ensuing 37 years. The economic study was completed in the summer of 1951 and published by TIAA in December 1951, under the title *A New Approach to Retirement Income*, by William C. Greenough.[4] It was the first study of an accumulating diversified stock fund and, of course, the first study of a variable annuity.

Because credible statistical studies of funds accumulated through steady, periodic investment in common stocks were nonexistent, we had to start from scratch. Robert M. Duncan, actuary, and Ida Cepicka, security analyst, organized the data and statistical methods, working with the author. Once the study was under way, I sought technical review from economists at the National Bureau of Economic Research: Dr. R. J. Saulnier, director of the Financial Research Program for the National Bureau of Economic Research, and his colleagues Dr. W. B. Hickman and Dr. David Durand. Dr. Saulnier later became chairman of President Eisenhower's Council of Economic Advisors; Dr. Hickman became president of the Federal Reserve Bank of Cleveland; and Dr. Durand became professor at MIT's Alfred P. Sloan School of Management.

We decided to study how a variable annuity would have worked as far back as adequate data were available, which turned out to be 1880. By studying the period from 1880 to 1950, we were able to include two world wars, a great depression, and three or four monetary panics or lesser recessions. We could cover long periods of reasonable economic stability, periods when the cost of living was going down because of growth in the economy and its productivity, and periods of inflation.

---

[4]*A New Approach to Retirement Income.* An Economic Report prepared by William C. Greenough, Ph.D., vice president of Teachers Insurance and Annuity Association of America, as background for its proposed College Retirement Equities Fund; A new method of providing retirement income through periodic investments in common stocks and the payment of a variable, or unit, annuity in combination with a fixed dollar annuity (New York: TIAA, 1951).

The general description of the new approach was:

The method of investing planned for the College Retirement Equities Fund combines a number of well-known principles into a broad new pattern. The principle of *diversification among issues* of equity investments would be obtained through pooling a portion of the annuity savings of many employers and individuals into a substantial fund invested in hundreds of companies in many industries. The principle of *diversification over time* would be obtained by accepting small payments, month by month and year by year, over a major portion of each participant's working lifetime. These payments would be directly related to salary and therefore would continue at all levels of common stock prices. Effective use would be made of the principle of *dollar cost averaging* whereby more shares of stock are purchased at low prices than at high. . . .

Perhaps the most interesting development is the *unit annuity*. Few individuals can accumulate enough by retirement time to live entirely on the earnings from investments. Under ordinary conditions, the retired individual dares not dip too deeply into principal because he has no way of knowing how long he and his wife will live. Some people die soon after retirement; others live 30 years or longer. By use of the traditional life annuity, an individual can, with safety, use up capital as well as interest earnings and thereby obtain a substantially higher income throughout the remainder of his life.

The unit annuity directly applies that same principle to a new area of investment, common stocks, allowing the individual the assurance again that he can use up both capital and dividend payments without danger of outliving his income.[5]

Three compelling conclusions emerged from the economic report:

1. It is unwise to commit *all* of one's retirement savings to dollar obligations, since decreases in the purchasing power of the dollar can seriously reduce the value of a fixed income annuity. Increases in the purchasing power of the dollar, on the other hand, improve the status of the owner of a fixed income annuity.

2. It is equally unwise to commit *all* of one's retirement savings to equity investments, since variations in prices of common stocks are much too pronounced to permit full reliance on them for the stable income needed during retirement. Changes in the value of common stocks and other equities are by no means perfectly correlated with cost of living changes, but they have provided a considerably better protection against inflation than have debt obligations.

3. Contributions to a retirement plan that are invested partly in debt obligations and partly in common stocks through an Equities Fund providing lifetime unit annuities offer promise of supplying re-

---

[5]WCG, *A New Approach*, pp. 12–13.

tirement income that is at once reasonably free from violent fluctuations in amount and from serious depreciation through price level changes.

These conclusions were based on 70 years of retrospective data from 1880 to 1950. Actual experience of CREF over the ensuing 37 years has confirmed and strengthened all three conclusions. Perhaps they are a partial answer to the question asked at the start of this section: "Has CREF worked as expected?"

There were several subsidiary conclusions, given here in full because of their continuing relevance to individual, employer, and pension system decisions:

4. The Equities Fund should make no dollar guarantees. Its liabilities should always be directly valued in terms of its assets. This is a cardinal point of the suggested arrangement for two principal reasons:

a. It assures that the Equities Fund is "failure proof" in the technical sense and cannot be forced into liquidation of its assets at a low point in the market. Whether the market be high or low, the Equities Fund obligations are automatically limited to the then market value of its assets. Typical pension plans whose liabilities are expressed in dollar guarantees and whose assets are partially in fluctuating securities, such as common stocks, are vulnerable in this connection.

b. It assures the individual participant his full prorata share in any rise in the net asset value of the Equities Fund. Under typical pension plans invested partially in common stocks, the employer gives a fixed dollar pension assurance to his employees. Any appreciation in common stock values is normally used to reduce the employer's cost or to create reserves, whereas it is needed in a period of rising prices as an increased benefit for the employees. Through a common stock fund free from the confinements of dollar promises, a participant can have a wider opportunity to share in the development of the American economy with part of his savings. Obviously, this opportunity to share in rises must be accompanied by a willingness to share in falls of the net asset values.

5. Common stock investments obtained through purchases month by month, at low prices as well as high, would have provided a very effective method of investing a portion of retirement funds. Most of the difficulties in individual investing in equities arise from lack of diversification *among shares* and *over time*. So long as the period of regular payments into a fund invested in common stocks was reasonably long, so long as each person owned a portion of a large, well-diversified fund and so long as there were no substantial shifts either into or out of equities at a particular moment, the experience was normally considerably better than that of a fund invested wholly or principally in debt obligations.

FIGURE 8–1 Amounts of Accumulation and Annuity (resulting from investment of $100 per year)

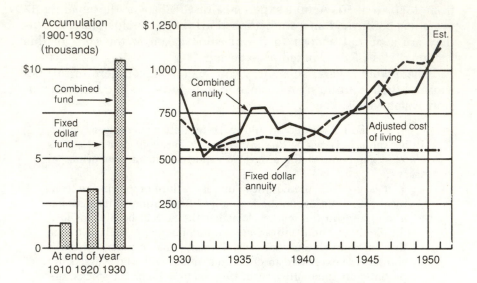

6. Substantial problems exist whenever an individual has the option to invest a large *single* payment in *either* an equities fund or a fixed-dollar fund. If he had invested $10,000 in common stocks in 1929, he would have seen it drop in value to $2,600 in 1932. (Since the price level was also falling, the purchasing power value would have been $3,250.) Likewise, if he had invested $10,000 in government bonds, a savings account, or a life insurance fund in 1914, it would have declined in *purchasing power value* to $5,000 in 1920. (Both figures exclude interest and dividend additions.)

The economic report contained a number of charts and data tables so the diligent reader could check all conclusions and dig as deeply as he or she wished. Reproduced here are the most frequently reprinted chart, Figure 8–1, and the table with the source data, Table 8–1, chosen because it gave the worst experience, that of an individual who paid in contributions to purchase annuities from 1900 to 1930 and then retired just at the outset of the Great Depression and the collapse of common stock prices.

As shown in the bars on the left side of Figure 8–1, the participant would have paid in $3,000 between 1900 and 1930, and this would have accumulated to $6,499 in a fixed-dollar fund and $10,469 in the combined bond and stock fund.

When the participant then retired, he or she would have received a fixed-dollar annuity of $552 throughout retirement. A combined annuity of stocks and bonds would have started munificently at $907 in 1930, dropped to a low of $503 in 1932, and then risen to $1,007 in 1950.

In the figure, the adjusted cost of living line shows the size of annuity income that would have perfectly hedged against inflation occurring both before and after retirement.

TABLE 8–1 Amounts of Accumulation and Annuity 1900–1950

	Amounts of Accumulation Resulting from Investment of $100 per Year 1900–1930		
Accumulation Period	Fixed Dollar Fund	Common Stock Fund	Combined Fund
1900–1910	$1,228	$ 1,439	$ 1,333
1900–1920	3,188	3,333	3,261
1900–1930	6,499	14,437	10,469

Amounts of Annual Annuity 1930–1950
Purchased by Above Accumulations

Year	Amounts of Annual Annuity			Adjusted Cost of Living Annuity[1]	Purchasing Power Comparison[2] 100% = Constant Purchasing Power		
	Fixed Annuity	Unit Annuity	Combined Annuity		Fixed Annuity	Unit Annuity	Combined Annuity
1930	$552	$1,263	$ 907	$ 724	76%	174%	125%
1931	552	824	689	659	84	125	105
1932	552	454	503	592	93	76	85
1933	552	587	570	560	98	104	101
1934	552	670	611	580	95	115	105
1935	552	720	636	595	93	121	107
1936	552	1,009	780	601	92	168	130
1937	552	1,019	786	622	89	164	127
1938	552	773	662	611	90	126	108
1939	552	834	693	602	91	137	114
1940	552	787	670	607	91	129	110
1941	552	736	644	638	86	114	100
1942	552	661	607	706	78	94	86
1943	552	874	714	749	74	117	96
1944	552	951	752	761	72	124	98
1945	552	1,150	851	778	71	148	110
1946	552	1,315	933	844	65	155	110
1947	552	1,169	860	965	57	121	89
1948	552	1,198	875	1,038	53	115	84
1949	552	1,194	874	1,025	54	117	86
1950	552	1,462	1,007	1,038	53	140	97
1951[3]	552	1,785	1,168	1,119	49	159	104

[1]The adjusted cost of living column shows the amount of annuity necessary each year so that the fixed-dollar annuity would have adjusted to cost of living changes occurring during both the accumulation and the annuity period.

[2]The purchasing power comparison is obtained by dividing the amount of annual annuity provided by each of the three funds by the adjusted cost of living annuity.

[3]Estimated to October 1951.

The economic study was undertaken to test the idea of CREF without contemplating that it would be published. But the idea did not sell itself; it required much explanation, and crucial people had to be convinced it would have worked and had a high probability of working in the future. And they wanted the data, charts and tables and all, as developed in the original study. So the study was published and was used widely to explain CREF and convince doubters.

Actuarial Task Force

The second of the four task forces was the actuarial task force, under the direction of Wilmer A. Jenkins, TIAA administrative vice president and later president of the Society of Actuaries from 1961–1962, and Robert M. Duncan, also a fellow of the society and TIAA actuary.

Jenkins and Duncan had to design several basic departures from the life insurance industry and from pensions as then known. For example:

1. A life annuity contract with *no* guarantees—no investment, no mortality rate, no expense guarantees.
2. A *fully participating* annuity contract—not just dividends in an amount selected by a board of directors; rather, complete distribution of all dividend earnings, and all realized *and unrealized* capital gains and losses, credited currently and determined by formula.
3. Formulas for computing the new accumulation unit values and lifetime annuity unit values that credited all dividend earnings and all net capital changes credited currently to participants.
4. An issuing company without contingency reserves or surplus for adverse mortality, expense, or investment experience.

This necessitated a company that would reverse the normal insurance valuation procedures. Although it did not gain much attention at the time, it was a startling change. Instead of adding up the total liabilities of the company and then hoping there were enough assets on hand to cover them and additional reserves for prudent management, the process would be reversed. The total assets would be added up first, and then that amount would by definition be the total liabilities, to be allocated among participants by formula. There would be no contingency reserves.

All of these objectives were accomplished in the original CREF design.

Duncan and Jenkins then set to work on the operating formulas for CREF. They worked out the detailed formulas for valuing the accumulation and the annuity unit values at all times. This included holding the annuity unit value steady for a year and then changing it as of March 31 each year. They designed the precise valuations for persons starting an annuity in the middle of a year after stocks had either risen or fallen from their starting point.

How to handle longevity? Traditional annuities had not been handled well by insurance companies, including TIAA for its first 18 years, or by pension funds. They had used retrospective mortality tables that underestimated life spans. Once their mistakes caused substantial losses, they began to build in reserves and frequently to overestimate life spans.

Neither approach would be good for CREF participants. Here, for the first time, groups of participants could be awarded their fair share of the total fund. The valuation methods for the annuity unit would choose an annuity mortality table expressing current longevity rates, neither conservative nor liberal. Then at the end of each year, the actual mortality experience of CREF annuitants would be used to adjust values for the coming year. Every five years a change in the mortality base would be considered and necessary adjustments made. Thus, small changes would be made each year and each five years to reflect actual mortality experience of annuitants.

Wilmer Jenkins outlined the proposed operation of CREF at the April 1952 meeting of the Society of Actuaries for informal discussion,[6] and Bob Duncan presented a seminal paper on the variable annuity proposal at the society's June meeting.[7] Duncan's paper reprinted much of the economic study and then presented the many formulas he and Jenkins had worked out for handling the fund.

DESIGNING THE CONTRACT

CREF was to be a true "new approach" to both common stock investing and to retirement annuity investing. Much uncharted territory lay ahead. In designing a new financial product as complex as a variable, lifetime annuity to fund college retirement plans, a large number of decisions had to be made and had to be made quickly, sensibly, and correctly. This section will describe the major questions and the reasons certain decisions were made. Many of the questions are as relevant today as they were at the start of CREF.

Designing the contract for the variable annuity proved to be a challenge, but one well met by Wilmer Jenkins and Robert Duncan.

---

[6]Duncan, "Discussion of Unit Annuity at Meeting of Society of Actuaries in Washington, D.C.—April 24th and 25th," May 1, 1952, WCG Files; the published account is: "Digest of Informal Discussion: Retirement Plans," *Transactions of the Society of Actuaries* 4 (1952), pp. 160–65.

[7]Duncan, "A Retirement System Granting Unit Annuities and Investing in Equities," *Transactions of the Society of Actuaries* 4 (1952), pp. 317–44; discussion, pp. 770–88.

In structure, in philosophy, and in provisions, it was to be unlike any annuity contract previously devised. The new contract would be expressed in units, not dollars. It would not guarantee any specific number of dollars. But it would guarantee fair and equitable treatment on the new actuarial variable annuity bases and proportional participation in the new funds.

Jenkins and Duncan recommended two funds for CREF, one for the accumulation of individual and college contributions before retirement and the other for pooling the annuity rights of participants. The first would be expressed as accumulation units, the second as annuity units. The actuarial methods of valuation of the two funds, and participants' share in them, would be determined by "rules of the fund," separate from the annuity contract itself but specified in the contract. The contract would be under the supervision of the New York Department of Insurance, its regulatory authority, and periodic examinations to assure fair and equitable treatment of participants, as specified in New York insurance law, would be carried out.

The final step in designing a new contract was to bring together a draft prepared by the TIAA Actuarial Department, incorporating all the necessary actuarial provisions, with a draft prepared by the Law Department. The actuarial draft had to provide precise methods for valuation, which originally were in the separate Rules of the Fund. The legal draft had to conform as closely as possible with existing insurance law, but it had to deviate in important respects appropriate to the new variable annuity.

The first effort to merge the actuarial and the law drafts resulted in a complex, technical, wordy form. We already were having trouble explaining the variable annuity. If we served up to our prospective participants an amalgam of actuaries' and lawyers' words, we would multiply the difficulty. TIAA solved the problem in a unique— unique for insurance policies, at least—way. In a memorandum to George Johnson, head of the legal task force, I suggested:

> I wonder if the first page could not be a very simple statement of the broad outlines of the plan, eliminating all unnecessary words, legal qualifications, and the like. Could it not be merely descriptive in nature, rather than summary? For a certificate of this sort it seems particularly inappropriate to have a 154-word sentence as contained in the fifth paragraph on the first page.[8]

As I tried in one meeting to make sense out of what the lawyers and actuaries were saying, I wrote on a lined pad a general description of the new annuity contract. We decided that if it helped me, it might help the policyholders. So my rough draft, smoothed up a bit,

---

[8]WCG to Johnson, May 8, 1952, re CREF Certificate.

became the first page of the final annuity contract. This General Description at the outset specified that it was not a part of the contract, but an effort to describe just what a variable annuity was in nontechnical language. It has served this purpose over the years and helped to avoid the frequent criticism of insurance policies that they are not understandable and are filled with fine print. The *National Underwriter's* issue of August 15, 1952, complimented CREF on the readability approach of the General Description and added:

> If the plan is well received by the certificate-holders and does not involve a significant amount of litigation, it might well be the answer to the often-heard criticisms that insurance policies are so full of legalistic phraseology that it takes a good lawyer to understand one.

This was a double-edged sendoff, but more than 35 years later the General Description is an accepted part of the CREF contract.

Participants in the new plan would own units, not dollars. How would this work?

Why Two Units?

There are two quite different periods of participation by CREF participants, each accounted for by different units—the accumulating period before retirement when they are purchasing their future annuity income and the retirement period when they are receiving a lifetime annuity they cannot outlive. The accumulation unit value reflects only investment and expense factors, while the annuity unit also reflects lifetime annuity experience. It would be more equitable to spread the gains and losses on annuitant mortality experience only over the retired group. The decision to keep the retiree's income from CREF steady for a year at a time also required two units.

The choice of separate units for the pay-in and the pay-out periods also allowed a transition to daily valuation of the CREF accumulation unit, commencing April 1, 1988. When CREF was established in the precomputer era, it was a major job to record accumulations for all participants once a month. The introduction of computers has, for TIAA-CREF and the entire financial world, caused a revolution in providing useful information to participants.

Ever since 1952, early in each month and especially in April, there was practically a line at the door of Warren Carter, TIAA-CREF second vice president. From the start, he has been in charge of computing the accumulation unit and the annuity unit values of CREF in accordance with the formulae. Warren Carter is one of the very few employees still at CREF who was "there at the creation."

Value of Accumulation Unit

For each premium paid to CREF, the participant is credited with a number of accumulation units. The number of units credited depends on the current value of the accumulation unit. The value of the accumulation unit is determined each month by dividing the current market value of all common stocks in CREF's accumulation fund by the total number of accumulation units outstanding. Thus, the participant buys fewer units for the same premium amount when the accumulation unit value is higher; more units when it is lower. The value of the participant's total CREF accumulation rises and falls with the monthly change in the value of the accumulation unit.

For the first 35 years of CREF, the accumulation unit value changes were based solely on changes in capital values of the common stocks in the fund, with dividend income being used to purchase additional accumulation units. This allowed participants to see the number of accumulation units they owned increase from time to time by dividends. It allowed an easy separation of the investment performance into its components of capital gain and dividends. As of December 31, 1986, these values were combined so the accumulation unit value changes now include both capital values and dividend income. This was not a substantive change; there was no change in the value of the individual's participation in CREF. The original decision to separate the capital values and dividend income was a sort of flip-of-the-coin choice. The new method of combining dividends and capital items in valuing the accumulation unit makes real sense for CREF, because CREF uses a true "total return" concept. This means a dollar of investment return, after expenses, is now credited precisely the same way whether it is capital or dividend income.

Value of Annuity Unit

When a participant retires, his or her CREF retirement income is expressed not as a fixed number of dollars, but as a fixed number of annuity units payable each month for life. The dollar value of the CREF annuity unit changes from year to year to reflect the market value and dividend income of the fund's investments in excess of a 4 percent assumed earnings rate that is credited to participants as part of their annuity income payments. Small factors in the valuations are expenses and a life annuity mortality computation.

Why Is the Annuity Value Kept Constant for a Year?

It would be reassuring for individuals if they could plan their budgeting for a full year. It would be more economical for CREF to manage the individual accounts in the precomputer era. The more the TIAA planners looked at this question, the less they thought the annuity unit value needed to be changed during the year. All that would do would be to impose a series of little squiggles in monthly annuities paid to participants.

We considered withdrawing from the CREF common stock fund the total amount of annuity payments CREF would have to make during an ensuing year and placing that amount in short-term money market type investments. But when we compared the performance of those normally very low interest rate investments with the higher returns on common stocks, we found variability would not be reduced much, and what reduction there was would not compensate for the loss of the higher total returns over time on common stocks. So the final decision was made to hold the annuity unit value constant for a year at a time and to keep fully invested in stocks.

Why the March 31 Date for Changing the Annuity Unit Valuation?

March 31 was a neutral date on which to value the annuity pay-out unit—there were no tax implications or other persistent biases in common stock performance on that date. Actually, TIAA tested December 31 and other possible dates and could not find persistent biases with them but concluded they might develop, from tax or other reasons, in the future. We considered using three month-end values to smooth the amount of benefit payment somewhat, but found over a long period that it did not result in much smoothing. It did, however, cause further lags in reflecting current common stock experience.

Why Not Average the Pay-Out Benefits?

One of the more frequent proposals over the years has been: why not smooth out the annuity benefits and their upward and downward movements from year to year? Any averaging creates a lag in the payment of the fully participating benefits. This would delay adjustment to inflationary forces for retired people who may already be trying to live comfortably on an impaired income. Furthermore, a lag would not give equitable treatment among participants. And such a smoothing process would necessitate some kind of reserves, contrary to the full participation design of CREF. Nonetheless, careful computations were made with three-year running averages, weighted averages of, say, 1–2–3 for three years, and other more sophisticated arrangements, but each of them meant that whenever there was a trend in common stock prices, the variable annuity would be slower to reflect it in the benefits. This was deemed not appropriate.

ORIGINAL RESTRICTIONS

When CREF was new, it was considered prudent from the standpoint of pension funding and politically necessary with regulatory authorities, college officers, and trustees to make sure participants had a strong base of Social Security benefits and TIAA savings before venturing into the new system. Originally, participants and their colleges could put any amount up to 50 percent, but not more, into the CREF variable annuity. If an individual participated and then dropped out, he or she could not re-enter for five years unless the dropping out was in connection with a leave of absence, transfer to another employing institution with different rules, and so on. Transfers from CREF to TIAA were originally allowed only over age 60.

These rules were a direct result of the newness of CREF. No one knew how individuals or their employing institutions would react to this new approach to retirement income. No one could assure the colleges, individuals, the state insurance department, or anybody else as to whether individuals' participation would be responsible or quixotic. Memories of the 1929 and the 1937 periods in stock investing were not reassuring regarding reactions of the general public, or professionals for that matter. Would individuals and colleges accept new methods of month-by-month, year-by-year investment in equities? Or would they try to play the market with their own and the college's retirement contributions? When the market went down, would they then rejoice at low prices for buying new units or panic and drop out? When stock prices were higher, would they keep investing steadily or suddenly go euphoric and decide to invest much more heavily, shifting funds from their fixed-dollar savings?

We concluded restrictions could be placed at the start and then dropped if not necessary, but they could not be imposed later. We incorporated restrictions and then monitored the experience—following individual choices as to the probable reason for dropping out of CREF, or changing the allocation during a year, or making large single-sum payments, or starting to participate in it. Few of the changes made by participants seemed to be a result of playing the market. The substantial majority of individual changes were related to employment factors—change in jobs, sabbatical leaves, temporary assignments, retirement. We reported the facts to college officers and trustees, and after appropriate consultation, the limits were dropped.

By far the most important of the original limits was the one restricting participation in CREF to half of the total retirement contributions being made on behalf of a participant. This 50 percent limit on contributions was strongly supported by college faculty, administrators, and trustees as the most basic of all the initial controls. It was suggested by the economic studies as a realistic balance between the greater volatility of stocks and the greater risk of inflation for fixed-dollar investments. And finally, it was highly unlikely that approval of the various necessary public authorities could have been obtained without the limit.

After careful monitoring over the years, the 50 percent limit on CREF participation was raised to 75 percent January 1, 1967, and 100 percent July 1, 1971. In 1989, nearly all of TIAA's 4,300 participating institutions permit full choice of up to 100 percent either to TIAA or CREF.

WHY NOT A BALANCED PORTFOLIO?

At the time CREF was started, there was much discussion of balanced portfolios for college endowments, for mutual funds, for other institutional investors. The idea was that finance committees would decide on allocation of funds from time to time between stocks and bonds. This matter came in for careful study at TIAA. The decision was overwhelmingly in favor of separate funds for TIAA and CREF.

The most important consideration was that hundreds of thousands of individuals would be starting their participation in college retirement plans at various times during the year and over the years, would be changing jobs and TIAA and CREF participation, would be changing their own allocations according to their individual needs from time to time, and would be retiring at different times. The separate fund approach allows maximum choice by individuals for their participation. Otherwise, the allocation of investment of their retirement savings between equities and fixed-dollar assets would be decided by the fund and they would have no choice.

There also were investment reasons. In a balanced fund, based for example on a 50-50 split between stocks and bonds, the investment manager is continually cutting back on whichever investment category is doing well in order to rebalance the fund. This is defended as a useful discipline for investment managers in the short-run business cycle. But it works poorly for long-term savings programs such as pensions. For instance, from 1932 to 1968, the fund would have been cutting back on its common stock investments to balance with fixed-dollar assets most of the time. The only time the system would have provided discipline to increase common stocks materially would be fairly short periods such as in 1937, during World War II, and 1974, plus a few even shorter opportunities. (The 1974-to-present period is discussed later.) A balanced fund can lead to lost opportunity whenever a major movement to a new level of either stock or bond prices and yields occurs over a period of time.

TRANSFERS TO TIAA AT RETIREMENT

Should participants be allowed to transfer part or all of their CREF accumulation to TIAA at retirement? In 1952, this was a real question. Two task force heads, Jenkins and Johnson, thought no such transfers should be allowed. They were right, philosophically. The author's memorandum at the time describes the rationale for TIAA's final decision:

> If at any one moment in the process a large shift of money can be made out of or into common stocks, there are real dangers that the shift will be made at the wrong time. . . .
> 1. Many persons will want a fixed-dollar income after retirement. They are perfectly willing to take the chances in common stocks while they are working, but feel that their risk-taking days should end when they retire. . . .
> 2. If a person has been investing his premium over a long period of time, say, 30 years, then, historically speaking, he would not be hurt badly if he transferred all of it out even in such poor years as 1932, 1937, 1942, etc. . . .
> 3. There is a question as to how far the policyholder should be protected from his own bad decisions, with the result that he is prevented from making good decisions such as transferring out of the market at the right time.[9]

I find it especially interesting, 37 years later, that we had very early concluded that protecting participants from their bad decisions also may prevent them from making good decisions. But note that the decision left to the individual on the basic college retirement plan still assured him a lifetime income and not cash lump sums.

The rule put into effect in 1952 provided that participants could transfer amounts accumulated in CREF at any time after age 60 or earlier upon early retirement. TIAA recommended transfers be spread over several years to minimize investment risk, but few participants have done this. The age limit was later lowered to 55 and then dropped in 1984.

LIFETIME RETIREMENT INCOME

The protection of the basic retirement annuity benefit as a lifetime payment has always been a cardinal principle of the college retirement system through TIAA-CREF and has its roots deep in pension philosophy and practice. It is precisely because TIAA and CREF contracts have protected the institution's interest in assuring its staff members of an income that they cannot outlive during retirement

---

[9]WCG to Johnson, "CREF Catechism," March 7, 1952.

that, in turn, the college or university has been willing to place substantial amounts of money in annuity contracts wholly owned by individuals.

The TIAA and CREF contracts were purposely designed to assure participants of their full ownership of pension contributions and to assure the colleges that all pension contributions would be used for this specific purpose, to discharge the institution's responsibility to provide retirement income. The no-cash-value and lifetime income provisions have protected the rights both of the colleges and of the individual participants.

One useful adjustment was made starting January 1, 1972, when the retirement transition benefit was added. This benefit allows an individual to withdraw up to 10 percent of the total accumulation at the time of retirement. This has provided, as its name states, a retirement transition benefit to help in moving to a new location, buying a new home, taking a trip, or readjusting office or other expenses.

In 1973, both CREF and TIAA introduced new supplemental retirement annuity contracts so individuals could supplement the basic benefits of their college retirement plan with their own personal savings. These new contracts provided all of the options and provisions of the regular annuities, plus cashability.

Recent changes in TIAA-CREF cashability options are discussed in Chapter 26.

CHAPTER 9

Structure, Controversy, Final Success

An intelligent, well-informed person would not have given very good odds on the chances of getting CREF into operation in 1952. All that was being proposed was provision of an annuity based on 100 percent common stock investments, whereas New York insurance law had permitted no common stocks for life insurance companies from 1906 to 1950 and then only a trifling amount. The new company would have no reserves, or surplus, or any tests for solvency. It would be a limited-eligibility, nonprofit pooling arrangement available only within the nonprofit world of higher education. Finally, at the federal level, there were difficult individual and corporate tax issues to resolve, regulatory questions with respect to the SEC, and status as a nonprofit institution.

One of the challenging aspects in developing CREF was that the plans had to be kept secret during the early months. This was not, as in the usual case, to keep proprietary information from competitors. It was more that the idea was likely to be exceedingly attractive to TIAA policyholders, and it would have been a disaster if the plan could not go forward. TIAA and its policyholders and cooperating colleges were already chafing under limitations imposed by investment and other laws and regulations designed for life insurance, not pensions. Imagine what would have happened if TIAA had publicly announced its plan, found that the proposed CREF was overwhelmingly popular with policyholders, which it proved to be, but something intervened to prevent its launching?

There were many ways to fail: opposition by the New York superintendent of insurance, the legislature, the governor, the insurance industry, the banks engaged in trusteeing pension funds, the mutual fund industry, or federal authorities, especially the taxing authorities. It could have been catastrophic if we had been blocked.

LEGAL TASK FORCE

The job of planning and guiding CREF through the white water ahead fell to George E. Johnson, head of the legal task force. TIAA's extraordinary vice president and secretary (later general counsel) was legally blind, normally considered a substantial handicap for a lawyer. George worked especially closely with outside counsel Root, Ballantine, Harlan, Bushby, & Palmer[1] in devising new contract wording to accomplish the objectives already outlined, a legal structure for the new corporation, and a viable method for federal taxation. George also produced the "Catechism." This was a management device well ahead of its time—a PERT fast-track analysis. It helped keep the task forces on schedule, and it organized all the decisions that had been made and those known still to come, including those not wholly within our control—legislative and governmental.

Complex questions arose immediately. Should the new organization be a pension or some other kind of a trust, a special act corporation, part of TIAA, or a coordinate organization? Much thought and many memoranda later, the final form of Special Act Corporation companion to TIAA was chosen.

Why a Special Act Corporation?

During the spring and summer of 1951, Johnson and John Good of TIAA's Law Department, working with Root Ballantine, had investigated the legal problems facing establishment of an equities fund. One of the earliest alternatives discarded was that of a Section 200 retirement system under the New York code because it would still be limited by the New York State investment restrictions for life insurance companies. It quickly became apparent that the only devices at all appropriate were a mutual investment company, a pension trust, or a special annuity company.

The mutual investment company form had serious disadvantages for the proposed fund. It would be under the SEC and its enabling statutes, which would require that all income be paid out annually and all shares be freely assignable, both inappropriate for a long-term pension fund.

Ordinary pension trusts were designed for single-company pension arrangements. They would be clumsy and expensive for the multi-employer TIAA system and would introduce tax complexities.

By far the best alternative turned out to be a Special Act Corporation, established by the New York State legislature as a companion organization to TIAA.

---

[1]Now Dewey, Ballantine, Bushby, Palmer & Wood.

One of our objectives was to eliminate all investment restrictions. A memorandum from Good stated:

> We strongly recommend that no limitation upon the investments of the new agency be incorporated in any legislation, since such provisions would be difficult to change in the future if new conditions should prove them to be undesirable. The experience of trusts has shown that it is impossible to set forth at the beginning what will be wise 20 or more years in the future, and in many cases such provisions have been a serious source of embarrassment to trustees.[2]

It was the rigidity of life insurance regulatory laws that was causing TIAA to have to seek the Special Act legislation.

Why a Separate Company?

Initially, TIAA had to assure everyone that TIAA and CREF were entirely separate, financially speaking, and that establishment of CREF would not impair the financial stability of the tried-and-true TIAA pension fund. As announced in *A New Approach to Retirement Income,* "Where the college and its staff members are not interested in the new Equities Fund, they can continue their present TIAA plans without change." Participation in the new fund was to be entirely voluntary. This proved to be a crucial decision, psychologically and politically. The New York Insurance Department made clear that this was its conclusion, and TIAA probably would not have achieved support except by establishing a separate company. College business officers and trustees also made it clear this was the way to go.

The separate company idea worked well because of the sui generis nature of TIAA. It was possible to assure coordination and common management for two different companies by appending them both to the Trustees of T.I.A.A. Stock, an existing Special Act Corporation set up by the New York State legislature in 1937. If TIAA were starting a variable annuity fund in 1989, it could set it up within TIAA, but it would be expensive and unnecessary to change now because the present structure is just as viable as one company.

Why a Companion Organization?

The most important incorporating decision with respect to CREF was

[2]Good to Lloyd, "Form of Organization for TEAF," April 13, 1951, TIAA-CREF Archives, Law Department Files. TEAF was another of the early working names for CREF—Teachers Equity Annuity Fund.

that it would be a companion organization to TIAA, a retirement fund, designed with the same basic objectives as TIAA. To be sure, it would issue a wholly new kind of annuity based on common stocks and varying with the performance of common stocks. But otherwise, it would be parallel to TIAA.

The companion organization decision meant the continuance of one low-cost, efficient college pension system. It meant one set of officers and staff, one set of annuitant records, and avoidance of much duplication.

The decision meant that CREF also would limit its eligibility to staff members of colleges, universities, independent schools, and educational and scientific organizations in the nonprofit world. Like TIAA, CREF's annuities would be portable, fully vested and owned by the individual, contractual, and designed to provide retirement income.

This fundamental decision meant CREF and TIAA would become hyphenated, would together be the TIAA-CREF college retirement system, with no basic change necessary in college retirement ages, age of participation, total amount of premiums for individuals, or any of the other generalized pension decisions that had been made over the years by the colleges.

CREF contracts, like TIAA contracts, would be wholly and immediately vested in the individual; they would be portable from college to college; they would have flexible premium arrangements; options in the event an individual died before retirement; annuity income options; flexible retirement age; and all of the services of TIAA. The only difference would be the investment choice, which would be made available by the college if it wished and then used by the individuals if they wished. This arrangement also allowed the reassurance of all interested parties that TIAA was not being changed by this radical innovation in pension funding, so if colleges or participants wanted nothing to do with the new idea, they did not have to participate.

College employment tends to be more flexible than employment elsewhere. The flexible premium arrangements, optional income choices, and flexible retirement ages facilitated by TIAA were carried over intact to CREF.

ORGANIZATION TASK FORCE

This effort, under the direction of McAllister Lloyd, had to do with the corporate organization and the selection of trustees. As described below, the New York Insurance Department was adamant that TIAA had to establish a separate corporation to handle the new variable annuity. TIAA was not to be changed in any corporate way, thus assuring policyholders and others that the existing legal reserve fixed-dollar annuity company would continue as in the past. TIAA then decided to seek a Special Act Corporation, and this was authorized by the legislation signed on March 18, 1952, by Governor Dewey, establishing a membership corporation. Each of the seven members of Trustees of T.I.A.A. Stock and their successors were designated as Members of CREF. This assured coordinated management of two separate corporations with separate operating boards.

Lloyd then talked with many people about how to govern the new organization at the trustee level. It was decided to elect all then current policyholder-selected trustees of TIAA as policyholder-selected trustees of CREF, with all subsequent elections selecting a different person as trustee for TIAA and for CREF. All other noninvestment trustees of TIAA would be brought on the initial CREF board, to be gradually succeeded by new CREF trustees. CREF needed different investment expertise than TIAA for its finance committee, which would determine investment policy.

The decision to make CREF a separate but companion organization to TIAA brought out the question of how to handle administrative costs efficiently. Management decided CREF would have no staff of its own, and its officers would be paid by TIAA. All accounting, purchasing, personnel, and other such services would be combined to the extent feasible. Through time allocations, CREF would reimburse TIAA for all salary costs, and all other costs would be allocated similarly. All of this was accomplished by CREF and TIAA under a nonprofit expense allocation arrangement. And TIAA would take over the entire Carnegie Teachers Investment office to provide the necessary expertise in common stock investments. This arrangement has proved economical and feasible.

These new approaches, new decisions, and new designs completed the architecture of the new variable annuity and the company to be established to provide it.

REGULATING A REVOLUTION

The first big hurdle for the proposed fund was the New York Insurance Department. The major block, of course, was that no insurance company domiciled or licensed in New York State had been allowed to own any common stock investments from the time of the Armstrong investigation in 1906 until 1950, and then only a token amount. TIAA was asking for the right to invest annuities 100 percent in common stocks. And it was asking for all of the other revolutionary differences—a structure that could not become insolvent; one that valued participants' shares in units, not in dollars; and one that had no reserves.

On May 29, 1951, Chairman Lloyd and Messrs. Johnson, Duncan, and Greenough trooped into the office of the New York State superintendent of insurance, Alfred Bohlinger. Our timing was off. During that period, Superintendent Bohlinger was engaged in a difficult fight on automobile premium rates in New York. He greeted the delegation courteously and listened as well as he could between telephone calls and interruptions. It was clear when the group left that we had made little progress. All that the TIAA representatives hoped for anyway was to have the superintendent of insurance stand aside and not oppose their effort in the legislature. But apparently even that was too much to hope for.

Not only was the superintendent preoccupied, but also his staff had concluded the proposed common stock fund was not an insurance company and could not come under the control and supervision of the department and should not be allowed. At this meeting and subsequent meetings, staff members showed interest but repeatedly questioned the establishment of the new organization and the appropriateness of its supervision by the Insurance Department. One of their points was that because CREF would always be solvent by definition, the department really would have no function in its triennial examinations. Incredibly, there TIAA was, a private pension system, arguing vigorously that the New York State Department of Insurance should regulate the new enterprise, and the department was arguing that it should not. This was a remarkable reversal of roles of regulator and regulatee. It must have been some kind of a "first" in the history of regulation.

TIAA pointed out that the department would have major responsibilities for assuring fair and equitable treatment of participants, accuracy of records, and conformity to all provisions of insurance law except inappropriate sections such as investment limitations. (Later, the department asked TIAA to help in writing instructions for the state examiners when they examined CREF, and George Johnson complied.)

With the roadblocks TIAA was running into, it could only hope that astute philosopher Casey Stengel was right when he said: "They say you can't do it, but sometimes that doesn't always work."

As soon as the results of the detailed task force studies were in hand, a second conference with the superintendent was held. This time, after greeting the TIAA representatives, Superintendent Bohlinger said, "I know each of you has your speech set to explain this to me and your desires to serve the college world. But I've read the economic and actuarial reports carefully, and I wonder if I could ask a few questions first?" There followed about a three-hour session during which Superintendent Bohlinger indicated thorough familiarity with the material, asked many sophisticated questions, and ultimately indicated his support of the proposal.

From that time on, despite the negative recommendations of several of his key deputies, Superintendent Bohlinger supported and even promoted the effort to charter the College Retirement Equities Fund. During the autumn of 1951, TIAA officers and the staff of the New York State Insurance Department met to draft the necessary legislation. In late November, Superintendent Bohlinger informed the New York State Senate Finance Committee that he was ready to support a pending bill, with minor revisions.[3]

Meanwhile, Johnson was working with various New York governmental departments that might raise some questions. This included William A. Lyon, commissioner of banks; Dr. Lewis A. Wilson, superintendent of education; Frank C. Moore, lieutenant governor; and leaders and committee chairmen in the New York legislature. He also touched base with the Department of State to learn of any conflicts with the name College Retirement Equities Fund.

The next step was Governor Thomas E. Dewey. Superintendent Bohlinger and many educators in the state and across the nation indicated their support to the governor's office. Governor Dewey became excited by the idea. The Senate Bill to establish CREF became S 1, a "must" administration bill. Senator Walter J. Mahoney of Buffalo, N.Y., introduced it on January 9, 1952, in the New York Senate. A strong Republican leader, he was chairman of the Senate Finance Committee and formerly chairman of the Joint Insurance Committee of the New York Legislature. Representative Justin C. Morgan introduced an identical bill in the House. The TIAA executives could then relax somewhat; Governor Dewey's first 10 bills each year were "musts" and they did not fail. Carroll V. Newsom, then associate commissioner of education, recalled: "The governor, then Thomas E. Dewey, was most interested in the measure. . . . Since he was an imaginative person, he quickly saw merit in the concept that was proposed. . . . So he approved the measure without any great question."[4]

TIAA met some resistance from one unexpected source: the State Board of Regents. Because the bill pertained to higher education, it was the usual procedure for Associate Commissioner Newsom to present it to the regents for discussion, and then make his recommendation to the governor. Several veteran members of the board and the board's counsel, raised objections. Newsom was convinced of the merit of a variable annuity, and eventually the regents agreed not to

---

[3]Bohlinger to Fred R. Spreeman, secretary, Senate Finance Committee, November 28, 1951, TIAA-CREF Archives, Law Department Files; also minutes of TIAA Management Committee Meeting of December 6, 1951, TIAA-CREF Corporate Secretary Files.

[4]C. V. Newsom, "Some Comments on the Origin of the College Retirement Equities Fund," undated personal communication, WCG files.

oppose the measure.[5] The final CREF charter contained a provision that CREF "shall not issue any certificate or contract to any person by reason of his being an employee in the public school system of the State of New York. . . . "

On March 18, 1952, a Special Act New York Corporation, incorporating the College Retirement Equities Fund, was approved.

Tax Status

Meanwhile, during the summer and fall of 1951, TIAA raised tax questions in Washington. The first necessity was to assure that the new organization would be tax free. This should not have been a problem and it was not. Pension plans of all kinds, except insured plans, were tax exempt. The Bureau of Internal Revenue informed TIAA there was every reason to believe the new organization would be declared tax exempt when formed, and it would waive the usual 12-month waiting period for such designations as being inappropriate. The bureau did so, when the time came.

The attempt to get a preliminary ruling that contributions by the colleges to the equities fund would not be immediately taxable to the individual raised difficulties. All initial rulings were adverse. The bureau took the position that an annuity by definition involved payment of a fixed sum, and, therefore, a payment that varied could not be considered an annuity. Conferences with bureau officials suggested they viewed the TIAA application as a potential Pandora's box, which might be cited later as precedent in other less valid circumstances.[6] TIAA asked for a rehearing in order to present a brief and further evidence in support of the variable annuity contract.

TIAA management was also prepared to legislate the variable annuity into existence, if need be, with an amendment to the Internal Revenue Code. After meeting with a number of congressmen and their assistants, TIAA filed a request in August with the Senate Finance Committee for consideration in the pending general revenue bill.[7] With pressure from the legislative flank and submission of

---

[5]Ibid.; also "OCC [O. C. Carmichael] and George Johnson," memorandum of an interview at Carnegie Corporation regarding passage of the bill, January 15, 1952, Carnegie Corporation Archives, TIAA File.

[6]Good to Lloyd, "Results of Conference at Bureau of Internal Revenue, April 16, 1951 re: TERF," April 23, 1951; Johnson to Harry G. Guthmann, July 5, 1951, TIAA-CREF Archives, Law Department Files.

[7]Good, "Memorandum of Trip to Washington by Mr. Johnson and Mr. Good July 30—August 2 to Work on Matters Connected with TERF," August 9, 1951; Johnson, "Request by Teachers Insurance and Annuity Association of America to Amend Section 22(b) (2) (B) of the Internal Revenue Code," August 2, 1951, TIAA-CREF Archives, Law Department Files.

TIAA's legal brief, the bureau saw the company meant business. Johnson agreed to "call off the dogs" on the proposed amendment if the bureau would give the company a written ruling.[8] On September 19, 1951, the Commissioner of Internal Revenue ruled the payments were annuities. TIAA then withdrew its proposed amendment.

After a number of conferences, the Internal Revenue Bureau in Washington and TIAA worked out appropriate methods for taxing the new annuity. Many problems had to be addressed. The concept of a variable annuity also caused difficulty in the determination of a taxable method for those persons receiving annuity income, but this also was satisfactorily resolved.

CREF and the SEC

When CREF was established in 1952, it was a new financial instrument. It was to be used only for retirement income purposes and in connection with nonprofit educational employer benefit plans. It was to issue life annuities, basing periodic benefits upon mortality tables constructed from life insurance company longevity experience. Under a special act of the New York State legislature, CREF was placed under the jurisdiction of all relevant articles of the insurance law. And CREF itself was a not-for-profit charitable and educational institution. All of these factors were considered in a Root Ballantine memorandum concluding that CREF was clearly exempt, on several grounds, from SEC jurisdiction.

Jumping ahead a few years, the Supreme Court decided in the VALIC (Variable Annuity Life Insurance Company) case in 1959 that variable annuities were securities for purposes of registration under the 1933 Securities Act and the 1940 Investment Company Act. This decision did not change CREF's exemption as a nonprofit charitable and educational institution. At the request of the SEC in the mid-1960s, CREF and the SEC held thorough talks as to whether CREF should register under the 1933 and 1940 acts. CREF filed briefs and supporting information. The American Council on Education, the Association of American Colleges, the American Association of University Professors, and other associations and individuals presented strong statements in favor of continued exemption.

One of the convincing facts to emerge was the large number of noncommercial variable annuities not under SEC jurisdiction. Specifically in the college world, in addition to CREF's broad coverage, some public institutions were included under state teacher and public employee plans modeled on CREF and providing variable annu-

---

[8]Good to WCG, "TERF—Legislative Approach—Federal," August 28, 1951, TIAA-CREF Archives, Law Department Files.

ities in Wisconsin and New Jersey; some college employees were covered by such plans provided by the Southern Baptist Convention and the American Baptist Convention; Harvard University provided an option funded in its General Investment Account, and the University of Rochester did the same for its academic employees. The non-life insurance plans for Long Island Lighting, Chemstrand, and many others, and the common stocks held in the AT&T, GM, or other industrial pension plans were not under the SEC.

Representatives of the educational associations and of CREF met with senior SEC officials. Afterwards, CREF continued to rely on its exempt status and the issue remained in that posture until CREF approached the SEC in connection with its new funds, starting with the money market annuity in 1985. To clear any possible future doubt as to its long-term reporting status, CREF decided to register with the SEC in 1985. This is discussed in Chapter 26.

Public Regulation Was Flexible

Public regulation can inhibit innovation. The necessity of dealing with so many public authorities made TIAA's job difficult and even dangerous to the pension system, when considering the chances of failure somewhere along the line. There were disappointments, such as officials who disapproved on the first round. There were officials who never were convinced TIAA was on the right track. But uniformly they approached the decisions with genuine concern for what was best for the public interest as they saw it. They frequently had difficulty with a situation that did not fit established pigeonholes, that was basically different. They never delayed just to delay; they never played games with their substantial power to destroy. And in a remarkably short time, they approved the entire CREF proposal, at both the state and the federal level.

FRIENDS AND RELATIONS

Family members can become very upset by the radical actions of their offspring. Usually, in such situations, not all the family members agree. So it was with the Carnegie Corporation, or at least with two of its eminent trustees, and TIAA's proposal to establish CREF. Randolph Burgess, later Undersecretary of the Treasury, and Russell Leffingwell, former chairman of J. P. Morgan & Company, were on the Carnegie Corporation board. Their deserved reputations were as towering as their physical presences. They both opposed establishment of CREF. Both of them raised the question of possible legal or moral responsibility of the Carnegie Corporation in case CREF did not work out well. They harked back to the huge expenditures by Carnegie because of overly generous pension promises in connection with the Carnegie free pensions and to grants made to TIAA because of financial problems dating back to Carnegie control of TIAA. But Mr. Leffingwell's objections went beyond that; he believed CREF was not a good idea.

Carnegie Corporation and the Carnegie Foundation no longer had power over TIAA affairs in 1952, but their opinions carried considerable weight. Other Carnegie trustees and staff members favored CREF. Oliver C. Carmichael, president of the Carnegie Foundation, wrote in August, 1951, "It is an excellent device. . . . I congratulate TIAA on its imagination and inventiveness."[9]

What was the attitude of the New York Stock Exchange to CREF? Keith Funston was president of the exchange from 1951 to 1962, the gestation period and early years of CREF. He came to the exchange from the educational world; he had been president of Trinity College in Hartford, Connecticut, a TIAA cooperating institution. As soon as he heard about the CREF proposal, he requested all material on it and expressed his personal enthusiasm. He was a popularizer of the concept "invest in America." He saw great potential in CREF for making common stock investments more broadly acceptable. But he reported to us that the exchange family was opposed to the idea, especially when it started to spread to other pension systems and the life insurance industry. Member firms feared continued institutionalization of the stock market, which they considered against their interests. This did occur. However, neither the exchange nor its member firms actively worked against TIAA, so far as is known.

To gauge the reaction of college administrators, TIAA executives invited the following group to sit down with them on April 4, 1951, to discuss the proposed funding agency:[10]

William Bloor, assistant treasurer, Columbia University

Boardman Bump, treasurer, Mount Holyoke College

F. Morris Cochran, vice president and business manager, Brown University

Lewis H. Durland, treasurer, Cornell University

W. H. Lane, Jr., controller, Columbia University

Gail A. Mills, controller, Princeton University

Laurence G. Tighe, treasurer, Yale University

In general the reception of the plan was highly favorable. . . . Mr. Tighe was particularly strong in this opinion. . . . Mr. Mills was

---

[9]O. C. Carmichael to WCG, August 23, 1951, Carnegie Corporation Archives, TIAA file.

[10]Good, minutes of TIAA Conference on New Pension Agency, April 4, 1951, WCG Files.

somewhat more reserved since he felt that a fluctuating annuity might be a dangerous thing. . . . He was still somewhat doubtful as to the ability of all faculty members at an advanced age to make an intelligent choice. . . . Mr. Bump thought that options . . . should be limited . . . to present a simple and saleable plan. . . .

It seemed to be generally felt that the equity fund could be explained to the faculty members participating, that it would be understood that there was a possibility of loss as well as gain, and that the colleges could live with the plan through periods of lower market values. . . .

The first long discussion of CREF at a TIAA trustees meeting was on April 27, 1951. The tenor of the meeting may be gleaned from the report on Trustee Shirley W. Smith, University of Michigan: "Smith: Earlier in the day he argued against [CREF], stating many objections. At the dinner-meeting he stated a few milder reservations and at the close of the meeting stated that most of his own investments were in common stocks."[11]

"Great idea, CREF! But isn't the market too high to start it now?" TIAA kept running into that refrain in 1951 and 1952. As an example, Dr. Joseph H. Willits, a TIAA trustee and director, the social sciences, the Rockefeller Foundation, sent comments made by one of his colleagues:

What disturbs me, however, is that the idea of launching an equity fund . . . should mature at this particular time. For a period of nine years the prices of common stocks have had an almost uninterrupted advance, and during that time one of the most widely used averages [the Dow Index] has advanced from 93 to 265. . . . The buyers' psychology of the "new era" . . . is beginning to become prevalent again. If an equity fund were available from which purchases would be made only when no one else had any confidence, the net gain to the professor would be great.[12]

My detailed letter of August 22, 1951, to Dr. Willits outlined the case for proceeding despite the "high level of common stock prices."[13] It pointed out that CREF was a new approach to retirement savings, including contributions month after month, year after year, thereby achieving diversification over time. I said: "We likewise agree it would have been fine if CREF had been established in 1932; what a spectacular 20-year history it would have had! In all probability,

---

[11]Johnson, "Notes on Dinner-Meeting at Harvard Club, Friday, April 27, 1951," May 3, 1951, WCG Files.

[12]Quoted in Johnson, "Comments by Trustees at the Meeting of the Board of Trustees on October 19th," October 29, 1951, TIAA-CREF Archives, Law Department Files.

[13]WCG to Dr. Joseph H. Willits, August 22, 1951.

however, we would have had trouble selling the plan to the colleges and the professors in 1932."

Henry R. Hayes, financial consultant and industrialist, was another TIAA trustee who had his doubts:

> Based upon our very unsound domestic economy, fraught as it has been and still is with fallacious theories and practices, I conclude it is not a propitious time to establish such a fund. . . .
>
> To believe, with assurance, that future annuitants can be safeguarded now from future ravages of serious inflation by equity investments is not to appraise adequately, I think, existing and prospective federal fiscal and monetary policies.[14]

Mr. Hayes telephoned me the morning of a crucial TIAA board meeting. We discussed the "economy, fraught . . . with fallacious theories and practices." I was getting nowhere, until I said: "Mr. Hayes, you are worried about 'all the socialists and communists on college teaching staffs.' Wouldn't it be a great idea if they all owned some common stocks, a share in capitalism, through participating in CREF?" Mr. Hayes moved the adoption of CREF that afternoon!

When TIAA started CREF, common stocks were yielding about twice as much as bonds. This was the risk premium for owning volatile stocks. This actually made 1952 an excellent time to start a stock fund.

INSURANCE INDUSTRY HURDLES

During the gestation days, we had to watch out for possibly dangerous opposition from any quarter. A crucial factor would be the attitude of the commercial insurance world and the regulatory authorities. We would make our research available without limit, as is the tradition in the educational world, and this was done. In addition, we decided to design an amendment to the New York insurance law that would allow TIAA, and any other New York-domiciled insurance company that wished to do so, to set up a new variable annuity fund.

This effort was not successful. We were told it would be opposed by the New York Insurance Department and the insurance companies. As Dr. Davis Gregg, president of the then American College of Life Insurance, later put it: "By opening the equity option, CREF had thrust at the heart of the life insurance industry." The superintendent of insurance, Alfred Bohlinger, told us quite accurately that, while TIAA had studied in depth the effects and implications of setting up a variable annuity fund for its limited eligibility group, college employees, we had not made a broader study of the implications for the

---

[14]Henry R. Hayes to Lloyd, September 27, 1951, TIAA-CREF Corporate Secretary Files.

entire insurance industry. But Superintendent Bohlinger reported the department would support TIAA if it would limit its request to the college world.

Chairman McAllister Lloyd asked Devereux Colt Josephs, president of the New York Life Insurance Company, to sound out the life insurance world as to its attitude if TIAA were to propose a change in the New York statutes to permit any life insurance company to establish a variable annuity fund. Josephs had been TIAA's investment officer from 1939 to 1943 and its president from 1943 to 1945, when he became president of Carnegie Corporation of New York. He became president of the New York Life Insurance Company in 1948.

Josephs reported the insurance industry would stand aside if TIAA were to limit its request to the establishment of a variable annuity fund for its own limited eligibility group, but if it were to propose a bill permitting any company to establish such a fund, it would be exceedingly controversial and probably take many years before passage. He pointed out that some companies, including Metropolitan, the largest New York company and then the largest in the world, would be vigorously opposed. Others, such as the Prudential Insurance Company, then second in size and now first, would be eagerly in favor. Not wishing to wait for years and still less eager to be crushed in a giant nutcracker between the Met and Pru, TIAA limited its request to the New York legislature to the establishment of a Special Act nonprofit corporation with eligibility restricted to the college world, and this became the College Retirement Equities Fund.

Josephs was prescient. Even though CREF broke the main barriers, only three companies were established within the first five years to write the new variable annuities. PALIC (Participating Annuity Life Insurance Company) of Arkansas was incorporated in 1954. VALIC (Variable Annuity Life Insurance Company) and EALIC (Equity Annuity Life Insurance Company) came soon after, in the District of Columbia, where the existing laws could accommodate them. George E. Johnson, TIAA-CREF general counsel who left in 1955, was the principal designer of both of these companies. Prudential, the first existing commercial life insurance company to be authorized to issue variable annuities, finally obtained legislative approval in New Jersey in 1959 after a vigorous fight and issued its first policies in 1964.

Lloyd also undertook major contacts with the insurance industry. He recalled: "I learned that Frederick Ecker, head of the Metropolitan Life[15] . . . was strongly opposed to the CREF idea. He did not think it

---

[15]In calling Ecker head of the Metropolitan, Lloyd had it right in substance but wrong in detail. By then, Frederick H. Ecker was honorary chairman, but not what might be called silent in either company or insurance industry affairs; his son was executive vice president and heir apparent.

was appropriate for insurance companies to own common stocks. He remembered the depression days of 1929 and 1930."[16] Lloyd arranged through Ecker's son, Frederic W. Ecker, a friend of his at Harvard, and Haley Fiske, Jr., to talk with the senior Ecker. After that conference, Ecker "agreed not to object to the establishment of CREF, saying we were not part of the insurance industry, that we were a separate pension fund." Lloyd also called on the presidents of the Equitable Life, New York Life, and Mutual Life.

Concurrently, TIAA sent out *A New Approach to Retirement Income* to many life insurance companies, seeking their reactions. Their officers were generally greatly interested and wrote, for example, this was "an intriguing approach . . . bound to arouse much interest and study during the next few years";[17] "a very interesting development in the pension field"[18] and "a fascinating outline and program."[19]

George Johnson and I were also meeting with small groups of officers at the large eastern life companies. Johnson's notes related interesting reactions at two companies. At the New York Life Insurance Company on November 28, 1951:

> Mr. Greenough and I surmised that these men [six top officers] were instructed to gather as much information as possible about the CREF proposal, looking forward to the possibility of New York Life doing something about it in a year or two. They appeared eager not to cross any wires with us or detract in any way from our efforts to obtain the necessary restricted legislation for CREF.[20]

In that meeting, the New York Life people were most interested in the application of CREF to investment of the proceeds of life insurance policies, not annuities. The "year or two" turned into 32 years. New York Life's actuaries developed a design for a variable life policy, presented at the 1969 meeting of the Society of Actuaries, but management decided not to go forward because of current federal government regulations on agent commissions.[21] A variable life insur-

---

[16]TIAA-CREF Oral History interview of Lloyd by Bob Lord, July 17 and 19, 1979.

[17]Daton Gilbert, actuary, The Connecticut Mutual Life Insurance Company, to WCG, January 8, 1952.

[18]J. Frederick Bitzer, assistant actuary, Aetna Life Insurance Company, to R. E. Fisher, January 23, 1952, WCG Files.

[19]David W. Gordon, financial vice president, Monarch Life Insurance Company, to WCG, February 8, 1952.

[20]Johnson, "Conference at the New York Life Insurance Company re CREF—11/28/51," November 30, 1951, WCG Files.

[21]Charles W. V. Meares, *Looking Back: A Memoir of New York Life* (New York: New York Life Insurance Company, 1986), pp. 118–22; *Variable Life Insurance: Current Issues and Developments,* ed. Douglas G. Olson and Howard E. Winklevoss. Proceedings of the National Conference on Variable Life Insurance, March 1971 (Philadelphia: University of Pennsylvania, 1971).

ance product was finally offered by New York Life in 1983, seven years after the Equitable marketed its first variable life policies.

On January 3, 1952, at the Mutual Life Insurance Company, we met with a group of six, including Lewis Dawson, president. Johnson's report says: "The officers of the Mutual Life Insurance Company asked many questions and are extremely interested in TIAA's proposal. They seem to think it has great merit."[22] For themselves, they thought it a way to spawn corporations and set them free with large chunks of assets, because "the greatest profit in life insurance companies came from the side of the business which was less of an asset builder, i.e., the life insurance side." They were not interested in annuities. They did not implement the "spawning" idea.

PRESENTING CREF IN PUBLIC

The philosopher Schopenhauer said innovations tend to pass through three distinct phases. "In the first stage, the new idea is ridiculed; in the second stage, it is severely opposed; in the third stage, having been accepted, it is considered as self-evident."

By September 1951, CREF was halfway through the second stage. The time had come to drop the mantle of secrecy and to expose the new plan to the public scrutiny of outside actuaries, economists, lawyers, finance and investment experts, public officials, and especially the college world.

Explaining Variable Annuities

We had not anticipated much difficulty in explaining the new variable annuity: "It is just like a regular life annuity, except that it is based on the investment experience of common stock and so varies up and down with that experience." At first, the message was not getting across. We finally realized Americans for years had been taking life annuities and their pension plans for granted but had no real idea how they worked. With the new variable annuity device, they wanted to learn everything about annuities—how mortality tables, assumed interest rates, and expense factors worked. And they wanted to know how the variable annuity is different. This new interest was all to the good, because annuities then represented most of the savings for many people.

We had to develop three levels of explanations of CREF: one for mathematicians, physicists, and actuaries interested in how our for-

---

[22]Johnson, "Luncheon Meeting re CREF at the Mutual Life Insurance Company office on 1/3/52," January 7, 1952, WCG Files.

mulas worked to produce fair and equitable treatment; one for finance professors, economists, and college business officers who were mainly interested in the validity and results of the economic studies; and one for the college staff members who would have to decide whether to add participation in CREF to their plans for retirement security.

The first action in going public was the appointment of a Special Commission of Educators and Laymen, composed of outstanding college officers and professors, authorities on investments, top business leaders, and public figures. Dr. Henry M. Wriston of Brown University and president of Trustees of T.I.A.A. Stock, sent invitations to proposed members in August 1951 for a October 5 meeting. A great deal of material was presented to them before the long session at the Harvard Club of New York, where the new plan was presented in detail. Most of the commission members, in addition to studying the material themselves, had asked their staff experts to analyze it. After thorough discussion, the commission adopted the following resolution, concluding:

> That the Trustees of T.I.A.A. Stock and the trustees and officers of TIAA should proceed with all possible dispatch to set up a College Retirement Equities Fund, looking to the establishment of the Fund as an operating entity in 1952. . . .

Members of the Special Commission

Arthur S. Adams, President, American Council on Education

S. Sloan Colt, President, Bankers Trust Company

Ralph E. Himstead, General Secretary, American Association of University Professors

Horace S. Ford, Member of the Corporation, Massachusetts Institute of Technology

Devereux C. Josephs, President, New York Life Insurance Company

LeRoy E. Kimball, President, Association of American Colleges

Deane W. Malott, President, Cornell University

John S. Millis, President, Western Reserve University

William Saltonstall, President, Phillips Exeter Academy

Herman B Wells, President, Indiana University

John H. Williams, Nathaniel Ropes Professor of Political Economy, Harvard University[23]

---

[23]The Special Commission's report was reprinted in the TIAA *Bulletin,* "Should TIAA Establish a College Retirement Equities Fund?" November 1951.

TIAA called a special meeting of its board of trustees for October 19, at which it unanimously approved "in principle the establishment of an Equities Fund. . . as a companion organization to TIAA."[24]

During October, TIAA invited groups of actuaries, lawyers, economists, investment experts, and other specialists to long, exhaustive discussions—usually dinner meetings—on the proposed fund. TIAA asked those present to comment in detail, especially if they had any misgivings or suggestions. This generated helpful discussion, criticism, and enthusiasm.

The noted actuary and author Joseph B. Maclean cited CREF as one of the few fundamentally new developments in the long history of insurance organizations, on a par with the adoption of group life insurance in 1912.[25] Actuaries made another observation. Noting that CREF was designed so it could not become insolvent, they called it "an actuary's dream." That was the idea—under no circumstances should CREF have to sell common stock investments during a depressed point in common stock or other equity prices. All experience had shown that such periods were a grave danger for investors who could not or would not hold through the low period, but an opportunity for those who could or would continue buying during such a period.

TIAA met at the University Club with the top legal counsel of New York life insurance companies on October 31.[26] Johnson reported, "In general, the proposal seemed to be well received by the group." Most of the discussion was on investment matters and how much leeway should be permitted.

TIAA's most important announcement came with the publication of a bulletin in November 1951, sent to all policyholders and cooperating institutions, titled, "Should TIAA Establish a College Retirement Equities Fund?" This bulletin explained CREF, how it was to be structured, how it would operate, and presented charts and economic analysis from A New Approach to Retirement Income. It then asked policyholders and college officers to react, giving their candid opinions as to whether they thought CREF would serve the colleges and their participants well, whether they thought the idea was viable, and whether they would expect to participate.

TIAA's job at this juncture was to explain CREF forcibly enough that traditional, stereotyped views of common stocks as risky investments were placed in a new perspective. We did not want to oversell

---

[24]Minutes of Special Meeting of Board of Trustees, TIAA, October 19, 1951.

[25]Joseph B. Maclean, "Variable Life Income Certificates," The Insurance Educator, April 23, 1955, pp. 1059–60.

[26]Johnson, "Meeting at University Club on October 31st to discuss CREF with the legal counsel of life insurance companies," November 8, 1951, WCG Files.

CREF, so we had to restrain our substantial enthusiasm. But if we either underexplained or undersold it at this point, we might risk losing the entire effort before it was even tested.

Reaction of college presidents and business officers as to adding a CREF option was overwhelmingly favorable. Only two of the first 192 replies received were opposed or not interested.[27] The reaction of potential participants was favorable; the files show enthusiastic readiness of TIAA policyholders to take up the new pension approach. This gave the organization a strong mandate to proceed.

Public Announcement

"Bill Ties Pensions to Stock Earnings" was the front-page article in the *New York Times* on January 12, 1952, announcing the introduction of a bill in the New York State Legislature to establish CREF. Excerpts:

> ALBANY, Jan. 11—Legislation designed to offset the impact of inflation on the pensions of employees of 600 higher education and research institutions has been introduced in the Legislature by Senator Walter J. Mahoney, Republican of Buffalo and chairman of the Senate Finance Committee.
>
> The bill envisages a new concept for annuities by substitution for half of the present fixed-dollar pensions a variable portion that would depend on the earnings of common stock investments.
>
> The proposal is being watched closely by insurance companies and large corporations maintaining pension plans for their employees.
>
> Introduction of the bill was requested by the Teachers Insurance and Annuity Association of America. . . .
>
> A study, going back to 1880, of common stocks made last summer by the association indicated that an investment policy such as is now proposed would have provided yields that largely would have kept pace with the rise of the cost of living. . . .
>
> William C. Greenough, vice president of the association, said that the 600 affiliated institutions had been asked for their views on the proposal and that of 250 replies, only three had been unfavorable.[28]

When everything was ready, in the late spring of 1952, TIAA faced the job of thorough and comprehensive communication with all cooperating institutions and all policyholders in a very short time. College officers, trustees, and interested staff members were invited to central locations to discuss CREF. The meetings turned out to be lively, interesting, and helpful.

---

[27]Cobb Memorandum, November 14, 1951, WCG Files.
[28]Copyright © 1952 by The New York Times Company. Reprinted by permission.

THE FIRST MONTHS

CREF commenced operations July 1, 1952.

The alacrity with which CREF was accepted by educational institutions was uneven across the country. Many educational institutions welcomed the opportunity to diversify investment of pension funds and to participate in equity growth. At universities where economics and business school faculty took an interest, acceptance was high; at others, frequently much lower.

At a number of institutions, college trustees were reluctant to "risk the retirement security of their faculty members on equity investments." It was interesting to note the reluctance of some of the leaders of American business and industry to place reliance on their own beliefs in capitalism and free enterprise. Faculty members frequently accepted the CREF idea much more quickly and vigorously than some college trustees.

CREF sent out the first report of individual participation in the fund as of March 31, 1953. It also revalued the annuity income being paid to CREF participants, the first time such a fund was ever revalued. Thus, March 31, 1953, could have been a big day in CREF's life. What if the stock market had boomed upward during the first year? Or more interestingly but more nerve-rackingly, downward? What about the first six recipients of annuity income? How would participants receive their first jolts or good news in this new fund that figured the value of their savings in units instead of dollars?

No extremes occurred. The accumulation value on March 31, 1953, the end of the first nine months, was $10; it had been slightly higher, $10.43 when CREF started July 1, 1952. But that small change caused not a ripple.

The lowest value ever reached by the accumulation unit value was for August 1953, when it reached $9.35. The annuity unit value, which started out at $10.00, dropped to $9.46 on March 31, 1953, its low point. The following year-end it was $10.74. The first annuitants' income varied proportionately but caused little comment.

Of the 613 educational institutions funding their pension plans with TIAA in 1952, more than half, 334, had made CREF available to their staff members during the first nine months of its inception. This required action by the board of each institution. Ninety percent of these made participation entirely optional with the staff member. Thus, the college staff member could allocate one fourth, one third, or one half of the total premium (his or her own and the college's contribution) to the new variable annuity. Or the member could stay entirely with TIAA. But at that time, no one could go more than half in CREF.

Total assets of CREF by March 31, 1953, reached just over $1.8 million. By the end of the first 21 months of CREF, 432 of the 635 TIAA cooperating institutions were permitting CREF participation. By the end of CREF's second year, 29 of its 30 largest cooperating institutions permitted staff members to participate (the last one was the University of Washington, where legislation was pending).

A NICE TOUCH

Now for a nice touch that in a very human way ties everything together, the Carnegie pensions, TIAA, and CREF. During the first year, six persons purchased CREF annuities commencing immediately. I was curious as to whether any of them are still alive, 37 years later. There was, a professor who at a fairly young age had purchased a small immediate annuity. Now, 37 years later, he continues to receive his regular checks, but they are more than eight times as large as in 1952. Because the cost of living is less than five times as high as in 1952, CREF has provided a useful hedge against the cost of living for him. But the coincidence that ties this all together? I thought the professor's date of birth sounded familiar: April 16, 1905. Sure enough, this was the day Andrew Carnegie made his stunning announcement, a $10 million gift for free college pensions, leading to TIAA, and then to CREF.

CHAPTER 10

_____ Spread of Variable Annuities _____

The second variable annuity plan to be established was a bank trusteed plan set up by the Long Island Lighting Company at the end of 1952. It was developed by Curtis Henderson, a lawyer, and Howard Hennington, an actuary at the Equitable Life Assurance Society but acting as an independent actuary in this case. Soon after, airline pilots became interested in the concept. They were highly paid, highly trained professionals who had to retire at age 60 or earlier upon encountering health problems. By mid-1959, over 12,000 airline pilots were covered by variable annuity plans, as well as employees at Northrop Corporation, Boeing Airplane Co., Cornell Aeronautical Laboratory, and Wisconsin state and local governmental employees. Even the federal government was active indirectly, through a plan in effect at the Tennessee Valley Authority.

The first adaptations in the life insurance industry were by three new proprietary companies established initially solely to write variable annuities. The first of these was Participating Annuity Life Insurance Company (PALIC) of Fayetteville, Arkansas. Established in 1954 under the more liberal Arkansas insurance laws by Professor Harold Dulan of the University of Arkansas, PALIC was profitable from the start but tiny and was eventually sold to the Aetna Life and Casualty Company of Hartford in 1967.

The second commercial company was Variable Annuity Life Insurance Company, established in 1955 by TIAA's former general counsel George Johnson, teaming with John Marsh, a life insurance agent and entrepreneur. For incorporation, Johnson chose the insurance laws of the District of Columbia, which were broad enough to permit variable annuities. VALIC prospered and was sold to American General Life Insurance Company of Houston. The third company, Equity Annuity Life Insurance Company, was incorporated in 1957 by its founder, George Johnson, and modestly financed by American General. It was amalgamated with VALIC in 1967.

REGULATORY DEVELOPMENTS

The Prudential Insurance Company worked diligently toward getting approval to write variable annuities. Led by Carroll Shanks as president and Meyer Melnikoff, the Pru first checked all of TIAA's economic research and then introduced enabling legislation in the New Jersey legislature. This legislation was opposed by the New York Stock Exchange, the Metropolitan Life Insurance Company, and the National Association of Investment Companies, among others. It took the Pru five years to achieve the June 18, 1959, passage of the measure by the New Jersey legislature, and Governor Robert Meyner signed it. But the Pru did not write its first variable annuity contract until 1964.

One problem was that, in March 1959, just before the Pru's legislation, the Supreme Court in the VALIC case reversed by a 5–4 vote a lower court decision and held that variable annuities were not "excepted securities" under the 1933 Securities Act. Thus, the exemption of the McCarran Act for life insurance was not available, and affected variable annuity companies would have to register under the SEC. Justice William O. Douglas, a former chairman of the SEC, wrote the majority opinion, saying variable annuities "guarantee nothing to the annuitant except an interest in a portfolio of common stocks or other equities—an interest that has a ceiling but no floor.[1]

This was a curious upside-down conclusion—a portfolio of equities might conceivably lose all value, so there is a floor of zero, but theoretically no ceiling. Nonetheless, most variable annuities issued by financial institutions were thereafter under SEC jurisdiction.

During the fight by Prudential to achieve enabling legislation in New Jersey, its adversary in the cause, the Metropolitan Life Insurance Company, conducted a survey that concluded: "More than 80 percent of the nation's life insurance companies are opposed to variable annuity policies."[2] The announcement was made by Frederic W. Ecker, president of the Met, and son of the Frederick H. Ecker who had opposed establishment of CREF. "Mr. Ecker noted that of the 257 respondent companies, 210, or 81.7 percent, said they did not believe

---

[1]Securities and Exchange Commission v. Variable Annuity Life Insurance Company of America, 359 U.S. 65 (1959).

[2]"Varying Annuity Opposed in Poll," *New York Times*, June 17, 1959.

that sales of variable annuities to individuals would help the insurance business. . . . Only 28, or 10.1 percent, said they believed that variable annuities would be in the best interests of the life insurance companies."

One of the Eckers' objections had always been that policyholders would take credit for themselves when the market was up, but blame the insurance company when it was down. Ecker asked only the question of whether variable annuities would be good for the insurance industry, not whether they would be good for participants and therefore a worthwhile service to provide.

Once the legal maneuvering was over, a number of life insurance companies set up variable annuity plans. Group variable annuity plans could by 1966 be established in 27 states and the District of Columbia and bank trusteed plans in these and many other states. By July 1967, *The Wall Street Journal* could headline an article: "From Orphan to Cinderella; Variable Annuity Policies Are Becoming Darling of the Life Insurance Industry."[3] And the *Journal* article reported: "Even one of the most conservative of the major life insurance companies, Metropolitan Life Insurance Company of New York, has apparently found the lure of variable annuities irresistible."

By 1984, more than 125 insurers offered variable annuities, and they were utilized in a large number of trusteed pension plans and state and local plans. Variable annuity plans now cover health and hospital workers, public utility workers, airline pilots, a number of church groups, public employees, and, of course, colleges and universities. The Southern Baptist Convention was the first extensive denominational plan to be established, and this was followed by the American Baptist Convention.

By 1965, most of the airlines in the country, many companies, and various groups of state and local employees had VA plans. In 1958, Wisconsin public employees became eligible for a variable annuity option. In 1964, the New Jersey retirement plans for teachers, police and firefighters, and other public employees added a variable annuity option. In 1968, some 40,000 of the 58,000 teachers and administrators of the New York City public school system chose to start putting about $100 million a year into a new variable annuity plan.[4]

The precipitous drop in common stock prices during 1974, reaching their lows in October, led to a pause in variable annuity development. *The Wall Street Journal* on September 10 trumpeted "anguish,"

---

[3]*The Wall Street Journal*, July 26, 1967.

[4]John P. Mackin, *Protecting Purchasing Power in Retirement: A Study of Public Employee Retirement Systems* (New York: Fleet Academic Editions, Inc., 1971), pp. 208–18; Robert Tilove, "The Variable Annuity Program of the New York City Teachers' Retirement System," *Pension and Welfare News* 4 (February 1968), p. 2ff.

"nightmare," "struggling," and reported falling enthusiasm for the variable idea.[5] It reported,

> Many of the hundreds of companies that instituted the plans in the 1950s and 1960s—including Mobil Oil Corporation, Bank-America Corporation, Monsanto Chemical Company, UAL Inc., Boeing Company, and Prudential Insurance Company of America—are now considering dropping or modifying them.

The Prudential cut back its offerings sharply at this time and effective January 1, 1976, gave its employees the opportunity to withdraw from the variable annuity option, though it did not eliminate it. The very low common stock prices of the mid-1970s were a great opportunity for variable annuity purchasers, but few people or organizations—even the Pru—saw it that way.

As stock prices rose in the late 1970s and 1980s, growth of variable annuities resumed.

LIFE INSURANCE COMPANIES DISCOVER PENSIONS

Life insurance companies in the mid-20th century were rapidly losing the race for the expanding pension market. In 1950, contributions to insured pension funds were 81 percent as much as to noninsured trusteed plans, but by 1960, they had dropped to 44 percent.

By the 1950s, life insurance companies were faring badly in the competition for group pension plans for industry, and they had none at all for public employees. Various restrictions made them noncompetitive with bank trusteed pension plans. Most of the huge life insurance companies were licensed in New York and, therefore, were limited by the New York insurance law in the categories in which they could invest policyholder funds. New York State also required allocating interest rates at a flat portfolio rate no matter when a premium was received, making New York-licensed companies essentially noncompetitive in annuities and pension plans. Only well after the CREF breakthrough did New York permit the "investment year" method of allocating investment income.

Insurance companies suffered two tax burdens that other pension plan providers did not have to pay—federal income taxation, particularly a capital gains tax, and, in over half the states, a state premium tax. These negative factors were unfortunate because the insurance mechanism, with its guarantees and ability to provide life annuities, was well suited to providing pension plans, especially for smaller and medium-sized employers.

---

[5]Victor F. Zonana, "Shrinking Benefits: Retirees Who Picked Inflation Insurance See Pensions Wither," *The Wall Street Journal,* September 10, 1974.

I believe it is accurate to say the establishment of CREF was the trigger that caused, over the next 30 years, a booming reentry of the life insurance business into pensions and annuities. Its major contribution probably was removing the fear and establishing the acceptability of common stocks for funding conservative long-term pension obligations. Its second major contribution was establishment of a new industry, variable annuities, available to funders of pension plans and to individuals saving on their own for retirement needs.

Even before the Prudential finally received approval to proceed with variable annuities, separate accounts were established to permit much broader choice of investment vehicles for company pension plans. These accounts freed insurance companies to include equities in their assets underlying pension plans. The John Hancock Life Insurance Company received authority from the Massachusetts legislature and established its first separate account in 1962.

Separate accounts gave life insurance companies a strong competitive tool in funding corporate pension plans, allowing them to compete directly with bank trust accounts. The assets of the life insurance company separate accounts grew phenomenally, from a little over $1 billion in 1967 to $10 billion five years later. After slumping to $9 billion at the low in equity prices in 1974, the assets rose dramatically, year after year, to $112 billion in 1987.[6] Now that such plans are common, and every state in the union permits separate accounts, it is becoming difficult to remember the vigor of the arguments against equity investments for pensions that TIAA had to meet in the 1950s in establishing CREF.

With respect to individual annuities, by 1988, hundreds of life insurance variable annuities were available to the general public. They had been joined by hundreds of mutual fund offerings. By then the name *variable annuity* had been added to money market, fixed income, equity, and flexibly managed annuities. Lipper's 1988 variable life and annuity survey included 173 equity funds and 57 flexibly managed funds.[7] Total net assets were nearly $22 billion. Investment performance of the equity funds varied widely. Over a five-year period ending June 30, 1988, the average gain of the top five funds slightly exceeded 100 percent, while two of the lowest five were minus 20 percent, and the other three ranged up to 13 percent gain.

VARIABLE ANNUITIES ABROAD

The first overseas publication of *A New Approach to Retirement Income* was in Germany in 1953, a country unusually sensitive to the

---

[6]American Council of Life Insurance, *Life Insurance Fact Book 1988*, p. 92.
[7]*National Underwriter*, July 25, 1988, p. 41.

ravages of inflation on annuities. This led to correspondence with various people in Germany concerning CREF and how to set up similar funds.

A letter in TIAA files tells the story for Japan, more powerfully because it is written in the then current Japanese-English:

> We, Japanese, had had a bitter experience that policyholders of the life insurance were suffered great damage from the inflation after the war. Today a cry for making the annuity life insurance is becoming larger and larger, and especially the variable annuity is strongly desired.[8]

The chief actuary of the Meiji Mutual Life Insurance Company of Tokyo wrote early in 1954 a letter that sounds quaint, knowing that the Japanese Stock Market (Nikkei 225 index) stood at 356 at the end of 1954 and 32,100 in March 1989:

> In Japan, fluctuation of currency value has so sensible effect upon prices of common stock that people feel it too much speculative to invest large part of their funds in common stocks. Also it is widely accepted idea that real estate hold on its value during the inflation time.[9]

One of the first foreign expressions of interest in the variable annuity was from Dr. A. H. Langeraar of N. V. DeWaerdye in Holland, who considered whether his company should establish such a plan.

In 1957, the London and Manchester Assurance Company Limited established the first annuity fund based on equities in England. It was an investment trust providing retirement annuities based on common shares for professional men.

Also in the late 1950s and early 1960s, much correspondence occurred with actuaries and others in Germany, Switzerland, Austria, Spain, Sweden, and England.

Canadian employers and government agencies began to develop interest in the variable annuity in the early 1960s. CREF received requests for information and guidance from the Canadian Taxation Division Staff Association, the Royal Trust Company of Toronto, the University of Manitoba, the Society of Ontario Hydro Professional Engineers, Canadian Airline Pilots Association, Crown Zellerbach Canada Limited, and various professionals in the pension field. The interesting fact that appears in riffling through the correspondence is the number of expressions of interest by employee groups in addition to employers.

---

[8]Ichizo Abe to WCG, August 25, 1960.
[9]Kiyoshi Sugawara to WCG, March 22, 1954.

And, dear to my heart as a former teacher, was the large number of requests for information about CREF from doctoral candidates working on their dissertations.

CONCLUSION

My Harvard Graduate School economics professor, Joseph Schumpeter, considered innovation as the driving force of capitalism. The noted actuary, Joseph Maclean, considered CREF the most important innovation in the life insurance and pension business since the introduction of group insurance in 1912. It would be pleasant to conclude that higher education in America has well served the general public and a very important business, life insurance and pensions, by the introduction of equity-based products.

PART THREE

Investments

INTRODUCTION

Influence of Investments

Financial security for older people and the capital growth of America are now inextricably commingled. In America, the great growth of pension fund assets and the substantial reliance on private pensions for retirement income has changed from dream to partial reality only in recent decades; this is still not generally found even in advanced countries.

The job of an *individual* saving for retirement is huge, and the job of a *nation* to finance the retirement security of its older citizens is gigantic. Perhaps half of this task can be accomplished through a social contract between generations. The American Social Security system is that social contract, transferring vast amounts of income from workers to retired people. Reliance for most of the other half is placed on employer pension plans. Private savings are also crucial and growing, much of it encouraged by favorable tax treatment through IRAs, Keoghs, ESOPs, and other tax-deferral methods.

Private pension plans now have over $1.5 *trillion* of assets. These savings for old age are actively financing jobs, housing, transportation, recreation, infrastructure, and production of goods and services. In turn, these investments and earnings on them are providing retirement security for the pension savers.

Interest Rates and Savers

In many ways, savers are not treated as well by the American economic and political structure as they should be. During and after World War II, and in other more recent years, interest rates were controlled at artificially low rates. This has led to serious damage for savers both through the lower income from their thrift and through the inflation resulting from such monetary policy.

There are repeated demands from domestic business and labor unions to reduce the value of the dollar and make imports dearer to protect American industry and jobs. Still other voices suggest lower interest rates to stave off a business decline. Translated, these voices are all saying: "Don't worry about the saver, the pensioner, the thrifty person hurt by low interest rates, the consumer hurt by a cheapening dollar. Force them to subsidize business, the borrowing of governments, the protectionists, through slim or negative real rates of interest on their fixed-dollar savings." Although not often recognized, this has been a major cause of America's dangerously low savings rate, near the bottom of the developed countries.

Some turnaround has occurred. During the 1980s, real interest rates have been positive and strong, averaging about 5 to 6 percent. Savings for retirement income has in many years been the only increasing source of savings for capital investment.

Leverage of Investment Earnings

College teachers and other professional people generally have to save enough during each two years of working life to support themselves and spouse for one year in retirement. This simply would not be feasible were it not for the leverage of investment earnings from savings for retirement spread over the many decades of the working and retired years.

For example, the first $1,000 saved by a young instructor at age 25 could grow sixteenfold, to $16,000, at age 65, 40 years later! All that is required is an interest rate of just over 7 percent, earned continually through productive investment.

The leverage of investment earnings over the long-term investment periods involved in annuities is enormous. The Rule of 72 is a handy and dramatic way of expressing this power. *To find how long it takes for money to double, divide 72 by the interest rate earned.* That is, savings will double in a little over 10 years at 7 percent interest. Or savings will double in a little over 7 years at 10 percent interest. The young professor's original $1,000 saved at just over 7 percent grows to $2,000 by age 35, to $4,000 by age 45, to $8,000 by age 55, and to $16,000 by age 65. The figure for the accumulation of $1,000 for 40 years at 7 percent compound interest would be $14,974, of which $13,974 is interest.

Annuities are generally purchased by periodic payments related to increasing salary amounts during most of a working lifetime. Early payments have as much as 40 years to accumulate, while some of the later ones have only a few months. As an oversimplified example, a periodic payment of $100 a month for 40 years—a total payment of $48,000 invested at 7 percent—would accumulate to $247,154. The great power of investment earnings suggests that primary effort should be given to the type, risk factors, and yields of the investments supporting pension savings.

Inflation and Pension Fund Earnings

Investment policy can do much to meet the extra needs for retirement income caused by inflation. TIAA has provided substantial protection for participants against inflation through emphasizing long-term higher yield investments and investments with equity participations. TIAA annuitants can also take advantage of the inflation protection mechanism of the graded annuity (discussed in Chapter 16), a payout structure that allows part of the extra earnings from the annuity accumulation to be deferred until later retirement years.

CREF, of course, was the first pension plan designed to help ameliorate the financial effects of inflation on retired educators.

CHAPTER 11

CREF Investments

CREF, 37 years after its birth, is the world's largest fund invested solely in equities. With TIAA, it is the largest nongovernmental pension fund in the world. It holds the first, second, or third largest block of stock in many of the world's largest companies. Perhaps it is America's largest single owner of foreign stock. It has become a force in the financial markets, a highly visible entity. Its vote on proxy proposals of companies, whether on social or economic issues, commands substantial interest and even power. All of this seems incredible to those of us who have been with it from the start.

BACKGROUND

CREF Investment Philosophies

A major challenge at the start of CREF was to develop a set of investment philosophies appropriate for a variable annuity company. Should they be different from those applicable to a college endowment, a charitable foundation, a mutual fund, a bank trust account, or a traditional fixed-dollar private pension fund? The size of the fund to be invested would matter. How large would CREF become? When? Should the investment philosophies be set in concrete, or should they be flexible? Which ones? How flexible?

A quick, general answer can be given to some of these questions. CREF could expect a remarkably smooth flow of funds from its participants right across the business cycle, so it could use dollar cost averaging effectively for participants. It could avoid the risks of timing. Institutions like colleges, relying on gifts for endowment growth, have an uneven flow, tending to increase when equity prices are high, so they must give some attention to spreading out their investments on a different pattern from the inflow of gifts.

On the outflow side, most organizations have fixed-dollar obligations—budgets to meet, buildings to pay for, projects to finance. For them, it is not handy to have to dump large blocks of stock on the market in a year like 1974 (or 1946 or 1929). Mutual funds often experience substantial inflows or outflows of funds. There tend to be large inflows of cash when the market is rising or high and large redemptions during periods of declining or low common stock prices. This requires greater liquidity, for which there is an investment cost.

On the outflow side, CREF was designed to avoid any fixed-dollar pension promises, so its financial solvency at any stage of depression or prosperity is unassailable, regardless of level of outflow or inflow. Participants who stayed in CREF for the annuity period would receive income in low, high, and intermediate years, without having to sacrifice large blocks of their equity units to meet payments stated in dollars. All of these factors provided an opportunity for CREF's par-

Normal day on NYSE floor (NYSE Archives)

ticipants to benefit in far more effective ways from common stock investments.[1]

Several fundamental investment philosophies were incorporated in CREF at the start.

Charter Provisions

CREF's status as a Special Act Corporation freed it from the "3 percent or one third of surplus, whichever is smaller" limit on equity investments mandated by the New York insurance law. The CREF charter contained some subsidiary limitations: stocks purchased had to be listed on a national securities exchange (at least a partial indication of quality); there was a prohibition, now lifted, on investing in shares of bank or insurance company stocks (intended to prevent interlocks of financial institutions); no more than 5 percent—now 10 percent—of the outstanding shares of a company could be owned, except CREF can own 100 percent of a real estate company. Where appropriate, these limits have now been changed or eliminated.

CREF Fully Invested in Equities

CREF was designed so the valuation of its assets and its liabilities would move together, as the value of the underlying investments moved. The purpose was to make equity investments available on a large scale without any danger that the pension fund could become insolvent. But we decided not to require, in CREF's charter, that its assets be invested in any particular way. We wanted the new annuity fund to be flexible enough, even many years in the future under different situations, to adjust to changes in the capital markets, in availability of other types of equities such as real estate or international investments, and in other economic conditions. We did not want to run into the inflexibilities of insurance law restrictions designed for a specific type of life insurance or annuity policy.

At the same time, we believed strongly and our studies supported our conviction that CREF *should* be fully invested in equities at all times. There should be strong control over ill-considered, poorly studied, or even panicky changes in investment policy. The mechanism we used to achieve this control was to place a strong investment

---

[1]All of these principles continue to prevail in the late 1980s for CREF and for those participants who send a reasonably level flow of premiums to CREF during their working years and who receive a CREF variable annuity during retirement.

CREF now allows transfers to and from a money market account as well as to TIAA. Those who avail themselves of these options will tend to do better or worse according to market levels when they shift. CREF is already having larger variations in its cash flow, but this does not matter since CREF's equity investments are always valued at market.

policy statement in the CREF constitution, which is a separate document from the legislatively granted charter:

> The following statement of investment policy is a guide and not a limitation on the investment powers of the corporation:
>
> (a) It is desirable that the corporation keep its assets invested at all times exclusively in investments having equity characteristics.
>
> (b) It is desirable that the corporation take advantage of the principle of dollar cost averaging by periodic purchases as funds become available, keeping as fully invested at all times as is practicable since:
>
> (i) the normal participant in the benefits of the corporation will make regular monthly contributions over a period of many years and will receive monthly retirement benefits for life;
>
> (ii) there is no need to anticipate demand for large sums of cash at any one time since the certificates of participation do not provide for cash withdrawal.
>
> (c) It is desirable that the corporation's funds be diversified as to type of industry and growth and yield characteristics.[2]

The CREF constitution can be changed by the Members of CREF if certified by the superintendent of insurance of the state of New York as being lawful and equitable. Recently, this flexibility has proved useful in a way CREF's originators would not have dreamed of—establishment in the CREF corporation of a separate money market fund. This is the direct opposite of a common stock fund but has been incorporated within the flexibilities of the original design of the Charter and Constitution. It is discussed in Chapter 26.

The economic studies for CREF demonstrated that if participants in common stock funds would stick to long periods of steady investment, they would do well. But efforts to time purchases of common stocks had not proved rewarding. From the outset, therefore, a basic element of CREF's investment policy was to keep its funds fully invested in equity-type securities at all times. Nothing has happened in the ensuing years that suggests a change in that conclusion. Studies of institutional investors' attempts to time when to go into and when to drop out of or lighten up on equity investments have shown disappointing results. Over most time periods, some two thirds of investment management firms do worse than the Standard & Poor's 500 Index.

The stunning rise of short-term market interest rates during the inflation of 1980 to 1982 is an example. Many individuals and money managers chose to move into cash and cash equivalents, such as money market funds and short Treasuries, seeking the higher yields.

---

[2]Constitution of College Retirement Equities Fund, adopted May 26, 1952, as amended November 9, 1979, Article VI, Section 1, Investments.

Both the yields and the movement peaked in July 1982. As yields on Treasuries and money market funds receded, so did the income of those who had chosen the temporarily higher yields. By then, they had missed the opportunity to buy long-term bonds at the highest yields ever prevailing and had also missed the early rise in common stock prices. The farther bond and stock prices rose in the next few months, the more these investors lengthened their bond maturities "in order to lock in yields" that had already fallen three or four percentage points and to "catch the bull market" that had already moved substantially.

A fully invested position avoids the temptation of "locking the barn door" after some horses have escaped, or trying to "catch the bull" market half way across the field, or to avoid "missing the boat" that is already well offshore, or to be "fast on our feet" after we have already tripped. These are the standard clichés of investment managers who did miss the boat. So called riskless short-term obligations demonstrated during that period the heavy costs of lost investment opportunity. During any such period, of course, there are some contrarian investors who happen to catch the swing and do well.

DIVERSIFICATION

CREF uses four different types of diversification, each of which reduces risk: diversification over time, among companies, among industries, and among countries.

Diversification over Time

Of all the changes in approach to investment philosophy led by CREF, perhaps the most important is *diversification over time*. CREF did not invent diversification over time. CREF was not the first to use diversification over time. But it was the first to set up a structure that allowed a million participants to diversify their own savings over their working and retired lifetime in a pattern that maximizes the opportunity to benefit from the long-term growth of the American economy. CREF participants can achieve a major reduction in investment risk by this system of investing month after month, year after year, decade after decade, and then drawing their annuity month after month, year after year, decade after decade, so long as they (and their spouse) live.

Dollar cost averaging (or dollar averaging) was a term that came into general use in the press and investment circles in the early 1950s. It meant investing approximately equal amounts of money in stocks at regular intervals over time. This would result in an average *cost* for shares owned lower than the average *price* at which the shares were purchased. The advantage is that a given number of dollars purchases a larger number of shares of stock when prices are low than when they are high, making for a lower average cost of the shares.

TIAA found when it studied dollar cost averaging that hardly anyone actually used it, although many talked about it. Mutual fund purchasers *could* buy on a regular basis but generally did not. College endowments and other such institutional investors can do the same but do not. Their inflow of funds is irregular, and so usually is their investment. The most powerful indication was the lack of competent studies of accumulating or dollar cost averaging diversified funds.

TIAA consciously designed CREF to maximize the opportunity and probability for participants to diversify their investments over time. Data given elsewhere show the remarkable success of the effort.

Diversification among Companies and Industries

Diversification is a primary way of reducing risk. At the end of its first year of operation in 1953, CREF owned common stocks in 53 companies in 14 industries. The list grew steadily, providing growing diversification among companies and industries and geographically in the United States, until it contained 170 stocks in 37 industries in 1973. In that year, CREF started its worldwide diversification by making its first purchases of Japanese stocks. In 1989, CREF was diversified among more than 2,400 companies in many industries in 21 countries. The domestic portfolio contains 1,500 companies; the international portfolio, 900 additional companies.

INTERNATIONAL INVESTING

CREF from its early days owned a few foreign stocks like Royal Dutch and Unilever. It commenced a regular program of international investing in 1973 and owned $72 million in such equities by 1978, almost entirely in Japanese stocks. In 1977, CREF announced to its participants, "We anticipate an extension of the Fund's investments into sectors of the world market and types of companies not found in many traditional pension portfolios." The following September 1978, the CREF finance committee approved a target of 10 percent foreign investment by 1984 by investing $12 million a month. This again was a prudent following of the principles of diversification over time and diversification among issues.

There is strong rationale for international investing. It opens up rewarding world markets and productive capacities and provides additional investment diversification. It gives CREF participants a share of the strong economic growth of certain foreign economies. It makes

CREF a prominent player in the global economy and in the 24-hour financial markets.

For CREF participants, it has a significant smoothing function. World economies do move somewhat in the same direction, at the same time, and by the same amount. But these movements are by no means parallel. As a result, an internationally diversified fund will vary up and down less than a single country fund, and a variable annuity income for retired people will be steadier, while at the same time probably improving investment performance. International investing also brings in an additional reward/risk factor, that of exchange rates. For the first years of the program, the U.S. dollar was generally declining in value, with mostly a long downward sweep in the value of the dollar, providing additional substantial gains for participants. This source of gain has vanished in more recent times.

CREF's investment law staff, headed by Peter Clapman, had to accomplish much innovative and complex legal work to obtain relief from withholding taxes on dividends from a number of foreign countries, meet or change state or federal fiduciary requirements, and handle accounting and safekeeping needs. The law staff worked with the Ford Foundation and Yale University in this effort. In addition, the law staff also obtained two major interpretive letters from the SEC that enabled CREF to participate in foreign privatization offerings, rights issues, and other investment opportunities previously denied U.S. investors.

By the end of 1979, CREF had approximately $166 million, or 2.6 percent of portfolio holdings, invested abroad. Ten foreign exchanges were included—Australia, Belgium, France, West Germany, Hong Kong, Japan, the Netherlands, Spain, Switzerland, and the United Kingdom—and shares of 321 companies were owned. CREF reached its initial 10 percent target for foreign investments in 1983.

CREF INVESTMENT STAFF

By a bit of historical good luck, CREF started with a common stock investment team already in place. For decades, a separate investment office, the Carnegie-Teachers Investment Office, had handled TIAA's fixed-dollar investments as well as those of several of the Carnegie trusts including the largest, Carnegie Corporation of New York, and the Carnegie Foundation for the Advancement of Teaching. These trusts were investing partially in common stocks. When CREF was established, TIAA-CREF took over the entire office, creating its own Investment Division, headed by Richard F. F. Nichols. Separate departments were established for CREF's common stocks and for TIAA's securities, mortgages, and real estate.

During this period, the CREF trustee finance committee was active in management of CREF investments as well as in setting policy. As CREF grew, the finance committee gradually increased its emphasis on monitoring effectiveness of strategies, choosing investment methods, and setting investment policy.

By 1957, CREF had grown to the size that warranted a separate CREF investment unit. It was placed under the direction of Harry B. Freeman, Jr., vice president. Ida Cepicka and Leonard Brooks, Jr., were assistant investment officers. Freeman was succeeded in 1960 by Gerard van Amerongen, vice president, who was the top CREF investing officer until 1965. He presided over a major expansion in analytical staff as CREF's assets rose from $127 million at the end of 1959 to $448 million at the end of 1964. During all of this period, CREF used traditional value-oriented analysis in choosing common stock investments.

Dr. Roger F. Murray joined CREF on February 1, 1965, as vice president and economist, to head the CREF investment operation. He was, and continues to be at 80, one of the top equity theoreticians and practitioners in the country. He was elected chairman of the CREF finance committee and executive vice president of CREF in 1967 and served in these capacities until 1970. He had already served on the CREF board for nine years and on the finance committee for five years before joining the staff full time.

For several decades, Dr. Murray commuted between the academic and the investment world, having become an investment administrator with the Bankers Trust Company in 1932, rising to vice president and economist before becoming associate dean and professor at Columbia University's School of Business in 1956. During his entire career, he continued to teach at Columbia, returning there full time after his five-year period at CREF.

Under Dr. Murray's leadership, CREF's investment staff developed a deep knowledge of the literature on risk management, modern portfolio theory, and actual portfolio management. He established an extended research program using both inside talent and university research facilities.

CREF became active in the mid-1960s in university and financial market projects to develop computer technology as an aid to investment management. CREF incorporated the more promising techniques into its own operations.

One of the first such applications was in security selection within the public utilities industry. The use of evaluation models saved analysts' time and achieved a more favorable rate of return.

CREF was one of the first institutions to execute purchases and sales through Instinet, in December 1969. Instinet was the first national computer network designed to make possible direct negotiation for block sales of securities among banks, mutual funds, college endowments, pension funds, life insurance companies, and other institutional investors. CREF at the time concluded it was too early to tell how large a role such networks could play but they held promise.

CREF used Instinet for a number of years and then discontinued it. In more recent years, technological improvements have occurred in the so-called fourth market, or more direct seller-to-buyer trading of common stocks. Instinet's introduction of Crossing Network, Jeffries' Posit Network, and other developments are in place and are being used by CREF again in its experimental trading program.

CREF continued to grow exponentially. By 1966, the number of college people receiving payout CREF variable annuities exceeded 5,000, so it was starting to have some impact on the payout side. But the challenge was in the stunning growth in assets. CREF's assets crossed the half-billion-dollar mark in 1965, reached $1 billion in 1968, went back and forth across the line a couple of times as the market fluctuated, and passed $1.5 billion in 1970.

One of the challenges for a not-for-profit, public service organization such as TIAA-CREF is recruiting and holding of able professional staff and organizing them into an effective team. The problem was how best to organize for effective investment of the enormous assets that would be accumulating in the 1970s. The CREF board established two special committees under the direction of Dr. Murray to make an intensive study of methods of organizing for large-scale equity fund management. Working with Dr. Murray, Theodore R. Lilley, vice president and senior investment officer, interviewed dozens of top officers of institutional investors, investment advisors, and academics.

At that time, competitive investment teams were popular with many large institutional investors. Three, 5, 10, or in the case of the Ford Motor Company, over 25, or at AT&T, over 100, outside investment managers would be assigned parts of the portfolio. Or internally, two, three, or five teams, each with one or two top investment officers and a group of security analysts, would be established on the institution's payroll. These teams were to compete with each other, on the assumption that the virtues of competition would achieve exceptional investment performance.

As chairman and CEO of CREF, I made one strong input to these deliberations—I would have nothing to do with setting up three separate competitive teams, each with a big staff, to keep secrets from each other, one to perhaps be buying General Motors or IBM at the same time that another was selling it. This was silly. Rather, all CREF people would be on the same team, sharing ideas and knowledge, helping in the single job of good investment performance for participants. What the trustees and I wanted was a group of first-rate investment experts whose job would be to compete with all the rest of the investment world, not with each other.

CREF decided it would be much more productive to establish cores of specialists and security analysts with substantial research capability to work as a unit toward good investment performance. They would be supported by talented "quants," as the computer whizzes who specialize in quantitative analysis are known, by economists, by an expert trading desk, and by supporting staff. Each of these expert centers would use outside research from brokerage firms, economic statistical services, and academic research. Much of this structure continues today, materially expanded as CREF's assets continue to expand.

CREF extended its staff at the start of the 1970s after the Murray-Lilley recommendations. Burt N. Dorsett, vice president for investments at the University of Rochester and a graduate of Dartmouth and Harvard, was brought in to head the expanded operation. He was joined by four vice presidents, all holders of M.B.A. or master's degrees and relevant investment experience: Leo C. Bailey from William Hutchinson and Company, Inc.; Timothy G. Dalton, Jr., from the Enterprise Fund; Mr. Lilley; and C. Oscar Morong, Jr., from Morgan Guaranty Trust Company.

Dr. Murray asked to be relieved of his duties as CREF investment head after the new team was in place so he could return to the Columbia University School of Business to the S. Sloan Colt Professorship of Banking and Finance, which he did in 1970.

Quantitative analysis and international investing were initially handled as integral parts of the CREF operation, each function gradually growing in size of staff and significance. Ida Cepicka Ohler and James Farrell were early specialists in statistical methods. In 1976, a separate Department of Portfolio Systems and Quantitative Research was established, with Leo Bailey in charge. He was succeeded by Robert Ferguson in 1979 and, in 1983, by Eric Fisher. A division to handle the burgeoning international investing, under the direction of Henry A. Frantzen, was established in 1979.

James S. Martin joined CREF in August 1974 and has headed the CREF investment operations since March 1979. He is now executive vice president and chairman of the CREF finance committee. He was previously with Chase Investors Management Corporation, a subsidiary of Chase Bank. Oscar Morong was one of the original expanded staff in 1970 and heads domestic active security research. Virgil Cumming has headed international investments since May 1987. He joined CREF as a domestic securities analyst in 1971 (from Connecticut Bank and Trust Company). Eric Fisher joined the company in June 1978 from Telestat Systems. He is responsible for the passive components of the portfolio, discussed later, and quantitative research activities. Diane Axelrod joined TIAA as a systems analyst in December 1971 and transferred to CREF Investments in December 1976. She is vice president in charge of administration and trading.

An invigorating and enlightening asset during those years was the extraordinary group of trustees: Paul A. Samuelson, Institute Professor at MIT and the first American Nobel laureate in economics; William Forsyth Sharpe, Timken Professor of Finance at the Graduate School of Business, Stanford University; and Richard R. West, dean and professor of finance, the Amos Tuck School of Business Administration, Dartmouth College, and now dean of the School of Business at New York University. They were joined on the board by several of the outstanding investment practitioners, heads of trust banks, investment firms, and college financial officers. And they were preceded by other academics such as Milton Friedman and Walter Heller.

The questions asked, the intellectual input, the vigorous discussions, all added immeasurably to the growth and effectiveness of staff's consideration of the major policy decisions (and, I might add, to the delight of working for TIAA-CREF). It is impossible to give deserved credit to each trustee's ideas but not impossible to emphasize the totality of influence of such a board of trustees.

RISK, BETA, AND VARIABILITY

During these years, investment risk was becoming an important subject for economic analysis. Academicians were developing the idea of risk-adjusted investment results and chose Beta, or variability, as the proxy for risk. The assumption was that risk-averse people do not want volatile investments, which at times sell for depressed prices. An informal CREF trustees luncheon club developed, with Samuelson, Sharpe, Walter Blum, and Richard West who were expert on this subject; these were long, involved discussions.

I did not and do not believe that variability alone is a satisfactory proxy for investment risk in a long-term fund like CREF, although it may be a keen measure of short-term psychological attitude toward risk. I have just reread some correspondence I had with Milton Friedman in 1971 that clearly states the question, although it did not end the discussion. Friedman wrote:

> I believe the criterion of variability . . . is utterly unsuited to CREF. It measures the variability of annual rates of return. It is appropriate for someone who is contemplating getting in and out of the market at fairly frequent intervals, so that it does matter to him what returns he will get for a period as brief as a year. That clearly applies to essentially none of CREF's policyholders, certainly not during the accumulation. During that period, nothing could be of less interest to a CREF policyholder than the year-to-year variations in rates of re-

turn. But what does interest him is the mean rate of return that he will earn over the period during which he is accumulating funds. . . . [A]s you increase the period of time for which individual returns are measured, from one year to two years to five years to ten years, the variability would diminish very sizably.[3]

Neither Friedman nor I was saying there is no risk in common stock investments. But we were saying the widely used proxy for risk, variability, measured by volatility of *annual* or even quarterly rates of investment return, should be irrelevant for the long-term investments in CREF. That is one of the times I wished I could return to academic scholarship to see if I could develop better proxies for risk for CREF and other truly long-range funds.

Following Friedman's board service, he suggested in a letter dated July 6, 1971, that CREF should eliminate all investment analysis and "adopt a mechanical formula whereby CREF simply bought into a Standard & Poor's 500 index." This was an intriguing and early suggestion for indexing the fund to the larger American corporations. But by then, it would have reduced CREF's diversification; in 1971, CREF already held a number of the 1,000 stocks listed on the New York Stock Exchange that were not included in the S&P 500 index, and it also held stocks listed on the AMEX and NASDAQ. It was soon to start an international investing program. We decided not to limit diversification to the S&P index stocks.

SOPHISTICATED INVESTMENT METHODS

CREF continued its intensive study of the academic and Wall Street literature pertaining to equities investment and, where possible, built on it. Phrases like modern portfolio theory, capital asset pricing theory, Beta and other measures of risk, indexing, dividend discount models, and covariance and its application to international investing were frequent topics of study and discussion. All of them came to have a significant part in CREF investment practice.

In seeking to combine sound investment theory with the practice of effective portfolio management, CREF uses a number of measurement techniques for quantitative analysis and control of the investment process: performance and strategy review, risk measurement, and portfolio activity analysis.

Relative Valuation Model

A major development in CREF's investment management came with the introduction of its dividend discount model as its principal secu-

---

[3]Friedman to WCG, August 31, 1971.

rity selection method. It was introduced in mid-1976 and fully implemented in March 1977. The fund attempts to make a practical application of capital asset pricing theory through the utilization of a "market line" that compares estimated market risk with returns projected by the valuation model. It maintains a computerized system for analyzing comparative values and arriving at investment choices in the managed section of the portfolio. It brings a highly disciplined methodology to selection of companies to be represented in the portfolio. The CREF valuation process has gone through a number of significant modifications since its introduction.

These efforts, plus rigorous quantitative research and international investing, began to show strong results. Starting in 1977, CREF performance exceeded that of the S&P 500 each month for 30 months, an unusually long run, until mid-1979.

But performance slumped from mid-1979 through 1980, trailing the S&P by nearly 600 basis points, or six percentage points, wiping out much of the gain of the previous period. CREF had taken a large position in high dividend-yield stocks, recommended by research showing them to be good long-term investments for nontaxable investors like pension funds. An underweighted position in energy stocks, lightened up in late 1979, especially contributed to the weaker performance. This helped lead to heightened interest in indexing part of the portfolio.

Partial Indexing

One of the significant decisions in CREF investments was implemented in mid-1981, a decision to index about 70 percent of the portfolio. CREF trustees and officers had discussed the possibility of indexing for some time, but wanted much broader diversification than a single index like the S&P 500.

When Paul Samuelson was elected to the CREF board in 1974, he immediately became interested in its investment philosophy and practice. He emphasized diversification and was both ally and goad in CREF's moves toward passive management of portions of the portfolio. He encouraged participation in the non-S&P parts of the American market and in extending diversification in foreign equities markets. He was a strong supporter of moving, in 1981, to indexing a major part of the fund while intensively managing the other part through the dividend-discount system installed in 1977.

The several investment leaders from money management firms, banks, and mutual funds who served on the finance committee were central in forming the 1981 system of active-passive investment management. Staff made a comprehensive study of the questions of volatility and further control over the portfolio and proposed to the finance committee adoption of an active/passive approach to the domestic portfolio. The CREF finance committee approved, in May 1981, the basic structure still in use.[4] It is added to the dividend discount model and other stock selection methods implemented earlier, and together they form the CREF investment strategy:

1. Indexing 80 percent of the domestic portfolio.
   (a) Using the S&P 500 index for about 90 percent (now 85 percent) of the indexed portfolio, representing the S&P stock weights among all stocks.
   (b) Using non-S&P New York Stock Exchange, American Exchange, and NASDAQ stocks for the other 10 percent (now 15 percent).
2. Vigorously managing the other 20 percent of the domestic portfolio.
3. Continuing to increase the international fund to about 10 percent of CREF's assets (new target approved in April 1988—15 percent).

This strategy continues to be central to the CREF investment management. It gives room for seeking better-than-average performance while containing risk, defined as variability and deviation from the market, well within a level appropriate for pension funding.

OPPORTUNITIES OF SIZE

Do large or small common stock funds do better? CREF was once a small fund and now is huge.

Small, specialty, undiversified funds *may* do spectacularly well for their investors—if they hit a significant industry development, make a major bet on energy at the right time, choose the right corporate takeovers, elect to concentrate on a growth industry at the right time in the economy, or some other specific factor. But on the same list with the high performers will be small specialty funds that have done spectacularly poorly. With remarkable frequency, the spectacular up leaders, small or large, at one time are the spectacular down leaders during the next period, and vice versa. These are high-reward high-risk volatile funds and are appropriate investment choices for those in a position to assume high risk. A "prince or pauper" investment approach is not for pensions.

A large pension fund does not match this kind of spectacular up- or downswing. Almost all pension funding, whether large or small,

---

[4] *1981 Chairman's Report to the Boards of Trustees,* TIAA-CREF, p. 17.

seeks much less volatility and is limited by the Employee Retirement Income Security Act (ERISA) in the types of risk taken for participants. The concentration of risk in a small, undiversified fund is not an advantage for pensions. Very large funds by their nature tend to be well diversified. CREF achieves national and international diversification through its size and investment methodologies. Its core portfolio closely tracks the indexes, and its managed portion seeks additional reward without losing the safety of diversification.

There are a number of advantages of size that can give a large fund an investment edge over a small fund. Size permits a fund to employ a better research staff, to have an effective stock lending operation, to obtain better service from brokers and Wall Street firms, to conduct more research—the list can be long. CREF can take advantage of modern portfolio theory, dividend discount models, capital asset pricing theories, and it can develop its own specialized methods. It has large programs using computerized portfolio optimizers to maximize expected return.

Securities Lending

CREF uses a number of sources of additional income that are especially productive for large funds. One of these is securities lending. A number of universities, notably Washington University of St. Louis, the University of Chicago, and Yale University, had pioneered in securities lending in the mid-1970s. CREF started a securities lending program in 1981 as soon as the Department of Labor ruled that ERISA-regulated pension funds could engage in such activity. It expanded this to the international field in 1983 with an emphasis on Japanese securities. CREF is strongly established as a major lending source. Its inventory is monumental in size. This essentially risk-free activity has provided $48 million of incremental income since the program began.

Experimental Trading System

Another such opportunity of size is the experimental trading system. This computer system is designed to achieve small incremental trading differences by using CREF's large inventory of stocks. It plays on small differences and trading at an incredible one or two cents a share. This program was applied to the passive component of the CREF portfolio in 1987 and 1988, generating $14 million of extra earnings, and is now being used in the active component.

CREF takes advantage of corporate dividend reinvestment programs in which it receives a discount to maintain its positions.

Investment Expenses

In 1987, CREF earned enough extra income from exploiting its advantages of size to offset a large portion of its investment expenses. When these savings are added to the reduced expenses from the elimination of high, fixed commissions on stock transactions, the savings are substantial.

DOWN PERIODS: DISASTER OR OPPORTUNITY?

The year 1973 was one of disappointment in the stock market. Economic growth was too high to be sustained; stock prices had risen rapidly. The slump at the end of the year resulted in a net total rate of return on CREF's investments of minus 18.1 percent, compared with plus 17.1 percent in 1972. Uncertainties were gathering, CREF informed its participants.

CREF's net total rate of return for 1974 was minus 31.0 percent, by far the largest one-year drop in value since CREF began. This compared with a minus 27 percent for the S&P index. CREF was more volatile than the market; it had risen faster, and it declined faster.

The 1974 stock market fall was precipitous. Month by month that widely published index and determinant of public sentiment, the Dow-Jones Index (DJI), was reaching new lows, dropping to 585 on October 4. Its high had been 1,052 in January 1973. The press was full of the slump; its stories were usually of the "end of the world" type. And to top it off, or bottom it out, New York City was going under financially.

This was the first test of whether the new approach to equity investing presented by CREF would weather a recession. Would participants and colleges panic, as did many stock owners in all previous crises? When establishing CREF, we had concluded, so far as participant psychology was concerned, the good years when stock prices were high and rising could take care of themselves; the problem of mass psychology had to do with the declining and low years. Our presentations of CREF would try to prepare participants for such years. But for over 20 years, the stock market had boomed along with scarcely a dip, rising from its July 1, 1952, level of 275 on the Dow to 1,052 in January 1973. We were sometimes accused of crying wolf.

CREF and its participants (and Greenough too) came in for a share of unsought public attention. Dan Dorfman included a short piece in his regular column for *New York* magazine, published October 14, 1974. The first few sentences will illustrate:

A Cruel, Costly Lesson

The College Retirement Equities Fund, which manages a multi-billion-dollar portfolio for some 380,000 educators across the country, is about to teach its participants a hard lesson. The CREF portfolio shows a paper loss of some $800 million in paper profits in the last nine months. While that would be bad news for anyone, it is especially tough on the 25,000 retired educators who, having faithfully paid into the fund during their working lives, are now drawing monthly checks from it.

To William Greenough, 60-year-old CREF chairman, falls the task of teaching his hard-pressed constituents the virtues of patience.

The public was pulling its money out of stocks and mutual funds. Mutual funds were selling stocks and building up cash. Earlier in the same column, Dorfman mentioned that fire and casualty companies were panicking out of stocks, one company "going on a binge last week, dumping over $100 million in equities in just a few days" (and, by the way, causing the Dow's October low). There were far more sellers than buyers. CREF executives hoped the long preparation of its participants would work, and that they, lonely among the gathering crowd of sellers, would stick with CREF's buying policy. They did.

A Bonanza for the Professors

The week in which Dorfman wrote his article proved to be the low in the market on the Dow index. The autumn of 1974 proved to be the lowest point for a quarter-century—from 1963 to 1988—in common stock prices. It was a most rewarding time to buy, as CREF continued to do and to pass on the bargain prices to its participants. Writing in 1988, Curtis Henderson, equity benefits consultant, put the mid-1970s period in perspective:

> In the disastrous common stock years of 1973 and 1974 . . . the supposedly unsophisticated academic community kept its cool and its common stocks, so that pension plan participants enjoyed the subsequent substantial increases in common stock prices. In contrast, in the business community many of the employers who had adopted an equity annuity plan became so concerned about employee reaction that they replaced their equity annuity plan with a fixed-dollar annuity.[5]

Participants who bought or held tight to CREF units at $4.35 in September 1974 could be very happy they had not listened to the general pessimism of late 1974. At the end of 1975, their units were worth $6.48, by the end of 1980, $11.71, and by 1988, $36.74, all total return figures including capital gains and dividends. So the premium-paying participants in CREF enjoyed a more than eightfold increase in funds they invested with CREF at the bottom of 1974. The

---

[5]Curtis R. Henderson, unpublished manuscript, Haddonfield, New Jersey, 1988.

contrarian philosophy and the long-term, hold-steady philosophies paid off well. CREF was working spectacularly well for its 332,000 premium-paying participants.

Annuitants Hurting

But in the mid-1970s, CREF's 27,000 annuitants were feeling bruised. Their CREF incomes had gone down by 12 percent in 1973; a further 17 percent in 1974; and the further drop of 17 percent in 1975 was still to come, all representing slumps in monthly annuity checks starting May 1 each year. As expected, CREF's annuitants were truly receiving a variable annuity.

On the longer horizon, from its starting point of $10 in 1952, the annuity unit value had reached a high of $35.74 in 1972, thereby more than tripling the actual dollar income of participants who had started a CREF payout annuity at the beginning. From there it fell to $31.58 from 1973, to $26.21 for 1974, and to $21.84 for 1975. Thus, the pleasure that should have been felt in 1974 by one third of a million premium-paying CREF participants because of the low prices at which they were accumulating common stocks was somewhat balanced by the reduction in income of the 27,000 CREF annuitants. I say "should have felt" because newspaper headlines and market psychology do result in substantially less euphoria when stock prices are low than when they are high. My best friends have a tendency, during events like 1974 or the October 1987 plunge, to say, "Bill, explain to me again how happy I am that common stocks are doing so badly? Oh yes, I remember, I'm buying the units at such low prices."

A fair amount of the opposition to CREF when TIAA was setting it up had to do with concerns about low periods in common stock prices. Frederick H. Ecker, of the Metropolitan Life Insurance Company, as already reported, exemplified this approach. He concluded people do not blame the insurance company, or fixed-dollar assets, for inflation, but they will certainly come down hard on variable annuity companies during low prices of stocks. When stock prices are high, the individual will take full credit for "success of his good choices." When prices are low, the hindsighters will bitterly blame the fund for its "poor performance." Experience has shown that Ecker was not completely wrong in that conclusion.

There is another facet to public opinion and the business press. The stock market is "not doing well" unless it is setting daily new highs on the Dow index, not a good index but the one that dominates the headlines. The Dow index almost hit 1,000 in late 1968. The extraordinary level of 1,052 in January 1973 represented an "overpriced" market. In 1976, the market "tested," as the phrase goes, its 1973 high but missed by a bit. It did not rise above 1,052 until 1982.

Therefore, in headlines and in many people's opinion, the market was doing badly from 1968 to 1982. The more sophisticated observers recognized that those 14 years treated both CREF participating and retired annuitants *well indeed* compared with fixed-dollar annuities.

The first low common stock market since CREF was formed in 1952 presented a challenge to communicate effectively with participants concerning how best to use this still-new development. The 1975 *Annual Report* contained a discussion of the importance of long-time equity investing, concluding:

> The retirement funds of educators who participate in both TIAA and CREF continuously over long periods of time benefit from a high degree of investment diversification over time.... Continuous, long-term participation ... is especially important when economic conditions are fluctuating widely.

Stocks Finally Take Off in the 80s

The 1970s were a rewarding time to be buying common stocks through a CREF-like fund, rewarding for those who recognized a bargain when they bought one. The 1980s have brought the euphoria. From a January 2, 1980, start of 824.6 on the Dow, stocks rose vigorously to a mid-1987 high of over 2,700. During this entire time, the CREF accumulations of workers continued to grow rapidly, and the annuities of CREF's retired family were marching up steadily. CREF investments also were doing well, exceeding the performance of the S&P index by a comfortable margin on a 1, 3, 5, and 10-year comparison.

In October 1987, it hit again. The phrase "stock market crash" was resurrected from old 1929 and 1974 newspaper files and again splashed across the front pages throughout America. There was widespread handwringing, especially by those who had finally built up their courage to get into the market at the high point in the summer of 1987. Wall Street was in partial shock. As to CREF, of course there were some frightened, a few angry, and a number of temporarily disappointed CREF participants. But the vast majority took the event in stride. The "stock market crash" of 1987 was largely a nonevent to CREF premium-paying participants. At the end of 1987, their CREF accumulations were worth about 5 percent more than at the start of the year.

CREF AND THE AMERICAN ECONOMY

The expectations and hopes of the founders of CREF that it would lead to major increases in economic security for college staff members

FIGURE 11–1 CREF Accumulation Unit Value (total return)

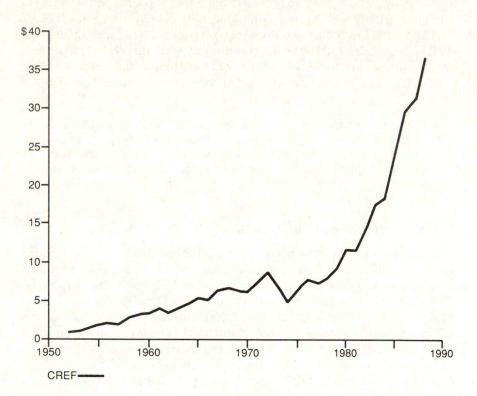

CREF——

have been amply realized. The leaps forward in retirement income produced by Social Security, TIAA, and CREF are discussed in Part Four. National publications and TIAA-CREF material present full lists of CREF's 2,400 common stocks, its month-by-month unit values, and its performance compared with other investors. Such material is voluminous and goes out of date rapidly, so it will not be reproduced here.

Two charts will provide the essence of this history. CREF's objective is to transfer to its participants a share of the productivity of the American economy, as shown in Figure 11–1. A little over $1 invested in CREF in 1952 was worth, at the end of 1988, nearly $36.74. An investment of $6 in 1970, or $11.70 in 1980, would also have reached the $36.74 level.

Figure 11–2 shows annuity unit values in CREF. An individual can take a starting point anywhere on the chart as the retirement date and follow what would have happened to annual income from then to the present. An individual starting his or her CREF annuity in

FIGURE 11–2 CREF Annuity Unit Value

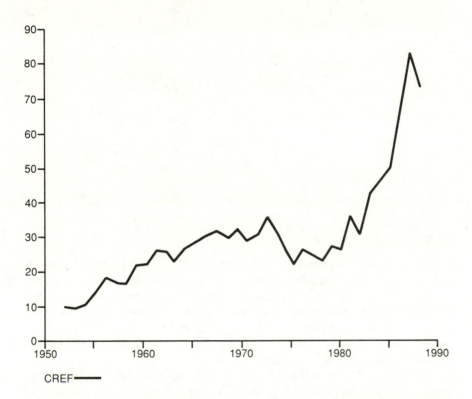

CREF——

1952 at $10 would enjoy its increase to $26.13 in 1962, and $35.74 in 1972. After a slump to $21.84 in 1975 it would have risen to $26.27 by 1980 and $73.58 by 1989. As already mentioned, one of CREF's first six annuitants is still alive; his annuity is now more than eight times as large as he received at the beginning; the cost of living is less than five times as high.

CHAPTER 12

_____ TIAA Investments _____

INVESTMENT POLICY

During the decades after World War II, TIAA put increasing effort and sophistication into its investment operations. In 1946, TIAA's investments were earning just about at the life insurance industry's average rate, 3.04 percent for TIAA compared with the industry average of 2.91 percent.[1] By 1963, TIAA had gained first place among the 25 largest life insurance companies and it continued in first place except for 1967 and 1985, when it was second.

The spread in interest rates for TIAA over the life insurance industry average, as seen in Figure 12–1, has meant literally billions of dollars added to annuities. Between 1963, when TIAA topped out the industry, and 1987, the additional earnings for TIAA amounted to $3.3 billion available for participants.

A primary reason for this record was the early and long-continued emphasis on mortgage investments and on direct placement loans to business and on a contrarian investment policy that enabled TIAA to benefit from certain disadvantages faced by many other institutional investors.

PHILOSOPHY

An important responsibility of the investment committees and staff of TIAA is to allocate funds between mortgages and real estate on the one hand and securities investments on the other, according to economic trends and opportunities.

---

[1]TIAA, _28th Annual Report,_ 1946, p. 10; _29th Annual Report,_ 1947, p. 11.

FIGURE 12–1 History of Net Interest Rate Earned

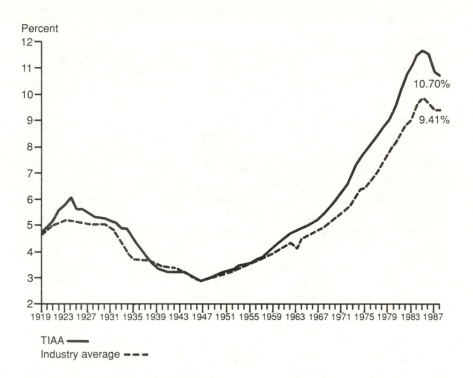

Percent

TIAA ——
Industry average – – –

One useful investment opportunity for TIAA is to manage commitment rates for new loans on a "contrarian" basis. TIAA, as a true pension fund, has a remarkably steady flow of funds to invest. Its major service to participants is the productive investment over many years of their reasonably regular premium payments, followed by payment of annuities over their remaining lifetimes. This long liability structure provides TIAA with the widest latitude in the selection of investments and stands in sharp contrast to most institutional investors. Savings banks and savings and loan institutions traditionally had taken what turned out to be demand deposits, that is, withdrawable on demand, and then invested them in long-term, illiquid mortgages. Whenever short-term rates moved well ahead of long-term rates, many depositers would shift their funds to money market obligations or certificates of deposit issued by commercial banks, leaving the savings institutions badly exposed. This effectively removed them from the market for new loans just at the time new loans provided the highest rates of interest.

A parallel situation existed for the life insurance companies. Policyholders could cash in their policies or take out policy loans at 6 percent, or in some states 5 percent, interest and immediately invest the funds at higher rates. Thus, even the life insurance companies were forced to reduce their lending activity right at the high points in interest rates.

Disintermediation always occurs during periods of rapidly rising interest rates and usually results in heavy withdrawals from savings institutions. This is a time of opportunity for pension funds; when other savings institutions are decreasing their commitments, TIAA is increasing its new loan acquisitions and commitments. During 1971, for example, TIAA made $94 million more in new conventional mortgage loans than it had made in 1970. As another example, TIAA worked down its forward commitments in direct placement loans from $523 million on January 1, 1977, to $283 million on January 1, 1978. Subsequently, as interest rates rose, forward commitments were increased to $440 million on January 1, 1979.

The most traumatic period occurred in the early 1980s, when savings institutions suffered hundreds of billions of dollars in withdrawals during a short period because U.S. interest rates were at historic highs. Life insurance companies suffered less, but still severely, through policyholders cashing in their policies or borrowing on them. The life insurance companies had net withdrawals of $18.1 billion during the 1980–82 period. This resulted in a large missed investment opportunity for these institutions. During the same period, TIAA increased its total investment commitments by $7.2 billion to take advantage of the high prevailing interest rates.

During the following spectacular drop in interest rates concurrent with the drop in inflation of the early 1980s, TIAA's direct loan commitments were allowed to drop from $430 million on January 1, 1982, to $274 million, or 37 percent less, the following year.

INVESTMENT STAFF

For 35 years, TIAA enjoyed a unique opportunity, for an insurance company, of participating in the Carnegie-Teachers Investment Office. As mentioned previously, the TIAA investments approved by this office were limited by the restrictions of the New York insurance law, but for the other Carnegie trusts and endowments, there were no such limitations. Thus, members of the office were involved in a broad spectrum of investment outlets, with greater than usual opportunity to study relative values and reward/risk relationships. When CREF was established, with its broader investment powers, TIAA-CREF took over the entire office and has managed it since.

Superior investment performance demands superior information and analytical techniques, superior investment policy and philosophy, and, most of all, superior people. TIAA has had a succession of unusually talented investment people, including two of its presidents, Devereux Josephs and McAllister Lloyd. My colleagues are generous enough to include me in this list. But more particularly, TIAA has had a continuing flow of extraordinary talent directly in the investment operation. Much of this has come about through a vigorous recruitment, training, and retention effort to develop a young and skilled staff and early providing them with broader-than-usual responsibilities.

Walter Mahlstedt joined TIAA in 1929 and headed the TIAA Securities Department from 1953 until 1962 and from 1959 also headed the Mortgage and Real Estate Department. He was in charge of all TIAA investments from 1963 until his retirement in 1975 as executive vice president. He continued on the board and as chairman of the TIAA finance committee until 1979. I can speak with admiration about many people at TIAA over those years—senior officers like Rainard Robbins, Wilmer Jenkins, Robert Duncan, and others too many to name as TIAA grew larger. Robbins had a Ph.D. from Harvard and taught mathematics at half-a-dozen institutions before coming to TIAA. Jenkins had a master's in mathematics from Michigan and taught there and at Harvard and was a Fellow of the Society of Actuaries and its president in 1961–62 while serving as TIAA's top actuary. Mahlstedt, by way of contrast, never received a college degree, although over the years, he took advanced investment courses at New York University and Columbia and became a Fellow in the Life Office Management Association.

Mahlstedt ferreted out talent from inside and out; he recruited and trained astutely; his colleagues considered him a superman. Do you suppose any noncollege graduates can now rise that far?

The second head of TIAA investments who merits exceptional mention is Walter G. Ehlers. Following his receipt of an M.B.A. in finance from Rutgers, he was with the Prudential Life Insurance Company for 12 years. In Mahlstedt's 19 years with TIAA, he served as chief investment officer from 1975 to 1984, then becoming president, but continuing to have top responsibility for investments until his retirement in 1988. He was a driving force in developing TIAA's equity-related investments. He helped TIAA establish its reputation for leveraged buyout investments before they were popular. This helped TIAA's capital gains to exceed $320 million in 1986 and 1987. He pressed forward on contingent interest mortgages, thereby sharing in equity profits. Under his guidance, TIAA's investments grew from $4 billion to $19 billion and consistently attained top ranking in investment returns.

Current head of TIAA investments is J. Daniel Lee, Jr., executive vice president. He received a B.A. degree from Duke University and an M.B.A from the University of North Carolina. The challenge to Lee was the super-high interest rates of the early 1980s, when corporations were making every effort not to issue any long-term debt instruments. The negotiation of adjustable interest rate loans in the securities division placed many loans on the books that otherwise could not have been made.

Successive heads of the securities division were: Richard F. F. Nichols, Walter Mahlstedt, Henry B. R. Brown, James M. Trucksess, James F. Straley, Walter Ehlers, Frank J. Pados, J. Daniel Lee, and David B. Bullett. The equally talented leaders of the mortgage and real estate division were: Richard Hurd, Lester Giegerich, Miles Babcock, William H. Jenson, Martin J. Cleary, and John A. Somers. Other significant contributors to performance have been: Gloria T. Addamo, John M. Baldwin, James F. Blair, Alice M. Connell, Leonard J. Franck, James A. Hallock, Joan Herman, Herbert Mann, Kathleen Nelson, Carol D. Nichols, Steven Olexa, Elsie G. Sautner, Matthew J. Smokovich, Daniel J. Sullivan, Jr., and Suzanne E. Walton.

COMMERCIAL AND INDUSTRIAL LOANS

TIAA came out of World War II with an investment portfolio divided as follows:

U.S. and Canadian government bonds	31%
Public utilities	34%
Industrials	13%
Railroads	10%
Guaranteed mortgages	6%
Other assets	6%

During the first 10 years after World War II, TIAA's emphasis in securities investments continued to be on high quality, publicly traded, nonequity bond investments. No common stocks were owned—New York law did not permit that until 1951. There was very little real estate and no extra income from equity participations in either mortgages or securities.

Its publicly issued, high-quality security investments were almost entirely traditional. Yields acceptable for pension funding were achieved by seeking investments of very long maturities.

From the end of World War II to the early 1960s, TIAA's main investment growth was in mortgages—mostly guaranteed. As a percentage of invested funds, mortgages rose to a high of 53.5 percent in 1965. Initially, it was both the size and quality of the mortgage program that brought TIAA up toward the top of the life insurance industry in earnings performance. Direct placements including some with equity participation carried TIAA the additional distance to the top of the industry.

Starting out the 1970s, TIAA was investing twice as much of its new money in mortgages ($257 million) as in direct placement loans ($129 million). All other categories, publicly offered bonds, common stocks, and real estate, accounted for only $84 million. By 1976, this ratio had almost reversed itself. In that year, TIAA made direct placement loans of $471 million at a gross yield of 10.29 percent and conventional mortgage loans of $271 million at a gross rate of 9.51 percent. (The latter rate represents the interest rates prevailing two to three years earlier when the mortgage commitments were made.) Publicly offered bonds were becoming more attractive relative to other investments and were available for immediate purchase. TIAA purchased $125 million of public bonds in 1975 at a rate of 10.80 percent and $152 million in 1976 at a rate of 9.56 percent.

Direct placement loans generally provide a rate of interest and special features such as equity participations that are usually not available on large bond issues of very high-quality companies underwritten by investment bankers and offered for sale in the public market. Initially, TIAA's direct placement loans to industry ranged in size from $1 million to $10 million and were made for a term of 15 to 25 years. The loan agreements are tailored to meet the individual requirements of the borrower while protecting the financial interests of the lender.

Public bonds have taken on greater interest for TIAA in recent years as cash flow has increased and become somewhat less predictable. Still, because a pension fund like TIAA does not generally need liquidity, it can seek the higher yields available on less liquid obligations.

During the 1950s and 1960s, TIAA was smaller than the huge institutional lenders. As a result, TIAA frequently found itself a small participant in large negotiated loans, with the interest rate, maturity, and other terms generally being fixed by the lead lenders. These loans would be presented by the underwriter to lending institutions that would "circle," or express interest, in a given portion of the loan. Prudential, Metropolitan, Equitable, or John Hancock would be the largest purchasers. However, TIAA's growth trend line was strongly up, and it rapidly entered the ranks of the mammoths. As it grew, TIAA became a major participant and ultimately assumed the role as the lead lender in large direct placement loans. As lead lender, TIAA could negotiate the provisions it deemed appropriate and be more in control of its lending.

The year 1975 saw TIAA make two of the largest direct placement loans it had ever made. The first was the $75 million Alaskan Pipeline Capital Inc., financing at 10⅝ percent interest with a guarantee from Sohio/British Petroleum maturing in 1993 and 1998. The other large purchase was $50 million for the Hydro-Quebec project, a huge hydroelectric power development in the James Bay watershed in Canada. This loan was at a 10¼ percent interest rate maturing in 1996.

TIAA made some major investments in the transportation sector during the early 1970s. At the time, shipping, rail equipment, trucking, and other such loans were made on the basis of cash flow analysis. The basic credits were not always particularly strong, but the cash flow from the equipment itself would cover the loan, with safe margins.

In 1975, TIAA financed two large tankers for Mammoth Bulk Ltd. to be leased to Amoco. The loans were for $40 million at a 9½ percent interest rate. As an aside, I was on a TIAA business trip when the Amoco Cadiz bumped into France and split open, causing a huge oil spill. This was a serious environmental crisis. In addition, I knew TIAA had financed two of the three sister ships leased to Amoco. Was the Cadiz one of them? I could not remember. I fretted the rest of the trip but returned home to discover our investment people, with their usual superior judgment, had financed the other two Amoco's, not the Cadiz.

TIAA's experience in lending to the transportation industry included some investments that turned out to be less successful, for example, Qualpeco and Richmond Leasing. Our 1974 LBO financing of Qualpeco, the trucking division spun off from U.S. Industries, resulted in a near total loss of our $6 million unsecured investment, as transportation deregulation reduced the value of the company's routes. In the case of Richmond Leasing, a specialized railcar leasing company, deregulation, overbuilding at the company's parent manufacturing company, and recession-induced shrinkage in the railcar leasing market combined to bring this firm to grief. In this case, however, thanks to our security interest in certain rolling stock, and the patience and hard work of our asset recovery group, we recovered about 96 cents on the dollar.

Loans with Equity Features

In 1968, TIAA embarked on a program of direct placement lending that sought equity participation wherever possible. This was accomplished by taking warrants, conversion privileges, stock purchase at nominal cost, contingent interest, or additional income in some form on as many loans as possible. This usually but not always meant giving up something in fixed interest rate or in quality on the loans, but it proved a small price for the added performance. TIAA sought and continues to seek equity kicker investments within its reward/risk parameters, although availability of these loans varies widely with business conditions and interest rates.

The high point of new direct loan commitments in securities that had equity components was reached in 1969, when 56 percent of TIAA's bond loans had such features, compared with 8 percent for the industry. Starting in 1974, depressed common stock prices made it difficult to negotiate good equity participations. In 1976, only 2 percent of TIAA's loans contained such participations, but this rose to 8 percent in 1977. In 1987, 17 percent of new direct loans had such kickers.

Gains on these investments sometimes develop quickly but more often build up over the years. By January 1972, with the program only four years old, $5 million in realized and $23 million in unrealized gains had accumulated. In 1986 alone, TIAA realized a $150 million net gain on equity-related investments, the highest in the 20 years the program has been in operation. Sales of Tele-Communications, Signode, and Wometco contributed $81.9 million of the gains in that year. An additional $140 million was realized in 1987. Sales of Calgon Carbon and Kings Entertainment were the main contributors that year. Over the years, TIAA's equity program has significantly increased its portfolio yield.

A growing segment of the equity kicker market that has blossomed in recent years is leveraged buyouts (LBOs). In the beginning, such loans were generally used to restructure a family-owned company that had grown large—frequently beyond the management talents of the succeeding generation of family members. This vehicle also permitted private owners to realize financially on their previously illiquid ownership. TIAA first went into leveraged buyouts in 1969. As time passed, buyouts changed in size and nature and became increasingly available. TIAA's activities in this lucrative field continued to grow with the market because it matched well with TIAA's interest in equity participations. Approximately 68 percent of TIAA's equity commitments in 1986 were associated with leveraged buyouts.

Problem Loan Monitoring

With its steady, predictable cash flow, TIAA established in the early 1960s an investment policy of seeking higher yield investments by selection and management of somewhat higher risk securities. As an added measure of safety, in addition to the normal loan valuation review and loss reserve requirements performed by the New York State Insurance Department, TIAA carefully monitors the financial performance of all of its borrowers and was one of the first insurance companies to establish separate workout units. TIAA might be said to have established a combination diagnostic and CPR unit, the former to sense early an irregular heartbeat and the latter to revive any weakening instrument. This group provides special attention to loans with companies experiencing financial difficulty in order to maximize recoveries from these securities.

Problem loans as defined by the National Association of Insurance Commissioners have averaged about 1.5 percent of TIAA's fixed income portfolio over the past eight years—about equal to the average of the 12 largest life insurance companies. During the 1982 recession, this percentage reached a high of 2.6 percent. Actual losses realized in these cases were only a small fraction of that percentage. During the same eight-year period, TIAA's net earned rate averaged 10.86 percent—190 basis points higher than the 12 company average of 8.96 percent—reflecting the more innovative and aggressive loans TIAA made.

Higher levels of risk have been assumed in the securities portfolio, where loan writedowns peaked at 1.9 percent of the bond portfolio in 1986 as an aftermath of the 1982–83 recession. A comfortable balance is provided by the high-quality mortgage portfolio, where problem loans have averaged well under 1 percent during the period and losses have been nonexistent. Both divisions maintain early warning lists developed from their ongoing portfolio review. Through timely action in conjunction with company management and other lenders, loan losses have been minimal.

COMMON STOCKS

Common stock investments for TIAA have never been significant. TIAA's guarantees are in fixed dollars. Although it makes substantial efforts to get equity participations of various kinds on both mortgages and securities, essentially its investments are fixed-dollar obligations.

TIAA started a small common stock program in 1951, when New York insurance law was changed to permit it, and gradually built up a portfolio over the next 30 years, within the limits of the New York law. It reached $130 million by 1979, including both listed stocks and the equity-kicker program for direct placement loans. In a sudden shift of policy in 1980, the TIAA listed common stock program was eliminated, and $100 million was sold within a few months, with the sale completed by August 1980. The listed stocks in the program had been accumulated on a dollar-cost-averaging basis as one more form of investment diversification. Since the portfolio was sold over a short time just before the long bull market of the 1980s, the substantial opportunity for gain over the next years was lost.

In addition to the listed stocks, TIAA has a continuing portfolio of stocks accumulated through its direct placement loan program. This was part of the successful policy of obtaining additional investment income from equity participations for direct loans to business and on mortgages.

MORTGAGES AND REAL ESTATE

Early Mortgage Investments

In seeking investments that met TIAA's special opportunities, the trustees rather early chose mortgages as ideal. Mortgages usually are long-term illiquid investments; this makes them undesirable for many investment purposes where quick access to cash may be important and be worth giving up some yield. Conversely, mortgages are especially useful for pension savings but were largely overlooked or avoided by other pension plans until recent years.

TIAA first expressed interest in mortgages at the very depth of the Great Depression, 1932. Farm and city mortgages, and of course most other investments too, were in disarray. In 1932, the board of TIAA instructed the finance committee

> to consider and report . . . as to whether or not there is undue danger from inflation because of the large proportion of the Association's investments which are in rate regulated industries (railroads and public utilities) and whether or not any shift in investments should be made to meet this situation.[2]

Henry James, acting president of TIAA, reported this interest to Carnegie Corporation, including his interest in employing a mortgage expert. The corporation's vice chairman and treasurer, Robert A. Franks, cautioned Carnegie President Frank P. Keppel, "The sooner the corporation sets a limit, the wiser it would be." Keppel answered, "Under James's direction, he was confident the expenses would be kept within a reasonable limit."[3] This is a revealing exchange, in view of the Carnegie-induced parting with Glover as president of TIAA the previous year and the coming effort of both the Carnegie Corporation and TIAA to work out a satisfactory arrangement for TIAA to emerge on its own. Years later, Russell C. Leffingwell, a trustee of the Carnegie Corporation, questioned the appropriateness of TIAA having 53 percent of its assets in mortgages, but stated: "These are delicate

---

[2]Minutes of the Board of Trustees, April 15, 1932.
[3]Memorandum of Interview, "FPK and Mr. Franks," August 4, 1933, TIAA file, Carnegie Corporation Archives.

questions, and we have no right or obligation to review TIAA's investments."[4]

TIAA actually began investing in real estate mortgages in 1934. TIAA's mortgage investments during the later Great Depression years were distributed among loans on income-producing urban real estate and on dwelling loans insured by the Federal Housing Administration. The commercial loans, 80 percent of the total, were located in the environs of New York City. The FHA loans were in Detroit, Atlanta, Toledo, and Cleveland. The loans totaled nearly $7 million and earned 4.20 percent. "Less than $30 of the interest on these various mortgages was more than 30 days overdue on December 31, 1939."

By the end of 1941, mortgages had reached 10 percent of total assets.[5] Few mortgages were available during the war years, and nearly all of TIAA's new money was invested in government bonds. Thus, between 1942 and 1945, total mortgage investments grew by only $2 million, and coming out of the war, the percentage of mortgages to total assets had dropped to 11 percent from its 1942 high of 13 percent.

At the end of World War II, America was suffering from a severe shortage of good housing. The federal government established several additional guaranteed or insured mortgage programs at that time. The GI and VA programs were designed to be useful to returning servicemen. The FHA program was greatly extended and led to large, cookie-cutter but economical housing developments such as Levittown in New York and Pennsylvania. Additional federal programs emphasized multiple dwelling high rise and garden apartment houses and attached townhouses. TIAA participated extensively in these programs.

TIAA's portfolio changed dramatically during these years. Between the end of 1946 and 1950, mortgage and real estate investments grew from 17 percent of total assets to 50 percent.

Mortgage Committee

TIAA took a significant and early step toward its mortgage investment program when, in 1934, it established a separate standing committee of the board. This new mortgage committee was charged with guiding the mortgage and real estate investment programs, under the general direction of the finance committee. McAllister Lloyd, upon becoming president of TIAA in 1945, gave strong support to the mort-

---

[4]Russell C. Leffingwell to Charles Dollard, April 25, 1951, TIAA file, Carnegie Corporation Archives.

[5]J. W. Ahern, "Mortgage Investments Memorandum," February 14, 1939; Henry James, "Memo as to Investment Problems," February 15, 1939, TIAA-CREF Archives, Carnegie Teachers Investment Office file.

gage investment program, especially the shopping center investments and the issued mortgages.

The move into government-guaranteed or insured mortgages was not without controversy. Two TIAA board members, neither of whom was on the mortgage committee, took special exception. Henry R. Hayes wrote to Mac Lloyd on June 5, 1950: "If TIAA still seeks investment in the mortgage field arising out of the government-promoted housing boom, then I want to be heard in opposition."[6] This led to extensive correspondence, with no yielding on either side. H. M. Addinsell, of the First Boston Corporation and a member of the TIAA board and of its finance committee, also vigorously opposed the program, saying the federal government had insulated itself from the guarantees and they would never be honored.

Because TIAA was early in this type of investment, it was also one of the first companies to suffer a foreclosure on an FHA obligation in the late 1940s. Neither TIAA nor the FHA handled the bureaucratic paperwork efficiently. At each meeting of the finance committee, Mr. Addinsell would say: "Have you received those government-guaranteed bonds yet?" And month after month the answer was: "Not yet." Finally the time came. At a particular Thursday morning finance committee meeting, Mac Lloyd quietly sat in wait for Mr. Addinsell to say: "Have you received . . . ?" At that point, Joel Per, investment attorney for TIAA, stepped forward and spread on the board table the government bonds exchanged for the foreclosed mortgage. The government had come through, despite the skeptics. The government-guaranteed program served TIAA's policyholders well for the time, but as we grew, other mortgage investments became more rewarding, and we slowly reduced the government program participation.

A number of educators have served on the mortgage committee. During recent years, the following three policyholder-selected trustees have served: Uwe Reinhardt of Princeton, Jack Guttentag of University of Pennsylvania, and Leonard Simon, now of Rochester Community Savings Bank. Dr. Joseph L. Fisher was elected directly to the board in 1965 with the view that he would bring to the mortgage committee deliberations a very long-range perspective. Dr. Fisher is an economist; before he was elected to Congress in 1974, he headed Resources for the Future, a foundation-funded economic analysis organization involved in trying to discern economic, social, and environmental trends decades into the future, a relevant factor for mortgage investments.

Dr. Fisher, with his long-range perspectives, was in a sense paired on the board with Albert C. Blunt, president of Melville Realty and

---

[6]Hayes to Lloyd, June 5, 1950, TIAA-CREF Corporate Secretary Files.

then of Hanover Shoe Realty. Because of his responsibility for renting shoe outlets, Mr. Blunt knew an astounding amount, in detail, about many of the premier shopping centers and shopping center developers in America.

Shopping Centers

One of the most successful single classifications of TIAA investments in 70 years has been shopping centers. In the late 1940s, the TIAA mortgage and real estate committee considered and approved a few shopping center loans. They seemed neatly to meet TIAA's needs for high-interest, long-term loans that did not have to be marketable or liquid. By 1970, 16 percent of TIAA's total assets and 30 percent of its

Country Club Plaza, Kansas City, Missouri (© Wilborn & Associates, Kansas City)

total mortgage and real estate portfolio was invested in shopping centers, and by 1980, 24 percent of its total assets and 49 percent of its total mortgage and real estate portfolio was so invested.

TIAA's first shopping center loan was made in 1948 to refinance the legendary Country Club Plaza in Kansas City. That well-designed and handsome plaza was America's first shopping district constructed for the automobile trade. It was developed by the J. C. Nichols Company beginning in 1922. Many shiny tinsel shopping centers built decades later have already been torn down or redeveloped, but Country Club Plaza still has its original charm.

During the immediate post World War II period, TIAA made a number of shopping center loans to Edward DeBartolo, a U.S. Navy Seabee, who became America's largest shopping center developer.

TIAA extended its reach to other fledgling developers who also became America's leaders—Ernest Hahn, James Rouse, A. Alfred Taubman, Jacobs Visconsi and Jacobs, Leonard Farber, and Melvin Simon. TIAA financed multiple centers with each of these developers.

Fortunately for TIAA, the idea of shopping center investments did not become popular with other major lenders until the mid-1970s. This meant TIAA did not have much competition for loans, and this in turn meant there was a favorable reward/risk ratio on such loans for the policyholders. The large developers were showing TIAA their centers first, frequently giving it first choice among the loans as to which to finance.

The important feature of all of the effort was that TIAA was achieving from one to two percentage points premium interest on its extensive shopping center investments, a premium that gradually declined as shopping centers became more popular investments for other institutional investors.

Are They Risky?

Interestingly, for many years shopping center loans were classified with other real estate loans by many investors as undiversified and risky. Most real estate investments have to "stand on their own bottom," as the anatomically uncomfortable cliché has it. Other lenders assumed shopping centers were in that category, and it helped to reduce the competition for the kind of loans TIAA sought. The fact is that shopping center loans tend to be unusually safe precisely because, if well done, they are diversified and with major residual value in event of problems. TIAA normally requires a certain proportion of national tenants in the shopping centers it finances. This means that if a particular center does not turn out well, the leases held by its major tenants will be supported by other stores in that system around the country.

TIAA's officers originating shopping center loans became well known in the industry for leadership in this lending field, and in the International Council of Shopping Centers. TIAA's top investment lawyer, Francis P. Gunning, later to become executive vice president and general counsel, helped set the prevailing pattern for mortgage indentures.

Total foreclosures in the multibillion-dollar shopping center portfolio from 1945 to 1988 were only $7.3 million, with full recovery of principal and most interest. The only large loan ever to be foreclosed was a center in Florida on which TIAA made a loan in 1986 of $68 million. It is too early to determine recovery on this loan.

Columbia, Maryland

One of the most imaginative and rewarding investment relationships has been with James Rouse and the Rouse Development Company. TIAA made its first Rouse loan, on the mall at St. Matthews in Louisville, Kentucky, in 1962. In the last 25 years, TIAA has been the major lender in approximately half of the 45 centers the Rouse Company has developed throughout America, for a total investment of $1.2 billion, including the $500 million joint venture in purchasing the large Baltimore real estate portfolio of McCormick Spice Company.

I made it a practice to meet with the heads of our largest repetitive borrowers so I, along with our mortgage officers, could get an idea of depth of management, long-term economic and social viewpoints, and soundness of approach to development projects. On one of the mortgage trips, halfway through a luncheon with James Rouse and his top group, Rouse said, "Bill, we have a major new project that might interest TIAA—a New Town. The Rouse Company has purchased over 15,000 acres of land between Washington and Baltimore, and we plan to build a new town from scratch. Would you be willing to talk with us about the next phase of financing?"

We were, and we did.

The Connecticut General Life Insurance Company, with which TIAA has cooperated in financing several real estate ventures, had

Downtown Columbia, Maryland (© *Tadder/Baltimore, Courtesy of The Rouse Company)*

bankrolled Rouse in secretly acquiring the original 15,000 acres. TIAA then came in to finance the infrastructure—the underground electric and telephone cables, the roads, and some of the facilities. It also financed the striking regional shopping center, Columbia Mall, the Teachers office building, and several other investments in Columbia.

Rouse's grand design resulted in the new town of Columbia, Maryland, now of 67,000 population and 43,000 related job opportunities. It is a town with minimal interior automobile traffic, with maximum green space, with neighborhood schools, with religious facilities jointly owned and sharing parking with the village centers. It has many housing units available to less affluent residents under a cooperative arrangement with various churches.

Columbia, Maryland, is a grand concept that has realized most of its original promise. It is unfortunate it has been seldom replicated. The Irvine Ranch in Orange County, California, covers an area of 68,000 acres and now has a population of approximately 90,000 with 133,000 related jobs, but it does not include the traffic patterns, village centers, school system and other innovative parts of Columbia. Jonathan, just outside Minneapolis, Minnesota, covers about 4,000 acres and is now starting to develop. There are a number of large retirement clusters, including Sun City and Paradise Valley, Arizona, but none of these reaches the potential of true New Towns. The European efforts, including the stunning new town of Tapiola, Finland, and the green-belt towns built around London after the war, have not been widely imitated.

Other spectacular investments resulting from the TIAA-Rouse cooperation have been in markedly unusual centers: Faneuil Hall Marketplace including Quincy Market, in Boston; Harborplace in Baltimore; and Jacksonville Landing in Florida. TIAA passed up the financing of South Street Seaport in New York.

Faneuil Hall Marketplace

When I was a graduate economics student at Harvard in the middle 1930s, Scollay Square in Boston was a degraded, ugly area, noted only for the Old Howard burlesque theater and, many decades before, for the house where Paul Revere hammered out his classic silver bowls and occasionally started out on after-dark horseback rides.

In 1972, the Historic Faneuil Hall District was only an idea being developed by the Rouse Company. The vision included restaurants, small shops, a nautical museum, and freestanding booths and boutiques—no major credits as tenants; no Filene's, Macy's, Sears, as anchors; no vaulted weather-free mall with fountains and full-grown trees transplanted from somewhere else; too many food dispensers;

not enough stores; very little parking; none of the absolutely essential features of successful shopping centers.

But the dream of Quincy Market had a major plus—an excellent development company, Rouse. It might become a major tourist attraction. The financial projections, if they could be believed, showed real promise, and the interest rates and other provisions of the loan from the lender's viewpoint showed an excellent reward/risk ratio. So TIAA suspended all its usual tests for this investment and has been happy about it ever since. TIAA provided financing of $24.1 million at a 10.25 percent rate of interest.

Now millions of tourists, nearby government and other office workers, and shoppers visit Quincy Market and Faneuil Hall each year. And TIAA policyholders are the better for it.

A primary source of investment for TIAA is financing industrial parks. Financing of clean and light industrial buildings in the Carolinas; Puerto Rico; King of Prussia, Pennsylvania; Route 128 and 495 in Massachusetts; Silicon Valley, California; and other strong real estate and mortgage investments resulted from this effort. In several of these ventures, TIAA financed the purchase of a large tract of land and, as industrial buildings were developed, took back mortgage loans on them.

OWNED REAL ESTATE

Because of its nonprofit structure, TIAA does not benefit from depreciation and other favorable tax aspects of owned real estate investment. Hence, in normal economic times, other investments have a yield advantage over owned real estate. It tries to be active contracyclically, purchasing during real estate depressions like the mid-1970s. From 1973 to 1980, TIAA made total real estate purchases of $227 million.

Towering Fiasco

At 1166 Sixth Avenue, a 44-story, 1.4 million-square-foot office building on Avenue of the Americas in New York City a revealing case study in real estate depressions and long-term investment opportunities is provided. *Fortune* magazine, in a February 1975 article,[7] highlighted the real estate catastrophe that was helping to paralyze New York City. It showed a full-page picture of 1166 Sixth Avenue, unfinished, with red ink pouring out of an accountant's bottle and down the 500 foot sides. *Fortune* went on to say the total loss from the co-

---

[7]Eleanore Carruth, "The Skyscraping Losses in Manhattan Office Buildings," *Fortune*, February 1975.

lossal office-building binge of the previous decade "undoubtedly approaches a billion dollars . . . the biggest white elephant of them all, the World Trade Center," as well as many other mega-edifices that were underleased and overfinanced.

Furthermore, New York was in its frightening financial crisis, the stock market had reached a low of 578 on the Dow index in December 1974, and, every month or so, another Fortune 500 company announced relocation of its headquarters out of Manhattan. More than three years later, a drawing of 1166 Sixth Avenue graced the cover of the July 31, 1978, New York magazine. The headline was "TOWERING FIASCO! The empty skyscraper that devoured $100 million and haunted Sixth Avenue for four years."[8]

The building was topped out but not filled in, either with partitions, furniture, or tenants. Tishman Realty was taking a large pretax loss; Citibank wrote off its loan of $40 million; and that was only the start of troubles to come for the building.

We decided that if TIAA could buy 1166 "marked way down," it would make a good addition to the real estate portfolio. For two years, TIAA watched 1166 go through wringers.

Finally, the moment came. TIAA purchased the building in a condominium arrangement with New York Telephone Company for $37 million. TIAA then financed its completion and rented the space it owned to International Paper Company for its corporate headquarters and to additional small tenants.

The total amount the previous lenders and Tishman lost on 1166 was more than $100 million. Having purchased its interest for $37 million and received an internal investment rate of return of 31.55 percent for the years 1978 to 1985, TIAA then sold it for $153 million, a profit of $116 million. If only all our purchases could work out that well!

Seagram Building

A special prize was the purchase of the Seagram Building, which TIAA contracted to purchase in 1979 from Joseph E. Seagram and Sons, Inc., for $73 million, yielding initially 7.9 percent but with low rental leases expiring quickly.

The Seagram Building, spectacularly set back from Park Avenue at 52nd Street in New York City, has won acclaim as the pinnacle of excellence in design of the International Style modern skyscraper. Designed by Mies van der Rohe and Philip Johnson, it is acclaimed the finest commercial structure in the United States by the American Institute of Architects.

---

[8]Peter Hellman, "Towering Fiasco," New York, July 31, 1978.

Seagram Building, New York City (Ezra Stoller © Esto)

In deciding in 1979 to purchase the building, TIAA committed itself to seek landmark status as soon as possible. Many real estate investors do not want impediments on their holdings; TIAA thought landmark status was not only appropriate for such a singular building, but that it also would be an economic asset. Its heritage and location make it an outstanding real estate investment, commanding the highest overall rental rates. As the *New York Times* reported in April 1988:

Seagram Landmark Move Is Backed

After 30 years as an unofficial landmark of modern architecture, the Seagram Building on Park Avenue now appears likely to become an official landmark as well.

The designation would be unusual in several ways, not only because it would add a modern bronze-and-glass skyscraper to the ranks of more classical landmarks, but also because the landlord of a major commercial property in mid-Manhattan actually favors such a move.

Indeed, the Teachers Insurance and Annuity Association-College Retirement Equities Fund, which has owned the building since 1979, said that it had requested landmark status. The Landmarks Preservation Commission will consider the matter next month.

The Seagram Building was designated a New York City landmark by the Landmarks Preservation Commission on October 3, 1989.

Other Projects

The Pacific Design Center in West Hollywood, California, speaking with its own promotional emphasis, admits to assuming "the position of leadership in the western architectural and design communities. . . . PDC is unique in the industry. . . . [Its annual design conference has an] audience of more than 20,000 architects, designers and manufacturers" from around the world.

TIAA's commitment to the PDC, first made in 1973, is now about $68 million at 10 percent interest with additional contingent interest for this single use, unusual building. TIAA's commitment on a second PDC building is $132 million, with 30 percent contingent interest.

The largest current project being financed by TIAA is 900 North Michigan Avenue in Chicago. This $400 million mixed use project includes the first Bloomingdale department store in the Midwest, 200,000 additional square feet of retail space, 500,000 square feet of office space, and a 346-room Four Seasons Hotel.

Losses

From 1950 through 1981, TIAA invested $5.9 billion in conventional mortgages. During this time, $101 million, or about 2 percent, was foreclosed, with a resultant loss of less than $4 million, or less than 0.1 percent.

WHY DID IT WORK WELL?

It is a fair question to ask what factors led to good investment performance for TIAA policyholders. The following brief comments, some necessarily subjective, apply to the entire investment portfolio, but especially to unusual aspects of it, such as the heavy reliance on shopping centers. It does not attempt the sophisticated analysis and reward/risk considerations made by the TIAA Mortgage and Real Estate Department before each loan is made.

The Mortgage Committee of the Board of Trustees always includes a mix of academic members with a broad and long-range view of the American economy and demographic trends and business leaders in retail space leasing and other lending institutions, fully knowledgeable about immediate mortgage and real estate investment factors.

The small staff has always been lean and mean. It is a young staff, with high academic attainments and relevant experience either with TIAA or other lenders. TIAA's total expense rate is only 45 basis points, or less than one half of 1 percent of investment funds. The expense rate for the other 11 largest insurance companies is twice as large, 95 basis points.

TIAA believes its mortgage investments, while leaving the major ownership equity stake with the developer, should share in equity returns—hence the *kicker deals*. Overage rentals and other such deals started for TIAA in 1953. They gradually grew to be a larger and larger part of the mortgage activity until, in recent years, TIAA has made no long-term mortgage loans without kickers. In 1987, the extra income from participating mortgages was $19 million.

A group of long-term developers provides TIAA with much of its regular mortgage portfolio.

TIAA allows leeway to adjust to opportunities. The TIAA mortgage department has guidelines as to various aspects of an acceptable mortgage loan. Two examples are: a specified ratio of parking to retail sales space, and a specified ratio of national or prime credit tenants to total tenants. But then along comes an opportunity like Quincy Market-Fanueil Hall in downtown Boston or Baltimore Harbor. Such projects meet none of the usual criteria for success, but they have something different going for them. This requires flexibility, judgment, and willingness to consider unusual situations.

Value is emphasized, not cost. On many types of loan, TIAA's mortgage operation does not care too much about cost of the property on which a loan is made, but on economic value, on income stream.

An exasperating illustration (chosen from long ago so it will not cause current friction with the New York Insurance Department) was a commercial freezer plant in Leesburg, Florida. TIAA made a mortgage loan on the plant, leased mainly to Minute Maid. The credit was good; the rental was good. At the next triennial examination, the insurance examiners criticized TIAA in their report because it did not have detailed records on the cost of the land or building. We argued that it is the rental stream and the certainty of that stream that really matters on most loans. We pointed out, tactfully of course, that if the Empire State Building had been built in Beanblossom, Indiana, its cost would have been irrelevant; it would have been worse than worthless. The insurance examiners were underwhelmed by the cogency of that argument. They required a writedown of the loan by 10 percent to reflect its valuation of the physical asset. The fact was that earnings on the freezer plant that year were over 27 percent, so TIAA wrote the loan down 23 percent, just from excess earnings.

THE FUTURE

TIAA's enormous growth rate, doubling every four and one half years, will continue to demand broad diversification of loans, imaginative approaches to new sources of investment, a skilled staff of unusual talent, and finance and mortgage committees of breadth and investment knowledge for the policy decisions to be made. TIAA expects to make about $30 billion of new investments over the next three years.

All the present sources of good loans will have to continue to be developed. Foreign investments in both securities and mortgage and real estate opportunities may become a substantial source of loans, as foreign common stocks are already in CREF.

The need for TIAA-CREF policyholders to store up earning power for their retirement years again fits into the capital development of America over the coming decades.

CHAPTER 13

_____ Socially Responsible Investing _____

By the 1960s, American business had come a long way from the turn of the century days of the robber barons, "the public be damned," Ida Tarbell and the muckrakers, Theodore Roosevelt galloping forth to bust the trusts, and Pinkerton guards floating down the Monongahela River shooting at striking Carnegie Steel Company workers. Of course, even those days were tame when compared with events described in Miriam Beard's _A History of the Business Man:_ "In 1496, for example, to settle a dispute, it was agreed to execute 10 leaders of the miners and 3 of the company officials."[1]

DOING WELL WHILE DOING GOOD

During the mid-20th century, interest broadened from keeping industry from "doing bad", to also challenging it to "do good". College student and faculty interest in social investments started in the mid-1960s. Students and faculty began asking whether college endowments owned investments in munitions plants, other defense industries, companies doing business in South Africa, environmental polluters, or companies that failed to follow fair employment practices. What about product safety, and infant formulas sold abroad? They wanted to know what was being done to finance ghetto housing, environmental improvements, and conservation.

On many campuses, these efforts led to rallies, sit-ins of college offices, and demands that trustees alter endowment investment poli-

---

[1]Miriam Beard, _A History of the Business Man_ (New York: The MacMillan Company, 1938), p. 221.

cies. This frequently meant disposing of all investments in the 50 largest defense contractors or companies with any business in South Africa.

As holders of large concentrations of investments, TIAA and CREF, and their policyholders, took an early interest in the many facets of "socially responsible investing."

The Institutional Investor of October 1968 had a feature article on Dr. Roger Murray, then CREF's executive vice president and chairman of its finance committee:

> One of the stockholders, a thin, white-haired man who looked like a family doctor walked up to the stage and took the microphone. He was Dr. Roger F. Murray, an economist, executive vice president, and chairman of the finance committee of the $1 billion College Retirement Equities Fund, which owned 181,500 shares of Kodak. He began by saying that he realized there were no resolutions to vote on at this meeting, but he had a few words to say anyway. The crowd grew still. Then he brought up the controversial subject. "The 225,000 educators who are policyholders of CREF have great confidence in what education can do," he said, "and great confidence in what Kodak could do to bring the hard core unemployed into an employable position." The crowd roared, and it may be the only time that ever happened for an institutional investor.[2]

One of the first social investing questions to arise was in the field of housing. The Federal Housing Administration's mortgage program did not guarantee mortgages in severely depressed housing locations. During the Lyndon Johnson administration, the life insurance industry established a $2 billion program of financing FHA housing in depressed areas, after the government changed its rules. TIAA was one of the first life insurance companies to meet its goal in this program. TIAA also was a primary investor in the new town of Columbia, Maryland, designed by James Rouse to include integrated, quality housing for low-income people, as well as being a new middle-class residential, industrial, and office city.

Correspondence with policyholders and college officers built up during 1970. Vehemence was equally distributed. One side would have TIAA-CREF avoid all South African investments, subsidize low-cost housing, and avoid the 50 largest military contractors and all environmental polluters. The other side stated that TIAA-CREF had one job and one job only—to invest policyholders' funds for the largest return possible within the law. It seemed useful to avoid radicalizing either side. TIAA-CREF wanted to go about investing funds entrusted

---

[2]Penelope Orth, "Roger Murray: Portrait of the Professor as a Fund Manager," The Institutional Investor, October 1968.

to it in a responsible manner with due regard for fiduciary and social factors. The Charter of TIAA gave its purpose as "providing . . . benefits . . . on terms as advantageous to the holders and beneficiaries . . . as shall be practicable."

In the spring of 1970, the author gave a talk at the Southern Association of College and University Business Officers. One of the ensuing letters, received April 24, 1970, was from the dean of administration at the University of Alabama, Dr. Franklyn H. Sweet, saying in part:

> I enjoyed and appreciated your presentation at the SACUBO meeting in Atlanta recently. . . .
>
> I was quite disturbed and more than a little irritated by the questions put to you on the part of a very limited number of individuals as to whether or not the Association invested in companies that would be considered "socially" acceptable. I am fully aware of all the connotations back of this sort of thing and take umbrage at the whole bit. In writing to you as an individual I wish to express a very pointed personal opinion that I feel the Association must regard as its number one obligation the care and protection of the retirement resources of all the participants, and all its investment activities should be directed to that end. . . . [3]

On the other side of the question, that espousing social investing, a particularly detailed letter was received from Daniel Kohl, assistant professor of biology at Washington University in St. Louis. Dr. Kohl asked many questions as "one of a group of TIAA-CREF policyholders who believes that our investments must serve the social goals which we hold as a central focus of our lives." He then asked TIAA to

> respond to the following proposition as a possible policy statement which would serve as a guide to the professional managers of the fund:
>
> "The investments of TIAA and CREF and their participation as shareholders in the companies in which they have substantial holdings shall reflect a concern for peace and the brotherhood of man. As several concrete examples of the many possible manifestations of those concerns (1) they shall not own stocks in corporations which do a substantial fraction of their business with the Department of Defense, (2) they shall require detailed programs of affirmative action for fair employment practices as a minimum prerequisite for supporting current management, (3) the pattern of their real estate holdings and mortgages shall contribute to better housing for poor people and residential integration, and (4) 3 percent of the current investment shall be made in projects or corporations whose pro-

---

[3]Franklyn H. Sweet to WCG, April 24, 1970.

grams do an outstanding job of promoting the objectives of peace and/or brotherhood of man even though these investments may yield a suboptimal return. . . . "[4]

TIAA-CREF sent Dr. Kohl a large amount of material that he asked for and detailed answers to his many questions.[5] We also gave a number of examples of TIAA-CREF investments that would clearly fit within his social tests and were also high yield investments—housing loans, medical care facilities, rehabilitation of central cities, and a number of pollution control companies that were high yield precisely because they were in a strong new field of endeavor.

Similar long correspondence was held in 1971 with Professor Ralph A. Loomis, president of the Michigan Conference of the American Association of University Professors, with respect to whether the chapters should "insist that . . . [the] trust fund managers of TIAA-CREF apply social criteria as well as profit criteria to their investments and support the actions of national groups that are seeking to promote corporate responsibility." I responded, "The answer is clearly no" to the question of whether any outside organization representing students, faculty, trustees, administrative, church group, and so on, should impose on TIAA-CREF its statement of investment judgment.

In my letters to Loomis and to Kohl, I used three examples of why efforts to establish particular investment restrictions should be avoided. The first example was the restrictive state laws limiting investments of life insurance companies, well-intentioned laws but ones that made investing of pension funds like TIAA less effective for participants. These laws made the creation of CREF far more difficult. This illustrated the problem that restrictions designed for particular situations—pension systems, college endowments, church endowments, mutual funds—frequently did not fit outside their particular structure.

The second problem was one of definition and action. Social criteria to one group means not investing in the largest 50 defense contractors; to another, avoiding any company operating in South Africa; to another, it means investing substantial sums in subsidized housing; to another, avoidance of any company that contributes to air, water, and land pollution; to yet another, avoidance of discrimination on the basis of race, religion, sex, or age. The problem of sorting among usually worthy and strongly felt objectives would become impossible. And much of the American economy would be off limits for investing, for one cause or another.

---

[4]Daniel H. Kohl to WCG, February 4, 1970.
[5]WCG to Kohl, February 27, 1970.

The third example was the change in the nation's social objectives over time:

> [A] quarter of a century ago, TIAA was one of the earliest companies to participate vigorously in the FHA and VA single family and multiple dwelling home loan programs. We made a large number of these loans. They seemed essential in order to house our returning servicemen, to make up for the great deficiencies in home building that occurred during the 1930s, and to try to upgrade the living conditions of Americans. This was a widely applauded social goal.
>
> I now look upon our sprawling cities in America, spread out in suburban communities endlessly over the horizons. I see the ribbons of concrete and asphalt slashing their way through these communities, spawning their trivia of gasoline stations, neon-signed hamburger stands, and a proliferation of used car and used-up car lots. It makes me wonder if the nation's social objectives were quite as clearly defined as they seemed to be at the time.

I commented that TIAA and CREF's major goals were to innovate and lead social developments toward retirement security and the strengthening of higher education. And finally, that I saw no conflict between social objectives of quality higher education and good pensions supported by high productivity fiduciarily chosen investments. The exchange of correspondence was useful and led to greater understanding and support for TIAA-CREF policy.

But something I said in the long letter to Dr. Kohl worried Dr. Joseph T. Sneed, a CREF trustee and conservative law professor at Stanford Law School. I used the term *social productivity*, and perhaps it was not helpful. Dr. Sneed concluded I was being inconsistent in claiming TIAA-CREF could maximize return and "serve society" at the same time. I confirmed that was exactly what I was saying, and that TIAA's record for many years at the very top of life insurance investment returns with "decent" investments proved it could be done.[6]

Dr. Sneed's activity among his fellow law school deans and economists brought many letters to my desk. Wrote one professor: "It is my view that the sole business of TIAA-CREF is to make money, and I would deeply resent the use of my investment in it for any other purpose."[7] And another: "I strongly oppose an investment policy based on any principle other than maximization of financial return to policyholders.... Any policy which departs from this

---

[6]Joseph T. Sneed to WCG, February 26, March 25, March 26, April 8, 1970; WCG to Sneed, April 2, 1970; discussion by Dr. Sneed, Record of the TIAA-CREF Educator-Trustee Advisory Committee Meeting, April 30, 1970, WCG files.

[7]Edwin G. Schuck, professor of law, Columbia University, to WCG, April 1, 1970.

objective is in violation of the fiduciary duty the board owes to policy holders."[8]

It took some time to convince the law deans that TIAA-CREF was aware of its fiduciary responsibilities and that its investment policies fell well within what they wanted. But the incident did provide an opportunity for widespread discussion of a crucial policy matter.

This really was the only letter-writing campaign that occurred. TIAA-CREF's detailed responses to both sides were accepted.

At that time, there was a deep-rooted feeling that social invest-ments were not good investments. The underlying assumption with respect to social investing went something like, to overstate it: Investments fall along a continuum from high investment yield "harmful" loans to low investment yield loans that subsidize some "good" activity.

This is not the way it is.

During those same years, some of TIAA's best performing invest-ments were "good" investments—pollution control companies like Keene Corporation, in water pollution control; Southwest Cryogenics, eliminating carbon dioxide discharge; and other companies producing cooling towers, wet scrubbers, and electrostatic precipitators. Some companies cause certain deleterious effects that need to be elimi-nated, and they then become good investments. Institutional inves-tors, by their prodding, can help speed these developments.

The vast majority of investments are good investments. They pro-vide employment, and they produce a useful product or service that people want.

Letters and conferences, and the resulting discussions with the TIAA-CREF boards, help to confirm and communicate TIAA-CREF's policy to participants and educational institutions.

VOTING CORPORATE SHARES

Mostly CREF, Some TIAA

For generations, the dullest piece of paper corporations sent to their owners—the shareholders—was the proxy. It had two squares marked "yes" or "no" on election of a management-selected slate of directors and appointment of an auditing firm. It did not make sense to vote against auditors, and there was no choice on the management slate of directors.

Controversial social proposals began to appear on proxy state-ments for large corporations in the late 1960s. One of the first big tests

---

[8]Charles J. Meyers, professor of law, Stanford Law School, to WCG, March 12, 1970.

was the General Motors proxy and annual meeting in the spring of 1970. The Educator-Trustee Advisory Committee of TIAA-CREF was a good place to discuss this controversial subject. This meant that 14 educators—presidents of state universities and private colleges, philosophy professors, economists, college business officers, finance professors, and futurists—would attack the issues. The resulting spirited discussion led to about an even split between supporting GM management or the proxy proposers.

The time had arrived to challenge the Wall Street approach of "vote for management or sell the stock." To sell 608,700 shares of GM stock (CREF's holding in 1970) because CREF's board agreed with, say, seven management recommendations on proxy proposals but disagreed on one or two or three made no sense. If a church group, or a Ralph Nader, or management of General Motors had a good idea, TIAA-CREF would vote for it, without thereby indicating it was voting for or against management. The organization would henceforth vote for or against a proposal, not for or against its sponsor.

The TIAA-CREF boards instructed me, as chairman and CEO, to express their views to General Motors. The letter I wrote to James Roche, chairman of GM, May 13, 1970, shows there was considerable difference of opinion within the TIAA-CREF boards in the early days of corporate activism. Because it was one of the first letters from an institutional investor to a giant corporation on the subject of social issues on corporate proxies, it is reproduced in part here:

> We enclose our proxies covering 608,700 common shares owned by College Retirement Equities Fund and 29,000 common shares owned by Teachers Insurance and Annuity Association for the Annual Meeting on May 22, 1970. . . .
>
> The issues presented in Proposals #4 and #5 in this year's proxy statement were of such significance that they were discussed fully by the finance committees of the TIAA and CREF boards, by our educator-trustee advisory committee, and on recommendation of both groups, referred to the full boards meeting jointly for discussion and decision. On Proposal #5, to increase the size of the General Motors board, 9 of 16 CREF trustees present and 8 of 15 TIAA trustees present voted against the proposal. On Proposal #4, to establish a Committee for Corporate Responsibility, the CREF trustees' vote was 10 out of 16 against and the TIAA vote was 9 out of 15 against.
>
> It was generally agreed that the mechanisms incorporated in the proposals were faulty, but the objectives were applauded. No enthusiasm was expressed for General Motors' past response to public concern about the pressing problems of safety, environmental quality, minority group employment and mass transportation. . . .
>
> The concluding remarks in General Motors' defensive *Record of Progress* state that 'A corporation can only discharge its obligations to society if it continues to be a profitable investment for its stock-

holders.' Surely it is time to rearrange these priorities: A corporation can only continue to be a profitable investment for its stockholders if it discharges its obligations to society.

Much is said of maximization of profits as if it is a concept incompatible with improvements in quality of life. Not at all—especially not in the long run. . . . We want and expect the companies in which TIAA and CREF invest to take leading roles in solving economic and social problems related to the products these companies produce. We are confident that this will be the only way to maximize the long-range profitability of those companies and justify our continuing investment in them as a means of enhancing retirement security of college teachers.

This led to a good deal of discussion with Roche and a February 1971 visit to the GM proving ground to study their responses to environmental, safety, and employment issues appearing on proxies. A funny thing happened at the proving grounds. Roche and I were standing by an experimental car when a shotgun blast went off. Noise, and the smell of gunpowder, took me back to younger days of quail and rabbit hunting with my father. "WHAT was THAT?" THAT shotgun blast was deployment of a pioneering new passive restraint system, to be called an air-bag system. "We've got to make it quieter," Roche said, to general agreement.

Two months later, Roche and I joined the same side of a challenging situation, as 2 of the first 10 public members of the board of directors of the New York Stock Exchange, on which we both served for a turbulent decade.

The New York Times on May 2, 1971, published an analysis of TIAA-CREF's approach to voting corporate shares and social issues in investing.[9] My article, "The Power of Institutions," recommended the organization's new activist role in which institutions would vote, not for or against a corporation, but for a good idea or against a bad one, no matter who the sponsor. This was so much a break with tradition that the voting part of the article is reproduced here:

It seems to me that there are seven options available to the institutional investor who must decide how the shares he holds are to be voted.

He may decide to not vote the shares. This may have been a viable approach once; certainly it is an easy way of handling things. But it is no longer acceptable. What it means, when shares of a corporation are 30, 50, or even 70 percent institutionally owned, is a vacuum in the responsible exercise of a corporate power.

---

[9]WCG, "The Power of Institutions. They Can Influence Corporate Role in Society," *The New York Times*, May 2, 1971. Copyright © 1971 by The New York Times Company. Reprinted by permission.

He may follow the common practice and always vote for management-sponsored propositions. Advocates of such a policy claim that institutional owners should either have enough faith in management to vote for all of management's propositions or should sell the stock. . . .

Institutions can vote selectively on the propositions [my recommended approach]. . . .

Institutional management may decide to abstain actively. . . . The causes for abstention can be presented to management and, if desired, to a larger public.

Some have suggested that institutions might pass voting rights through to their clientele. I suspect that in most cases the expense to the institution would be prohibitive. . . .

Institutions might initiate propositions. This is an option rarely used except in a takeover bid. Its potentials for good are great, but so also are its dangers of misuse. Clearly institutional investors should not be trying to manage American business, nor to give specific directives through frequent sponsorship of propositions. But there are occasions when such initiative would be both practical and helpful.

An institutional investor may use any of the options discussed and add a letter to management. Such letters explain the votes of the institutional investor on either controversial or noncontroversial items, and bring out the thoughts of the investor and his clientele. . . .

When social issues attained prominence, CREF separated the financial issues and had them voted under the instructions of the finance committee but took the social issues to the full board. The 1971 TIAA-CREF *Annual Report* stated, "Over the past five years CREF votes were cast on [49] occasions contrary to the recommendations of management on particular proxy proposals."

Trustee Committee on Shareholder Proposals

As the number of proxy proposals involving social issues increased rapidly, it became impractical to take them all to the full TIAA or CREF boards. So an Ad Hoc Trustee Committee on Shareholder Proposals was appointed in 1972. This committee, and since 1988 a successor standing committee, now named the Joint Committee on Corporate Governance and Social Responsibility, spends many hours each year studying the various proxy proposals and deciding on the vote. It then reports the votes to the full boards and publicly. Meanwhile, the financial matters continue to be voted by the CREF finance committee or by the analyst handling the stock, voting under policy decisions set by the finance committee.

Frequently, CREF writes management letters to corporations expanding on the reasons for its votes or requesting review of corporate response to environmental or other concerns. Virtually without exception, the corporations indicated in their response an appreciation of the trustees' careful consideration of the issue highlighted by the proposal. Often the companies indicated that, although the proposal was defeated, they had taken or would take steps in the direction suggested by the proposal.

Successive waves of proxy issues have appeared since the early 1970s. Church groups, college students, faculty members, and others became active in environmental, fair employment, racial, and other issues, and proposed many items for inclusion in proxy statements.

Investor Responsibility Research Center

Because of the growing interest in social investing, individual colleges and TIAA were making repetitive trips to corporations, to South Africa, and other sources of information. Responsible institutional investors needed some central fact-finding organization. In 1972, under the leadership of TIAA-CREF, Amherst College, Harvard University, and others, the Investor Responsibility Research Center (IRRC) was established, with original funding from the Ford, Carnegie, and Rockefeller foundations. Its mission was to make impartial fact-finding surveys of pending social issues within the scope of social investing and report to its member institutions. Dr. Roger Conant was TIAA-CREF's representative on the IRRC from 1972 to 1979, as the center established its reputation in research and analysis on shareholder resolutions and through special reports on issues such as U.S.-Soviet trade and surface mining of coal.

The IRRC continues to be an active force in this field and has expanded both its focus and the array of information available through data bases, newsletters, directories, and reports. The center provides subscription services in three main areas: social issues, South Africa review, and corporate governance. It also has taken the lead in reporting on new issues of concern to investors, such as animal testing, ozone depletion, foreign military sales, and U.S. companies in Northern Ireland. One measure of the IRRC's success is its growth: from an operating budget of $160,000 in 1973 it has grown to a 1988 budget of $2.7 million.

TIAA-CREF has subscribed to IRRC since its inception and supported its development through service on the center's board. A TIAA-CREF officer, Albert J. Wilson, has been a member of the IRRC board since 1979 and chairman of the center's board from 1985 to 1987. Wilson is now vice president, corporate secretary, and associate general counsel of TIAA-CREF and continues to coordinate the social responsibility effort.

South Africa

One of the world's most intransigent human rights problems has been apartheid in South Africa. One of America's ways of trying to influence South African policy has been through U.S. corporations doing business there. For a number of years, TIAA-CREF supported the presence of a corporation in South Africa as long as it could be a positive force for change. As a minimal first step, TIAA-CREF asked companies to sign and implement the Sullivan principles. In 1978, the TIAA and CREF boards approved their own separate set of principles to be presented to managements with respect to their South African operations. This statement went well beyond the Sullivan principles, especially in calling for the right of South African labor to unionize, in opposing technology sales to the South African government, and in supporting blacks' "basic human right to live within a family unit."

Wilson first made a fact-finding mission to South Africa in 1982. As a black representing a large institutional investor, he was uniquely able to move between the two worlds in that painfully divided country and to achieve an unusual depth of understanding of the apartheid system. Following his second mission in 1986:

> The pension companies concluded that the long-term economic interests of its participants would be best served by urging all 160 portfolio companies with operations in South Africa to withdraw from the country as expeditiously as possible.[10]

TIAA-CREF trustees also decided to begin submitting shareholder resolutions in support of its new policy.[11] Following discussions with corporate managements, a number of additional companies withdrew. Newmont Mining Corporation, a large gold producer based in New York, was one of the first managements approached by CREF, in the late 1960s, about its very heavy dependence on South African operations. Newmont announced on March 30, 1988, it was selling its interests in Tsumeb and O'Okiep Copper.

Takeovers, Poison Pills, and Acquisitions

The 1980s saw a wave of new economic issues on corporate proxies. The main financial issues are poison pills, anti-takeover devices, mergers and acquisitions, "greenmail," secret proxy ballots, and executive compensation including golden parachutes.

---

[10]TIAA-CREF, *1986 Annual Report,* p. 20.
[11]TIAA-CREF News Release, July 23, 1986.

CREF's guidelines now direct that it oppose proposals that tend to limit shareholder rights without offering a clear benefit in return. In CREF's view, anti-takeover devices fall into this category. CREF also opposes greenmail, or proposals that give a small group of stockholders a higher-than-market price for their shares without extending the same offer to all shareholders. In addition, CREF initiates shareholder resolutions that oppose adoption of poison pills without shareholder votes.

CREF Initiates Proposals

CREF made a major change in its use of shareholder power when it decided in 1985 to initiate proposals on corporate proxies. South Africa became the first arena for proposals; CREF filed 10 such proxy proposals in 1985. Soon, takeover preventatives—poison pills—became a major initiative, and, by 1986, CREF made 10 proxy submissions on that issue. In 1988, CREF continued its resolutions on South Africa and poison pills and filed resolutions with an additional five portfolio companies calling for the adoption of secret balloting on corporate proxies and other relevant stockholder matters.

The wave of mergers, acquisitions, and buyouts in the late 1980s raised a real challenge to efficient market theories and to institutional commitments to long-term investment in any one company. When the equities market has placed a value of approximately $12.5 billion on RJR-Nabisco and the final buyout price was about $25 billion, some adjustment needs to be made in prevailing theories and practices.

CREF analysts scrutinize all executive compensation plans for reasonableness and potential to achieve positive corporate objectives, voting against those deemed to be exceedingly generous or not designed to improve the performance of the company.

For the future, it looks as if proxy proposals on social and financial matters will continue to grow. The entire subject of voting corporate shares, responsible institutional investing, and social questions is important and challenging for TIAA-CREF and other institutional investors.

In addition to voting TIAA and CREF shares and initiating appropriate shareholder resolutions to be filed with selected portfolio companies, this committee also develops specific policy positions on selected issues for consideration by the full TIAA-CREF boards of trustees. This interaction between the joint committee and the boards allows continuing and increasingly sharp focus on vital shareholder issues.

PART FOUR

Economic Security for College Staff Members

CHAPTER 14

Setting Pension Philosophy

The purpose of TIAA-CREF and of the effort expended by the college world in its benefit plans is financial protection from the predictable and chance events that occur to an individual over a lifetime. There are many subsidiary financial objectives: minimizing taxes, accumulating an estate, temporary savings for many purposes, good investment performance, good family expenditure control. But the real purpose that drives the effort is financial security.

Nonfinancial aspects of college benefit planning are crucial too. The college needs to be able to attract, motivate, and hold talented academic and staff employees and, when necessary, to part with them in a socially acceptable manner (a 1940s euphemism). The employees need to know they will be secure during the vicissitudes of life. And the system of higher education needs to be able to attract an adequate supply of the finest academic teaching and research talent available.

These objectives of employers, staff members, and the system are compatible. This has led to an unusual joint effort among them and the principal manager of their benefit plans, TIAA-CREF, over seven decades, to develop benefit contracts and plan provisions that best fit the needs of all parties, as determined by themselves.

This world of higher education generally agrees on its desire to provide fully vested, fully funded, contractual, portable, defined contribution basic retirement benefit systems. Within these broad elements, it demands substantial variety and flexibility in certain provisions of retirement systems—retirement ages, contributions toward annuity contracts, participation rules, and flexible arrangements during leaves of absence, number of months receiving salary during the year, leaves for government or other service, and receipt of contributions from more than one employing institution.

"Before you lock the door, Mr. Absent-Minded
Professor, do you have the keys, all our luggage,
the plane tickets and our accumulated pension
rights in TIAA-CREF?"

Reprinted with permission from MODERN
MATURITY. *Copyright 1981, American Association of Retired Persons.*

Both the generally accepted core provisions of retirement plans
and the various flexible arrangements have been studied repeatedly
over the years, first by the Carnegie Foundation for the Advancement
of Teaching and then by educational associations, TIAA, individual
scholars, and others. It is doubtful that any other industry or employment category has had the same amount of careful analysis as to what
should be included in good retirement planning.

TIAA STUDIES

TIAA's studies of retirement planning evolved from the Carnegie
Foundation's pioneering studies on pensions. During the 1920s, when
Henry Pritchett was president of both the foundation and TIAA, the
studies were published in the Carnegie Foundation's annual reports
and in several foundation *Bulletins.* Following Dr. Pritchett's retirement in 1930, one sign of TIAA's gradual move to independence was
the decision by the foundation in 1931 to formally turn over responsibility for external pension studies to TIAA.[1]

---

[1]Savage, *Fruit of an Impulse,* pp. 204–6.

TIAA's first analysis was published under the title *Retirement Plans for College Faculties* in 1934, by Rainard B. Robbins. He put forth the following "fundamental principles" for college retirement planning:

> 1. It is not important to determine a quarter of a century before a man retires how many dollars he will receive as a retirement allowance.
> 2. It is important to provide a substantial allowance, and there is very little practical danger of the provision being too liberal.
> 3. It is important that accumulations to meet old age benefits be made while the prospective pensioner is in service and that these accumulations shall be carefully safeguarded.
> 4. It is important that the accumulations to support retirement benefits for a particular individual shall be so controlled that they can neither be dissipated nor confiscated.[2]

The next study was a more inclusive one, also written by Robbins, titled *College Plans for Retirement Income* and published by Columbia University Press in 1940. Robbins' study concluded, with respect to salient provisions:

> Retirement income should be funded through joint contributions of employer and employees under a plan applying in an obligatory manner to as nearly all classes of staff members as is practicable. A normal retirement age should be announced, and contributions should be as large as seems practicable—certainly not less than 5 percent of salary from the member and as much from the institution. Benefits should be funded through noncashable, nonforfeitable retirement annuity contracts that belong to individuals and provide for adjustment of the date at which annuity payments shall begin and the kind of annuity that shall be received—whether a single life annuity or one that will provide benefits to dependents as well as to the pensioner himself.[3]

The first broad analytical and statistical study of college benefit plans, including insurance as well as retirement plans and the effect of Social Security, was written by William C. Greenough and published in 1948.[4] It was based on a combination of data from a questionnaire and direct analysis of college benefit plans throughout the country. The study was accepted by Harvard University as this author's Ph.D. dissertation.

---

[2]Rainard B. Robbins, *Retirement Plans for College Faculties* (New York: TIAA, 1934), pp. 50–51.

[3]Robbins, *College Plans for Retirement Income* (New York: Columbia University Press, 1940), pp. 179–80.

[4]WCG, *College Retirement and Insurance Plans* (New York: Columbia University Press, 1948).

The study and its data showed the trends and status of retirement benefit plans and insurance plans by 1948:

> Two thirds of the colleges, universities, and state teachers colleges in the United States, employing over 85 percent of the total number of faculty members, now have retirement plans, as do over half of the Canadian institutions. Thus a considerable majority of college faculty members may now look forward to some measure of security after retirement. . . .
>
> Other than the inauguration of plans at institutions where none now exist, the major problems with respect to college retirement plans at present are the inadequacy of benefits provided by most plans and the provision of retirement benefits for classes of employees not now protected. . . .

This postwar study presented data on actual provisions in college plans and gave qualitative analysis of those provisions and recommendations for consideration by the colleges. The data showed the strong trends toward interest in staff benefit plans that developed in the immediate postwar period. The study especially helped lead to flexible retirement ages in the colleges, to more adequate contribution rates, and to the start of a strong trend toward life insurance and other benefit plans. And it led to an interest by the colleges and their associations in developing rules of acceptable practice in academic retirement and insurance plans.

AAUP-AAC STATEMENT OF PRINCIPLES ON ACADEMIC RETIREMENT

The educational associations in Washington—the Association of American Colleges, the American Association of University Professors, the Association of American Universities, and the National Association of State Universities—were deeply involved in the deliberations leading to establishment of TIAA. During the ensuing years, they and TIAA were in frequent contact on matters of fundamental pension policy. They encouraged the publication of TIAA's early studies on benefit plans in the colleges.

An instance of useful cooperation among employers in a broad, nationwide group came with the joint action of the American Association of University Professors (AAUP) and the Association of American Colleges (AAC), reporting in 1950, and recommending carefully thought-out philosophy and provisions for college retirement plans.[5]

---

[5]"Academic Retirement and Related Subjects. Report on a Study Conducted by a Joint Committee of the American Association of University Professors and the Association of American Colleges," *Association of American Colleges Bulletin* 36 (May 1950), pp. 308–28.

The first Statement of Principles on Academic Retirement and Related Subjects evolved after many meetings of the AAUP and AAC committee members. They studied a large amount of material provided by the colleges and by TIAA; they asked TIAA officers to meet with them on several occasions. Much statistical work was provided, and the deliberations were exhaustive. For example, there was vigorous discussion as to whether colleges should have a fixed retirement age beyond which there were no extensions of service, in which case the age should be high, or a more flexible arrangement of normal retirement at age 65 with extensions on specific action of the board of trustees to some such age as 70.

The original joint committee members were acutely aware of the problem of inflation and its effect on retired and near-retirement staff members. "In many cases," the 1950 report observed, "the present situation of those retiring varies from a disappointingly stringent financial condition to the tragic." The committee could make no definite recommendation to counter inflation, stymied by "the wide variations in the financial problems of American institutions and the legal limitations placed upon them."

The establishment of CREF as a partial protection against inflation was welcomed with relief and enthusiasm. The fund was barely six months old when the AAC's Committee on Insurance and Annuities in January 1953 urged institutions with fixed-dollar benefits to "study this new development carefully" and recommended that the Statement of Principles be amended to acknowledge the "purchasing power" of a retirement annuity.[6] The AAC formally approved this revision, as did the AAUP Council soon afterward.

Though not so widely felt as inflation, the possible hardship caused by major illness or disability was also of grave concern. These forms of insurance are especially complex to write. TIAA's efforts to develop major medical and disability insurance received financial support from the Ford Foundation in 1956. They also quickly received formal policy support from the AAUP-AAC Joint Committee. The 1958 revised statement included specific recommendations for insurance programs, and even the title of the Statement of Principles was expanded to emphasize the importance of provisions for insurance as well as for retirement. The 1958 Statement of Principles is an especially important document for the history of TIAA and CREF. Its basic principles continue to be generally accepted for professional employees (with the important exception of now legally mandated restrictions on retirement age, as noted below). It is reprinted in full here:

---

[6]"Report of the Committee on Insurance and Annuities," LeRoy E. Kimball, chairman, January 6, 1953, Association of American Colleges file, TIAA-CREF Archives.

Academic Retirement and Insurance Programs

Institutions of higher education are conducted for the common good and not to further the interest of either the individual teacher or administrator, or even of the individual institution. The policy of an institution for the retirement of faculty members and administrators and its plan for their insurance benefits and retirement annuities should be such as to increase the effectiveness of its services as an educational agency. Specifically, this policy and plan should be such as to attract individuals of the highest abilities to educational work, to sustain the morale of the faculty, to permit faculty members with singleness of purpose to devote their energies to serving their institution, and to make it possible in a socially acceptable manner to discontinue the services of members of the faculty when their usefulness is undermined by age.

The following is recommended practice:

1. The retirement policy and annuity plan of an institution, as well as its insurance program, should be clearly defined and be well understood by both the faculty and the administration of the institution.

2. The institution should have a fixed and relatively late retirement age, the same for teachers and administrators. The length of training of college teachers, their longevity and their health generally are such that in the present circumstances the desirable fixed retirement age would appear to be from 67 to 70.

3. Circumstances that may seem to justify the involuntary retirement of a teacher or administrator before the fixed retirement age should in all cases be considered by a joint faculty-administration committee of the institution. This committee should preferably be a standing committee, but in the consideration of specific cases, no interested person should be permitted to participate in its deliberations. (The above is not meant to indicate that the involuntary return of an administrator to teaching duties need be regarded as a retirement.)

4. The recall of teachers on retired status should be without tenure and on an annual appointment. Such recall should be used only where the services are clearly needed and where the individual is in good mental and physical health. It may be for part or for full time. Such recall should be rare where the retirement age is as late as 70.

5. The institution should provide for a system of retirement annuities. Such a system should:

(a) Be financed by contributions made during the period of active service by both the individual and the institution.

(b) Be participated in by all full-time faculty members who have attained a certain fixed age, not later than 30.

(c) Be planned to provide in normal circumstances and in so far as possible for a retirement life annuity (including Federal Old Age and Survivors Insurance benefits) equivalent in purchasing power to approximately 50 percent of the average salary over the last 10 years of service if the retirement is at 70, and a somewhat higher percentage if the fixed retirement age is younger.

(d) Ensure that the full amount of the individual's and the institution's contribution, with the accumulations thereon, be vested in the individual, available as a benefit in case of death while in service, and with no forfeiture in case of withdrawal or dismissal from the institution.

(e) Be such that the individual may not withdraw his equity in cash but only in the form of an annuity. (To avoid administrative expense, exception might be made for very small accumulations in an inactive account.) Except when they are small, death benefits to a widow should be paid in the form of an annuity.

6. When a new retirement policy or annuity plan is initiated or an old one changed, reasonable provision either by special financial arrangements or by the gradual inauguration of the new plan should be made for those adversely affected.

7. It is desirable for the insurance program of an institution to include the following:

(a) Life insurance on a group basis, in addition to survivors' benefits under Federal Old Age and Survivors Insurance.

(b) Insurance for medical expenses, including major medical (catastrophic) insurance.

(c) Disability insurance, covering long-term total disability for any occupation for which the staff member is reasonably fitted, and paying half-salary up to a reasonable maximum during disability before retirement as well as continuing contributions toward a retirement annuity.

The policy statement has always emphasized the purpose of benefit plans as being "to attract individuals of the highest abilities to educational work . . . and to make it possible in a socially acceptable manner to discontinue the services of members of the faculty when their usefulness is undermined by age." Among the crucial features emphasized is full vesting of the individual and institutional contributions, with investment earnings, but the annuity should "be such that the individual may not withdraw his equity in cash but only in the form of an annuity." The latter statement has been liberalized to permit a reasonable payment of a "retirement transition benefit," now 10 percent of the accumulation, at the time of retirement. The Statement of Principles was revised by subsequent AAUP-AAC joint committees in 1968, 1980, and again in 1987–88.

RETIREMENT AGE

The purpose of a college retirement plan is to make it possible for staff members to retire with dignity, fairness, and financial security when they want or when they should and to make it possible for the college to part with its retiring staff members in a dignified and acceptable manner. Another purpose is to assure the rights of students and the public to expect continued high performance for their tuition, tax, and charitable expenditures.

But at what age should college staff members retire? As in other problems in human relations, no formula will at once deal equitably with all persons concerned. Perhaps yardsticks will sometime be available to measure physiological age as nicely as chronological age is now measured, to measure the intangibles of mental elasticity, artistic, and scientific awareness, sensitivity to the problems of youth, and the variety of capacities that make up the good teacher, but they are not yet available. Who is to say when Titian became old? At 98, he painted his "Battle of Lepanto." Or Goethe, who at 80 completed *Faust*? Benjamin Franklin, Oliver Wendell Holmes? Claude Pepper, Margaret Chase Smith, Albert Einstein, Marie Curie, George Balanchine, Margot Fonteyn, Barbara Tuchman, and "the oldest U.S. president to serve"? Who is to say when they should have retired? (Other than the voting public, or the Constitution, or the marketplace for art?) But these conspicuous examples are exceptional, and merely serve to support the generally held conclusion that the ravages of time take their toll of most people in their middle 60s or early 70s.

Before the advent of federal and state legislation limiting age-mandated retirement, colleges usually chose either a fixed retirement age, usually higher than 65, with no extensions or a "normal" retirement age of 65 with board-approved extensions to age 70. Many institutions with flexible ages for academic staff required retirement of all administrators at age 65; all others had to retire from administrative duties at 65. Under many retirement plans, annuity income does not have to start at the time of retirement, except as required by Internal Revenue at or above age 70½.

Retirement ages first came to attention when Bismarck over 100 years ago established age 70 as the minimum retirement age for receipt of German social benefits.[7] In 1906, the Carnegie Foundation designated age 65 as the first age at which the free benefits were available. The 1932 International Labor Conference recommended the pensionable age be set at not more than 65 years.[8] (Opinion in labor circles on this tends to change with the economic cycle.) Originally, U.S. Social Security used age 65 as the first time benefits could be received. In 1956, the age for wives and widows was reduced to 62 with reduction in benefits, and this was extended to men in 1961.

---

[7]Robert J. Myers, *Social Security,* 3rd ed. (Homewood, Ill.: Richard D. Irwin, 1985), p. 240.

[8]Margaret Grant, *Old-Age Security: Social and Financial Trends.* A Report Prepared for the Committee on Social Security (Washington, D.C.: Committee on Social Security, Social Science Research Council, 1939), pp. 29–30.

Until the advent of the Carnegie Foundation, most college staff members taught until ill health prevented their continuance or the college told them to leave. As professors' financial security improved with stronger pension plans, the decision of when to quit gradually shifted to the individual. As benefits became more adequate under retirement plans, colleges were able to impose mandatory retirement ages. Most continued to be flexible; academic staff members still had considerable choice of when to retire between age 65 and 70. The really good level of financial security reached in recent decades has given staff members the option of retiring earlier than a college's stated normal retirement date. Financial considerations no longer drive most decisions on when to retire.

Flexibility in retirement practices at the colleges served well during the surge of GI enrollment right after World War II and into the 1950s, when faculty was in short supply. The first post-World War II census of college retirement ages was published in 1948, showing a general preference—47 percent of college plans—for a "normal" retirement age *with extensions allowed*: 37 percent at age 65 and another 10 percent at ages 66 to 70.[9] A smaller percentage of plans, 36 percent, set a retirement age *where extensions were not mentioned*: 22 percent at age 65 and another 14 percent at ages 66 to 70.

The AAUP and AAC were active with retirement age recommendations during the ensuing years, although the recommendations in the 1950 and 1968 Statements of Principles on Retirement generally conformed to the 1958 statement. These minor modifications resulted in no material shift in practice by 1980; 65 continued to be the most commonly used retirement age, especially at private institutions.[10]

With legislative action in 1967, 1978, and again in 1986, Congress helped to decide when people in America should retire. A number of states also passed their own retirement age legislation. This has not been all bad or all good. It has limited flexibility and allowance for differences in employment situations. The 1978 amendments to the Age Discrimination in Employment Act of 1967 (ADEA) prohibited employers, after January 1, 1979, from mandating retirement at an age earlier than 70. Among the exceptions were "bona fide" executives and policymakers, where compulsory retirement was permitted at age 65 under specified conditions. Retirement at age 65 was also allowed for tenured employees at institutions of higher education, but only until July 1, 1982.

---

[9]WCG, *College Retirement and Insurance Plans,* p. 234.

[10]See Table 3–20, "Stated Normal Retirement Age, Four-Year Institutions of Higher Education, by Type and Control," in Francis P. King and Thomas J. Cook, *Benefit Plans in Higher Education* (New York: Columbia University Press, 1980), p. 102.

Further amendments in 1986 removed the age 70 cap for *most* employees covered by the law: among the exceptions, compulsory retirement at age 65 for "bona fide" executives and policymakers continues to be allowed. A special rule also allows compulsory retirement at age 70 for tenured employees until December 31, 1993, unless Congress concludes after study that it should be extended.

Throughout all these sometimes hotly debated legislative intrusions into setting retirement ages, professors have gone about their teaching and research, working about the same number of years, and retiring at about the same age as in the past. No discernible trend has surfaced; most professors retire about age 64 to 66.

Congress in 1986 also mandated that contributions to an employee's account in a *defined contribution* plan cannot be discontinued and the rate of contributions cannot be reduced because of the attainment of any age. This substantially limits the flexibility of colleges and their staff members to design retirement plans to meet their needs. It also has a major impact on costs and effectiveness of retirement plans. Under *defined benefit* plans, the benefit accrued to an employee cannot be reduced or discontinued based on age. Employers with defined benefit plans may, however, have a benefit maximum as well as a limit on the number of years of service or participation that are taken into account—but without regard to age.

These factors bring to the forefront discussions of the need for inducements for early retirement and for phased retirement or tapering off of regular duties. Much has been written on retirement ages and retirement decisions in college employment through TIAA-CREF research conducted by Dr. Francis P. King, Thomas Cook, James Mulanaphy, and others; by officers of educational associations; and by college people. Much material is available regarding other employments, social security here and abroad, and individual ideas.[11]

It seems appropriate once again to draw attention to the durability of the college world's original pension planning. The fundamental idea evolving from the 1916–18 Carnegie Commission studies envisioned that the colleges and their staff members would make the decisions as to retirement age, participation in the plan, level of

[11]In addition to the works cited above, see, for example: Henry James, "How to Determine the Retirement Date," *Association of American Colleges Bulletin* 31 (December 1944), pp. 542–51; Rainard B. Robbins, "Issues in Retirement: A Collection of Views," *Association of American Colleges Bulletin* 36 (December 1950), pp. 534–51; George E. Johnson, "Contemporary Opinion: Is a Compulsory Retirement Age Ever Justified?" *Journal of Gerontology* 6 (July 1951), pp. 263–71; Thomas J. Cook, "College Benefit Plans and the Age Discrimination in Employment Act Amendments," *Academe* 67 (October 1981), pp. 308–12; James M. Mulanaphy, *Lessons On Retirement* (New York: TIAA, 1984); Commission on College Retirement, *Retirement Ages for College and University Personnel* (New York, 1986); Kevin Gray, *Retirement Plans and Expectations of TIAA-CREF Policyholders* (New York: TIAA-CREF, 1988).

contributions to support benefits, and all other employment decisions. And they would make the basic decision as to the retirement plan that best suited their needs. The great majority chose TIAA.

The TIAA plan provided the flexibility needed to accommodate different retirement ages, level of contributions, and participation. In turn, the TIAA contract would provide for the investment of the pension savings, the optional forms of income at retirement, the protection from creditors, and the wide range of other protections incorporated in the contract.

It is striking how well all the basic philosophies of college retirement plans and the contracts issued by TIAA have adapted to changing conditions of the ensuing seven decades. A current necessity is to adapt to the increasing variety of investment options available, the changing demographics of college staffs, the growing interest of the federal government in pensions generally, and the substitution of federal decisions for those the college used to make—when participation will occur, whether contributions will continue after age 65, what the retirement age can and cannot be, who must be covered in the plan, and a number of other matters.

CHAPTER 15

Social Security Extension

INITIAL EXCLUSION OF COLLEGES AND UNIVERSITIES

Many groups of American workers were not included under Social Security initially: farmers and other self-employed persons; farm workers; domestics; employees of charitable, educational, and religious nonprofit organizations; ministers; and local, state, and federal government employees. The reasons for exclusion ranged from practical problems to important philosophical questions.

Social Security was thus not originally available to college and university staff members. In a few instances, fundamental disagreements with the basic philosophy of Social Security led trustees and faculty members to oppose it. But the compelling factors lay in deeply rooted elements of American society. Church-related institutions were not included because of concerns about separation of church and state and worries about taxation of religious organizations. Other private colleges and universities were not included because of concern over academic freedom and anxiety related to taxation of private nonprofit entities. State universities were not included because of constitutional questions about federal taxation of state and local entities, including state employees.[1]

These important questions were ultimately resolved only after such actions as changing the word *taxes* to support Social Security to *contributions;* making participation initially voluntary by ministers; and making initial participation voluntary in one way or an-

---

[1] I remember, with nostalgia, that for the first two years of my teaching and administrative experience at Indiana University in the late 1930s, I did not have to pay any federal income tax, a saving at that time of about $40 a year to a young bachelor. That provision of the Internal Revenue Code was changed in 1939.

other for employees of each college whether denominational, private, or public.

TIAA's officers were convinced it would be good for colleges if their staff members were covered by Social Security. They also believed each of the philosophical or practical problems could be solved. TIAA set out on what proved to be a 15-year campaign to inform the college world about Social Security and later to work with the educational world and the federal government in achieving coverage. It was unusual for a pension-funding agency to support the extension of Social Security. One of the arguments used by the colleges was that they were happy with their existing retirement provisions through TIAA and did not need or want Social Security. This was pleasing, of course, but TIAA believed it overlooked an opportunity for the colleges. So part of TIAA's effort was to show how colleges could meet part or all of the Social Security cost by cutting back on their TIAA plans, if they wished.

A memorandum of TIAA President Henry James in November 1937 reported on his attendance at meetings of the Association of American Colleges in Dallas and Birmingham at which he "did not hesitate to explain my view that the colleges had made a mistake in getting themselves exempted from the law."[2] But he also concluded, "Most of them now think that they are well out of the Social Security legislation and that they don't want to stir up any discussion that might bring them in."[3]

A year later, James again addressed a regional meeting of the Association of American Colleges at Dr. Guy Snavely's invitation, meeting with a more informed response. When Congress adopted the broad 1939 amendments, TIAA intensified its educational effort, with detailed analyses of the law and recommendations. Dr. Rainard Robbins, vice president and secretary of TIAA, wrote to Professor J. Douglas Brown of Princeton University, one of the half-dozen most important Social Security pioneers: "I think our most formidable antagonist is President [Henry M.] Wriston of Brown [University], and he is especially important because he would be invaluable if he should change his mind."[4] Robbins reported that the president of Washington and Lee University was "dead set against having anything to do with the federal government."[5] James, President Wriston, and President James Bryant Conant of Harvard then corresponded

---

[2]Henry James, "Memorandum re Meetings of A.A.C. at Dallas, Texas, and Birmingham, Alabama," November 16, 1937, TIAA-CREF Archives, Association of American Colleges file.

[3]H. J., Memorandum, June 30, 1938, TIAA-CREF Archives, A.A.C. file.

[4]Robbins to Brown, March 12, 1940, TIAA-CREF, WCG files.

[5]Ibid.

concerning the philosophical and practical aspects of extending the federal plan to private higher education.

James wrote to Dr. Wriston on February 28, 1940, about Dr. Wriston's concerns over Social Security:

> Each of us fears more certain dangers which the other fears less. I should say that history teaches one relevant lesson very clearly. Social classes and institutional groups that do not know how gracefully and gradually to modify their status and accept obligations in place of exemptions when the world changes, end up by getting it in the neck.[6]

It was a colorfully expressed philosophical dispute over Social Security, not a personal one. President Wriston was elected a member of Trustees of T.I.A.A. Stock in 1942 and was issued CREF Certificate #1 when CREF started in 1952.

In 1935, when Social Security started, only a few institutions on TIAA's eligible list included nonteaching employees in their retirement plans. With the passage of the Social Security Act that year, and with its exclusions affecting colleges and universities, nonacademic employees were additionally without the protections afforded industrial and commercial workers in similar occupations. TIAA's view was stated in its 1936 annual report:

> The [college] president's secretary or the heating plant engineer or the grounds superintendent of a college is not reasonably to be distinguished from persons who are doing the same sort of work for factories, banks and other companies. Why should the legal status of the employer place the employee in an unfavorable social and economic situation?[7]

This inequity also put colleges and universities at a disadvantage in their ability to attract capable workers from covered employments and to retain their best staff members. A number of institutions subsequently inaugurated plans for nonacademic employees, including TIAA-sponsored plans, but Robbins and James were convinced Social Security represented a national movement for social reform. The 1939 amendments to the act, in the Old-Age and Survivors Insurance provisions, drove another wedge between covered and excluded employees.

Much discussion but little action on Social Security extension occurred during the early 1940s, caused in part by the war. After the war, TIAA's officers renewed their efforts on behalf of extension of

---

[6]James to Wriston, February 28, 1940, TIAA-CREF Archives, Association of American Colleges file.

[7]TIAA, *18th Annual Report,* 1936, pp. 5–6.

coverage through speeches, writings, and meetings with educators. The association also argued for extension in its annual reports:

> From the 1948 report: We believe coverage, especially of the Old Age and Survivors Insurance program, should be extended to persons in educational work. It seems quite unfair to exclude a most worthy occupational group from the benefits of the national program that will be supported not only from payroll taxes, but also in the long run partially from general tax revenues.[8]

The last prediction has not come to pass. In fact, looking into the future from 1989, it appears that Social Security taxes, because of demographic shifts, will indirectly be funding a considerable part of the federal deficit for years to come. The current hump of working-age Americans will probably build large annual excesses of income over outgo until the second decade of the new century, when the baby boom will be retiring, unless the Social Security Act is amended.

The 1949 TIAA report analyzed the various provisions of H.R. 6000, a bill that would increase Social Security benefits and extend coverage to many excluded groups, including college staff members. In February 1950, I testified before the Senate Committee on Finance on H.R. 6000, stating, "Coverage should be extended to employees without distinction as to whether they are on the teaching or the non-academic staff, whether they are employees of large colleges or small, publicly supported colleges or private."[9]

By this time the attitude in the college world toward extension of Social Security coverage had changed materially. The great educational associations in Washington—the American Council on Education, the Association of American Colleges, the AAUP—and a number of others favored and generally worked toward the extension. The National Education Association, more oriented toward public school teachers, was still opposed.

EXTENSION TO PRIVATE INSTITUTIONS — 1951

Coverage of Old-Age and Survivors Insurance (OASI) was extended by 1950 legislation to part of the educational world, effective January 1, 1951. Private colleges and universities could elect coverage regardless of the views of their employees; the employees present at the inception of coverage could, individually, opt out, but all new employees would be compulsorily covered. Publicly supported institu-

---

[8]TIAA, *30th Annual Report*, 1948, p. 7.

[9]"Statement on H.R. 6000 by Dr. William C. Greenough, vice president, Teachers Insurance and Annuity Association of America, before the Senate Committee on Finance, February 13, 1950."

tions could elect coverage only if they had no existing retirement plans (a relatively rare situation). The 1950 TIAA *Annual Report* commented, "While the new law leaves much to be desired, it helps many private colleges make substantial improvements in overall retirement and survivor benefits for their staff members." The report went on to state: "The greatest weakness in the extension to the educational world is the fact that staff members of publicly supported colleges and universities cannot be covered by OASI if they are in positions included under existing retirement systems."

State teacher retirement systems successfully fought against extension of Social Security to their groups. Because many such systems covered college faculty members at public universities, such faculty also were excluded from coverage. This hurt retirement benefits. It also meant a tariff barrier was erected between institutions that were and those that were not covered by Social Security. This was not too different from the barrier between institutions covered by the free Carnegie pensions and those that were not.

Making matters worse, as the TIAA publication pointed out, was that a faculty member shifting from a private university with Social Security coverage to a public one before having enough service to qualify for Social Security would lose all benefits credited to him or her from taxes paid by the member and by the institution. In addition, typical state teacher and public employee retirement systems provided no benefit to staff members who left before many years of service or before early retirement. So staff members could lose all benefits from the employer plan and frequently end long years as teachers without either Social Security or a teacher retirement benefit.

In addition to the discussions with educational associations, individual colleges and universities, and staff members, TIAA officers frequently testified in Washington and spoke about Social Security to large groups. Dr. Robbins often felt frustrated when testifying, as did I. Teachers Insurance and Annuity Association was invariably classified with state teacher retirement systems. TIAA was frequently the only pension plan on a given day presenting testimony supporting the extension of Social Security benefits to its part of the employment world.

The executive secretary of the Maryland State Teachers' Association, speaking also for the Maryland Educational Association and for the Civil Service Group—a combined total of 18,000 public employees in Maryland—testified that a voluntary election by individuals of coverage by Social Security for public institutions meant that, if 5,999 out of 6,000 members of a state teacher retirement system voted for Social Security coverage, they were forcing that one additional person against his or her own will into Social Security, a misuse of democratic power. The solution he offered? If one out of 6,000 voted against coverage, then none could have it. The founding fathers were diligent in protecting the rights of the outnumbered, the minorities, but this was going a bit far.[10]

EXTENSION TO PUBLIC INSTITUTIONS —1955

Congress acted in 1954, and state institutions with retirement systems finally could opt to include their staff members in Social Security, effective January 1, 1955, joining the private institutions on a voluntary basis. With the exception of a few states—Alaska, California, Illinois, Louisiana, Massachusetts, and Ohio—and separate public retirement systems in some other states, most joined quickly, and many have joined in subsequent years.

INTEGRATION FOR EARLY RETIREMENT BENEFIT

At the time that Social Security was extended to private colleges, its benefits started at age 65, and it provided no early retirement benefits. TIAA and other pension funds established an "integration for Social Security Benefit" option that permitted participants to elect, on an actuarially equivalent basis, a larger TIAA monthly benefit from the date of their early retirement to their age 65, to fill in the gap until the federal benefits started, and a lower TIAA benefit after age 65. This seems to have been one of those good ideas that does not work out in practice. Few people elected the arrangement, and it was dropped soon after Social Security initiated early retirement benefits starting at age 62.

COMMUNICATIONS WITH COLLEGE WORLD

The colleges, their associations in Washington, and TIAA had achieved extension of Social Security coverage for private and denominational institutions in the 1950 amendments. TIAA assumed the job of quickly communicating much technical detail to a large number of colleges and their staff members. Information to staff members was through written material, as usual for TIAA, with bulletins, annual reports, and pamphlets. TIAA has no agents; at that time, it was a relatively small pension plan with many small and some large institutions as participants.

In 1950, the first of what became a long series of "college institutes" was held. College officers, staff members, and trustees were invited to institutes, usually held on a college campus or in a large

---

[10]Report of William C. Greenough on meeting of Senate Committee on Finance, February 14, 1950.

central city, to share information on Social Security benefits, the technicalities of achieving coverage for faculty and staff, a description of the benefits provided, and answers to any questions. This efficient and effective method of meeting personally, but in groups, with the colleges throughout the country later proved efficacious when CREF was established; when TIAA major medical and disability insurances were set up in 1956; when additional attention was being given to adjustment to retirement; and when several other topics came up for discussion.

In 1950 and the following years, Social Security expanded vastly. In addition to college staff members, coverage was extended to other state and local employees, the self-employed, other nonprofit organizations, and domestics, until nearly all workers were covered except federal employees, a curious exception. They were finally brought in nearly 50 years after the act was passed.

Congress increased benefit levels 10 times between 1950 and 1972. It made a major benefit increase in 1972 and added the cost-of-living escalator. Total disability benefits for workers age 50 and over were added in the 1956 amendments; the age limit was dropped four years later. Congress added Medicare benefits in 1965. All of this had a significant effect upon the financial security of all college staff members.

Social Security had started out as a program for about half of American workers. It took 30 years for it to reach a maturity of providing substantial financial protection for the vast majority of American workers.

SMALL CLOUDS ON THE HORIZON

A number of political and business leaders are making some of the most misguided suggestions for Social Security that have ever been made in its long and remarkably successful history.

Only the tersest comments will be made here.

One misguided idea is that OASDI benefits should be paid only upon meeting a needs test. This would penalize the thrifty, wreak havoc with the hard-won security of all lower income and middle-class working Americans, and destroy the effective partnership between governmental Social Security benefits and private benefit plans, just for starters. This is a very bad idea. It probably would lead to far higher contributions from colleges and individuals to TIAA-CREF to make up for the loss of OASDI benefits, but this is not the way to go.

Another is that Social Security benefits should be fully taxed. This idea is half right. Under present law, only half of the OASDI benefits received are included in taxable income, and I believe this is how it should be. The employee's contributions to OASDI already have been taxed during working years and should not be taxed again. The present taxation of half the benefit, as coming from employer contributions, is arbitrary but reasonable.

However, OASDI benefits should be included in taxable income without the high threshold limit ($25,000 for single persons and $32,000 for married persons filing joint returns). This would not hurt the poor. And it would eliminate a special, unfair discrimination for Social Security income as against income from earnings or savings.

The retirement earnings test should be gradually restrengthened. Americans who continue to work should not, just because they are over age 65, receive additional income transferred from younger workers. The annual exclusion amount should be frozen at its present level ($8,880 in 1989 for those age 65 to 69). There really should be no age at which benefits are received regardless of continued employment, but age 75 (as against the present age 70) would be a reasonable compromise.

Many younger American workers do not believe Social Security will be there when they arrive at retirement. Steps should be taken now, coupled with the good changes made in the 1983 amendments, to reaffirm the strength and viability of the system.

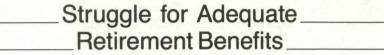

CHAPTER 16

Struggle for Adequate Retirement Benefits

Eighty years ago, most college faculty members were not financially secure in their old age. Forty years ago, the great majority of industrial and service-sector employees were not financially secure in their old age. In the last 80 years for colleges and the last 40 for industry, great advances have been made in old age security. Just in time, too, because for the first time in history, a large proportion of the population lives to retirement and then lives longer in retirement. This chapter will recount the several events, several mechanisms, and many efforts that add up to adequate retirement savings. It will not present statistical studies showing progress toward adequacy, relationships of pre- and postretirement income, or the other data TIAA-CREF publishes at frequent intervals.

In the college world, the main pension events have been these:

- Establishment of the Carnegie free pension system in 1905.
- Establishment of TIAA in 1918. The first college retirement plans with TIAA were almost all based on institutional and individual total contributions of 10 percent of salary. This provided, after a normal college career of 30 to 40 years, a modest retirement benefit during stable economic times.
- Broad-based effort, starting in the late 1930s and carried on through the 1960s, to provide larger pension contributions and therefore more adequate benefits. The better college plans moved up to about 15 percent of salary.
- Extension of Social Security to private colleges in 1951 and public institutions in 1955.
- Introduction of CREF in 1952.
- Vast expansion of TIAA-CREF among public colleges and universities, first with single retirement plans like in the private

colleges and universities and then with a flood of optional retirement plans providing a choice between TIAA-CREF or an existing public retirement system.

- Renewed emphasis on personal savings. This was encouraged by favorable federal tax laws, starting in the college world in 1958.
- Introduction by TIAA-CREF of:
  Unlimited CREF participation in 1971.
  Retirement transition benefit in 1972.
  Supplemental retirement annuities in 1973.
  TIAA graded benefit payment method in 1982.
  Money market account in April 1988.
  Bond market and Social choice accounts in March 1990.

CARNEGIE FREE PENSIONS

Andrew Carnegie and Henry Pritchett established a generous free pension system when the Carnegie Foundation was established in 1905. The original stipend was $400 plus half salary for those whose service made them eligible for full pensions. Because salaries of professors averaged about $1,800 a year, this meant a take-home ratio of 72 percent. Plus there were no federal income taxes to pay; they were not imposed until 1913. This take-home amount was more generous than retirement income objectives in use for the next half-century. The objective was well chosen, if only enough money had been there; only a few thousand professors actually received the half salary plus $400. Most received a reduced amount of $1,000 from CFAT plus a $500 Carnegie Corporation-purchased annuity.

TIAA FUNDED PENSIONS

The next attempt, establishment of TIAA in 1918, proved flexible and enduring. At first, the new plan was based on voluntary participation by individuals. It assumed, "The obligation to secure protection for himself and his family rests first upon the individual." The new plan recommended an equal sharing of contributions, 5 percent by the individual and 5 percent by the college, to purchase an annuity. With then prevailing interest rates and flattened salary scales, and the overly generous annuity mortality tables in general use, this would provide a sufficient annuity over a career to give a satisfactory standard of living in retirement. Those who elected to participate would-have far better protection than that available to other professional groups.

By the end of World War II, the college pension system was strongly in place, covering well over 300 institutions of higher education. But during TIAA's first 30 years, interest rates declined and more realistic mortality tables were adopted. This substantially reduced expected annuity income and rendered inadequate the prevailing contribution level of 10 percent of salary. By the mid-1940s, the 10 percent retirement plans were providing about one third of salary as a benefit for persons who were covered by the college retirement system for most of their working career.

TOWARD HIGHER CONTRIBUTIONS

By 1947, interest rates on long-term obligations of the type suitable for pension plans had declined to less than 3 percent. The life insurance companies in America were earning 2.88 percent on their assets.[1] TIAA's earnings, as they always have been, were above the average for the life insurance companies but at that time only slightly. Concurrently, there were substantial declines in mortality rates assumed for writing annuity plans.

These factors introduced a long effort by the colleges to achieve more adequate benefits through increasing their total annuity contributions to above 10 percent of salary. The first major institution to adopt a new schedule was Columbia University. In 1945, Columbia moved up to 15 percent total contributions shared equally between the participant and the university.[2] While Columbia was the first institution to move to this more generous level, it also was the last to discard a maximum benefit purchase. For many years, Columbia ceased contributing to a participant's annuity contract when a single life annuity of $4,000 a year beginning at age 65 had been purchased. This was a substantial annuity at the time. But such maximums, whether in college plans or in federal limits on IRAs, Keogh, or other plans, tend to reflect populist ideas as to "how much is enough" rather than the realities of inflation.

For the coming years, a strong trend had set in toward 15 percent contribution rates in the colleges, producing much more adequate benefits.

SOCIAL SECURITY AND CREF

Two crucial events occurred from 1951 to 1955. Social Security was extended to college employees, and CREF was introduced. The first half of the 20th century had produced substantial effort by the colleges and their staff members to build a sound, effective retirement system providing at least minimal financial security during retire-

---

[1]WCG, *A New Approach*, p. 51.
[2]WCG, *College Retirement and Insurance Plans*, pp. 99–100.

ment. The second half, inaugurating Social Security and CREF, would see the goal raised to generous, inflation-hedged, annuity income approaching the same standard of living in retirement as enjoyed in the highest earning years just before retirement. And the higher goal would be mostly reached by the early 1980s.

In adjusting to Social Security, most colleges with plans calling for 10 or 12 percent of salary contributions added Social Security taxes and benefits right on top. Most of those with 15 percent plans adopted step-rate plans with annuity contributions of 10 percent on the first $4,800 of salary (then the Social Security wage base) and 15 percent on salary above that level. Contributions in these patterns provided TIAA plus Social Security benefits after 35 years of service of nearly 80 percent of final salary for lower paid persons under the most generous plans to only 40 percent for higher paid staff members under 10 percent plans.

OPTIONAL RETIREMENT PLANS

A major development led to many more college staff members being covered by the portable retirement system. Large public institutions were early participants in TIAA. The University of Michigan was in at the start in 1919, and state universities such as Alabama, Arkansas, and Colorado in the 1920s, the four public colleges and universities in Indiana in 1937, and the three in Iowa in 1944 established plans over the years. Joining in the postwar period were the University of Vermont in 1946, Washington State University in 1948, and the University of Tennessee in 1955. In 1958, Detroit's city university, Wayne, became a state university and had to withdraw from the underfunded city retirement system, a complicated maneuver. It established a new TIAA-CREF plan. Michigan State University joined the same year. In 1961, five Kansas public institutions became participating institutions; in 1962, 11 West Virginia public institutions established TIAA-CREF plans to supplement the existing public plan.

With the phenomenal growth of public higher education in America, TIAA-CREF established a special force to work with the burgeoning institutions. The impetus came from the employees who wished to escape from limited-vesting public retirement plans under which they would lose much of their retirement savings if they left the employing institution. The state colleges and universities were interested in improving their competitiveness in attracting scarce academic talent. Associations of state college presidents or statewide faculty associations such as AAUP delegations usually led the effort to establish plans with TIAA-CREF.

In the mid-1960s, a new wave of public college and university interest commenced. Previously, public institutions were covered either by a public system, the most frequent arrangement, or TIAA-CREF, as the only plan. Now, state after state sought TIAA-CREF plans as an optional retirement plan (ORP) choice for its staff members. College staff members were allowed to choose to participate either in TIAA-CREF or the state teacher or public employee retirement system.

The first major plan of this kind was for the State University of New York. Governor Nelson Rockefeller decided strengthening public higher education was a keystone of his administration. As one of his actions, he approved on April 3, 1964, establishment of an ORP for 30 units of the State University. Dr. Samuel Gould, chancellor of the State University, was instrumental in the work leading to the new plan, which went into effect July 1, 1964. Of the 16,000 State University of New York employees currently eligible for the ORP, 12,000 have elected TIAA-CREF.

The City University of New York followed in 1967, as did the public institutions in Oregon. In 1968, the New York State Community Colleges established ORPs. The trend continued strongly throughout the 1970s and 1980s, with ORPs established for the Florida State University System in 1983 and the Virginia State system in 1984. By 1989, TIAA-CREF retirement plans were in effect at publicly supported colleges and universities in 36 states and the District of Columbia, including an optional retirement plan in 20 states.

The wave of public institutions with ORP or single TIAA-CREF plans led to stunning growth. The 600 participating institutions now account for about half of the policyholders in the system.

INDIVIDUAL TAX-DEFERRED SAVINGS

The college world was a precursor in the development of tax-deferred voluntary individual savings for retirement. In 1958, a small seed was planted by the college world; 16 years later, Congress extended the idea to Keogh plans, tax sheltered annuities, individual retirement accounts (IRAs), and other inducements to individual savings.

It happened this way. College contributions to participants' annuities have been "before tax" dollars to the individuals since the start of TIAA in 1918, as are employer contributions to qualified pension plans. This was formalized in broader amendments to the Internal Revenue Code in 1942. In the 1950s, the School of Medicine at Washington University of St. Louis, encouraged by Thomas Blackwell, university business officer, and the Johns Hopkins Medical School offered their medical doctors on the staff an arrangement whereby doctors could designate their entire salary or any part of it as annuity premiums, before taxes. Many doctors jumped at this chance. TIAA was concerned about this practice and challenged both its validity and wisdom, with good response from all but a handful of medical schools to which the practice had spread.

The IRS became interested, and a high Treasury official, Dan Throop Smith, a former professor at the Harvard Business School, pressed an amendment to the Internal Revenue Code that would limit tax-deferred college contributions to annuities to 10 percent of current salary. Congress considered this suggestion. The heads of several educational associations and I appeared before the staff of a joint committee. The discussion was not going well. The excesses of a few part-time doctors at a few medical schools were leading to an inappropriate threat to retirement security for large numbers of college employees.

I repeat the following incident because it makes a point about the far greater generosity of Congress and the IRS toward benefit plans for industry than for those in the nonprofit sector. I finally said, in exasperation:

> Look, Congress has given business concerns half-a-dozen ways for their people, especially top executives, to squirrel away sizable pretax savings. In a defined benefit pension plan, a company may have to contribute large amounts of money, *50, 100 percent of salary* for some years to fund benefits for a top executive who has many years of service. *In addition*, it can provide him a profit-sharing plan. *And* a stock option plan. *And* a bonus plan. *And* a few other plans. Colleges do not have these other opportunities, and you want to limit their pension plan contributions to a measly 10 percent of salary, only a fraction of what industry can do in its pension plan alone. Colleges have enough trouble competing for top brainpower without this!

The final result was a reasonable compromise, permitting annuity contributions of up to 20 percent of current salary, with a formula for past service. In the Technical Amendments Act of 1958, Congress added Section 403(b) to the Internal Revenue Code as a replacement for all that had gone before in the college world. It was a restricted substitute for "qualification" by IRS of pension plans in industry.

Section 403(b) clarified the status of employer contributions to retirement systems in the educational world. But the unexpected development was that the individual could *voluntarily* elect to fill the rest of the 20 percent if his or her employer was not contributing the full amount. The individual could transform part of his or her salary into "employer contributions" to an annuity under Section 403(b) by so-called salary reduction. By doing this, he or she could defer taxes until annuity income was received.

A clear distinction needs to be made between benefits provided by the basic college retirement plan supported by institutional contributions and those arising from the extra savings of individuals. The latter are fully the individual's own funds, to be used how, when, and where the individual wishes. Cash values are appropriate for extra contributions. If the extra contributions enjoy special tax treatment, they may be subject to substantial restrictions as to withdrawal and taxing.

Beyond the College World

The 403(b) action by Congress in 1958 for the college world turned out to be the first small step toward a number of significant moves by Congress to provide tax incentives to encourage individual savings for retirement. Congress and the administration became more interested in pension coverage for the large number of Americans not included under formal employer plans. In 1962, Congress established Keoghs through the Self-Employed Individuals Tax Retirement Act for small-business owners, farmers, professional practitioners, and their employees.[3] The emphasis was still on *employer.*

In 1965, a Cabinet-level study was released, titled "Public Policy and Private Pension Programs." Bills were pending in Congress, with Senators Jacob Javits, Vance Hartke, Ralph Yarborough, and others calling for earlier vesting, disclosure, fiduciary standards, and communications with participants in employer plans.

Pensions Are for People

The good experience in the college world with Section 403(b) led me to wonder whether this might be a pattern for encouragement and regulation of pensions and individual savings for the general public. Following my Huebner Foundation Lecture, titled "Pensions Are for People," at the University of Pennsylvania in January 1968,[4] I testified before congressional committees in March 1970 and June 1972. My crucial points were:

1. Some of the then focus of pension planning should be shifted from employer interests to protection of participant interests, helping achieve earlier vesting, more adequate funding, better portability.

---

[3]Emily S. Andrews, *The Changing Profile of Pensions in America* (Washington, D.C.: Employee Benefit Research Institute, 1985), p. 86.

[4]WCG, "Pensions Are for People. The 'ERITD' (Earned Retirement Income Tax Deferral) Approach to Federal Regulation of Pensions," in *Insurance, Government and Social Policy: Studies in Insurance Regulation,* ed. Spencer L. Kimball and Herbert S. Denenberg (Homewood, Ill.: Richard D. Irwin, for S. S. Huebner Foundation for Insurance Education, 1969) pp. 389–410.

2. Tax deferral for individuals on up to 20 percent of income set aside for retirement in approved systems.
3. Tax deferral only for funds actually set aside as pensions in the name of individuals.
4. Full disclosure of all pertinent facts regarding investing, plan provisions, management, and fiduciary responsibilities of approved programs.

When these conditions were met, qualifying contributions would be deductible by an employer as a business expense and tax-deferred for the individual until retirement.

By this time, many voices were to be heard in America recommending additional congressional encouragement of pension savings.

Action by Congress

In 1974, Congress took a major step toward encouraging personal savings for retirement. It established individual retirement accounts under the Employee Retirement Income Security Act of 1974 (ERISA). This extended the system of individual tax deferrals to workers not under an employer-sponsored plan. The Economic Recovery Tax Act of 1981 extended the IRA option to virtually all workers and their spouses. IRAs became enormously popular.

Congress established 401(k) plans in 1981, permitting employer-sponsored deferred compensation arrangements within certain parameters.

Thus, the system of tax encouragement for individual retirement savings that was initiated on a small scale in the college world in 1958 has helped lead to a half-trillion-dollar addition to the retirement savings of the American people. Individual annuity sales in America were $32 billion in 1987, up 30 percent from the previous year.

Just as things were going well in this area of savings and capital formation, the 1986 Tax Reform Act cut back severely on various individual savings and deferred income arrangements, a probable mistake in public policy.

INCREASED GOALS

A 1959 TIAA study provided a timely warning about offset plans:

Since Social Security taxes are scheduled to increase to 9 percent of covered salary by 1969, without compensating increases in benefits, a plan that continues to reduce annuity contributions by the full amount of the increasing Social Security taxes results in continually reducing benefit expectations, especially for new younger entrants to the retirement plan.[5]

Not only did the tax rate increase, but also the wage base escalated even more rapidly, so that in 1990, the tax rate for the old age, survivors, and disability portion is 12.4 percent total, shared between employee and employer, on a wage base of $51,300.

By 1969, the AAUP-AAC statement recommended an after-tax retirement income "equivalent in purchasing power to approximately two thirds of the yearly disposable income realized from his salary after taxes and other mandatory deductions during his last few years of full-time employment." And there should be "provision for continuing more than half of such income to a surviving spouse." The good college plans were exceeding this objective.

A special 1972–73 AAUP Subcommittee on TIAA-CREF recommended annuity contributions that are lower at younger ages and increase substantially in the 10 or 15 years before retirement, the "saving" years. A number of colleges provide this. This committee also recommended certain increases in cashable options, incorporated in the supplemental retirement annuity (SRA) policies of TIAA-CREF in 1973. It took special note of CREF's use of an assumed interest rate of 4 percent as the base for starting the computation of annuity benefits each year and suggested TIAA might use the same system.

RETIREMENT TRANSITION BENEFIT

In 1972, TIAA introduced a new option, the retirement transition benefit (RTB). Under this arrangement, retiring participants may take up to 10 percent of their accumulation in either TIAA or CREF, or both, as a lump-sum payment. The full 10 percent means a doubling (roughly) of the first year's retirement income, with a reduction of aggregate future retirement income by the same 10 percent. The act of retirement frequently brings extra expenses, for moving to a new house or city, for travel, for delayed maintenance (on either residence or self), for doing those things for which there has been no time.

Employing institutions were given a choice as to whether they wanted the option extended to their retiring staff members. Of the first 2,000 institutions acting, only 42 elected not to permit the option.

One out of five retiring TIAA-CREF annuitants elect the RTB. Not all of those who so elect take the full 10 percent.

---

[5]WCG and Francis P. King, *Retirement and Insurance Plans in American Colleges* (New York: Columbia University Press, 1959), p. 99.

SUPPLEMENTAL RETIREMENT ANNUITIES

TIAA-CREF in 1973 introduced special new supplemental retirement annuity (SRA) contracts so individuals could increase their own voluntary before-tax savings through employer cooperation. The SRAs provide cash values for policyholders who wish it in addition to or instead of an annuity. They have been widely used for individual savings.

USING INVESTMENTS

On Behalf of Savers

Politicians, businesspeople, economists, and the general public give much lip service to the importance of savings in the American economy. They talk with admiration of the savings rates in Japan and Germany; they complain that the United States is toward the bottom of the list of savers in the Western world. In the next sentence, they ask for lower interest rates to avoid a recession and to increase the competitiveness of American business, as mentioned in Part Three. Not content, they espouse a lower value for the American dollar in order to enhance the competitiveness of American products abroad. And public policy results in a Grand Canyon-sized federal debt, with its implications for inflation.

Someone should speak up for the American saver, the saver who defers consumption in order to be secure in old age. Low interest rates and a lower value for the American dollar hurt savers in three main ways:

1. Lower earnings on their savings.
2. Greater inflation, resulting from lower interest rates during some phases of business conditions.
3. Higher prices for imported goods and foreign travel and for some domestic goods, because of the depreciating dollar.

Perhaps part of the reason for the low rate of saving in America can be found here. Fortunately, during recent years, the saver is earning a reasonable real rate of interest.

Fixed-Dollar Annuity Inflation Hedge

Social Security directly links its benefits to the consumer price index. CREF provides a direct link of annuity benefits to the investment experience of equities, which over the long run has helped retirement income adjust to changes in the cost of living much of the time.

Here comes a surprise, and a welcome one. Fixed-dollar annuities used in defined contribution plans can provide a surprisingly large amount of protection from inflation for retired people.

The 1951 economic studies leading to the establishment of CREF shattered the illusion that fixed-dollar annuities were conservative, risk-free providers of retirement income. The studies brought out the fact that preservation of principal in dollar terms was not enough to provide economic security over the many years of retirement enjoyed by most people. More was necessary—preservation of income levels in terms of purchasing power; hence, CREF.

Hence, TIAA also, as it has turned out! During the last half of the 20th century, TIAA and other defined contribution plans have provided growing and now substantial financial protection for annuitants against inflation. This has come about partly because of the strong upward secular trend of interest earnings on long-term investments. Real rates of interest—nominal rates minus the inflation rate—turned positive for savers during most recent years.

During the post-World War II years, TIAA increased its investment earning rate rapidly as a result of rapidly rising interest rates and efficient investment policies. From a net rate of 2.96 percent on assets in 1948, it rose in the ensuing decades to 3.95 (1958), 5.45 (1968), 8.71 (1978), and 10.70 (1988). This rate of TIAA earnings provides savers with a reasonable real reward, or "rental value of money" of about 4 percent a year, plus about 6 percent a year additional reward to hedge against inflation. In addition to the strong performance of long-term interest rates, TIAA began in the late 1960s and early 1970s to obtain "kickers" on its investments, or shares in equity earnings. This included warrants to purchase stock, leveraged buyouts, escalating rentals from shopping centers, office buildings and industrial park buildings, and real estate ownership.

Now for the key question—can individuals defer some part of annuity income to their later retirement years in order to have that income adjust better to inflation as time passes? This the TIAA graded benefit payment method annuity option does.

TIAA Graded Benefit—Inflation Help

One of the most important and basic recent changes in life annuity income is the TIAA graded benefit payment method (GBPM), made available to policyholders January 1, 1982.

The GBPM option allows TIAA retirees to choose a low initial monthly payout when they first retire and then to receive increasing annuity amounts when TIAA adds retained and current dividends. This provides an option to the traditional type of fixed annuity that starts out much higher in dollar amount but tends to remain level throughout the retirement years. The GBPM option is essentially adapted from CREF, which uses an assumed interest rate of 4 percent, with the annuity amount paid each year depending on whether total investment experience exceeded or was below 4 percent the previous year.

The TIAA GBPM system also assumes that interest earnings will be 4 percent, and the first year's annuity is based on the 4 percent, providing a low annuity that year. Earnings over 4 percent are plowed back to purchase additional future lifetime income. The second year's annuity payment to participants equals the first year's payment plus an amount available from annuitization of the plowed-back savings. For example, during interest earnings at 1988 levels, payments under the graded method start out at perhaps 40 percent below high fixed benefits, but they can be expected to increase about 5 percent to 8 percent a year in the future.

This means annuity checks would double in 9 to 15 years and quadruple in 18 or more years. This can help materially in meeting the financial dangers of "living too long" in an inflationary economy. Because a husband and wife about age 65 have a future life span between them of some 27 years, they can expect substantial inflation and, if they have elected a two-life option with the graded benefit, a substantial compensating increase in annuity income from TIAA over the period as some protection against that inflation.

The GBPM option does not sell itself; relatively few TIAA annuitants choose it. "Why give up the early income; I'll never live that long!" Most people underestimate the typical life span. There is a better than 50-50 chance that one member of a couple age 65 will be alive a quarter of a century later, at age 90. The much lower initial income under the GBPM is immediately apparent to persons starting their annuities; the possible doubling of annuity checks in about 10 years and quadrupling in some 18 to 20 years seems a long way off.

The vast majority of the retirees transferring from CREF to TIAA at retirement choose the high levelized TIAA annuity payout. It may be that a concerted effort to explain and demonstrate the differences between a high level benefit and a low initial increasing benefit is necessary to have significant use of these devices to help protect retirement income against inflation.

This brings up the subject of quality of retirement benefit. Retirement plans used to be designed to provide level benefits throughout retirement. Even relatively mild inflation can seriously erode income over long periods. The CREF benefit based on an assumed investment rate of 4 percent plus the TIAA graded benefit with 4 percent assumed interest rate provide an opportunity for retirement benefits to increase substantially during retirement, and this may well be called "quality" of benefits.

Development of GBPM Annuity

In November 1978, we asked Thomas Walsh, then TIAA vice president and actuary, to make a detailed study of income patterns that would have been provided by TIAA if it fixed the assumed interest rate at 4 percent and used extra earnings to increase annuity dividends year by year during retirement. His studies confirmed the opportunities for substantial inflation coverage over the retirement years.

Support for the idea came from a paper given by John H. Biggs, then a vice chancellor of Washington University, St. Louis, in a paper presented in October 1980 to the Consortium on Financing Higher Education. COFHE was giving increased attention to retirement matters at the time. Biggs recommended that TIAA should, like CREF, also offer a 4 percent assumed interest rate, with excess earnings over the 4 percent rate increasing the annuity for future years. With his university background, he made a telling argument for such a plan. Universities, in their endowment management, try to plow back capital appreciation to help the endowment avoid depreciation from inflation; individuals should do the same thing with their retirement savings.

Biggs became a trustee of TIAA in 1983 and president early in 1989.

The graded benefit system when used in private pension systems has broad implications. Witnesses appearing before the President's Commission on Pension Policy, on which I served in 1979–81, stated emphatically that private pensions could not solve any material part of America's need for retirement income for its citizens; only Social Security could do much about inflation. Social Security does and should have its inflation escalator. But in addition, variable annuity defined contribution pension plans based on equity investments, plus graded benefit plans based on debt obligations, can help meet this pension need. Defined benefit plans also meet the needs for inflation occurring before retirement.

Winning Financial Security

For 70 years, the colleges and their staff members, the educational associations, and TIAA and then CREF kept moving the target back, as aim improved, as ability to achieve ever-increasing retirement income objectives developed. First, in 1905, it was adequate free pensions for a few thousand professors and their wives. Then it was contributory pensions for those in the profession who would participate with their college, but at a very modest level. Then it was gradual improvement in the level of pensions, through effort on the investment side and added contributions from colleges and participants. Then adequate income for spouses was achieved and protection from the erosion of inflation.

Each time the AAUP-AAC and TIAA moved the target, they did so to an achievable goal and, when achieved, moved it again. During the process, the college world built the $83 billion pool, TIAA-CREF, as part of their retirement and insurance savings.

Ninety eight percent of TIAA-CREF annuitants now receive Social Security benefits, and 90 percent receive some income from investments. Social Security and TIAA-CREF together provide two thirds of retirement income, with earnings supplying only 5 percent for persons already receiving retirement income.

With few exceptions, people near retirement age in 1989 are showing combined benefits above the 60 percent to 70 percent income replacement level if they have been TIAA-CREF premium-paying participants for 30 to 35 years. For persons now participating with 10 or more years of contributions ahead of them, many can look forward to replacement ratios of 75 percent or more. These developments have introduced a good new world of adequate lifetime annuities, one that lifts the largest financial risk from individuals, that of living too long, financially.

Financial security in retirement is, like democracy, a goal that must be rewon by each generation. So the job has only started.

IT'S MY MONEY

Dr. Richard Niebling chooses an intriguing medium to express his loyalty to his pension companies. This is a 1961 photo of Dr. Niebling, teacher of English at Phillips Exeter Academy, New Hampshire.

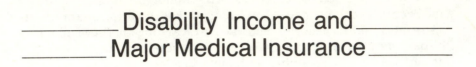

CHAPTER 17

Disability Income and Major Medical Insurance

THE NEED

As the colleges, their staff members, and TIAA-CREF worked together over the years, life became much more secure for retired college staff members. In general, pensions were adequate and, supplemented by Social Security, beginning to be comfortable, for long-service people who stayed within the fully vested, portable TIAA-CREF system throughout their careers—*if they remained healthy.*

But poor health sometimes intervened in two ways. A few, not many but a hard-hit few, college staff members became totally disabled before retirement. They not only lost their current income, but they usually also had heavy medical expenses. Moreover, their contributions to pensions may have stopped. Still other staff members were making it well on their salaries or pensions until major medical bills consumed their incomes or even destroyed their life savings.

The original Carnegie Commission in 1916–18 leading to the establishment of TIAA recognized the financial problems related to disability but not the heavy medical expense risk. It concluded, "The risk of disability will not at present be dealt with by the association, but will be provided for by the Carnegie Foundation." This was done in the Carnegie free pension system.

TIAA's original charter provided for insurance "upon the lives or the health of persons" as well as annuities. TIAA did not issue disability income insurance at the time, even though a number of commercial life insurance companies were doing so. This turned out to be a good financial decision for TIAA; commercial insurers suffered substantial losses on their disability income plans. This was especially true during the Great Depression when disability claims rose in proportion to the loss of jobs and the insurance companies found themselves providing a substitute for unemployment insurance. Commercial insurers almost ceased writing disability insurance during the 1930s. By the mid-1950s, some companies had returned to disability income insurances but issued only short-term "sickness" coverage. A few offered lifetime coverage for disability caused by accident, but only for five years in event of illness. This is a sort of "get them out of sight" provision that does not solve the problem of long-term disability income protection.

In 1953–54, the Ford Foundation's Fund for the Advancement of Education asked TIAA to study whether there was a practical way to improve financing the college education of faculty children. A study was published under that title by Dr. Francis P. King, TIAA research scholar.[1] The study concluded faculty members were concerned as to their ability to provide the same educational advantages for their children as they had had. But long-term economic risks also concerned them greatly. These included, along with adequate income for their retirement, income if they became totally disabled, income for their survivors in event of their early death, and insurance to meet catastrophic medical expenses.

In April 1954, TIAA invited a number of college business officers to an advisory conference to discuss disability income insurance. The purpose of the meeting was to test whether there was a demand as well as a need on the part of colleges and faculty members for disability coverage and whether such coverage would be feasible within college budgets. The question of whether such coverage could be written on a sound basis, after so much poor experience in the commercial world, was accepted by TIAA as its problem to solve. In general, the college business officers were supportive and even enthusiastic. A few indicated there were so few, or no, cases of disability on their campuses that they questioned whether the experimental premiums were too high.

The Committee on Insurance and Annuities of the Association of American Colleges under the chairmanship of Dr. Mark H. Ingraham was asked to consider the suggestion for new insurances. The head of the AAC at the time was Theodore A. Distler. The relevant committee conclusions from the report follow:

> (5) *Group medical insurance.* It is the judgment of the committee that the recent development of "Major Medical" or catastrophic medical insurance is of considerably more importance than the more limited medical insurance previously on the market. . . .

---

[1]Francis P. King, *Financing the College Education of Faculty Children.* A Study Conducted by Teachers Insurance and Annuity Association for the Fund for the Advancement of Education (New York: Henry Holt and Company, 1954).

(6) *Group disability insurance.* . . . To the institution this is of even greater importance than the catastrophic medical coverage since there is always the temptation, often a moral obligation, to keep an individual on the payroll for a prolonged period even though his services may be nonexistent or minimal. . . .

Disability insurance currently on the market is designed only for short-time protection. . . . We urge [TIAA] to use its offices to further plans for the initiation of [a long-term disability income program].[2]

TIAA decided to ask the Ford Foundation in late summer 1955 for support for development of a new program of major medical and disability insurance. Its first step was to conduct a market survey among 1,165 colleges, universities, and other educational institutions to help "determine whether there was a *real* and *effective* demand" for major medical and disability insurances. It also sought attitudes toward desired provisions of any new coverages. By the end of May 1956, half the colleges had responded.

The key question was: "What is your best guess as to whether your institution would establish within the next three years a TIAA plan covering Major Medical expenses?"

Thirty percent of all colleges responding would establish a major medical plan; 39 percent would not; and 31 percent were undecided or did not answer. The count by number of staff members came out about the same.

The market survey also disclosed that more than half the institutions establishing a plan would expect to cover all employees; 96 percent would make dependent coverage, that is, insurance for spouse and children, available to the staff; 40 percent would pay half the premium; nearly 30 percent would not contribute; and only 12 percent would pay the full premium.

The study was made in 1956, at which time it was found that 93 percent of colleges had basic medical coverage, mostly Blue Cross-Blue Shield, but only 11 percent had any form of major medical coverage. TIAA decided to move ahead and develop a major medical plan. TIAA did not consider its place in catastrophic medical coverage to be either unique or crucial, as it was with pensions and disability income. But since only 1 out of 10 colleges had major medical expense coverage for their staff members, TIAA concluded it had a function to perform, both in developing with the college world adequate catastrophic health care insurance and in extending such coverage to the institutions. TIAA confirmed its decision not to provide basic hospital and medical insurance because Blue Cross and Blue Shield were providing this coverage throughout the United States.

---

[2]Mark H. Ingraham, Committee on Insurance and Annuities, Association of American Colleges, extract from report, January 9, 1956, WCG files.

College demand for disability insurance was much lighter, with 23 percent answering "would establish," 44 percent "would not," and 33 percent undecided or no answer. While the indicated demand for disability income insurance was less than for major medical, the need for TIAA to establish disability income insurance was much greater because there was no equivalent to Blue Cross-Blue Shield to provide limited but valuable coverage, and the few commercial insurers that ever issued it had mostly given it up in the 1930s. Disability coverage could fill a pressing need for college staff members, one not being met at that time. It was a benefit plan that TIAA was uniquely in a position to provide successfully. TIAA could combine its annuities with a new disability plan to provide lifetime income in case of disability. Its knowledge of the college world could lead to developing an economical plan that met educators' needs.

TIAA's decision was to provide both major medical and disability programs for the colleges. After an initial push on major medical, TIAA would concentrate its long-term selling efforts on disability insurance. It would expect the disability income benefits to grow steadily over the years.

FORD FOUNDATION

With the results of the market survey in hand and its own analysis of the opportunities, TIAA requested from the Ford Foundation a grant of up to $5 million. Of this grant, $500,000 would be used for organization and development costs, and $4.5 million would be available for takedown over a 10-year period to provide contingency reserves equal to premiums in force for the two new kinds of insurance coverage. Thus, the foundation would pick up the research and development expenses, plus the initial contingency reserves and risk premium for TIAA's experimenting with total lifetime protection for disability and innovative provisions in major medical insurance.

Both the foundation and TIAA agreed that contingency reserves from the foundation were needed for experimental forms of insurance, especially the long-term total disability coverage. From its start, TIAA had concentrated on life insurance and annuity protection. Under both of these coverages, the only significant risk factor was to determine whether a professor was alive or dead, and we could almost always tell which. Under the new forms, large risks were undertaken on individual lives, without adequate data on which to set premiums or define disability.

Much of the actuarial analysis for the Ford Foundation submission was prepared by Robert J. Randall, associate actuary of TIAA-

CREF. Randall was the first black to become a Fellow of the Society of Actuaries and, when he joined TIAA-CREF in 1953, the first black to become an officer of a major insurance organization. This was a decade before the passage of the Civil Rights Act of 1964, and I was pleased that TIAA-CREF had taken a positive step forward in establishing an equal opportunity employment policy.

The board of trustees of the Ford Foundation approved the $5 million grant in July 1956. The Ford Foundation representative in the deliberations toward the grant was William McPeak, who had been head of the Ford Motor Company's foundation before joining the Ford Foundation.

There was almost universal applause for the announcement of the Ford Foundation grant to establish the new benefit forms. TIAA files contain copies of only two critical letters, both from life insurance agents from the same address in St. Louis, addressed to Henry Ford II. And the Ford Foundation received one questioning the grant. A letter prepared by TIAA on request from the foundation stated:

> The Foundation grant was made partly to enable TIAA once again to develop a "product" along the special lines required by its educational clientele. For example, long-term total disability income insurance is rarely found in benefit plans, either in industry or the colleges. Insurance companies have not generally made this type of coverage available on a group basis, but after the grant was made a number of insurers showed a renewed interest in offering protection in this area. . . .
>
> It seems probable that the life insurance companies will be interested in a carefully managed pilot experiment in long-term disability income insurance. The argument is heard often in Washington these days that private enterprise is not meeting the needs of the American public. Heavy pressures have been exerted on Congress to have the federal government take over this entire sphere of activity and recent Social Security amendments and proposals are indications of the effectiveness of such pressures. A well-conceived program by TIAA may help point the way toward meeting these needs through private enterprise.[3]

McPeak's studies had looked into the competitive questions and concluded as above. He noted a number of foundation grants, like the one to TIAA, that had led to the development of a new product for an entire industry. The grant to TIAA may well have been a key factor in opening the way for renewed interest in disability insurance throughout the economy.

The professionalism and diligence of foundation officers are most impressive. By the time he was through asking questions about

---

[3]Draft by TIAA of possible reply, September 8, 1959, WCG files.

TIAA, its proposed new benefit plans, its market survey, and its management, Bill McPeak was thoroughly conversant with all important aspects of the recipient organization. TIAA had gone through just such a thorough and professional analysis by Dr. James A. Perkins for the last of the Carnegie Corporation grants on behalf of the old annuity contracts in 1952 and by Carnegie for its previous grants.[4]

DESIGNING MAJOR MEDICAL COVERAGE

During the preliminary studies, TIAA used Wendell Milliman, experienced consulting actuary, for technical advice. When the decision to proceed was made, the first action was to bring in two able young group insurance experts from insurance companies to help design, install, and then operate the new coverages.

Charles E. Wilson, age 35, received his B.A. from the University of Iowa, was Phi Beta Kappa, and majored in actuarial mathematics. He formerly was with the Group Underwriting Department of the Equitable Life Assurance Society. Wilson was made head of the TIAA Actuarial Department in 1971, serving until his retirement in 1986.

James G. MacDonald, age 31, received his B.A. from Hobart College, and he was group underwriter with the New York Life Insurance Company. MacDonald became head of the TIAA Group Department and rose to the presidency of TIAA from 1979 to 1984, then serving as chairman to 1987.

TIAA's chairman in 1956, Mac Lloyd, appointed a Major Medical and Disability Insurance Committee to develop all aspects of the new coverages. Members were this author, Robert M. Duncan, Thomas C. Edwards, John Paul Good, Wilmer A. Jenkins, MacDonald, and Wilson.

Challenges and Solutions

Challenge: Should TIAA plans supplement Blue Cross-Blue Shield and other base plans or replace them?

By 1956, Blue Cross-Blue Shield had become a standard staff benefit plan in industry and in four out of five of the colleges. Most of

---

[4]I do remember one costly incident for me. One Monday I was working with a battery of lawyers from the Ford Foundation, TIAA, and the New York Insurance Department, regarding the final details of the grant to TIAA. My secretary sent in a little note, "Your wife called; call her if you can." It was not one of those days on which I could call her. Doris met me at the door that night with the attention-getting sentence: "You didn't call, so I went ahead and bought the piano." We hadn't even discussed a piano! I considered, but only for the briefest moment, sending the bill to the foundation.

the others had some form of basic hospital coverage. The Blues have served Americans well for 60 years.[5] They started out as a pioneering method of meeting medical costs, but they suffered from two major drawbacks: (1) they covered only in-hospital costs, and (2) they covered the first expenses but were not sufficiently comprehensive when expenses mounted and really began to hurt.

The committee proceeded to address the many aspects of the new coverages.

Solution: TIAA decided not to write base plan coverage because Blue Cross-Blue Shield was serving that market well.

Challenge: In 1956, major medical coverage was a confusing hodgepodge of miscellaneous benefit provisions. Varying from plan to plan were the maximum benefits, deductibles, types of coverage (per cause or calendar year), maximum dollar benefits per day in the hospital, coverage of osteopathic expenses, treatment of mental illnesses, coverage for retired employees, and on and on.

Solution: The solution arrived at was to develop an optimum plan. The studies of college preferences were used to choose from among the wide variety of available options and combinations of options the one pattern that TIAA would recommend to the colleges as achieving a desirable balance between benefits and costs.

To summarize the major standard provisions, the optimum plan would have a deductible amount of $100 to be paid by the individual before any benefits were paid; then the plan would pay 80 percent of the medical costs up to a $15,000 maximum benefit, and it would use the new TIAA continued expense approach. It could be the sole medical expense program, or it could supplement a Blue Cross-Blue Shield or other base plan.

Although TIAA offered a panoply of major medical options, over 95 percent of the institutions installing TIAA major medical plans in the early years selected the optimum plan. College officers and benefit committees reported that the decision to offer a recommended plan saved a vast amount of benefit plan committee time and helped fulfill TIAA's purpose "of counseling such institutions and their employees concerning pension plans or other measures of security."

Unfortunately, the uniformity and efficiency of TIAA's optimum plan has now been shattered by the dozens of mandated provisions that vary from state to state, as well as federally mandated provisions.

Challenge: In 1956, the usual maximum benefit available was

---

[5]The Blue Cross/Blue Shield system originated, like TIAA, in the college world, when in 1929 an administrator at Baylor University in Dallas, Texas, worked out a plan for hospital care for Dallas school teachers. The concept of community-wide prepayment plans spread rapidly.

$5,000; a few insurers offered $7,500; a rare one, $10,000. It was called a lifetime maximum benefit.

Solution: Fortified with the Ford Foundation grant, TIAA decided to offer a maximum of $15,000, with reinstatements under certain circumstances. Thirty years later, with typical plans providing maximum benefits of $1 million, the 1956 maximum seems quaint. But it required some courage to go to three times the usual maximum provided by the insurance industry, even with foundation support.

Challenge: Faculty members may be more concerned with psychiatric problems than with losing an arm, and yet no one was covering such problems then.

Failure: TIAA instituted psychiatric coverage without restrictions initially. Claims were excessive, and TIAA had to impose restrictions such as limiting the number of visits covered and the annual benefit amount.

Challenge: In 1956, there were two standard types of major medical plan, the *calendar year* and the *per cause*. Under *calendar year* plans, all expenses are accumulated during each separate year to meet the deductible. All expenses regardless of cause are grouped for the purpose of reimbursement and applying the one maximum.

Under the *per cause* method, each different illness requires meeting another deductible and the establishment of a separate reimbursement or benefit period. And each illness had its own maximum so the total benefits could be much greater. Both plans had arbitrary features and were difficult to explain to policyholders.

Solution: To meet these problems, MacDonald and Wilson developed a new form of protection, the continued expense plan. Under this approach, once the insured met the deductible, benefit payments continued for as long as expenses continued at a certain stated level, for up to three years. Any maximum benefit used up was automatically reinstated within a specified dollar amount at the end of each year, without requiring a physical examination.

Challenge: One of the problems the colleges complained about with existing plans was slow payment of claims by commercial insurers. This might have been a serious problem for TIAA, operating as it did without agents, without branch offices, relying entirely on the mails.

Solution: We decided to turn a possible Achilles' heel into an advantage by establishing a "same-day benefit system." The *1958 Annual Report* stated, "When you are sick it is important to get medical expense checks in a hurry; prompt benefit payments help avoid financial worry and anxiety. . . . Over 98 percent of all Major Medical benefit payments have been mailed out *on the same day* the bills were received by TIAA." This same-day service was adhered to for many years after the new plans were established.

Premiums and Benefits

TIAA established a very competitive rate structure. This meant a premium frequently below $1 a month for an employee and about $3 a month for family coverage supplementing Blue Cross-Blue Shield. If the reader finds this hard to believe, remember that the average daily cost for hospital rooms then was between $10 and $20 a day. TIAA made no change in this rate structure during the first seven years, a record not even approached in the double-digit medical expense inflation of more recent years.

Premiums for medical insurance in 1989 bear little relationship to the 1957 premiums. The coverage has expanded considerably, but premiums have soared. It would not be unusual for premiums for a major medical plan where there is no underlying basic plan coverage to be approximately $110 a month for individual coverage and $280 for family coverage. For a major medical plan that supplements basic medical coverage, the rates can vary dramatically, depending on the level of underlying coverage, but $40 for individual coverage and $90 for a family would not be uncommon.

DESIGNING SOUND DISABILITY COVERAGE

TIAA's announcement of its new total disability income plan in 1957 stated:

> The new disability coverage represents a fundamental advance, since long-term disability insurance is rarely found either in business or in the colleges. Such disability occurs rarely, but when it does, it exposes the individual and his or her family to a sustained and usually disastrous financial loss.

The financial loss is usually greater than the one that occurs when the individual dies.

The objective was to establish a plan whereby a college could install a disability income plan financed by premium contributions made jointly by the college and its employees. An insured staff member who became disabled would receive, after six months of disability, monthly benefits of half salary (later increased) up to a reasonable maximum, all the way to age 65 regardless of whether disability was caused by accident or sickness. Lifetime income coverage after age 65 would be provided by the plan's payment during disability of the individual's TIAA-CREF annuity premiums, keeping them in force and growing.

Meanwhile, a large and impressive outfit was working toward providing some disability income protection for American workers— the federal government through the Social Security system. Amid many predictions of disaster, Congress approved a modest program, effective July 1, 1957, providing benefits for workers over age 50 who met a strict definition of disability. Eligible disabled persons would receive Social Security benefits of up to $108.50 a month after a six-month waiting period, continuing during disability to their retirement age. This was to have a profound effect on disability coverage. The TIAA plan would be designed to coordinate with the limited federal plan. In 1960, Congress extended the Social Security plan to workers under age 50 and subsequently legislated several increases in benefits.

Commercial company experience was relevant to the TIAA studies. Montgomery Ward in 1911 purchased a disability income benefit plan that is generally regarded as the first group health insurance policy (group life insurance followed a year later).[6] Written by the London Guarantee and Accident Company of New York, the plan provided coverage for all Montgomery Ward employees under age 70, starting after three days of disability. There was a maximum benefit of $28.85 a week, continuing until the employee was able to return to work.

Other insurers soon began to offer short-term sickness benefits, occasionally reaching out to five years of benefits, and then later providing longer term benefits to age 65. Disability income insurance issued before the Great Depression generally had run into disastrous problems at that time and had been almost entirely discontinued.

At TIAA's request, the actuary Joseph Maclean analyzed the reasons for failure of disability income plans offered by life insurance companies before 1930. He concluded the companies did not know and did not guess very well as to how many workers would become disabled and how long disability would last. They used too short a waiting period and ended up writing temporary sickness insurance on top of the disability coverage. Benefits were payable for life—a very costly life annuity. Claims administration, including checking on recoveries, was lax. Finally, insurance was issued almost to retirement and then continued throughout retirement.

With all the problems, college employees nonetheless needed income protection during disability. Could TIAA, with the backing of the Ford Foundation appropriation, design insurance that would provide greatly needed protection in a viable program? The Major Medical and Disability Committee went to work. It could and did learn much from the outside about what did not work, but it had to figure out for itself what would work.

---

[6]Health Insurance Association of America, *Principles of Group Health Insurance* (Chicago, 1972), Part I, p. 23.

Because of the poor experience, experts in the field of casualty coverages had a deep and abiding suspicion of everyone when it came to claiming benefits, either major medical or disability. The committee embraced the idea that college faculty members and other employees are basically honest and that few would try to "pull fast ones"; that what the insurance industry calls *moral risk* would be less in the college world.

Thus, TIAA's approach to the new programs should be that of wanting to pay benefits, not fight claims. Of course, there should be thorough claims review; improper claims should be resisted; strict auditing methods should be put in place. But the vast majority of requests for benefits would be perfectly proper and valid. The normally used words *claims* and *your case* were dropped and *benefits* and *your payments* were substituted. This may appear to be only semantics, but words can have a powerful effect on the claim-processing employees' attitude toward insured individuals, on such individuals' perception of and approach to TIAA, and the general feel of benefit programs. They should be as positive as possible.

The committee then addressed the design of disability coverage.

Challenges and Solutions

Challenge: To develop a viable, actuarially sound, disability income coverage for college staff members.

Solution: With Ford Foundation backup, the solution was to propose an income plan as a substitute for earnings when disability intervenes, at a feasible cost for the colleges and staff members.

But to help make it actuarially sound, only partial replacement of income, say one half or 60 percent up to a monthly dollar maximum, should be provided to assure that the individual is better off working than languishing in a disabled condition—real or imagined.

Challenge: Provide lifetime income, even though it is impossible in many instances to decide what is total disability during retirement ages.

Solution: Use TIAA-CREF annuities to provide assured income after age 65. Keep them in force from the advent of disability payments until age 65 by having the disability plan pay the annuity premiums in addition to income benefits. This decision was a substantial breakthrough; it allows viable underwriting of an uninsurable risk above age 65, thus assuring lifetime income at reasonable expense.

Challenge: What is *disability*? Permanent? Total? Inability to be a college professor? Or to hold any job?

Solution: The committee concluded the program was not trying to cover short-term sickness benefits; it was better to administer them locally. It also would not cover partial disability; for instance, the loss of an arm or leg, serious as it may be, need not disable most professors. Permanent? Well, yes, except also "temporary long term" from which recovery might occur.

The following definition of disability was chosen: the inability by reason of sickness or bodily injury to engage in any occupation for which the employee is reasonably fitted by education, training, or experience.

Premium Rates, Intelligent Guess?

Little experience was available that could be used as a guide for premium rates. Insured group plans were almost nonexistent, and the only disability income being administered on a group basis was by state teacher and other retirement systems, with benefits provided through reduced retirement income. So the premiums developed under the direction of Robert M. Duncan, TIAA actuary, were in the nature of intelligent guesswork, plus a dollop of standard actuarial conservativism, all backed by the Ford Foundation appropriation.

TIAA estimated that a good disability income plan would cost about 1 percent of salary of participants, including monthly disability income plus current premiums for the individual's annuities. TIAA's experience with disability income insurance turned out well; as a result, premiums were reduced by 25 percent July 1, 1962, the first of several reductions. We finally overdid it and had to increase premiums. The real cost to each college was based both on premiums charged and dividends paid. The latter depended, for disability coverage, largely on the financial experience of all TIAA plans, but for very large institutions, there was a substantial reflection of the institutions' own experience.

THE NEW PLANS START

Two small warmup major medical plans started early—Carnegie Corporation of New York in October 1956 and American University Field Staff in November. Bennington College in Vermont and Union College in New York followed January 1, 1957.

By July 1, 1957, everything was ready for the introduction of disability insurance. Carter Davidson, president of Union College and also president of the Association of American Colleges, wanted Union College to be the first with both new plans and brought in Union College on July 1. The Council on Foreign Relations and West Virginia Wesleyan College also started that day.

Now came the communications effort. TIAA's booklets, pamphlets, articles in the educational press, and college services staff educated the college world to the new coverages in wholesale fashion.

But something more was needed. Once again, as in the case of CREF, TIAA decided to have a series of college institutes to communicate rapidly and efficiently with college officers, trustees, and staff members. From February to May 1959, the company invited college employees to institutes held in central locations to describe the still-new coverages to them. The initial surge had been helpful, and the institutes led to still further interest in adopting these benefits.

Three years later, Donald Willard, in charge of TIAA's college services division, decided to take a hard look at whether the marketing of the new coverages could be improved. This was a period of explosive growth of coverages throughout American employment. By 1960, TIAA was no longer alone in the disability income field; once it had broken the ice, other insurers took up the coverage quickly. Among the large companies were the Prudential, Metropolitan, Connecticut General, New York Life, Liberty Mutual, Equitable, and Continental Assurance.

A committee of TIAA officers analyzed all aspects of TIAA's group coverages and the manner of presenting them to the colleges. The committee concluded: "Our track record in broadening institutional participation in the major medical and disability coverages is not encouraging." And, " Creative plan design is not sufficient by itself to stir many institutions into adopting TIAA disability plans." A TIAA survey in 1960 received 1,232 responses from four-year colleges and universities. Of these, 1005 reported major medical plans, 216, or 22 percent, with TIAA. And 450 institutions reported disability income plans, 281, or 62 percent, with TIAA. Premium cost of disability plans versus the perceived risk was the main deterrent. One out of five major medical plans, and two out of three disability plans, was not bad, but compared with some 90 percent of the private institutions with TIAA-CREF retirement plans, it was not considered good enough. The committee recommended many changes in marketing methods and provisions of the plans, which were implemented.

In the mid-1960s and especially in 1977, TIAA established improved rehabilitation procedures for people suffering disabilities. TIAA started working closely with all disabled benefit recipients who could be helped toward renewed activity, and many recoveries have occurred. TIAA has now added a Social Security assistance program to help eligible people obtain their Social Security benefits.

FINAL FORD GRANT

The Ford Foundation in 1963 paid the last premium-matching installment, completing its $5 million grant three years ahead of time. TIAA's final report and grant request concluded:

The already substantial and growing number of colleges and other educational employers that sponsor these important forms of insurance protection for their staff members, and the expressed appreciation of colleges and individuals, attest to the effectiveness of the Ford Foundation appropriation. The staff and trustees of the Ford Foundation have not had the opportunity, as has TIAA's staff, to work directly with the colleges and their faculties in implementing these plans and seeing how they serve their intended purposes. This has allowed us some estimation of the great appreciation of these joint efforts among the people who are in higher education. On their behalf, TIAA thanks the Ford Foundation for making these coverages possible.

SUBSEQUENT DEVELOPMENTS

TIAA has made a number of major and minor changes in its health coverage for expensive illnesses over the years. Major medical coverage for pensioners was an especial help. It provides an exceedingly efficient source of retirement income protection. Average medical expenses during retirement are high, but their main problem is extreme fluctuation. One person will have painfully high costs; another very little. If everyone tries to accumulate enough retirement income to meet the possible but improbable very high cost of the few, an almost impossible goal is set. But if the cost can be shared by employers and active and retired people, it can be handled efficiently and reduce the total need for retirement income.

TIAA provided major medical coverage for retired people at the outset in 1957. It was for a small amount, a *$2,500 maximum, but medical costs were much less.* Improvements in the experimental benefit program were rapid. Social Security added Medicare in 1965.

Increased Coverage and Benefits

"Gapless" coverage was introduced September 30, 1968, for participants moving from one TIAA plan to another or while on leave for various purposes. Two decades later, gapless coverage was mandated by federal law under the continuation provisions of the Consolidated Budget Reconciliation Act of 1985 applicable to all medical insurance plans in industry.

In June 1969, maximum benefits available were increased to $50,000. The maximum was increased again to $250,000 ($50,000 for treatment of mental or nervous disorders) in October 1973. The maximum was increased in December 1981 to $1 million ($50,000 for treatment of mental or nervous disorders).

TIAA major medical insurance has gradually been extended to many areas not originally insured—licensed practical nurses, some forms of mental illness. Coverage now often extends to psychologists, home health care, alcoholic treatment facilities, outpatient surgical centers, preventive child care, birthing centers, and hospice care.

Control of Expenses

Medical science has advanced exponentially in recent decades. Some of this has caused health to improve and medical expenses to decline; witness the virtual elimination of tuberculosis and polio and the eradication of smallpox. Some of it has led to use of expensive new equipment to achieve improved diagnosis and treatment—CAT scans and magnetic resonance imaging machines. Some costs have risen because the public is demanding more and better services; some from unnecessary tests and procedures (often because of physicians' fear of malpractice suits) and regular costs rising much faster than the cost of living. Some cost increases have been due to the availability of third-party payment of medical expenses, Medicare, Medicaid, base plan coverage, and major medical insurance. This again has advantages— far greater availability of good care regardless of income level of recipient—but it also brought overutilization and escalation of charges.

TIAA has made many changes in administration and efforts to keep costs and benefits within acceptable limits. This includes such things as intensive review of covered fees against reasonable and customary standards, auditing inpatient hospital expenses, using peer review and consultants to review uncommon treatment patterns and fees, and case managing the more catastrophic and chronic disorders to achieve high-quality care efficiently and effectively in the appropriate setting. These along with other measures represent efforts to reduce the soaring cost of insurance without reducing quality of care.

TIAA's efforts have been led by Bruce L. Boyd, vice president, who has headed the group division since 1974 and who has become an insurance industry leader in trying to solve the problems of long-term medical care.

INSURANCE FOR SMALL GROUPS

Group insurance coverage for very small groups had not been generally available. Many commercial companies provided no insurance for employer groups of fewer than 50 or 100 participants; nearly all others stopped at 10. The magic of group insurance is that it makes it possible to insure all members of a large group of individuals associated with a particular employer. This permits insuring poor risks along with a large enough group of good risks to achieve somewhere near typical experience. This is especially needed in the case of income coverage for long-term total disability. Premiums are low because incidence is rare. But the value of one individual's benefits can be many hundreds of thousands of dollars.

TIAA from the start covered groups as small as 10 persons. As satisfactory experience built up within this pioneering coverage, TIAA decided to try to cover truly small groups—down to two. Some of the educational associations have only a few employees; state fund-raising organizations rarely have more than a few; many research and service arms and other extensions of colleges are tiny. And yet the professional staff members are drawn from and go back to larger educational institutions. The new micro-group coverage for as few as two employees was offered to small educational employers on September 1, 1965; it was greeted enthusiastically and expanded rapidly.

COST OF LIVING ADJUSTMENTS

Inflation can be a serious problem for some benefit plans. In major medical insurance plans, premiums and benefits are adjusted annually to reflect the increasing costs of medical care; the amount of insurance can be increased in group life plans. With disability income, premiums and benefits are a percentage of salary and so adjust automatically and in a controlled way as inflation affects earnings. But once a person becomes disabled and is receiving monthly benefits over a long period, the problem of inflation can become severe. With its history of trying to do something about inflation, TIAA in 1967 offered the colleges an option to automatically increase a disabled person's benefits by 3 percent for each year of disability. Later options of up to 5 percent increase were made available, then a cost of living escalator with a cap.

GROWTH OF MAJOR MEDICAL

TIAA's survey in 1956 indicated a huge market for major medical insurance in the colleges, but an imperfect one. As already reported, only 11 percent of the colleges had major medical insurance. But 93 percent had base plan coverage, a coverage TIAA did not believe it was well equipped to supply. So it was likely that TIAA's major medical insurance coverage would grow well at first and then slump as competition from the Blues and commercial companies developed. This is just what happened.

By the early 1970s, we decided not to continue to promote the coverage vigorously, partly because of the widespread conviction in the late 1960s and 1970s that national health insurance was just over the horizon. Once again, in 1989, national health insurance is being discussed seriously. The slump occurred as shown in Table 17–1. By

1972, at the high, 651 institutions provided TIAA major medical benefits for 150,000 insured employees and 86,000 dependent units. In 1988, 150 educational institutions had TIAA major medical plans, covering just under 40,000 employees and half that many dependent units. To illustrate the startling increase in medical costs in this country, annual premiums grew from $10 million to $25 million during those 15 years of decline in coverage, or, from about $72 a year per employee insured in 1972 to $626 a year per employee insured in 1988.

GOVERNMENTAL MANDATES

The federal government and many of the states have become major influences in determining provisions of staff benefit plans. Many of their mandates have served American workers well. But they have caused widespread requirements of specific provisions suggested by the exigencies of a moment, without regard to widely different needs of various classifications of workers.

In many cases, the mandates have required minor but administratively expensive changes under TIAA plans even though TIAA's approach was, in sum, more beneficial. They have caused differences in provisions from state to state, and the idea of TIAA's optimum plan, a recommended, economical, balanced benefit plan, became impossible to implement. Some of the more costly mandates required coverage for the treatment of alcoholism and substance abuse in facilities dedicated to such care. However, the number of days of inpatient care and outpatient visits in each calendar year varied from state to state. Other mandates that were more problematic to address under an in-

TABLE 17–1 Major Medical Expense Insurance Plans: Cumulative Figures

Year	Number of Institutions	Number of Employees Insured	Number of Dependent Units	Annual Premium
1956	2	47	28	$ 2,872
1960	235	44,000	27,000	2,300,000
1965	473	97,000	60,000	5,500,000
1970	630	131,000	82,000	9,000,000
1975	587	144,000	85,000	12,000,000
1980	372	119,000	66,000	23,600,000
1985	185	59,000	32,000	29,100,000
1986	166	54,000	30,000	28,000,000
1987	158	49,000	27,000	28,200,000
1988	150	39,000	22,000	24,600,000
1989	133	37,000	20,000	28,020,000

surance plan required coverage for the non-M.D. "allied medical practitioners" such as social workers, chiropractors, and speech therapists.

And the federal government during virtually every year for more than the past 10 years has enacted legislation that has had a major impact on employers' plans.

EXCESSIVE PAPERWORK

By the time the typical patient who has gone through some extensive medical procedure has filled out Blue Cross-Blue Shield forms, major medical, perhaps Medicare or Medicaid, the hospital's own forms, and contended with complex reports on deductibles met and not met, maximums reached, and limitations, he or she is about ready for another hospital admission. One can advance a number of persuasive reasons for not getting sick, and I now include on the list paperwork.

Having said that, the important thing is the remarkable developments toward better coverage and better medical care during the last 30 years in this country.

TIAA DISCONTINUES MAJOR MEDICAL

TIAA announced in September 1989 that it would gradually phase out its major medical coverages by the end of 1990, a third of a century after its introduction. When the major medical coverage was established in 1956, TIAA did not consider its function either crucial or unique, compared with its pension, life insurance, and disability coverage. In 1956, only 1 out of 10 colleges provided any kind of catastrophic medical care, so a major objective was to introduce the coverage on a sound basis.

Another objective was to make the coverage as effective as possible—hence the development of the optimum plan, a plan with standard provisions that would efficiently meet the needs of most colleges. This was so successful that 95 percent of the colleges adopted it. This effort collapsed in the face of differing state legislative requirements. Originally, TIAA offered broader coverage and a maximum three times as large as available elsewhere—$15,000 versus $5,000—but now all companies offer $1 million maximums. TIAA also established same-day benefit payments and gapless coverage. By 1989, most of these provisions were available from commercial insurance companies at competitive rates. In view of the total situation, TIAA announced its decision to withdraw from providing the coverage.

GROWTH OF DISABILITY INCOME PLANS

TIAA's disability income plans grew slowly until 1962, when good experience permitted a 25 percent reduction in premiums, the first of several changes. This triggered major growth in the coverage. By 1972, the high point of major medical coverage, disability had surpassed it, reaching 165,000 employees insured at 861 educational institutions. This service to the colleges continued to grow without pause to its 1988 level of 392,000 employees insured under 1,476 plans. In 1987, TIAA introduced a major decrease in premium rates and made a significant reduction in reserves required for the disability coverage. This generated another surge in coverage. Table 17–2 presents relevant figures. The strong growth of disability income plans represents a natural TIAA benefit program for lifetime security and supplement to the annuity coverage.

TABLE 17–2 Total Disability Benefits Insurance Plans: Cumulative Figures

Year	Number of Institutions	Number of Employees Insured	Annual Premium
1957	9	444	$ 49,908
1960	64	6,000	437,000
1965	284	34,000	1,400,000
1970	715	127,000	6,300,000
1975	1,052	242,000	16,400,000
1980	1,228	285,000	32,000,000
1985	1,290	320,000	44,000,000
1986	1,301	307,000	41,900,000
1987	1,395	343,000	29,700,000
1988	1,476	392,000	39,000,000
1989	1,507	407,000	50,000,000

CHAPTER 18

Survivor Benefits

THE NEED FOR SURVIVOR BENEFITS

The third great destroyer of income, in addition to retirement and total disability, is the death of the person[1] who used to be called the breadwinner or the head of the family. In event of retirement or total disability, a reasonable replacement of preretirement or predisability income is called for. Well-established patterns help determine how much income to provide through the employer plan and how much the individual should provide from additional savings. But in the case of survivor benefits, the individual carries most of the responsibility for providing an amount of protection that will meet the needs of his or her family.

The protection provided by survivor benefits for a single person with no dependents can properly be minimal. For the head of a family of two elderly people with good annuities, it may again be minimal. For the breadwinner of a family with five young children, however, the benefit needs to be enough to see the children through college, if that is the aspiration, plus provide enough income to protect a nonworking spouse until Social Security retirement benefits become payable and then to supplement the Social Security benefits. This can be a huge amount while the children are young, but it tends to decline rapidly with the years. Thus, individuals have widely differing needs for protection, and benefit plans should be designed to adjust flexibly to those needs.

What is the obligation of the employer? If the employer provides any plan for survivor benefits, what should it look like? Are there good patterns as in retirement benefits?

---

[1]Actually, "person" was a "he," and he never died, he "dropped out of the picture," in insurance parlance.

Until 50 years ago, employers' responsibilities were usually considered discharged if they provided a small amount of burial insurance. At least this was an advance from the days of passing the hat among the other employees.

The pioneering group life insurance plan was included in the benefit plan established for the employees of Montgomery Ward in 1912.[2] This was the first plan to provide insurance without medical examination to cover all, or a substantial proportion, of the workers of a single employer, regardless of their health. Like the Carnegie free pensions, Montgomery Ward found that it initially overpromised benefits—paying annuities to widows and children. In 1921, Montgomery Ward dropped its original plan and substituted a new plan with amounts related to service. This opened a huge new market for American life insurance companies and a new approach to employer protection of employees and their families.

Group life insurance, like the vast majority of pension plans, was and is designed for the personnel needs of each single employer. As written by the commercial companies, the coverage is not transferable among employers. When an insured leaves an employer, he or she either drops the insurance or has to convert it to high-premium permanent insurance. This has become far less a problem over the years as group insurance has spread, making it likely that a transferring employee will be eligible for the new employer's plan.

Dr. Rainard B. Robbins, TIAA's vice president, concluded in the 1930s that the typical group life insurance plans set up in industry were designed by executives for executives; they left the young family seriously underprotected. Typical group life insurance plans provided and still provide one or two or three times salary at all ages. This means that at age 30, when an individual's salary is likely to be low and his or her children young with their major expenses ahead of them, the insurance for the family is at a minimum. As the worker gets older, his or her children finish schooling and are on their own, and the annuity death benefits become large, the life insurance gets larger, not smaller as it should. It also gets much more expensive because of the far higher death rates at older ages.

Collective Decreasing Insurance

TIAA did not, in the early years, provide group life insurance coverage for the colleges. The colleges needed something designed to meet

---

[2]Louise Wolters Ilse, *Group Insurance and Employee Retirement Plans* (New York: Prentice Hall, 1953), pp. 25–45.

the needs of a mobile employment population and to coordinate with the large death benefits provided by the accumulations of fully vested defined contribution annuities.

In 1936, Dr. Robbins filled the gap. He invented a new form of insurance, to be called collective life or collective decreasing life insurance. These were the essentials:

1. The insurance would be issued to groups of college employees, without medical examination.
2. Each individual would have his or her own policy, not merely a certificate. And each could continue the same policy after leaving the group and would not have to convert it to a higher-premium form of permanent insurance, as in the usual commercial company group insurance.
3. The amount of insurance provided would be in units of insurance costing $1 premium per month each. Now that was the fun part of the new insurance! As an actuary, Robbins knew the pattern of mortality rates increasing with each year of a person's age. So he neatly reversed the mortality table, and set up a scheme based on providing whatever amount of insurance could be given by $1 a month premium. This provided a level *premium* at all ages and a decreasing *amount of insurance* as age increased.

This met the objective: high initial amounts of life insurance coverage that would reduce over the years as an individual and his or her spouse grew older, raised their children, sent them through school, and achieved an ever-growing annuity death benefit.

The introduction of collective decreasing insurance gave the colleges a useful tool for providing maximum total life insurance coverage for their staff members when they needed it, on a nonmedically examined basis so people in good and bad health were covered at very low cost with "no wasted insurance." But this idea of decreasing life insurance coverage never caught on even though it was economical and fair. It gave younger families the kind of a benefit plan of real use to them, at startlingly low cost. Because life insurance costs 25 times as much at age 65 as at age 30, the amounts available could be up to 25 times as high at age 30 for the same expenditure.

The trouble with collective insurance was that we never could sell much of it. Or rather, in the TIAA tradition, we never could get the colleges to see its strengths as clearly as we did. There are still 40,000 policies in force, but the coverage has for many years been eclipsed by regular group life insurance.

Collective life insurance proved itself over the years to be one of TIAA's imaginative, sensible, logical, and well-designed innovations. And a failure!

Wholesale Insurance

TIAA's next effort to design a nonmedical staff life insurance plan to meet the needs of the college world was even less successful than collective decreasing insurance. Here again, TIAA tried to provide individually owned policies that were portable, not just group insurance certificates. Wholesale insurance was introduced in 1950 and discarded in 1958.

GROUP LIFE INSURANCE

In 1958, TIAA belatedly joined the crowd and included traditional group life insurance among its offerings. Group life insurance is also available on a decreasing formula basis, but most colleges have installed the usual type of plan with benefits related to some multiple of salary. This form provides certificates stating the formula for insurance amounts. When a person leaves a particular employer, he or she can convert to higher premium permanent insurance, as available in commercial plans.

By the 1960s, driven by tax deductibility of employer premiums, the opportunity to supplement the substantial survivor benefits of Social Security, and increasing pressure on employers to provide "cradle to grave" insurances, group life forms started to grow rapidly. Growth in the colleges paralleled that in industry, although TIAA's late entry meant much of the market was already filled.

The first AAUP-AAC Statement of Principles on Academic Retirement and Related Subjects in 1950 called on colleges "to study the opportunities of collective and group life insurance" and recommended decreasing insurance. The 1958 statement recommended "Life insurance on a group basis, in addition to survivors' benefits under Federal Old-Age and Survivors Insurance." Each statement recommended more adequate coverage, and the most recent statement, of 1988, recommends:

> Life insurance providing a benefit considered sufficient to sustain the standard of living of the faculty member's or administrator's family for at least one year following death. Where additional protection is contemplated, consideration should be given to providing the largest amount of insurance at the younger ages, when the need for insurance often is greatest, with coverage decreasing as age advances and the death benefit from the annuity becomes substantial.[3]

The growth of TIAA's collective and group life insurances is shown in Table 18–1.

---

[3]"Statement of Principles on Academic Retirement and Insurance Plans," *Academe* 74 (January–February 1988), p. 8.

TABLE 18–1 Collective and Group Life Insurance: Cumulative Figures

Year	Number of Employees Insured	Amount of Insurance in Force
1945	2,126	$ 5,095,468
1950	10,000	50,000,000
1955	19,000	96,000,000
1960	36,000	232,000,000
1965	65,000	704,000,000
1970	107,000	1,492,000,000
1975	124,000	2,154,000,000
1980	135,000	3,193,000,000
1985	159,000	5,163,000,000
1986	169,000	5,656,000,000
1987	168,000	6,009,000,000
1988	169,000	6,433,000,000
1989	174,000	7,066,000,000

INDIVIDUAL LIFE INSURANCE

The original Carnegie free pensions provided lifetime benefits for widows of eligible professors, but no other survivor benefits. The Carnegie Commission leading to the formation of TIAA emphasized that the teacher and his family should be protected by both annuities and life insurance. They held that the individual was responsible for meeting his life insurance responsibilities. From the start, TIAA offered whole life and endowment policies, but it emphasized term insurance expiring at age 65 to protect family members if death should occur before retirement. The term policies would work side by side with the annuities in providing substantial survivor coverage at low cost. A good start on insurance issues by the fledgling company during its first two years of operations was explained:

> In the past it has been possible to write large numbers of insurance and annuity policies only by the direct solicitation of agents. Such progress as has been made in the last two years is due to the superior advantages offered to teachers by the policies of the Teachers Insurance and Annuity Association.[4]

All of the early TIAA annual reports carried tables comparing the costs of various types of TIAA life insurance with agency company issues, showing savings ranging from 15 percent to 45 percent. All of the comparisons were on life insurance; the agency life insurance companies did not become interested in annuities until several decades later.

[4]TIAA, *2nd Annual Report*, 1920, p. 3.

TIAA has two fundamental differences from commercial life insurance companies that largely account for its different history in issuing life insurance. The first is its nonagency structure; the second is its predominance as an annuity company.

Because TIAA employs no soliciting agents, its distributional activities are designed to promote insurance by mail and telephone. As to the annuities, TIAA-CREF annuities are wholly owned by the individual; they cannot be forfeited to the employer. As a participant advances through his or her career, the accumulation in the annuities increases substantially. In the years near retirement, the annuities may provide all the death benefit needed by the family. Consequently, the appropriate kind of protection is inexpensive term coverage, particularly coverage of decreasing nature, because it provides efficient coverage, concentrating on the years of family youth and greatest need for insurance and gradually diminishing as needs decline and the annuity accumulation grows.

TIAA issued decreasing insurance from the start. By the mid-1940s, TIAA issued three forms of decreasing life, one scheduled to begin decreasing at age 41; the second at age 51; and the third, introduced in 1948, at age 61. (I wonder how many more of these decreasing insurance policies we would have issued had we named them HIIP, for high initial insurance plan?)

The nonagency form was not overwhelmingly successful; note the plaintive comment in TIAA's *Annual Report* for 1936: "An erroneous impression that the TIAA writes annuity contracts only—not life insurance policies—is still encountered frequently." The report for 1945 whined:

> Many of our clientele still fail to appreciate the opportunities furnished by the Association. In spite of the fact that the Association has repeatedly called attention to the attractive low cost of its policies, it seems that many professors must be urged by personal interview if they are to buy the life insurance they need; too often they do not take the initiative when urged merely through correspondence.

Following World War II, the colleges expanded quickly and TIAA experienced a rapid growth in its pension business. Both the new president, R. McAllister Lloyd, and I as his assistant were interested in developing the sales of individual life insurance. We soon brought in two people who were to dominate the life insurance operation—Tom Edwards, who had been with Northwestern Mutual, managed the TIAA life insurance section from 1948 to 1955 before taking on broader responsibilities and Torrey Dodson, who led the development of life insurance sales for most of his 40-year career with TIAA.

Progress in life insurance came steadily in the late 1940s and 1950s. The year CREF was introduced, 1952, happened to coincide with two milestones in TIAA individual life insurance: $10 million of new insurance was purchased that year, and total protection in force rose to more than $100 million. But to put those milestones in perspective, they were about what one large agency of a commercial insurance company would have accomplished at the time. A notable difference, however, was that with TIAA, 60 percent of the insurance was term coverage; with a life insurance agency in 1952, it would have been less than 10 percent.

TIAA made a breakthrough in individual life insurance protection in 1956 when it introduced policy size dividend credits, the effect of which was to give cost discounts for larger policies. Sounds obvious enough, but previously it had not been permissible in life insurance, nor had it had been sought. It took several discussions with the New York Insurance Department before approval was received. TIAA's 55 percent increase in sales in 1955 can be attributed largely to this pioneering discount concept, which was subsequently adopted by many agency insurance companies.

I was always vitally interested in our life insurance program and how we could best encourage educators to take advantage of the opportunity TIAA offers. I had made a number of serious—but my colleagues considered them tongue-in-cheek—suggestions for advertising campaigns ("Term Insurance? We Give It Away!" And: "Maybe Our Actuaries Made a Mistake!"). But it was actually my wife, Doris, who hit upon a basic idea that we used in some of our promotions for a number of years. *"You mean you can buy $20,000 of TIAA life insurance for less than $100 per year?"* she exclaimed after looking over some TIAA cost information. That question captured the essence of the idea we wanted to get across to our readers—that life insurance just did not cost much; a faculty member could not afford to be underinsured. This was one factor contributing to the 36 percent increase in new insurance sales in 1958.

TIAA's average size new policy issued that year was $17,000. Through efficiency, product design, and good underwriting, TIAA was able to make remarkable changes to lower the cost of insurance over the years. In 1977, for example, TIAA's direct-mail advertising stated, "For a man aged 30 or a woman aged 35, $100 buys $78,431 worth of life insurance, and $200 purchases $176,470 of protection." By 1987, TIAA's average size life insurance policy issued was $162,000; a $100,000 five-year renewable term policy at age 35 cost about $140 a year, and new individual life insurance protection issued exceeded $2.2 billion. These are primarily term insurance policies, insurance to meet temporary needs while children are growing up, mortgages being paid, annuity accumulations growing.

In 1958, TIAA became the first insurance company to introduce lower premium rates for women than for men to reflect the longer life expectancies of women. Many years later when the Supreme Court decided annuity underwriters would have to charge the same premium rates and provide the same monthly annuity benefits to women as to men, it became appropriate to charge the same life insurance premiums to women as to men, and this was done.

In an innovative move to counter inflation, TIAA in 1973 developed a cost of living life insurance rider that prevents inflation from cutting the purchasing power of the policyholder's coverage. TIAA offers the policyholder the opportunity to purchase supplementary cost of living insurance annually in an amount based on the cumulative increase in the consumer price index since issue. No medical examination is required to purchase this supplementary insurance. It is offered as long as premium is payable on the base policy and the insured individual is under age 65 and has purchased the cost of living insurance offered each prior year. By 1989, a policyholder who elected the cost of living insurance rider when first offered in 1973 and renewed it each year since would have increased his or her protection by 191 percent, matching the increase in the cost of living over that period.

This life insurance provision together with CREF and the cost of living escalator available in TIAA's total disability benefits insurance programs are three examples of TIAA's efforts to help educators cope with the damage caused by inflation.

Money magazine, discussing the merits of various life insurance policies and companies, stated, "The best deal by far goes to policyholders of Teachers Insurance and Annuity Association." Many consumer-oriented publications, including *Consumer Reports* and *Changing Times*, have published comparisons over the years, consistently showing TIAA policies to be among the very lowest in cost.

In 1974, I appointed a small task force headed by Tom Walsh, actuary, with Neil Bancroft and Francis Figiel. Their charge was to analyze all aspects of individual life insurance operations with the objective of keeping TIAA in the forefront of the lowest cost major insurance companies in America.

The study produced a large number of recommendations designed to streamline the product portfolio and to increase the efficiency of operations. Ronald P. McPhee, who was vice president in charge of group insurance operations, was asked to take charge on October 1, 1974, of a newly formed individual life insurance operation that comprised Torrey Dodson's marketing, counseling, and sales division and Walter Nolan's underwriting and policy issue division.

As a result of the study and the reorganization, TIAA dropped many unpopular policies, seldom used services, inefficient operations, and complicated procedures. Ambitious short- and long-term marketing goals were set, and strategies and plans were designed to

FIGURE 18–1 Individual Life Insurance Amounts Issued 1973–88

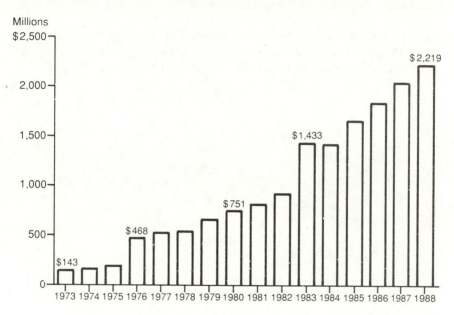

achieve them. Because of these changes, the anticipated economies of scale, continuing very low death rates among those insured by TIAA, and exceptionally low policy lapse rates, TIAA's already low costs were cut by an average one third in 1975. By the second anniversary of this insurance reorganization, the amount of new insurance issued had tripled to $468 million (the original objective was $300 million), the number of persons buying TIAA life insurance had more than doubled, and the average size policy educators bought had increased by 43 percent. The amount of insurance issued to women, for whom premium reductions were especially dramatic, increased fivefold over the period.

Further innovations that gave major impetus to life insurance issues came in 1982 with the introduction of the unique Mod One generation of life insurance policies. Under this concept, first-year premiums were substantially reduced, making it possible for people to begin large new policies with minimum outlay. Discounts up to 40 percent were offered on policies of $100,000 or more, and 50 percent discounts on very large policies were added in 1985.

TIAA issued 3,773 policies in 1974 that averaged some $41,300 of protection and produced $155 million of total new insurance. In 1988, 14 years later, the number of policies issued had increased by 3.6 times, the average new policy size was up four times, and the total amount of insurance issued exceeded $2.2 billion, or more than 14 times the 1974 level (see Figure 18–1). These latter amounts greatly exceeded the rates of growth in the life insurance industry as a whole. The number of educators covered by the cost of living rider has nearly tripled since 1974, and the amount of protection provided has vaulted to over 30 times the amount in force at that time. The importance of the figures is in the strengthening of the financial security of educational staff members and their families.

PART FIVE

Outreach

CHAPTER 19

Governance

TIAA's and CREF's governance, like so many other features, is unique. In some respects, it is designed to meet the distinctive needs of the college world and would not necessarily be replicable in other contexts; in other respects, its lessons are more widely relevant.

FOUR MAJOR EVENTS

Birth—March 4, 1918

TIAA is incorporated as a nonprofit legal reserve stock life insurance company under New York insurance law. The charter of TIAA specifies its purpose of serving higher education by providing certain benefit plans and then states it shall operate "all without profit to the corporation or its stockholders." Carnegie Corporation of New York donated $1 million and held all the stock in trust. Sixteen original trustees were named.

The first board of TIAA included among its members three persons connected with the Carnegie Foundation: Dr. Henry S. Pritchett, president of the Carnegie Foundation and unsalaried president of TIAA; Robert A. Franks, treasurer of Carnegie Corporation and unsalaried treasurer of TIAA; and Alfred Z. Reed of Carnegie Corporation. Reed left the TIAA board in 1923. Dr. Pritchett retired as TIAA president in 1930 and from the board in 1934. Mr. Franks' 17 years on the TIAA board ended with his death in 1935. Carnegie Corporation of New York held the controlling stock of TIAA for the first two decades of its life. This was a limiting situation both for Carnegie Corporation and for TIAA.

Since TIAA became freestanding in 1937, the only Carnegie officer to serve on the operating board has been Dr. James A. Perkins, who served on the TIAA board from 1957 until 1965, after assuming the presidency of Cornell University. John Gardner, president of Carnegie Corporation from 1955 to 1965, served as a Trustee of T.I.A.A. Stock and Member of CREF from 1968 to 1971, following his service as secretary of Health, Education, and Welfare.

Policyholder Trustees—1921

The Policyholders Nominating Committee was formed and balloting was instituted to put into effect the original Carnegie recommendations that some trustees be selected independently by policyholders. The board was increased in size to 20 to accommodate the policyholder-selected trustees.

Maturity—June 3, 1937

The act to incorporate Trustees of T.I.A.A. Stock was passed by the New York legislature and signed into law by the governor. The original trustees were John W. Davis, Lewis W. Douglas, Henry James, Jackson E. Reynolds, and George Rublee, who "are hereby constituted a nonprofit corporation by the name of Trustees of T.I.A.A. Stock."

CREF's Birth—March 18, 1952

Governor Thomas E. Dewey of New York signed into law the charter of a new membership corporation, College Retirement Equities Fund. This charter also carried a nonprofit provision "all without profit to the corporation." The original members of CREF were Laird Bell, Virgil M. Hancher, R. McAllister Lloyd, Irving S. Olds, Francis T. P. Plimpton, Henning W. Prentiss, Jr., and Henry M. Wriston.

RETIREMENT AGE FOR BOARD MEMBERS

The Trustees of T.I.A.A. Stock established a retirement age of 70 for operating board members and 75 for Trustees of T.I.A.A. Stock in 1953. For TIAA, the rule was that no one could be elected to the operating board for a term extending beyond his or her age 70. This rule has caused practically no controversy over the years, except for expressions of regret over individuals having to leave the board. It assured adequate turnover and a young enough board.

There was one problem. TIAA-CREF's main objective was to make life financially comfortable for retired college staff members, but none of them over age 70 could serve on the operating board. The board definitely did not want to eliminate the retirement age. Occasionally, we would puzzle over this problem or correspond with policyholders who felt strongly.

In 1979, Professor Morris E. Garnsey, joined by the Senior Faculty Association of the University of Colorado, led a vigorous effort to eliminate the retirement age for the board in order to have representatives of TIAA-CREF retired participants on the board. As was true of so many such puzzling issues, the answer came right out of the Educator-Trustee Advisory Committee. Professor Ben Friedman of Harvard's department of economics and a CREF board member said at the ETAC meeting in May 1979: "Why not allow a person who has never served on the board to be elected at any age, but to serve only one term if elected beyond the usual retirement age?" This did it. At the time of the election, the candidate would probably be in good health. There would be a regular terminal point four years later. Dr. David Truman, retiring president and professor at Mount Holyoke College, was so elected to the board in 1982.

POLICYHOLDER-SELECTED TRUSTEES

The parties to the setting up of TIAA contemplated policyholder democracy in the election of some trustees. They did not want a single, unopposed slate for trustee elections. They wanted adequate access to the ideas and talents of the various interests within the academic world.

In order to achieve the objectives, it was decided to have an independent, freestanding nomination process to designate multiple choices for nomination of one trustee a year for a four-year term. Thus, four policyholder-selected trustees would be serving at all times.

The mechanism chosen was the Policyholders Nominating Committee. First appointed by Carnegie Corporation after consultation with educators in 1920 and 1921, the self-generating committee existed from 1921 through 1988 and brought 69 policyholder-selected members to the TIAA board. Each year, the ballot asked policyholders to suggest names of candidates to be considered by the committee at its next meeting.

Beginning in 1921, the Policyholders Nominating Committee presented the names of five candidates each year, one of whom was selected for the board by weighted voting. The weighting was five points for first preference, three for second, and one for third. The weighted voting was dropped with the advent of CREF, and the number of candidates on each ballot was reduced from five to three in 1971.

Some of the contests have been close. In 1985, the margin was 570 votes out of 116,000 cast in the CREF balloting. Some votes were one-sided: in 1974, Paul A. Samuelson won by a margin of 32,000 CREF votes over his nearest competitor, a 42 percent advantage, in a balloting in which 76,000 participants voted.

Participation in the last 20 years has varied within a band of 8 to 30 percent of those eligible actually voting. The voting has been toward the low end in recent years. The percentages are about the same as alumni participation in contested races at large universities. The usual vote at the almost-never-contested elections for mutual life insurance companies is a tiny fraction of 1 percent. There almost never is a multiple-candidate election for mutual fund directors, where the overwhelming proxy vote is designated for management's candidates.

The question of whether policyholder-selected trustees effectively participate in TIAA's governance has a long history. There was an exchange of letters in 1940 between Henry James, president of TIAA, and Erwin Griswold, professor of law at Harvard (later dean and then U.S. solicitor general). Soon after the exhaustive inquiry into the life insurance and other financial industries by the Temporary National Economic Committee during the Great Depression, Griswold questioned whether policyholder-selected trustees had any real influence. Henry James answered:

> There has been a good deal of criticism of the system by which in mutual [life insurance] companies the policyholders vote and express their wishes. The T.N.E.C. took testimony on the subject, and incidental publicity showed that there is more form than substance to "policyholder participation" in the affairs of the mutuals. . . . It might be said that our system has more substance than form.[1]

Dr. Griswold was subsequently selected by the policyholders for the board. I can testify that there was no lack of effective participation on his part in board deliberations.

Every few years, TIAA and CREF governance is criticized on the grounds that all trustees should be elected, "as in mutual life companies or mutual funds." James' point about such company elections having more form than substance compared with TIAA's more substance than form was well taken.

Andrew Tobias, writing on *The Invisible Bankers:*

> In a recent election for board members of the Prudential, four vacancies were to be filled. Vying for these four spots were a total of four candidates, nominated by the board itself. Eligible to vote were 18.4 million policyholders. Of these, 323 did—virtually all of them em-

---

[1]James to Griswold, September 24, 1940, TIAA-CREF Archives.

ployees of Prudential. Later in the same year, policyholders of the Equitable were called upon to choose among a field of 11 nominees to fill 11 board seats. An estimated 3,250,000 policyholders were eligible to vote but were not informed of the election; 6,400, mostly Equitable employees, voted by mail. Seven showed up at the election to vote in person.[2]

Robert A. Beck, chairman of the board and CEO-elect of the Prudential Insurance Company, testified at 1983 congressional hearings:

> The policyholders do not actively participate in the governance of the company. . . . No one has been able to devise a feasible and practical method by which policyholders can become intimately involved in the decision-making process required in the operation of a business of the magnitude and complexity of Prudential.[3]

TIAA and CREF over the years have attracted far more voting than in mutual companies. In 1988, 75,834 policyholders of TIAA and 63,137 participants of CREF actually cast a vote and selected one of three independently chosen candidates for each board. Frequently, the CEO of TIAA-CREF has never met the new policyholder-selected trustee until after election, a happening that is nearly inconceivable in business or other insurance companies.

The balloting for TIAA and CREF policyholder-selected trustees for the last 20 years is shown in Appendix C. The tables show the winner's name and academic discipline and total votes cast.

The advent of CREF in 1952 changed the pattern of policyholder voting. Policyholders began asking: "What does he or she know about handling my money?" The pattern of voting by discipline of policyholder-selected trustee changed abruptly; no longer were sociologists, physicists, chemists, humanities professors, or other disciplines selected. The year of the economist and the finance professor arrived with CREF. From then on Nobel laureates in economics filled the board, as did finance professors, efficient market theorists, and members of the White House Council of Economic Advisors. Many Ivy League professors were selected, but almost none from small, private, liberal arts colleges.[4]

During their entire history, the TIAA board and the CREF board have been "outside" boards. Only one or two, and occasionally

---

[2]Andrew Tobias, *The Invisible Bankers: Everything the Insurance Industry Never Wanted You to Know* (New York: Linden Press, 1982), pp. 39–40.

[3]Beck in "Rights and Remedies of Insurance Policyholders," U.S. Congress, Senate Committee on the Judiciary, Hearing before the Subcommittee on Citizens and Shareholders Rights and Remedies, Part 2, The Role of the Policyholder in Mutual Insurance Companies, May 10, 1978 (Washington, D.C.: U.S. Government Printing Office, 1978), p. 966.

[4]Under CREF's agreement with the SEC in 1988, CREF trustees will be directly elected; see Chapter 26.

three, members of each board are officers of the companies; the other 17, 18, or 19 are outside trustees. When the offices of chairman and president are held by different people, both serve on the board. And when a particularly senior investment officer is available, such as Dr. Roger Murray or James Martin for CREF or Walter Mahlstedt for TIAA, the board adds them to its membership.

DIVERSITY

The policyholder trustee selection process has helped maintain a broad range of talent on the boards. This range includes diversity of academic disciplines, business and financial expertise, and management experience. And the boards' ethnic, sex, and racial diversity reaches back 50 years, a quarter-century before such diversity appeared on other boards.

The first woman to serve on the TIAA board was Ada Comstock Notestein, selected by policyholder balloting in 1940. Dr. Notestein, then president of Radcliffe College, had been dean of women at the University of Minnesota and at Smith College and president of the American Association of University Women from 1921 to 1923. Dr. Notestein was especially helpful in advising from the policyholder and institutional viewpoint on necessary service cutbacks by TIAA during World War II. The second woman trustee was Mabel Newcomer, economist and economic author, who took an interest in the postwar inflationary period and the developing economic climate that led to CREF.

As late as 1974, TIAA-CREF alone had 10 percent of the total number of women on Fortune 500 companies boards. By May 1988, *Catalyst* was able to report there were 427 women directors on the boards of the 1,000 largest companies, up from 46 in 1969.[5] And it notes that one company alone, TIAA-CREF, has 10 women directors.

The following women have served on the TIAA, CREF, or Trustees of T.I.A.A. Stock boards as either policyholder-selected or directly appointed members:

Trustee	Affiliation	Term
Ada Comstock Notestein	President, Radcliffe College	1940–44
Mabel Newcomer	Professor, Vassar College	1948–52
Sarah G. Blanding	President, Vassar College	1956–60
Anne G. Pannell	President, Sweet Briar College	1963–64
Grace E. Bates	Professor, Mt. Holyoke College	1965–69
Juanita M. Kreps	Professor, Duke University	1968–77
		1985–

---

[5]"Update: Women on Corporate Boards," *Catalyst Perspective*, May 1988.

Dr. Luther Foster, president of Tuskeegee Institute, first was selected by policyholders to the TIAA board in 1957. His administrative knowledge, having been the top business officer of Tuskeegee before becoming president, was invaluable. He served policyholders first as a trustee of TIAA, then of CREF, and subsequently on the Trustees of T.I.A.A. Stock. Trustees who are members of minorities include the following:

TIAA also had on its board from 1951 to 1955 Dr. Ralph Himstead, general secretary of the AAUP, the closest approach at the time to a labor group for the college world. Except for the Union Labor Life Insurance Company, this also was a rare mark of diversity in the life insurance business.

BOARD COMMITTEES

TIAA and CREF committees, like the composition of the boards, have always been composed largely of outside trustees. During the earlier years when TIAA was small, compensation, audit, and similar functions were handled by the executive committee or full board. As TIAA grew in size and complexity and as governance practices advanced, TIAA changed its committee structure. A nominating committee was put in place in 1941 to recommend new board memberships, officer titles, and salaries of officers and highly placed staff members. An audit committee was appointed in 1973 to take over this function from the executive committee. A compensation committee was established in 1986 to allow greater attention to salaries, benefits, and other compensation. In 1971, a separate committee on questionnaires was appointed to establish conflict of interest procedures. This committee, also of outside directors, recommends appropriate policy statements on conflict of interest, monitors adherence to the policies, establishes procedures to disclose any possible conflicts of interest, and in general protects policyholder and participant interests.

These trustee committees are drawn entirely from the nonmanagement members of the board. They include one or more policyholder-selected trustees. The CREF committees parallel these TIAA committees.

One unique additional committee is necessary. TIAA manages CREF under a nonprofit expense reimbursement arrangement, paying for all of CREF's expenses and being reimbursed under an arrangement that allocates expenses properly. Each board of trustees appoints a committee, its Committee on Expense Reimbursement Agreement, to monitor all financial arrangements between the companies.

INVESTMENT COMMITTEES

The investment committees of TIAA and CREF are directly charged, under general guidance of the full boards, with the investment policies of the two pension funds. Both TIAA and CREF have finance committees charged with overall investment strategy and policy and approval of all large loans for TIAA or common stock investments for

CREF. TIAA also has a mortgage committee, to set policy for mortgage and real estate investments and approve large transactions.

The membership of these committees includes those persons placed on the boards specifically for their investment skills and knowledge, plus those policyholder trustees whose experience is directly relevant to investment deliberations. The TIAA finance committee has experts in direct placement loans, public issues, allocation of funds among investment vehicles, and general strategy. The TIAA mortgage committee needs persons well informed on shopping centers, downtown business buildings, industrial parks, and other forms of mortgage and real estate investing.

STRICT ETHICAL STANDARDS

In the early decades, TIAA relied on usual inside and outside auditing procedures, staff memos, supervision, and climate to assure that each staff member and each trustee would operate in an ethically acceptable manner. Also, the New York State Insurance Department's periodic examinations are meticulous.

TIAA attracted to its board from the start persons with special knowledge regarding ethics in business. Elihu Root, Jr., the distinguished lawyer and civic leader, served on the TIAA board from 1921 until 1946. He was succeeded by Francis T. P. Plimpton, senior partner of Debevoise, Plimpton, who served on the operating and top boards of TIAA and CREF for almost a quarter of a century. Plimpton's long record of public service included five years as deputy U.S. representative to the United Nations under Presidents Kennedy and Johnson and his appointment by New York City Mayor John Lindsay as chairman of the city's Board of Ethics. Another longtime member of the TIAA and CREF boards was Cloyd Laporte, known as "Mr. Ethics," who also served as chairman of the New York City Board of Ethics under Mayor Wagner.

In the early 1970s, state insurance and banking departments and the SEC were becoming interested in eliminating conflicts of interest. And TIAA and CREF were becoming huge financial institutions. It seemed an appropriate time to develop and install the strictest controls possible. TIAA-CREF lawyers and board committees worked out a detailed and rigorous conflict of interest procedure and installed it in 1971. No amendments were necessary to conform it to the SEC and the Insurance Department regulations when they came out.

The procedure depends on a questionnaire filed periodically by each staff member and officer in a sensitive position, that is, one dealing with investments, accounting, purchasing, and so on. The questions cover any family connections that could lead to conflicts, other board or other outside activities, as well as internal items.

Questionnaires of staff members are scrutinized by the general counsel's office; those of officers, by a special Ad Hoc Joint Committee to Examine Questionnaires; and for board members, by a committee of the Trustees of T.I.A.A. Stock and Members of CREF.

During the insider trading scandals of the mid-1980s, these procedures were thoroughly reviewed and strengthened.

EDUCATOR-TRUSTEE ADVISORY COMMITTEE

Perhaps the most distinctive board structure for TIAA and CREF was the Educator-Trustee Advisory Committee (ETAC). Clearly, TIAA and CREF had unusual talent available in the educators serving on the boards. They were both participants in the benefit plans and outstanding teachers, administrators, and researchers at educational institutions. How could they participate most effectively in the governance of TIAA and CREF?

For several years starting in the late 1940s, all the educators on the boards were invited to an informal dinner before board meetings. The discussion took whatever tack the trustees wanted, just so it was on subjects of relevance to college benefit planning. The dinners were in the nature of brainstorming sessions. Trustees brought out ideas that were in the formative stage or items they wished discussed in more detail than usually possible in board meetings.

The informal dinners proved so useful and interesting they were scheduled with some regularity twice a year, the evening before board meetings. At the dinner, management briefly would present ideas in the development stage, projects or problems, or matters of policyholder communication. Then trustees would take over the discussion. No votes were taken; the trustee comments were for guidance and study of ideas and not necessarily for determination of policy.

Starting in November 1958, the informal discussions became even more a part of board sessions when the educator trustees began meeting for the full morning before meetings of the board in the afternoon. The name Educator-Trustee Advisory Committee (ETAC) was adopted in 1963.

The New York Insurance Department, in its quinquennial examination for the period ending December 31, 1964, recommended the committee be made formal and be included in the corporation bylaws, and this was done. Something of the brainstorming, or "thoughtful, involved people sitting around thinking" element of the original ETAC meetings was lost, but the usefulness continued.

While I was president and then chairman and CEO, from 1957 to 1979, I found ETAC exceptionally worthwhile in the governance and management of TIAA-CREF. It allowed strong trustee input early in the decision-making process without committing the organization to action until new ideas could be tested and refined. It eliminated the frustration on many boards where all matters coming to the board are ready for final approval, at too late a stage for board input except to oppose recommendations already decided on, a traumatic occasion if it ever occurs on most boards. It allowed management to get the advantage of board input at an early stage without becoming committed, and it gave board members a significant participation in early policy deliberations.

ETAC was the first part of TIAA governance in which certain aspects of the new variable annuity plan, or what became CREF, were discussed. It was the first group to discuss the cashable annuities, or what became the supplemental retirement annuities (SRAs). Policyholder communications concepts frequently were items of intense discussion. And the original questions relating to voting of corporate shares by CREF and TIAA were thrashed out in ETAC. Some other subjects discussed were new products and services such as the retirement transition benefit and the cost of living life insurance. During the 1950s, much attention was given to adequacy of benefits, with the trustees commenting on Social Security and its influence on TIAA-CREF and college benefit plans. Early retirement, nonacademic retirement plans, federal taxes, "doing business" problems, social investment issues, and many other subjects were discussed.

Trustees Carolyn Shaw Bell, Juanita Kreps, Charles Z. Wilson, Jill Conway, Leon Bramson, and Samuel B. Gould took special interest in improving policyholder communications. David Alexander, Luther H. Foster, W. Robert Parks, Charles Odegaard, Wilbur K. Pierpont, and the late David M. Pynchon emphasized the important interests of cooperating institutions and keeping them in tune with the developments of good pension planning. A number of trustees served especially well in investment performance reporting, how to tell the inflation story, and leverage of savings; these included Edward Kane, Harry Sauvain, Paul Samuelson, Bill Sharpe, and others. CREF was fortunate in having two outstanding law professors, Walter J. Blum and Stanley S. Surrey, at hand during much of Washington's interest in developing pension regulation. TIAA's major part in establishing the Common Fund was encouraged and guided by John Meck. Such a list is hopelessly inadequate.

The most divisive and uncomfortable issue brought before ETAC repetitively was that of fair annuity benefits—the question of equal monthly benefits for men and women. The deep and pervasive convictions on both sides of the question made it difficult. Even with this complex and emotion-filled subject, the committee gave it civil deliberation, with only occasional civil disobedience and rare uncivil disputation. This subject is discussed in Chapter 21.

ETAC performed an important function for four decades. Its functions were melded into other committees during a broad restructuring of the boards in late 1987. Some of its most important functions were assigned to the new Joint Committee on Products and Services.

CURRENT INTEREST IN GOVERNANCE

In recent years, governments, stock exchanges, business leaders, academics, and the general public all have become more interested in the governance of America's business enterprises.

The old school tie, the 100 percent inside board, the CEO who dominates the board, even the golf and country club buddies are vanishing. Reporting to the board on major policy changes after implementing them, and otherwise treating boards with arrogance, is declining. After much work by the New York Stock Exchange, corporations, the SEC, and concerned business leaders, the principle of audit and compensation committees being composed only of outside board members is well established.

The Notre Dame Lawyer published an article in 1981 titled "The Role of Independent Directors in Corporate Governance" written by this author and Peter Clapman, senior vice president and associate general counsel of TIAA-CREF.[6] The article cautioned against the growing adversary relationship between some boards and management, pointing out that representative board members and special-interest pressuring may not be productive in the boardroom. It said:

> Vigorous discussion, even tension, is to be sought after; continual contention is not. . . . Effective corporate governance requires a creative, zestful, and dynamic board. . . . [The board] should consider how to achieve enough turnover to develop new ideas and to replace persons who have lost their creativity or interest.

STUDIES OF TIAA AND CREF GOVERNANCE

TIAA and CREF governance is of importance and interest to policyholders, participants, and cooperating institutions. Periodically, the trustees and educational groups such as the American Council on Education, the AAUP, and other Washington educational associations, and interested policyholders study the governance of TIAA and CREF and make recommendations. At the start, Carnegie Corporation sought the ideas of educators on the voting process. At turning points thereafter, the educational associations, colleges and universities, and participants were asked for their suggestions. In addition to major de-

---

[6]WCG and Peter C. Clapman, "The Role of Independent Directors in Corporate Governance," *The Notre Dame Lawyer* 56 (1981), pp. 916–25.

velopments such as the establishment of TIAA, the organization of the Trustees of T.I.A.A. Stock, and the establishment of CREF, a number of fine-tuning changes have been made over the years.

1969–70 Study

In 1969, Congress was considering tightening the rules for private foundations. In order to assure that TIAA-CREF would not be affected unfavorably, the trustees appointed a special Committee on Trustee Elections composed of Francis T. P. Plimpton from the Stock trustees, Harry Sauvain and Sharvy Umbeck from the TIAA board, and Robert Keeton and Wilbur Pierpont from the CREF board. On March 30, 1973, the Internal Revenue Service determined TIAA met the 509(a) (3) tests and was not a private foundation. No further action by the committee was needed. It did make a recommendation that conformed with the AAUP committee, next discussed, "that there be an increase in the proportion of TIAA and CREF operating board trustees selected by policyholder ballot."

AAUP Subcommittee on TIAA-CREF

One of the most thoroughgoing outside considerations of TIAA-CREF's governance was by the AAUP in 1972 and 1973.[7] Following a motion presented by the Rutgers University chapter of the AAUP to the 58th annual meeting of the association in the spring of 1972, Bertram H. Davis, general secretary of the AAUP, appointed a special committee. Its members were Robert Summers, University of Pennsylvania, chairman; Anthony Y. C. Koo, Michigan State University; Gail Pierson, Harvard University; Giulio Pontecorvo, Columbia University; and William B. Woolf of the Washington AAUP office staff. The committee met a number of times with TIAA and CREF staff and conducted its own studies on a broad range of topics.

The AAUP committee focused most of its attention on TIAA-CREF governance. The objective, as stated in the vote, was "more formal faculty representation on the boards of TIAA and CREF." Its first tentative suggestion was that 18 of the 20 members of each board be popularly elected in multiple-candidate balloting among policyholders. Only the chairman and the president of TIAA-CREF would be elected to the boards by the Trustees of T.I.A.A. Stock and Members of CREF.

The AAUP and TIAA-CREF thoroughly discussed the possibility of representative board members. There were far too many publics to

---

[7]"Report of the Subcommittee on TIAA-CREF," *AAUP Bulletin* 59 (Summer 1973), pp. 259–65.

make this feasible: faculty members and staff; instructors and full professors; large public universities and small private colleges; many organizations representing faculty—the AAUP, the NEA, the UFT, and various disciplines; many associations of colleges and universities having at least some claim to representation, such as the Association of American Colleges, the American Council on Education, the National Association of College and University Business Officers, the College and University Personnel Association, and many others. No outside organization represented more than a small fraction of TIAA-CREF policyholders or cooperating institutions. Of even greater significance, the TIAA-CREF boards had already concluded that all board members are fully responsible, in a fiduciary and management sense, to all policyholders, and none are beholden to or *representative* of only a portion of participants.

The TIAA-CREF Committee on Board Membership and the board concluded that the proposal that nearly all trustees on each board be popularly elected in a multicandidate ballot did not adequately address the need for experienced investment and other financial skills among persons elected to the boards. It was not sensitive to the fiduciary nature of a financial organization. Finally, the colleges and universities, as participating institutions, pointed out they did not have and had never requested representation as such on the boards, but would have to if the requested changes were made. The colleges' stake was large; the contributions they made to participants' annuities substantial; and they relied on balanced composition of the boards and on the terms of the contracts to protect institutional interests.

The final AAUP report stated, "The subcommittee acknowledges the need for financial expertise . . . and wishes to allow for such expertise on the boards." The subcommittee finally recommended that 12 of the 20 be elected on each board.

This recommendation still was considered as not meeting the governance requirements of the TIAA and CREF boards, but a goal of at least 8 on each board, or a total of at least 16 on the two boards, could be achieved by a different method.

At the time of the AAUP committee meetings, the Policyholders Nominating Committee followed a rule of one term only for nominations as policyholder-selected trustees. The only exception to this was Howard R. Bowen, who served two CREF policyholder-selected terms, 1960–64 and 1966–70. The rule made sense; it assured turnover and new ideas continually coming in from policyholder trustees. It did pose problems of continuity, familiarity of policyholder trustees with a complicated insurance and pension program, and development of the various skills needed in governance. The nominating committees of the operating boards generally followed the same practice, although on occasion they returned a policyholder-selected trustee to the board after the expiration of a four-year elected term. Luther H. Foster and Harry C. Sauvain were so returned to the boards before the AAUP's report.

The option of reelecting previously selected policyholder trustees provided the key to achieving more policyholder representation while maintaining continued board experience and expertise. To meet the various suggestions and needs, it was decided to double, to eight, the number of persons serving on the operating boards who were originally brought to the board by policyholder nomination. The first action was for the nominating committees of the TIAA and CREF boards regularly to consider for reelection the policyholder-selected trustee whose term was expiring. At the November 1974 board meetings of TIAA and CREF, Paul Samuelson and Josephine E. Olson joined the boards as newly elected policyholder trustees. They succeeded Walter J. Blum and Joseph E. Slater, who were then reelected by the boards under the new policy. The number of policyholder trustees was quickly brought up to seven on each board and when possible eight or nine.

Another recommendation had to do with the Trustees of T.I.A.A. Stock and Members of CREF. The AAUP subcommittee recommended, "As vacancies occur on that body, trustees representative of the policyholders be appointed thereto until they hold at least three seats thereon." This was implemented by adding Howard R. Bowen in 1973, Luther H. Foster in 1983, and Juanita Kreps in 1985 to the top boards.

The AAUP committee considered a number of other matters. It gave considerable attention to adequacy of retirement benefits, to investments, to policyholder services, and to the developing controversy over women's annuity benefits. Committee members spent many hours meeting with TIAA-CREF officers considering the questions carefully, doing their own research, and preparing their recommendations. In addition, William Slater, then TIAA vice president, and this author (I have continued my nonvoting AAUP membership since my teaching days at Indiana University and recently received a certificate of 50-year membership) attended annual meetings of the AAUP and were available for vigorous discussions from the floor and in committee meetings.

The entire process of communications was useful in coming to helpful conclusions on the governance of the college pension plans. After all the spirited discussions, the AAUP report stated:

> The subcommittee wishes to conclude this report by restating a fact that frequently gets lost in discussions of specific features of the operation and structure of TIAA and CREF: Those college and university faculty members who are covered by TIAA-CREF are participants in one of the finest retirement programs available in America.

Its combination of immediate vesting, complete portability, and current full-funding has become the standard to which other plans aspire. The recommendations made in this report are made in light of this excellent record, and in the spirit of the continued mutual search for even better service to the profession.

1977 Study

In planning for my own retirement in 1979, I hoped to leave a somewhat less complicated governance structure for my successors. TIAA-CREF asked Francis T. P. Plimpton, of Debevoise, Plimpton and former ambassador to the United Nations, to study the legal ramifications of change. Plimpton had served for 32 years on the operating TIAA board and also on the Trustees of T.I.A.A. Stock and Member of CREF boards. He reviewed all previous governance studies and new ideas. Careful study was given to having overlapping boards. This would be accomplished by increasing each board to 28 members, with 24 overlaps, giving a total of 32 board members for the two organizations. This could, somewhat clumsily, provide for the investment and other specialized talent needed for the two organizations.

As a result of the study, it was concluded by Plimpton and all concerned that the advantages of such a change were substantially outweighed by the disadvantages, and the idea was dropped.

CREF agreed to make major changes in its governance in response to requirements of the SEC during the registration proceedings in 1988. These are presented in Chapter 26.

CHAPTER 20

Governmental Relations

STATE REGULATION

A good, high-minded, carefully considered decision of the founders of TIAA has served policyholders well, but at considerable expense, difficulty, and even danger to the portable pension system. This was the decision to place TIAA under the New York insurance law and the supervision of the New York State Insurance Department.

The special Carnegie Commission in 1916–18 recommended the new, contractual annuities be placed under third-party supervision. This simplified the decision because the only such supervision then available was state insurance regulation. At the time, it was concluded that licensing TIAA in only New York State, and using the mails for formal communication with the colleges and their staff members, was feasible and acceptable to everyone.

The recommended form of incorporation met all of the objectives established by the Carnegie Commission, the educational associations, and the college world. Under it, the new pension arrangement could achieve:

- Nationwide uniformity of contract.
- Portability.
- Fair and appropriate tax treatment.
- Right to operate without agents.
- Accessibility to public as well as private and denominational educational institutions.
- Low expenses.

For 40 years after TIAA was started, it lived harmoniously with the one-state supervision arrangement. It operated under the strict

New York insurance law and the competent supervision of the New York State Insurance Department. It maintained voluntary compliance with fiduciary and other relevant standards of all state laws. It was able to serve academic institutions even in states where only one small private educational institution was interested and where the usual forms of licensing would have been prohibitively expensive. It limited eligibility for its contracts strictly to the narrow category of higher education within the nonprofit world and received appropriate tax relief.

Things started to unravel in mid-century. In determining in the 1944 Southeastern Underwriters case that insurance is commerce and when it crosses state boundaries is *interstate* commerce, the Supreme Court opened up the possibility of federal regulation of insurance. Congress then passed the McCarran-Ferguson Act in 1945, providing that so long as the states performed adequately in regulating insurance, the federal government would not interfere. But several unethical—*fly-by-night* was the strikingly descriptive term used— mail order insurance companies were preying on the public. They would issue hundreds of policies by mail, usually health insurance, and then vanish as claims started to roll in. They were hiding behind the mail order method of operating. This complicated the situation for the ethical and sound companies such as TIAA.

In 1950, TIAA took a positive step to distinguish itself from the fly-by-nighters. The charge had occasionally been made that policyholders and colleges could sue TIAA only in New York, a potentially troublesome matter. So TIAA took the proactive step of incorporating in all contracts a "service of process" clause, and this was included in all CREF contracts from the beginning. This conferred on aggrieved parties the contractual right to sue TIAA or CREF in their own state or federal court.

The first real crisis for TIAA occurred in Wisconsin in 1961 when a bill was introduced that was designed to regulate and tax insurance transacted by mail. The bill was not aimed at TIAA but nonetheless seriously conflicted with its operating method. With the leadership of educators in Wisconsin, especially Dean Mark Ingraham of the University of Wisconsin, the legislature provided an exemption from the Wisconsin code for a nonprofit life insurance company serving educators by mail. Such an exemption protected both the tax status of TIAA benefit programs in Wisconsin and the nationwide uniformity of those programs. Some years later, Wisconsin, in revising its insurance code, provided for tax exemption and uniformity but with licensing, and TIAA licensed.

Another challenge arose the same year when West Virginia University and other publicly supported institutions in that state wished to establish TIAA plans for their staff members. The state of West Virginia taxed life insurance and annuity premiums. TIAA was paying no annuity taxes in any state and no insurance taxes other than to the state that carried the costs of regulating it, New York. (In 1941, the New York legislature exempted from tax insurance premiums received by TIAA on policies issued to persons not resident in New York State.) After a great deal of effort by educators and public officials in West Virginia, that state approved a law exempting TIAA life insurance and annuity contracts from premium taxes. In order to serve the state institutions, TIAA would have to license, which it did in 1962. West Virginia, thus, became the first state other than New York in which TIAA was licensed, but it was without taxes and with assurance of uniformity of contract, an essential part of the agreement.

These two patterns, the Wisconsin pattern of exemption for TIAA and its college services from taxes and jurisdiction of the state insurance code, and the West Virginia pattern of licensing in the state but with exemption from premium taxes and any restrictions on contract uniformity, became important precedents.

In 1962, the U.S. Supreme Court decided the Todd Shipyards case favorably, and this was strongly in TIAA-CREF interests. The state of Texas was attempting to impose a tax on premiums paid to a nonadmitted (mail order) insurance company by Todd Shipyards. TIAA's general counsel, Clarence E. Galston, recognizing both a threat and an opportunity, had the Dewey Ballantine law firm prepare an amicus brief. The success of this case gave TIAA time to fight its various battles and finally to achieve nontaxable status in the states.[1]

But the ticklish situations began to escalate. They were caused by the discriminatory situation in which the life insurance industry across the country found itself. In the 19th century, a single state seeking a source of tax revenue imposed an excise tax on all life insurance premiums within the state. This was perhaps the only excise tax on any kind of savings, bank accounts, mutual fund deposits, bond purchases, pensions, or stock purchases.

The insurance companies operating in that state decided it would be cheaper to spread the tax over all their policyholders nationwide rather than separating the policies issued in the taxing state and adding the tax solely to them. This was an invitation to all other states to institute the same kind of tax, as a good revenue raiser and to dump part of their tax load on life insurance policyholders from all the other states.

State premium taxes spread throughout the country and in many states included annuities as well as life insurance. The states that had such taxes imposed a 1, 2, or 3 percent excise tax on every dollar sent

---

[1]TIAA-CREF Oral History interview of Clarence E. Galston by Robert W. Lord, June 23, 1980, addendum on Todd Shipyards by Galston.

in as premiums on annuities. No such taxes were imposed on bank-trusteed pension plans, union plans, self-funded arrangements, or public employee systems, comprising over 90 percent of the retirement plans in force. It was a clear case of discriminatory taxes against one industry, insurance, and one among several ways of funding pension plans. But it mattered little to the insurance industry; it was not heavily into pensions and its stake was becoming smaller each year. The discriminatory taxes, the investment restrictions, the low prevailing interest rates, and the relative lack of interest by insurers in pensions all combined to cause the poor showing of the industry in pension plans.

For TIAA-CREF, the situation was strikingly different. The overwhelming preponderance of their services to higher education was the retirement plans. During the 1950s and 60s, state colleges and universities in many states wanted to establish a full TIAA-CREF plan or at least an option for their staff to choose TIAA-CREF instead of the nonportable state teacher or public employee plans. But when the state colleges and universities attempted to set up a TIAA-CREF plan, questions would be raised about insuring with an "unauthorized" insurer, and another crisis would explode. Commercial insurers would align themselves against the state educational institutions and TIAA-CREF. At that time, this industry had not been asked to fund a public-sector retirement plan, except in higher education. The upshot was that usually the public institutions were able to establish the desired TIAA-CREF plans, but only after much expense and effort by the educational world and TIAA-CREF.

Life insurance agents also triggered several of the crises by complaining of TIAA's very low costs and tax-free status as unfair competition.

As already mentioned, the life insurance industry was discriminated against by premium taxes, especially in the case of annuities. In their anger at the discrimination against them, parts of the industry attacked their own close relative, TIAA-CREF. It was legitimate anger but misdirected. The industry would have been better advised to try to solve its own tax and multiple regulation problems, rather than trying to inflict its virus on its relative.

Faced with the odds aligned against TIAA-CREF, many executives would have given up and licensed; to TIAA-CREF, it seemed to be a wholly unjustified cost and lack of uniformity for higher education to have to bear.

Texas was the next state to pose a serious threat. This was the only instance in which the "doing business" problems ended up in a full-scale jury trial. After an adverse opinion from the attorney general of Texas, TIAA sought in 1964 a declaratory judgment from the court as to its rights under the Texas insurance code. TIAA's principal counsel was Leon Jaworski of the Houston firm Fulbright, Crooker, Freeman, Bates & Jaworski. Jaworski later served as special Watergate prosecutor. At the time, TIAA-CREF benefit plans in Texas were small, covering fewer than 750 participants at 13 private institutions. But the precedent was important. A jury found against TIAA-CREF in December 1966, and the subsequent judgment meant TIAA would have to license and be taxed in order to serve any educators in Texas.

At that time, Dryden's "Johnnie Armstrong's Last Goodnight" came to mind:

> Says Johnnie, "Fight on, my merry men all,
> I'm a little wounded, but I am not slain;
> I will lay me down for to bleed a while,
> Then I'll rise and fight with you again."

The Texas State Legislature about that time had become concerned about the adequacy of retirement plans at state-supported colleges and universities. A special State Senate Committee on Faculty Compensation submitted its report in January 1967, commenting favorably on the TIAA-CREF system. That year, the state legislature enacted an optional retirement bill that included a tax exemption provision for any life insurance company, including TIAA-CREF, insuring college staff members. Governor John Connally supported the effort vigorously against the strong insurance lobby in Texas. Wilfred Wilson of the TIAA legal staff was also instrumental in achieving the Texas result. After passage of the new legislation, TIAA sought and obtained a license in Texas.

California for many years imposed a tax on annuities, although contracts issued under qualified retirement plans were taxed at a lower rate. Unlike in Texas, many strong private institutions, including the University of Southern California, Stanford, the Claremont Colleges, University of the Pacific, Occidental College, Rand Corporation, California Institute of Technology, and a large number of individual policyholders at the state and other universities were TIAA-CREF policyholders. The stakes both for the national system and for the many cooperating institutions in California were high.

California educators got busy. In 1968, TIAA sought legislative and constitutional approval for a tax exemption. The California State Assembly and Senate unanimously approved a constitutional amendment, exempting from state taxes premiums for retirement benefits for employees of educational and nonprofit research institutions. Under

California's unique proposition system, the measure appeared as Proposition 6 on the November 1968 ballot. Despite endorsements from substantially all of the California daily newspapers and from most of the significant endorsing organizations in the state—among them the California State Chamber of Commerce, the California Taxpayers Association, the California League of Women Voters, and some unions— the measure failed. It and a statewide bond issue for higher education apparently fell before voter indignation against student activities in 1968.

At the request of the Association of Independent California Colleges and Universities, TIAA met with representatives of the California Department of Insurance and the then-Insurance Commissioner Richards D. Barger to determine if TIAA could qualify under those provisions of the California insurance code relating to grants and annuity societies. It was determined that TIAA could so qualify, and TIAA then applied for a certificate of authority to act as a grants and annuity society, which was granted in 1969. Because the certificate did not cover group or individual life insurance policies, TIAA ceased offering these new contracts. In 1972, the state insurance department issued a certificate authorizing TIAA to issue group and individual policies.

One of the rewarding state efforts was in Oregon. The chancellor of the Oregon State System of Higher Education, Dr. Roy E. Lieuallen, gathered together the presidents of the University of Oregon, Oregon State University, Reed College, and others for meetings with Governor Mark Hatfield, later to become a U.S. senator from Oregon; James Faulstich, commissioner of insurance; and other state officials. There was no opposition from the insurance industry. Necessary legislation was passed in 1967 to authorize TIAA-CREF programs for the state universities.

Florida was another matter. The University of Miami, the State University, and others tried to set up TIAA-CREF plans but ran into demands that the companies be licensed. TIAA made its standard offer—it would become licensed if the state premium taxes were lifted for educational benefit plans, and if the nationwide annuity policy forms were approved.

I was learning many new things during these years, including the definition of *snow birds*—professional people such as lawyers, doctors, dentists, life insurance agents, and accountants, who work up north during the pleasant months and flock to the south at the first snow, continuing their practice there. At the instigation of its year-round professional people, Florida law contained unusually strict restrictions on out-of-state entities trying to serve Florida organizations and people. The colleges' efforts to establish TIAA-CREF benefit plans were shot down by the anti-snow bird legislation on the Florida books. Over the years, many Florida educators worked diligently to remove the obstructions. In 1979, the tax on annuity considerations was removed, and TIAA applied for and received a license to do business in Florida in 1980.

Crises arising in Ohio, Oklahoma, New Mexico, Colorado, and other states each led to more or less satisfactory resolutions of the particular situations, but only after unwanted jeopardy and confrontations between educators and their state officials. The problem would not go away. It was proving expensive and exhausting for the college world. It was frequently forcing TIAA-CREF into a defensive position.

We were continuing to run into the "level playing field" argument. The demand to observe that cliché meant using the power of government to make all companies within an industry into carbon copies of each other and to eliminate the innovator. We repeatedly faced, "Your tax status gives you an unfair advantage." We tried to point out that TIAA-CREF was not being discriminated *for*, but the insurance industry was discriminated *against*. We emphasized that, among all the suppliers of pension plans, *only* insured annuities were taxed and forced into the varied and limited investment and contractual requirements of 50 states. The level playing field was not at all level. The "rules of the game" were 50 state rules, each slightly different, sometimes conflicting and destructive of uniformity. And they would have a drastically different effect on TIAA-CREF because of its preponderance of annuity business.

FEDERAL CHARTER EFFORT

We decided to go for a federal charter. We would remove ourselves from the line of fire in the insurance business. A federal charter would assure the nationwide uniformity of the college benefit plans. It would specify their nontaxed status, putting them on the same basis with all other pension plans except those provided by life insurance companies. It would remove the colleges and TIAA-CREF from the problems of mail order, nonagency communication.

One exciting idea was that TIAA would return to its mother's womb. The Carnegie Foundation for the Advancement of Teaching had a federal charter. Its functions were to "provide retiring pensions, without regard to race, sex, creed, or color, for the teachers of universities, colleges, and technical schools," and "in general, to do and perform all things necessary to encourage, uphold, and dignify the profession of the teacher,"[2] which was parallel to the powers granted in the TIAA-CREF charters to serve the college world. Perhaps small

---

[2]Savage, *Fruit of an Impulse*, p. 362.

amendments by Congress could turn the Carnegie Foundation charter into a sort of holding company for TIAA-CREF.

Carnegie groups were reluctant to shift the academic studies programs of the foundation to some other entity, studies that have continued in distinguished form under Dr. Clark Kerr and Dr. Ernest Boyer. It was also a time of congressional interest in, one could say harassment of, foundations, and it did not seem helpful to confuse the problems of foundations and the college world's benefit program. So the idea of using the Carnegie charter died an early and gentle death.

College Benefit System of America

On March 4, 1969, Senator John L. McClellan of Arkansas introduced with 13 cosponsors, including Senate Minority Leader Everett McKinley Dirksen, a bill, S. 1290, to incorporate the College Benefit System of America. The other 12 cosponsors were Senators Birch Bayh, Quentin N. Burdick, James O. Eastland, J. William Fulbright, Mark O. Hatfield, Edward M. Kennedy, Michael J. Mansfield, Claiborne Pell, Jennings Randolph, Hugh Scott, Joseph D. Tydings, and Harrison A. Williams, Jr. On March 17, a companion bill was introduced by Representative Emmanuel Celler of New York in the House of Representatives, H.R. 9010. Duplicate House bills were introduced by Representatives Jonathan Bingham, Donald Clancy, Silvio Conte, Edith Green, John Murphy, Thomas P. O'Neill, Bertram Podell, and Ogden Reid.

As Senator McClellan said in introducing S. 1290:

> The intent of the proposed charter is to preserve the private pension system of higher education so that it can continue to offer precisely equal services and benefits at equal cost to education in all 50 states, and to protect the principles of immediate vesting, full funding, and portability from fragmentation or unequal treatment under local law.[3]

Higher education rallied around the cause with great energy and unity.[4] TIAA-CREF proved to be a great unifier. Publicly supported, private, and church-related institutions; large colleges and small; faculty, administration, and staff; economists, comparative philolo-

---

[3]*Congressional Record,* Senate, March 4, 1969, p. S2279.

[4]See U.S. Congress, Senate, Committee on the Judiciary, Subcommittee on Federal Charters, Holidays, and Celebrations, *College Benefit System of America: Hearings on S. 1290,* 91st Cong., 1st sess., July 17, 18, 1969; U.S. Congress, House of Representatives, Committee on the Judiciary, Subcommittee No. 4, *College Benefit System of America: Hearings on H.R. 9010 and Related Proposals,* 91st Cong., 2nd sess., March 17, 18, 19 and April 22, 1970.

gists, and microbiologists; great scientific laboratories, independent secondary schools, and the educational associations in Washington all coalesced in support of S. 1290 and H.R. 9010.

But TIAA-CREF's power to unify was by no means exhausted. We managed to bring together in strong opposition to the federal charter proposal many of the disparate parts of the life insurance industry— the powerful insurance lobby of large companies and small, mutual and stock, and especially the agents—and the national insurance associations.

A powerful obstacle for TIAA-CREF was that, for decades, the word *federal* had sent the insurance industry into a frenzy of effort to protect state regulation. Our effort to get out of the line of fire was seen by the insurance industry as the camel's head under the tent (I can mix metaphors with the best of them). The industry pushed the state insurance commissioners out ahead of it, and it beat us. This was ironic, because the TIAA founders had sought state regulation initially, and when it started to prove dangerous to the system, merely tried to remove itself from the controversy, not change what anyone else was doing. TIAA went to considerable effort to assure the insurance world that we were not attacking the McCarran Act or trying to change the rules for anyone else; we were merely trying to retire to the sidelines and be quiet.

One of the things that hurt most was the testimony of Dr. John T. Fey, president of the National Life Insurance Company of Vermont, before the Senate subcommittee. He had been president of the University of Wyoming and then of the University of Vermont, which he emphasized when appearing for the American Life Convention and the Life Insurance Association of America against the bill.

The bill was buried in committee in 1970. We studied at length whether to try again in 1971 but decided against it. The efforts of the educational world and of TIAA-CREF, led by General Counsel Clarence E. Galston, Vice President Wilfred Wilson, and Counsel Louis R. Garcia, were by then bearing fruit at the state level.

Our federal effort had greatly improved the acoustics at the state level. The state insurance commissioners, in testifying against the proposed federal chartering, had stated they were accommodating the needs of the college benefit system. They pointed out that 30 states had provided relief without licensing or the necessary exemptions with licensing. They did not emphasize how much effort by the colleges had been necessary, over whose opposition the successes had been achieved, or that the exemptions even in successful states were repeatedly attacked. But the insurance witnesses, together with the state insurance commissioners, insisted that a solution to our problems was possible at the state level. So we took them at their word and dropped the federal effort. Things went much more smoothly after the federal attempt, and TIAA was licensed or had exemptions in 48 states by 1977.

Annuity Premium Taxes

During the early part of this period, annuity premium taxes were spreading rapidly in the states, reaching a high point of nearly 30 states imposing such levies. As TIAA-CREF successes mounted, the industry finally reversed its tactics and strived vigorously for tax relief on insured annuities and pension plans. The forward movement was stopped and the rollback, once it occurred, progressed quickly. Now, annuity considerations are exempt from the premium tax in 39 states; several additional states exempt premiums and considerations received under qualified and 403(b) plans. Life insurance companies do not pay federal taxes on such business.

Tax exemption and uniformity had been preserved for the colleges' pension system. It took a great deal of skilled, delicate, and vigorous effort by the educational world and TIAA-CREF to achieve this. But the rewards were vast. The college world was saved many tens—probably hundreds—of millions of dollars in inappropriate and discriminatory taxes on their scarce resources. A crucial aspect of the national market for academic talent was preserved. The ultimate result was so successful that the entire effort has now almost slipped out of memory as a dangerous crisis.

FEDERAL INCOME TAXES

One of the first actions taken by the founders of TIAA in 1918 was to seek tax-free status for the new central benefit arrangements for the colleges. The application to the federal government met with approval in July 1920 when the Treasury Department announced that TIAA "is exempt from income taxes under the provisions of Subdivision 6, Section 231, of the Revenue Act of 1918." Subsequently, the Treasury found that TIAA was tax exempt under Section 501(c)(3) of the Internal Revenue Code, the same tax-exempt provision covering all of the institutions eligible for TIAA services. This was tantamount to saying TIAA was part of the colleges, providing a service for each of them that in absence of TIAA they would have to provide for themselves, at greater cost and risk and without academic portability.

The federal government appropriately reviews tax-exempt status of nonprofit organizations from time to time. For nearly 70 years, the tax status of TIAA and CREF relied on the judgment of Treasury officials who came and went. TIAA's unique structure and operations complicated the issue and led to long and worrisome deliberations whenever the tax status was reviewed. The longest and most comprehensive review started in 1960. The end result was that the National Office of the Internal Revenue Service in March 1972 reaffirmed TIAA's exempt status under section 501(c)(3) of the code.

In 1985, a crisis arose that no one would have planned but that proved to be an unequalled opportunity. The proposed Tax Reform Act contained a provision eliminating tax exemption for "organizations engaging in the insurance business." The draft definition would have included TIAA. It specifically exempted the pension business of Mutual of America Life Insurance Company, which was the renamed, broadened eligibility National Health and Welfare Retirement Association that TIAA had helped set up after World War II to serve the social welfare and health world.

To tax the pension business of TIAA-CREF and to exempt Mutual of America was clearly incorrect. The educational world reacted vigorously and persuaded Congress to preserve the tax exemption in the code for the annuity issues of TIAA-CREF. James MacDonald, chairman and CEO of TIAA-CREF, joined with the educators to lead the effort to include TIAA-CREF in the H.R. 3838 exclusions. He offered the same preemptive capitulation, that is, allowing taxation of group and individual life insurance if annuities were free of taxation, that TIAA had offered 17 years earlier at the time of the federal charter effort. This time it was accepted. This time the insurance industry did not oppose and in significant ways was supportive of the effort. Much progress had been made toward accommodation over the years. Senators Moynihan and D'Amato of New York led the successful congressional effort. This final legislative resolution of the tax status ended the laborious struggle to retain the TIAA-CREF tax exemption for its service to the college world.

The tax status gives TIAA-CREF equivalent tax treatment to company-trusteed plans, church plans, self-funded plans, union-negotiated plans, plans covering governmental workers, and insured pension plans.

THE GOVERNMENT AND PENSIONS

Social Security's OASDHI is the government's way of assuring a basic level of retirement, disability, health and survivor income for all gainfully employed persons and their families. Supplementary Security Income under Social Security is one of the ways the U.S. government assures minimum financial security for those who fall through the *worker* safety net. The system is and should be a massive redistributor of wealth, from the young to the old, from small families to large, from single persons to families, from the healthy to the sick. In the United States, the latest major governmental action on Social Security was in 1983, to rescue it from threatened heavy deficits by the early years of the 20th century.

In its galactic-sized pension program, the government sets all of the rules in meticulous detail. It decides which workers (nearly all) must participate and when (all their working years), how much taxes their employer must pay on their behalf and how much they must pay (for most, their largest tax bill), when they can start to receive Social Security retirement income, and how much it will be. This is good. It is appropriate to have elected representatives make these decisions for a gigantic transfer system. It is a major social contract between the generations, redistributing income from current workers to the retired.

Government also has an interest in private pensions. In the United States and many other countries, tax laws are designed to encourage private pensions by making employer funding contributions tax-deductible and deferring taxation of such contributions and their associated investment earnings to the plan participants until they receive benefits. To qualify for these favorable tax treatments, certain government-specified tests must be met. The major test was to assure that plans did not discriminate in favor of highly paid employees. In the United States before 1974, this was essentially the only federal regulation of private pension plans. State regulation was sporadic, with almost no regulation of self-funded pension plans. Bank plans were regulated as trust arrangements and insured plans as an incident to life insurance company regulation.

About 15 years ago, the federal government took on the added crucial function of assuring that private pension benefits, if promised, are actually paid. The federal government reversed its largely inactive role in 1974 by enacting the Employee Retirement Income Security Act. ERISA required nongovernmental employers to comply with detailed requirements as to fiduciary standards, funding, investments, vesting, participation, reporting, and other aspects of private pensions.

ERISA was sweeping legislation, affecting most elements of pension plan provisions and their administration. It represented an effort to move single-firm retirement plans toward the type of protection for individuals that had always been provided by the colleges. In testimony in 1972 before introducing ERISA, Senator Jacob Javits said:

> We need tax incentives for multi-employer plans, which are most helpful in dealing with labor-mobility problems. We need to learn something from the success of the college teachers' retirement

system—TIAA-CREF—which would be a real model for private industry.[5]

To Javits, "multi-employer" and "mobility" were important concepts deserving encouragement.

With the tremendous impact of Social Security on the economy and its people, how much beyond ERISA should the federal government and the states go in prescribing the precise details of all other methods of saving for retirement income? Its effort to prevent abuses and assure fiduciary responsibility and adequate funding is clearly appropriate; should it go beyond this? Should it extend its reach to determine minute details of private plans as well? Should it make social judgments as to the redistribution of income through private plans?

The answer to all those questions given by Congress was yes. Congress had discovered a wonderful new world of social justice. Private pensions offered an area where, without any new taxes, Congress could have a strong impact on human welfare. With Social Security legislation out of bounds after 1983, Congress could turn with delight to mandating ever more detailed rules in micromanaging private pension plans and the choices to be made by employers and individuals. After ERISA there followed in quick succession ERTA, TEFRA, DEFRA, REACT, COBRA, TRA, OBRA, TAMRA, CHAOS. (The only one I made up was CHAOS.)

And there went the diversity of private pension plans, the flexibility, much of the ability to innovate, to design different plans for airline pilots, college professors, and auto workers. And there went the chance for reasonably simple, efficient-to-operate plans.

Each successive wave of legislation has caused greater problems and expense. The regulatory strictures have been aimed at single-employer plans and do not fit the design of portable pensions, even though they are trying to move toward greater portability in industry. They especially do not fit employers with two categories of employees, faculty and staff, with differing employment situations. So, in the college world specifically, the question remains, how to achieve the good things desired in private pension plans with adequate room for diversity and experimentation. Will there be room for pension systems that are decently different?

---

[5]U.S. Congress, House, Committee on Ways and Means, *Tax Proposals Affecting Private Pension Plans: Hearings,* 92nd Congress, 2nd sess., Part 1 of 3 Parts, May 8–9, 1972, p. 121.

CHAPTER 21

Fair Annuity Benefits

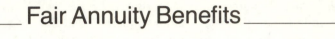

Can pension plans and annuities lawfully provide benefits on the basis of data-based actuarial tables that reflect the unequal longevity of similarly situated male and female annuitants? Or must they use "unisex" tables that provide equal periodic annuity benefits?

This issue started suddenly and caused serious disruptions for a long time. Dr. Eleanor Metheny, a professor at the University of Southern California, wrote a long memorandum in March 1969 to TIAA-CREF and to USC. She proposed that women with the same salary and employment history as men be paid the same monthly annuity amount as men, even though, as she noted, women live substantially longer on the average than men. She charged that TIAA-CREF's use of separate mortality tables for men's and women's annuity payments was a discriminatory practice under the Equal Pay Act of 1963 and Title VII of the Civil Rights Act of 1964. And she charged that the University of Southern California and every other TIAA-CREF institution "condones and supports such discriminatory practices."

This started a 15 year, difficult, divisive, and disturbing issue for TIAA-CREF, participating institutions, educational associations, men and women policyholders, women's action groups, state insurance departments, and the federal government. It was a deeply emotional issue. Everybody who could hid in the underbrush, even if their interests were severely involved. This included the insurance industry, which refused to take a stand until much later when its own interests were directly hit. It included most men and some educational associations. Vast time, effort, expense, and discomfort ensued. It was the only issue that tended to split TIAA-CREF clientele down the middle and that found educational associations on opposite sides of the question. For the first time, a chasm developed between TIAA-CREF and a substantial number of its clientele.

The Metheny letter was detailed and contained many of the arguments later used to promote the causes of equal monthly annuity benefits for men and women. Tom Edwards, TIAA's president, and Bud Galston, general counsel, wrote comprehensive responses to the actuarial and legal arguments made by Dr. Metheny.

Many state insurance codes had always required that the longer life span of women be reflected in individual annuity reserves. Others were silent on the question or required use of separate mortality tables for men and women under "fair and equitable treatment of policyholders" provisions. The tax laws and regulations of the federal government were based on actuarial tables reflecting mortality differences by age and sex.

A number of departments of the federal government that were responsible for regulating fair employment practices had been operating for many years under the "either/or" guideline. This provided that employers could have pension plans that either provided equal monthly benefits during the retirement years for men and women or provided equal contributions during the pay-in years, with benefits determined actuarially for males and females during the retirement years. The federal departments using the either/or guideline included the Equal Employment Opportunity Commission (EEOC), the Department of Labor, the Department of HEW, and the Office of Federal Contract Compliance Programs that determines which institutions are entitled to receive federal government funds.

On April 5, 1972, the EEOC, which administers Title VII of the Civil Rights Act of 1964, changed its guideline from the either/or position to requiring pension plans to provide equal benefits for similarly situated males and females despite the resulting difference in costs. Subsequent definitions of the guideline made it clear the EEOC was requiring equal periodic benefits, and it would not permit actuarially equal lifetime benefits. This placed the EEOC in conflict with regulations under the Equal Pay Act. The state insurance departments, directly supervising TIAA-CREF, had up to this time always approved the actuarial approach, which was acceptable to all but one of the federal agencies, the EEOC. The colleges and TIAA-CREF were caught between a rock and a hard place for more than a decade.

TIAA-CREF throughout these years supported the either/or guidelines, permitting either equal costs or equal periodic benefits. Its basic retirement system provided equal costs with actuarially determined equal benefits. Starting in 1972, TIAA-CREF worked on several ideas for providing equal monthly benefits. Some would require unequal employer costs for men and women, others would merge the separate mortality tables for men and women. At the outset, the educational associations in Washington supported a choice between equal costs and equal monthly benefits. Many of them had recently installed commissions on women or some other formal structure to consider the various issues concerning women.

The fair annuity benefits issue was a difficult one for the AAUP. The issue was one of deep concern to women; men, although expressing themselves in private as worried about the impact on their and their wives' annuity income, mostly remained silent in public. The AAUP Subcommittee on TIAA-CREF, whose 1972 recommendations on governance were discussed in Chapter 19, reported on the fair annuity benefits issue:

> After prolonged investigation of a wide spectrum of issues and points of view, the Subcommittee concludes that equity consider-ations in the last analysis demand the standard of equal pay for equal work. Equal total lifetime benefits appear most consistent with that standard because . . . equal annual benefits for women would re-quire larger employer contributions for women than for equally situ-ated men.

Two years later at its annual meeting, the AAUP changed this committee position and carried a motion to "direct the AAUP Coun-cil promptly to take action to implement the principle of equal monthly retirement benefits for women and men faculty." The vote was 149–69. Professor Mary Gray of the American University was a leader in the AAUP effort and chaired the AAUP's Committee W on the Status of Women in the Academic Profession.

The new AAUP position led to intensive discussions among the committees and the staff of the AAUP and TIAA-CREF. William Slater, head of TIAA's educational research; Tom Edwards, president; and I attended several AAUP annual meetings in the early 1970s. Dr. William W. Van Alstyne, president of AAUP, and I exchanged correspondence in 1975 outlining positions and factors involved for publication in the *AAUP Bulletin*.[1] This correspondence brought out the complex questions of fairness on both sides and is recom-mended reading for those who wish to revisit the issue. The deliber-ations were useful and clarifying, but the AAUP's Committee W continued steadfast in its opposition to the either/or guideline, and TIAA-CREF continued its steadfast support for giving the colleges a choice.

---

[1]"On Equal Monthly Retirement Benefits for Men and Women Faculty: Correspon-dence between the President of the Association, the Secretary of Labor, and the Chairman of TIAA-CREF," *AAUP Bulletin* 61 (December 1975), pp. 316–21.

The 1974 TIAA-CREF Chairman's Report to the Board of Trustees stated:

> TIAA-CREF continues to work with interested groups in clarifying the misunderstandings surrounding how the complicated pension mechanism works. Accordingly, in 1974, TIAA-CREF discussed the issue of fair annuity benefits with the American Council on Education Task Force on Equal Opportunity, representatives of the Washington-based educational associations, and representatives of an AAUP Committee. Additionally, representatives from TIAA-CREF appeared before the Special Subcommittee of the House of Representatives Committee on Education and Labor and testified at hearings held by the Department of Labor.

THE DEBATE, THE ARGUMENTS, THE BRIEFS

The name *fair annuity benefits* aptly expressed the issue during the early period but not its complexity. What is fair? Should women be penalized for living longer than men? Are men being penalized by living less long than women? Should men who not only live less long also have to give up some of their savings?

Equal monthly pension benefits for men and women certainly sounds fair as a starter. Do women not need the same monthly income as men? If actuarially equal benefits are paid, resulting in lower monthly benefits for women, are women being paid less than men for equal work? Since the lifetime cost of an equal monthly annuity for women is greater than for men, does payment of equal monthly benefits mean men are being paid less over their lifetimes for equal work? Or, with equal costs for men and women, is it fair to reduce the actuarially determined monthly benefits for men in order to increase the monthly benefits for women over their longer lifetime? Was the practice used in most defined benefit pension plans, public and private, fair, where only one option, the single life annuity, provided equal monthly benefits? If a retiree chose any other option, it was computed on the actuarial value of the single life annuity, which was higher for women than men. Thus, a female employee and her spouse received a larger monthly benefit than a male and his spouse.

How about couples? When two people have to live on the annuity of one worker for the rest of their lives, is it fair for them to get less monthly income than a single woman or man? If adjustments are to be made, where would the additional funds come from? The employer? Single men and women? Older men and women? The government? How about age discrimination? Should people who retire later receive larger monthly benefits for each dollar of accumulation than do their younger retiring colleagues?

Clearly Solomon was needed, and she was no longer available.

SEX-BASED OR DATA-BASED TABLES?

TIAA-CREF in one of its many reports to participants on the fair annuity benefits issue in 1972 wrote:

> The average expectation of life at age 65 is now about 21 years for a female annuitant, compared to 17 years for a male. Differences in male-female longevity are not unique to annuity owners, but are found in all general population surveys, Social Security studies, and life insurance experience here and abroad.
>
> As an example of the difference in rate of annuity payout, women who retire at age 65 and select a one-life income option will receive from 3 percent to 12 percent less *monthly* income (depending on the option used) than men retiring at the same age and under the same option, but over an average lifetime the women will receive from 5 percent to 10 percent more than the men because compound interest will be working for them about four years longer. Although differing in monthly amount, the income benefits for males and females are actuarially equal.

Although the problem was expressed in terms of sex-based annuities, it was not an accurate term. Gender is only one of the factors involved in setting annuity rates. They are also based on age. An argument could be made that pension plans should not discriminate among retirees on the basis of age. The younger people are when retiring, the more monthly income they need, not less as provided by actuarial tables. Their savings are less, their danger of suffering from inflation is greater, their younger age probably means more travel, more clothing, more entertainment. While age discrimination can be compared with sex discrimination, in the instance of annuities, the age discrimination argument fails because pension funds obviously cannot pay the same monthly benefit to a similarly situated person at age 55 as they can at 75. Other factors in establishing annuity rates are the powerful effect of investment earnings and the small factor of expenses.

One argument pressed by the advocates of equal monthly benefits was that pension plans did not make distinctions based on other factors known to affect longevity, for example, smoking, drinking, and eating too much. The answer given was that these voluntary and reversible factors are unreliable and therefore inappropriate to use in setting annuity rates.

Advocates of equal monthly benefits pressed hard on the claim that insurers discriminated against blacks by not giving them larger monthly benefits since their life span was shorter. Data showed that life span from birth was indeed shorter, but that was mostly accounted for by the unhappy frequency of violence among young black males, poorer medical care during pregnancy, and generally poorer living conditions. But census and other available data showed equivalent life spans of all races at retirement age. There were no data for only black annuity owners. Census figures show blacks who reach age 68 live longer than whites from that age. There is no evidence of racial as distinct from economic and social differences in longevity at any age.

DO WOMEN LIVE LONGER?

One of the first challenges was to the mortality tables. Why was it that female longevity from birth was about the same as for males at the turn of the 20th century, but it had increased dramatically more than that of males by mid-century? A specific factor was responsible—the remarkable decrease of mortality in childbirth during the first half of the century. But this was not relevant to the retirement years.

The next question was: Do not working women, under all the stresses of the workplace, have the same life span as men? This was one of the more difficult questions to study because figures were hard to obtain. The TIAA-CREF policyholder lists provided one of the few valid populations to study; only college employees could take out annuity contracts, so TIAA-CREF could make a mortality study of its policyowner experience. Robert Duncan, TIAA's top actuary, headed the study of this question, not knowing what he would find as actuarial facts. The data showed the same spread in longevity between working men and women as between all male and female annuitants. Interestingly, the TIAA-CREF system was self-correcting—if long-run mortality experience shifts between men and women occur, annuity and dividend rates would periodically reflect the changes.

The actuarial search also turned up a 1957 study by Father Francis C. Madigan addressing the particular subject of life span of males and females with similar stresses.[2] He studied teaching orders of monks and nuns. The Madigan study found the same mortality difference between monks and nuns as between men and women in general.

Census figures, data from around the world, specialized and general studies all showed the longer life spans of women, and this finally became accepted by everyone. Although data from the animal world do not prove what happens among humans, studies disclosed that with only rare exceptions, female mammals, birds, and aquatic animals also lived longer than males.

---

[2]Francis C. Madigan, S.J., "Are Sex Mortality Differentials Biologically Caused?" *The Milbank Memorial Fund Quarterly* 35 (April 1957), pp. 202–23.

COURT CASES

The question slowly shifted from vigorous discussion on both sides as to what is fair and from arcane mortality studies as to what are the facts on longevity, to the question of what is legal. This took control of the situation out of the hands of those immediately involved and placed it in the courts and the regulatory agencies, followed by a decade of conflicting regulations, laws, and court cases. The first, and the last, conflict was between state laws and federal departmental regulations and conflict among federal agencies themselves.

The first lawsuit was filed April 14, 1974. By 1976, TIAA-CREF was involved in three court cases, each of which led to important decisions: *Spirt v. TIAA-CREF and Long Island University; Peters v. Wayne State University and TIAA-CREF;* and *EEOC v. Colby College and TIAA-CREF.* Several cases not involving TIAA-CREF directly also were progressing through the courts. At this time, JoAnn Sher, associate counsel, was handed primary responsibility for fair annuity benefits litigation. She coordinated and organized the legal effort and some of the outreach work until the ultimate conclusion. The Rogers and Wells firm was added as outside counsel because of its background in civil rights work.

The court cases involved a basic conflict. The relevant civil rights laws and regulations are based upon discrimination against *individuals* in the workplace. Pensions, annuities, and all insurances are based upon probabilities of something happening to individuals *in their status as members of groups.* One of the arguments used by advocates of equal monthly benefits was that it did not matter if on the average women lived substantially longer than men; the question was what actually happened to individual women.

If some individual women died before some men, then they were discriminated against if they had not received the same monthly benefits as any man who happened to die at the same time they did. This was pressed by the overlap argument advanced by Professors Barbara Bergmann and Mary Gray that some 84 percent of women died at the same age as men, and therefore they were discriminated against if they had received smaller monthly benefits.[3]

There were those who, looking at the same set of figures, pointed out that Drs. Bergmann and Gray were using hindsight—matching dates of death that could not have been foretold. If death could be foretold, it would be easy to figure annuity amounts: a person who was going to live only one year would receive a huge annuity, and

---

[3]Barbara Bergmann and Mary Gray, "Equality in Retirement Benefits: The Need for Pension Reform," *Civil Rights Digest* 8 (Fall 1975), pp. 25–27.

one who was going to live 30 years, a very small annuity. The critics also pointed out that the Bergmann-Gray overlap calculations unequivocally proved that women lived longer than men. They emphasized that of the 16 percent of men and women not dying at the same age, every one of the men died before a single one of the women. Thus, even using the Bergmann-Gray approach, under unisex, 16 percent of men would be clearly discriminated against and 16 percent of women discriminated for.[4] But for the judges and the law, the simple argument of individual discrimination versus actuarial probabilities ultimately won out.

The issue consumed a great deal of time for the board of trustees, executive, public affairs, actuarial, and legal talent during the late 1970s. At one point, TIAA and CREF were simultaneously codefendants in 10 lawsuits and myriad administrative procedures, in addition to constant communication from interested women's groups. The conflict between state and federal and different federal departmental rulings was disconcerting and frustrating. It required much consultation with the equally frustrated and harassed educational associations in Washington. Although its interests were deeply involved, the insurance industry looked the other way until cases involved commercial insurers.

The first case to advance to the Supreme Court was the *Manhart* case.[5] The water and power company of the city of Los Angeles provided a defined benefit pension plan with equal monthly annuity benefits for men and women under the single life option, but a larger deduction was required from the take-home pay of women. This latter provision was rare and was the kind of bad case that makes bad law. The Court in April 1978 found the Los Angeles plan to be discriminatory because of this provision. It did not specifically address the issue of unisex tables, or, as they are also called, merged gender tables.

In the *Norris* suit in Arizona, the district court in March 1980 decided Arizona women state employees were discriminated against under the state's tax-deferred annuity and deferred compensation plans, because women choosing an annuity option were given smaller periodic annuity payments in conformity to their longer life expectancy.[6] TIAA-CREF filed an amicus brief in the *Norris* case. Other cases in which TIAA-CREF was not a party also were decided

---

[4]Robert J. Myers, "Forum: Pension Benefits and Sex," *Civil Rights Digest* 9 (Winter 1977), pp. 45–46.

[5]*City of Los Angeles Department of Water and Power v. Manhart*, 435 U.S. 702, 55 L.Ed.2d 657, 98 S.Ct. 1370 (1978).

[6]*Norris v. Arizona Governing Committee*, 486 F.Supp. 645 (1980). The lower court's decision was upheld on appeal, *Norris*, 671 F.2d 330 (1982) and ultimately went to the Supreme Court (see below).

in favor of using merged gender mortality tables for computing pension benefits for men and women.[7]

By the time I retired in mid-1979, seven cases were pending against TIAA-CREF. These included the *Spirt*, *Wayne State*, and *Colby* cases. *Spirt* and *Wayne State* had been decided adversely to the then-existing approach of sex distinct actuarially computed benefits, but *Wayne State* was reversed on appeal. *Colby* was the opposite—sex distinct actuarially computed benefits were upheld at the lower court level and reversed on appeal. More on these below.

Tom Edwards succeeded me as chairman and CEO on August 1, 1979. He had been with TIAA-CREF since 1948, as president since 1967. He had also been carrying much of the effort on fair annuity benefits. In an effort to combine the seven cases and to try for some solution to the problem, Edwards proposed TIAA-CREF adopt a merged gender table in early 1980, for all premiums paid on and after the date the new table was effective. All premiums paid before that date would carry the guaranteed rates provided by the original actuarial basis under which they were first paid. The announcement was made in December 1979. Implementation would require approval of the merged gender tables by the state insurance departments involved as well as by federal agencies.

By July 1980, TIAA-CREF had received all but one of the state insurance department approvals required for the adoption of a merged gender ("unisex") mortality table. State insurance department approvals would permit changeover to equal monthly benefit payments to men and women for all future premiums on annuity contracts; past premiums would provide sex distinct benefits because such premiums were remitted during years when no laws were being interpreted as precluding the use of sex distinct actuarial tables.

An EEOC commissioner drew up a charge against TIAA-CREF claiming discrimination against males for the future under the proposed TIAA-CREF rules because their benefits were to be reduced in order to increase monthly benefits for women under the merged gender tables. Furthermore, the EEOC charged TIAA had discriminated over all previous years back to its origin in 1918 and CREF back to its origin in 1952 by not using merged gender tables and that benefits should be adjusted for everyone on all annuity savings back to the start. The EEOC was planning to file separate charges against each institution participating in the system. Meanwhile, the court cases were on hold pending the outcome of discussions with the EEOC.

---

[7]Albert B. Lewis, "The Unisex Issue: What Price Equality?" *Best's Review* 16 (March 1982), pp. 10, 12, 115–17.

The EEOC opposed the use of the tables as announced and was adamant on two points:

1. Equalize not only the monthly benefits to be purchased from future contributions, but also all other periodic annuity benefits, whether for people retired or not yet retired, regardless of when the contributions were made.
2. Equalize monthly benefits for the future by raising women's benefits to the level of men's. Their wording on this was that equalizing benefits would violate the law if done by "reducing annuity benefits to individuals of one sex as part of a plan to equalize (benefits) between the sexes."

The problem was, where was the money to come from? These extreme moves were headed off by the Washington educational associations and individual institutions. The American Council on Education and its president, J. W. Peltason, were especially active, and the National Association of College and University Attorneys, the College and University Business Officers, the College and University Personnel Association, and others were also heavily involved. The EEOC situation was a distressing climax to the *Manhart* case in Los Angeles, in which the Supreme Court had said its purpose was not to "revolutionize the insurance industry."

A TIAA-CREF status report on July 22, 1980, to presidents, business and personnel officers of participating institutions by Chairman Edwards concluded:

> As you know, it has been our plan to move as quickly as possible to adopt the merged gender mortality tables for future premiums. However, as mentioned, the EEOC is now claiming that such a procedure in itself would be a violation of the law by TIAA-CREF and by each participating institution. . . . For the present, then, the only prudent choice is to postpone adoption of the new table.

Meanwhile, legal decisions were occurring. The EEOC case against Colby College and TIAA-CREF was decided in favor of Colby College and TIAA at the lower court level. Then the court of appeals in December 1978, commenting, "Like King Canute, neither Congress nor a court can change the forces of nature. 'As a class, women live longer than men. . . . ' " found "great difficulties" but nonetheless vacated the lower court summary judgment.[8] The *Peters et al. v. Wayne State University, TIAA and CREF* went back and forth through the courts, with the circuit court in October 1982 reversing on appeal the 1979 decision of the District Court for the Eastern District of

---

[8]*Equal Employment Opportunity Commission v. Colby College*, 589 F.2d 1139 (1978).

Michigan.[9] In the reversal, the court took cognizance of insurance principles, saying, "Annuity payments must be calculated prior to death" using "the only tools available to calculate payments, mortality tables," and "both men and women have the same probability of living to the predicted statistical age."

California stepped into the fray by a legislative prohibition against merged gender mortality tables for individual annuity and life insurance contracts issued in that state after January 1, 1981. And the New York State Insurance Department, after previously accepting a merged gender table, rejected the approach January 27, 1981, as being inconsistent with requirements of New York insurance law.[10]

EXHAUSTED BY IT ALL?

The reader must by now be worn out with the conflicts among the states, between states and the federal Government, among federal departments, and among the courts. The Supreme Court had settled the issue of whether employer pension plans would have to provide equal monthly benefits—they would. But it had not spoken decisively on whether the unisexing would be retroactive, and if so, how far. Many implementation questions remained. Much conflict and confusion was still to come. Much consultation, conciliation, and compromise was required on the way to solution. But perhaps it is time to proceed to the ultimate conclusion.

FINAL RESOLUTION

The Supreme Court spoke in *Arizona Governing Committee v. Norris*[11] regarding annuity benefits derived from employer-sponsored plans. The court's judgment, effective August 1, 1983, required, "All retirement benefits derived from contributions made after the decision today must be calculated without regard to the sex of the beneficiary."

On August 1, 1983, TIAA-CREF amended its pension system to provide sex-neutral benefits resulting from premiums paid on and after August 1, 1983. Effective January 1, 1985, all annuities for men and women who began receiving annuity income from TIAA-CREF after May 1, 1980, were placed on a sex-neutral basis. This retroactive action conformed to the Supreme Court's denial on October 9, 1984, of TIAA-CREF's petition to review the lower court decisions in the

---

[9]*Peters v. Wayne State University,* 691 F.2d 235 (1982).

[10]"Status Report on the Unisex Issue," TIAA-CREF *Participant,* March 1981.

[11]*Arizona Governing Committee v. Norris,* 463 U.S. 1073, 77 L.Ed.2d 1236, 103 S.Ct. 3492 (1983).

Spirt case.[12] A subsequent court order in *EEOC v. TIAA*, effective January 1, 1986, adjusted the future dividend portion of TIAA annuities started on or after March 24, 1972, and before May 1, 1980.

Once the courts chose sides in the complex and gripping problem, the TIAA-CREF mechanism made conforming to the new rules reasonably easy. Throughout the process, all of the contractual guarantees of all TIAA contracts stayed in place. All adjustments were made through the dividend payments TIAA was providing. To comply with the court decisions, TIAA changed the dividend amounts it was crediting on all payout annuities currently and prospectively for all annuities for persons not yet retired.

In CREF, the change was effected by adjusting the number of annuity units credited in order to provide equal monthly benefits. The largest financial impact of the changes was on persons choosing single life annuities. For example, women choosing a single life annuity in CREF to start at age 65 received about an 8 percent increase in their monthly payments, and men under the same conditions received about 8 percent less. Other options produced less change in monthly annuity amounts. Whether the monthly annuity amount for married couples was affected much either way depended on the ages of husband and wife and the last-survivor income options chosen.

UNISEXED INSURANCE?

TIAA announced new premium rates using merged gender tables resulting in equal premiums for men and women for life insurance effective February 1, 1984. But it is lonely in its consistency. Life insurance companies generally charge higher premiums for individual life insurance for men and lower for women, reflecting the actuarial facts of life. TIAA's group life, major medical, and disability insurances follow industry practice in using differential premium rates that are merged at the employer level to provide equal benefits to staff members.

---

[12]*Spirt v. TIAA-CREF and Long Island University*, 735 F.2d 23 (2d Cir. 1984), *certiorai denied* by the U.S. Supreme Court, 53 U.S.L.W. 3269 (1984).

CHAPTER 22

_____ Eligibility _____

TIAA was conceived as and continues to be a limited eligibility non-profit service organization for higher education. It developed out of the Carnegie Foundation, but it was designed to serve a much larger segment of higher education than did the foundation. Neither denominational nor public colleges and universities were initially eligible for Carnegie free pensions. Church-related colleges never became eligible, but public institutions were added almost immediately through a second grant of $5 million from Andrew Carnegie. Both categories were admitted to the TIAA system from the start. One of the early questions discussed was whether TIAA should have minimum quality standards and not take nonaccredited colleges. However, one of the tests used by accrediting agencies was whether a college had a TIAA plan. So TIAA accepts any nonprofit college or university.[1]

THE GRAND DESIGN

TIAA-CREF's purpose "is to aid and strengthen nonproprietary and nonprofit-making colleges, universities, and other institutions engaged primarily in education or research" by providing benefits. The full text of Article 8, "The Purpose," is given in Chapter 3.

This statement of purpose establishes the broad outlines of TIAA-CREF's eligibility requirements and its rationale. The limited eligibility policy has its roots deep in TIAA philosophy. Its writings over the years have emphasized that TIAA, by serving a defined clientele, could concentrate on the needs of that clientele. It could devise spe-

_____
[1]See President's Commission on Higher Education, 1947, and *TIAA 1947 Annual Report,* pp. 4–5.

cific services and products to meet those needs. It could write explanatory material, from tax information to benefit options, specifically for its clientele. It could study college benefit plan strategy, help to guide it, and respond to its specific needs. TIAA could know its market in depth and with precision, without trying or claiming to know other markets.

The grand design is to make the entire field of higher education a mutually supportive, cooperative venture in pensions. In sharp contrast to pension coverage elsewhere, the idea is to allow college employees the opportunity to develop their careers in a variety of institutions or only in one if they wish. All of the career moves can bring the individual into contact with other fine academic minds, enhancing teaching and research capabilities. Meanwhile, the crucial process of accumulating retirement income through fully vested annuity contracts continues. This makes the college world, for pension purposes, one vast employer, with full portability.

TIAA and CREF now cover completely or partially the faculties of 90 percent of the private colleges and universities in America. TIAA-CREF plans are the sole plan or an option at public colleges and universities in 36 states and the District of Columbia.

Although TIAA-CREF coverage is widespread in the academic world and is the world's largest private retirement system with over $80 billion in assets, it is only a small part of the total pension world. TIAA-CREF's market is about one tenth of the nonprofit world and none of the for-profit sphere. Total assets of private pension plans in 1987 exceeded $1.5 trillion: about $500 billion in plans with life insurance companies and $1 trillion with other plans.[2]

Limited eligibility, but intense concentration on the needs of the particular group served, has undoubtedly been responsible for a large part of TIAA-CREF's success.

ELIGIBILITY RULES

TIAA-CREF eligibility rules in effect in 1989 illustrate the rules from the start because only small changes have been made. The current rules, eliminating refinements and definitions are:

Eligibility for a TIAA Policy Contract
   A. An institution is eligible for TIAA services (including group insurance coverage for its employees and their dependents) if it is
      (1) organized or incorporated in the United States or Canada, and

---

[2]American Council on Life Insurance, Washington, D.C., *1988 Life Insurance Fact Book,* p. 54.

(2) nonproprietary and nonprofit-making, whether publicly or privately supported, and

(3) an institution which, if privately supported, . . . is exempt from federal income taxes as an organization described in Section 501(c)(3) of Internal Revenue Code of 1986 . . . and

(4) an institution which
 (a) offers a regular course of instruction as its primary purpose, or
 (b) conducts research or serves or supports education or research as its primary purpose, or
 (c) is ancillary to (a) or (b).

. . . [The foregoing] shall include an institution which is a public school below the college level for TIAA insurances, but not annuities. It shall not include any private foundation as defined in Section 509 of the Internal Revenue Code.

ELIGIBLE INSTITUTIONS

From the beginning, TIAA admitted to eligibility the employees of educational associations connected with higher education, the employees of some libraries, museums, scientific and research institutions, foundations, and independent schools.

A few examples of museums and libraries are:

Museum of Fine Arts, Boston.

Rochester Museum and Science Center, New York.

San Francisco Museum of Art.

Carnegie Library of Pittsburgh.

Pierpoint Morgan Library, New York.

Many research and scientific organizations, educational associations, and other institutions are small and are clearly within the nonprofit educational field. Some have 2 or 3 staff members; many others from 3 to 10.

Some examples of tiny TIAA participating institutions are:

China Medical Board.

Citizens Budget Commission.

New England Deposit Library.

Independent School Association of Massachusetts.

Institute for Foreign Policy Analysis.

Institute of Current World Affairs.

USS Constitution Museum Foundation.

Some of the noncollege participating institutions are large, including a few of the research laboratories. The total number of staff members employed by all such institutions is a small part of the total number of TIAA-CREF participants. Only nonprofit institutions that meet the requirements of Internal Revenue Code Section 501(c)(3) status are eligible and, within that group, only those meeting the criteria for membership established by the charters and board resolutions of TIAA and CREF. For example, charitable organizations such as the Salvation Army and the United Way are nonprofit under 501(c)(3) but are not eligible because they are not primarily education, research, or in support of education.

Scientific and Research Institutions

One of the interesting eligibility questions that arose had to do with major centers of scientific talent. In the early years of TIAA, such institutions as the Rockefeller Institute for Medical Research (now Rockefeller University) joined the TIAA list of participating institutions. World War II was a vast conflict on the battlefields and oceans of the world; but to a larger extent than ever before, the war was fought and won in great scientific laboratories. Many clusters of superb scientific talent existed: the famous group under the stadium of the University of Chicago; those who watched the first atomic explosion in the New Mexico flats; the groups such as Aerospace, Battelle Memorial Institute, and various ones in the Manhattan Project.

At the end of the war, the questions arose as to what would be the best way to utilize the brainpower collected under wartime auspices. Clearly, many of the scholars would go back to their colleges and universities or industries. But many others would wish to stay at the new scientific organizations and attack challenging questions in the physical and biological sciences. Some of the groups organized during the war were converted into permanent nonprofit research institutions, while others were newly formed, either as freestanding organizations or tied to one or more universities. In the United States, Congress established such organizations as the Oak Ridge Institute for Nuclear Research in Tennessee, Argonne Laboratories in Chicago, Associated Universities on Long Island, and Rand Corporation.

TIAA received a telephone call in August 1946 from the Columbia University treasurer's office, informing it about the formation of Associated Universities, Inc., to establish and operate a nonprofit research unit on Long Island.[3] This was to become Brookhaven National Laboratory, and Associated Universities was interested in participating in the TIAA retirement system for its staff members.

In the first instance, such a federally sponsored unit did not seem eligible under TIAA's rules. A few days later, TIAA executives met

---

[3]Brookhaven file, TIAA-CREF Archives.

with a representative of the laboratories to discuss the matter. It was pointed out that the new laboratory was sponsored by nine great eastern universities. Of these, eight—Harvard, Yale, Columbia, Cornell, Johns Hopkins, Pennsylvania, Rochester, and Princeton—already had TIAA pension plans for their academic staff, and the ninth, Massachusetts Institute of Technology, self-funded its benefits before retirement but then purchased lifetime annuities from TIAA for its staff.

The whole structure of the new laboratory depended on mobility of academic talent. Most of its scientists were expected to come from the associated universities for a two- or three-year stint at Brookhaven and then return, either to their former employing institutions or to others in the academic world. Their representatives stated it would be of great use in recruiting and in parting with staff members if they were covered by the college world's portable pension plan. Furthermore, they pressed the idea that it would be a good thing for higher education and for the country if employment at the new experimental national laboratories was linked with that of the universities rather than industry, so pure and untrammeled research as well as industrial research efforts could be maintained on a strong basis after the war.

The arguments made sense. Within a few months, Brookhaven, Argonne, Oak Ridge, and other such laboratories were brought into the TIAA system, and they have been part of the educational pension world since.

Independent Schools

Almost from the start, representatives of independent primary and secondary schools asked for and received eligibility for TIAA's services. They pointed out that public schoolteachers usually had state teacher retirement plan coverage and that both the Carnegie Foundation and TIAA encouraged it. But the private independent schools had no good alternative. So TIAA accepted them. Many church-related schools had pension plans; many did not. So TIAA was opened also to church-related schools below the college level.

Teaching Hospitals

Teaching hospitals owned by an eligible college or university have always been eligible for TIAA-CREF services. Many teaching hospitals are large institutions operating as part of a university and its medical school. An eligibility question arises when a teaching hospital is otherwise freestanding; how much teaching is "teaching"? Harvard University, University of Michigan, University of Washington, and many other institutions have both kinds of hospitals affiliated with them, and both kinds are eligible for TIAA-CREF services, if their primary functions are teaching and research.

SETTING THE BORDERS

Almost all of the institutions eligible for TIAA-CREF are clearly so; almost all of the institutions not eligible are just as clearly not eligible. Institutions not clearly in or out are considered, on their application, by a special eligibility committee.

The subject has largely been noncontroversial except for disappointed institutions that were rejected. TIAA's efforts to manage its eligibility rules appropriately can be emphasized by an example or two.

One of TIAA's eligible institutions—the Baseball Hall of Fame and Museum—became the subject of some controversy over the eligibility criteria. Commercial insurers questioned its eligibility. Its name does not conjure up visions of ivy-covered Gothic buildings with professors and students pursuing knowledge. But TIAA has not tried to make choices as to which nonprofit organizations doing primary research should be served—genetic engineering, plate tectonics, sex, economic forecasting, baseball. The situation cooled off somewhat when it was disclosed the Hall of Fame had only four employees.

TIAA-CREF appropriately tightened its eligibility rules in 1962 after receiving criticism from some agency organizations and life insurance companies. Bruce Shepherd, then executive vice president of the Life Insurance Association of America, told us his association objected to the fact that the chief executive officer of U.S. Steel, the Equitable Life Assurance Society, and others who had previously been college professors were eligible for additional TIAA policies long after they had left the halls of academe.

This "current policyholder" rule helped meet the needs of educators working on advanced degrees or working at temporary assignments in government or industry. However, it also made new contracts available to those who had left academic employment permanently but maintained their existing contracts. Few took advantage of this, but they could. TIAA also provided donor annuities with which colleges and universities, if they wished, could accept a gift from a donor and purchase for him or her a life annuity through TIAA-CREF to meet the college's obligation to provide a life income to the donor. Because this resulted in TIAA issuing an annuity for a noncollege employee, TIAA decided to discontinue the service to avoid any possible criticism. Few donor annuities were ever issued; the real service turned out to be to warn colleges how much their usual rather casual guarantee of a lifetime annuity to a large donor was costing them.

Effective July 1, 1962, the boards of trustees changed the eligibility rules to exclude persons not currently employed by, on official leave of absence from, or retired from an eligible institution.

Public School Teachers

Perhaps the most persistent of the eligibility questions has to do with whether to admit public school teachers. There was some talk of public schoolteacher eligibility while TIAA was being organized. At that time, the Carnegie Foundation was encouraging states to establish statewide retirement systems. This complementary approach was thought to be better than confusing the issues and objectives of the new college retirement system by admitting public school systems.

The early judgment to exclude public schoolteachers was confirmed by the TIAA trustees in April 1951. George E. Johnson, then vice president and secretary of TIAA, made an exhaustive review of both the legal issues and the history of board and executive committee votes on eligibility. Dean Mark H. Ingraham, a TIAA policyholder-selected board member who was dean of the faculties at the University of Wisconsin, pressed the idea that TIAA should open eligibility to all schoolteachers. After deliberation, the board voted, "Staff members of public schools below the college level shall not be eligible for TIAA's policy contracts solely by reason of their public school employment."[4] The reasoning was that portability for public schoolteachers was much more limited to, and was better served by, a statewide retirement system than was true of college teachers.

This question soon arose again during consideration of the CREF Special Act Membership Corporation Bill in the New York Legislature. A provision was added to that charter that CREF "shall not issue any certificate or contract to any person by reason of his being an employee in the public school system of the State of New York."[5]

The only change in this long-standing decision came in 1987 when eligibility for TIAA insurances, but not annuities, was extended to public schoolteachers.

Certain Hospital and Health and Welfare Organizations

A large number of hospitals are freestanding medical care institutions with only an incidental teaching or research component and as such are not eligible for TIAA. In addition, thousands of other health and

---

[4]Minutes of the Board of Trustees, TIAA, April 27, 1951.

[5]Charter of College Retirement Equities Fund, Chapter 124 of Laws of New York of 1952, as Amended March 8, 1972, December 15, 1972 and November 28, 1977, Section 7(b).

welfare organizations are also not eligible—Red Cross chapters, United Way, and various others.

The Community Chests and Councils consulted TIAA in 1937

> to ask if that experienced entity would make its retirement plan available to health and welfare agencies. . . . TIAA considered the request, but decided against offering its plans to employees outside the educational field. It agreed, however, to help CCC in its quest for retirement coverage for social workers and appointed its executive vice president, Dr. Rainard B. Robbins, to act as technical consultant to the committee.[6]

He worked with Ralph Blanchard, executive director of Community Chests and Councils, Inc., who was prominent in social work; with Gerard Swope, president of General Electric; and with other prominent citizens toward the eventual goal of a special retirement system for employees in the health and social welfare field.

The full-fledged National Health & Welfare Retirement Association began operations in 1945.

Because of similarity in objectives, a supportive relationship existed between TIAA-CREF and NHWRA in the early years. In addition to Dr. Robbins' original work, Wilmer A. Jenkins, executive vice president of TIAA-CREF, was asked in 1954 to do a broad survey of the products, procedures, and administration of NHWRA, and he later served on the board. In 1960, George Johnson, former vice-president and general counsel of TIAA and then a leader in commercial development of variable annuities, was retained by NHWRA to help form long-range objectives. He and Thomas C. Edwards, president of TIAA-CREF, also served on the board of NHWRA.

NHWRA converted to a mutual life insurance company at the end of 1978. In 1984, it changed its name to Mutual of America and also extended its eligibility to colleges and universities and many additional types of philanthropic organizations and public employees in social welfare fields.

Other Professional Groups

Many other professional groups have approached TIAA and CREF over the years requesting eligibility, which could not be extended, or seeking counsel, freely given, as to how to establish portable pensions for members of professions. The American Chemical Society did an especially exhaustive study, aided by Thomas C. Edwards, then president of TIAA. The objective was to work out a system whereby chemists, whether they were individual researchers on college staffs with

---

[6]Mutual of America History, manuscript in preparation.

the industrial chemical laboratories such as Lederle, Lilly, and Merck, or government employment, could participate in a portable, fully vested retirement system.

Other similar requests were made by police commissioners and school superintendents. Both groups pointed out that their promotions and new job opportunities frequently cross state lines, just as do college professors. Here again, the final partial solution to the problem was improvement and earlier vesting in the existing pension plans.

CHAPTER 23

Research, Communications, and New Ventures

RESEARCH

The college world and TIAA-CREF offer a good example of symbiotic organizations. TIAA-CREF's purpose is to be a part of the college world, to work with the colleges and college staff members and their benefit programs operating an efficient portable pension system across the college campuses.

This has led to extended research by TIAA-CREF covering all aspects of retirement and other benefit plans, foundation-financed research into many aspects of college professional career and personnel development, and studies of needs, wants, and aspirations of colleges and their staff members regarding retirement, professional careers, and effectiveness of services. TIAA-CREF has also worked with colleges and college staff members in establishing new service organizations to pool and invest college endowments, to help retiring college professors get new jobs if they wish, to provide a faculty children's tuition exchange, to facilitate taking overseas assignments, and to pool research efforts on institutional social investment questions.

TIAA's efforts have, when possible, focused on "how it ought to be," not just how it has been. Research to quantify provisions of college benefit plans proved most effective when used as preparation for cogitation by a joint committee of the AAUP or AAC in determining recommended future practice.

Benefit Plan Research

The longest continuing major research effort of TIAA is the approximately decennial studies of all college benefit plans. From the establishment of the Carnegie Foundation in 1905 until TIAA took over the benefit plan research in 1931, most Carnegie studies had to do with pensions in general, both in the United States and abroad. The Carnegie studies emphasized that pensions, mostly considered employee gratuities, were not well enough designed to cope with the growing needs for retirement income. They criticized the designs of plans that gave nothing to the withdrawing employee: such plans would not meet society's needs. And they concluded the country needed vast expansion of retirement plans.

The first publication after the Carnegie Foundation turned over the research charge to TIAA was a small 1934 booklet on college pension plans and their intelligent administration and policy.[1] The next study, by Dr. Rainard B. Robbins of TIAA, followed in 1940 and included nonacademic employee plan coverage, a discussion of Social Security, and the now familiar synoptic summary of provisions in TIAA plans, permitting direct comparisons among plans.[2]

Then came this author's 1948 presentation of a broader range of plans and benefits, including thorough description of all TIAA plans, public employee retirement systems covering state and municipal colleges and universities, denominational plans, and insured plans. It analyzed patterns and trends in retirement provisions. The study analyzed how to achieve adequacy of retirement income and discussed when retirement should occur. A new section covered survivor benefits. It became the core of my Harvard University Ph.D. thesis in economics.

By 1958, the health insurances were just getting started, so the next study, by Dr. Francis P. King and me, presented the initial figures on life insurance, medical expense insurance, and disability income insurance plans in addition to pensions.[3] It discussed the AAUP-AAC Statement of Principles. It also presented all the retirement plan descriptions—non-TIAA as well as TIAA—in tabular form, arranged in sections according to basic type.

A decade later, another study brought in detailed reporting of benefit coverage for faculty, administrative personnel, and clerical and service employees, as well as surveying current benefit plan policy and provisions.[4]

By 1979, an incredible 99.9 percent of America's faculty members and administrators were at colleges and universities with retirement

---

[1]Robbins, *College Retirement Plans.*

[2]Robbins, *College Plans for Retirement Income.*

[3]WCG and King, *Retirement and Insurance Plans in American Colleges.*

[4]WCG and King, *Benefit Plans in American Colleges* (New York: Columbia University Press, 1969).

plans. During the 1970s, colleges and universities made major strides toward financial security, as discussed in the study by Francis P. King and Thomas J. Cook.[5]

When a college is establishing a new or revising an existing benefit plan, it is interested in what the college world in general is doing. But it has intense interest in what institutions similar to itself have in the way of benefit plans. Before the advent of computers, TIAA had arranged the data so it could laboriously pull out or tabulate the information for "all private four-year colleges in Ohio," or for a particular provision such as retirement age or policy during sabbatical leaves. Now computers and regional TIAA-CREF centers have increased the availability and variety of such information.

One set of data especially interesting to faculty committees or college officers is the pattern of expected benefits for staff members. Projections of typical careers, showing the changing salary and annuity contributions, forecasts of interest rates, age at which participation begins and retirement occurs, and contribution rates, are now available for a wide combination of factors.

Sponsored Research

Many of the research projects that TIAA-CREF undertook were clearly within the range appropriate for the use of policyholder funds. But as its reputation for useful research grew, so did the suggestions for stepping outside the usual pattern of staff benefit research. This has led to a series of cooperative research projects with foundations, individuals, and others.

Financing college education. One of TIAA-CREF's earliest studies on a benefit plan *other* than insurance or annuities was a 1954 study, Financing the College Education of Faculty Children, conducted for the Ford Foundation's Fund for the Advancement of Education.[6] This study addressed a question of substantial importance for college faculty members: Will they be able to provide as good an education for their children as they themselves received? The study, by Dr. Francis P. King, TIAA research officer, recommended a number of actions. The report led directly to a grant by the Fund for the Advancement of Education in 1954 to assist the Faculty Children's Tuition Exchange. Dr. King subsequently served on the board and as its chairman.

---

[5]King and Cook, *Benefit Plans in Higher Education.*
[6]King, *Education of Faculty Children.*

The Outer Fringe. *"Salary is a very good way to pay people. . . . Yet salary alone seldom provides the most effective compensation." "The chief purpose of a benefit program is to enhance the educational services of a college or university."*

So says Dr. Mark Ingraham, author of *The Outer Fringe*, a 1965 study covering the various staff benefit plans that TIAA-CREF *does not* provide.[7] TIAA-CREF conducted the study and cosponsored it with the Association of American Colleges, with cooperation of the AAUP, and with primary financial support from the United States Steel Foundation; 757 colleges and universities provided data. Dr. Francis P. King of TIAA collaborated.

Ingraham was the well-informed and strong-minded professor of mathematics and then dean of the College of Letters and Science at the University of Wisconsin. Knowing Dr. Ingraham's abilities and proclivities, the head of the AAC, Theodore A. Distler; Princeton Dean J. Douglas Brown, chairman of its Commission on Faculty and Staff Benefits; and I agreed to an unusual request from Dr. Ingraham: there would be no committee meetings, no joint drafting sessions, no approvals by any organization, no watering-down of his fresh and frank statements of opinion.

The study reported on the availability of such fringe benefits as housing, educational privileges, personal loans, sabbatical leaves, status of retired faculty and widows, faculty club facilities, and travel expenses. Dr. Ingraham tried to omit the subject of parking, but it turned out there were 164,000 parking spaces available for faculty on college campuses and 189,000 were needed, which seemed to lead to problems.

About 60 percent of surveyed institutions owned housing they rented to faculty, with 14 percent of their faculty living in such housing. The problems of allocating housing led Dean Ingraham to a conclusion with general applicability in the educational world:

> It is better that a dean be considered a blackguard than that a man consider his departmental colleagues to be such. It is better for the head of a housing program to be thought a scoundrel than that the dean be thought such. The distribution of the objects of wrath in an institution is of importance and the optimal distribution is not always just.

Mirror of Brass. *The Mirror of Brass*, published in 1968, was the first comprehensive study of the total compensation, in salary and fringe benefits and working conditions, of the presidents and chief

---

[7]Mark H. Ingraham, with the collaboration of Francis P. King, *The Outer Fringe: Faculty Benefits Other Than Annuities and Insurance* (Madison and Milwaukee: The University of Wisconsin Press, 1965).

administrative officers of colleges and universities.[8] This Ingraham-King study probably was one of the first comprehensive studies of total compensation of executives anywhere. Here, even more than in the case of faculty, "the lure of well-advertised high salaries and stock option, profit sharing, and bonus plans in industry," as stated in the *TIAA-CREF 1964 Annual Report*, drew able people from the campuses. This study was supported by a grant from the Esso Education Foundation and participated in by the Association of American Colleges. Dr. Ingraham concluded:

> Few institutions can claim that the circumstances under which their chief administrators work either maximize the administrators' effectiveness or are attractive enough to persuade the ablest young persons to follow their footsteps.

Pension Plans and Public Policy. Pension plans came of age in the 1970s. They became a major part of the savings and retirement security for millions of Americans. They became substantial lenders to, as well as owners of, American business; they financed downtowns and suburbs. As a result, they started to attract major attention from legislators, economists, public interest groups, and the general public.

The TIAA-CREF boards took an interest in the broader developments and the joint lessons TIAA-CREF could learn and teach. In November 1972, the boards encouraged this author, despite being CEO of TIAA-CREF, to take some summer months and regular time (as it turned out, over a 60-hour week) to "continue the broad program of research and study undertaken by [Greenough]."

This seemed a timely opportunity for me and my co-author on other writings, Dr. King, to see if we could organize our thoughts and information on how America does, and how it should, prepare for the financial security of its elderly. Partially funded by the Ford Foundation and conducted by the TIAA-CREF Educational Research Department, the study was published in 1976.[9] It examined the three work-related systems on which most Americans increasingly depend for financial security after retirement: Social Security, pension plans of private employers, and public employee retirement plans.

Dr. King's and my hope was to have some influence on public policy. We selected for particular emphasis the vesting of retirement

---

[8]Mark H. Ingraham, with the collaboration of Francis P. King, *The Mirror of Brass: The Compensation and Working Conditions of College and University Administrators* (Madison, Milwaukee, and London: The University of Wisconsin Press, 1968).

[9]WCG and King, *Pension Plans and Public Policy* (New York: Columbia University Press, 1976).

benefits, financing of such benefits, and income objectives and retirement ages. Early in the century, neither public nor private employers felt much pension obligation to any employee who did not stay alive, stay well, and stay put until retirement. By the mid-1970s, this was seen as unacceptable public policy.

At that time, the pension reform act, ERISA, took the first federal steps forward on vesting and financial soundness of private retirement plans. *Pension Plans and Public Policy* recommended substantial improvement in vesting, concluding, "Nothing short of full and immediate vesting for all participants is appropriate for the long run." Congress and employers have now made substantial strides, lowering vesting to five years by 1987. A second recommendation was to prohibit cash withdrawals, especially where the employee had to forfeit all employer contributions if he took cash. Major steps toward this have been taken. A third recommendation was to establish a pooling arrangement for central management of small pension accumulations.[10] This has not happened.

The second most important set of recommendations had to do with financing: requiring adequate pension reserves, establishing fiduciary standards, and encouraging defined contribution plans with the employee owning the full accumulation.[11] Since 1976, both private and public plans, the former pushed by federal legislation, have made major strides in financing. But large problems remain with the Pension Benefit Guaranty Corporation, with some private plans, and with a number of public plans.

Inflation came in for vigorous language in *Pension Plans and Public Policy*. Dr. King and I emphasized, in 1976, just at the start of the worst inflationary period the country has ever had in peacetime or generally even in war:

> Rapid inflation should be recognized for what it is—a highly regressive tax that harms the economy and penalizes savers and pensioners. It is a tax that the elderly are especially defenseless against, a vicious social impost. The only fair and comprehensive way to meet this problem is through fiscal and monetary policies rigorously dedicated to keeping inflation at moderate rates. . . .
>
> Under the Constitution, private property cannot be expropriated without due process and adequate compensation; when government confiscates private land for public use, recompense is made. This concept is not applied to the consequences of inflation . . . but government policy can play a more decisive role in inflation control. Pending more determined application of appropriate measures, how-

---

[10]Ibid., pp. 172–75.
[11]Ibid., pp. 203–6.

ever, present pension plans may be expected to continue to try to improve their mechanisms for the provision of some protection against serious loss of purchasing power.[12]

This was, unfortunately, an accurate prediction of the inflation that occurred and the damage it wrought in the late 1970s and early 1980s, and probably of the next episode when it comes.

Extending the research focus. In 1975, TIAA-CREF decided to expand its research function substantially by initiating a major new program of research on age-related problems in higher education, to be supported by foundation grants. Juanita Kreps, a policyholder-selected CREF trustee, agreed to chair the Research Advisory Committee. The other members also were leading academic experts on the problems of the aged: Allan Cartter, Earl F. Cheit, Eli Ginzberg, Leonard Hayflick, Eleanor Sheldon, and myself. Consultants were Leon Bramson, James Morgan, Hans Jenny, and Herman Brotman. The Lilly Endowment, Inc., funded this planning effort.

The assignment to the committee was to select important areas of research to be carried out over three to five years, supported by foundation grants. The committee in 1975 designated 10 study areas for Phase I, ranging from academic labor market mobility, to midcareer changes among academic professionals, to impact of early retirement on individuals and institutions, to the social, psychological, and economic problems associated with women's longer life expectancy.

TIAA then sought out independent scholars to conduct the research on college campuses and helped arrange for grants from the Ford Foundation, Carnegie Corporation of New York, the Exxon Education Foundation, the Lilly Endowment, the Alfred P. Sloan Foundation, the U.S. Steel Foundation, the Edna McConnell Clark Foundation, and the Fund for the Advancement of Education. The Trustees of T.I.A.A. Stock also donated unneeded earnings on its small endowment to TIAA's educational research effort, and TIAA-CREF assisted the undertaking with staff time and financial support.

The program outlined by the Research Advisory Committee helped guide TIAA-CREF's effort for the remainder of the 1970s. To extend its reach still further, TIAA-CREF in 1977 brought in Dr. Peggy Heim from the Carnegie Council on Higher Education and Bucknell University. For a number of years, Dr. Heim, staff economist for the AAUP in Washington, D.C., had headed AAUP research into the economic status of the academic profession.

TIAA's contributions in furthering higher education research include developing the study agenda, contacting scholars, refining proposals, obtaining funds, administering foundation grants to TIAA,

---

[12]Ibid., p. 241.

shepherding projects, convening panels, arranging presentations, and in other ways facilitating dissemination of the studies and findings. Panels convened or sponsored by TIAA have drawn on the experience and knowledge of more than 40 scholars, presidents, provosts, deans, faculty members, association and foundation officers, and other higher education experts.

Research Dialogues. A new publication, *Research Dialogues*, started in August 1984, has become a major forum for reporting on TIAA-CREF's and other relevant research efforts in the benefit planning area. Articles have covered subjects such as long-term care for the elderly, voluntary participation in retirement plans in the colleges, employee assistance programs, and the "Our Aging Society" issue, based on an in-depth 1986 Carnegie Corporation study headed by Alan Pifer and D. Lydia Bronte.

Personal Planning for Retirement

What do people want in retirement? How do they fare in retirement? Financially? Psychologically? What do they do? How is their health? Some of the most rewarding and revealing TIAA studies have delved into these questions.

There were a few comments in early TIAA writings but nothing comprehensive until Henry James, TIAA's third president, wrote in the mid-1940s his *When to Prepare for Retirement: Testimony from Our Clientele with Notes by Henry James*. This was a sensitive tract on the challenges of growing old and less productive and active. James' successor, Mac Lloyd, commented to me several times that H. J. had given very good advice to TIAA's many policyholders, but that James himself did precious little slowing down. In fact, Lloyd reported that James, on his deathbed, was giving many helpful, pointed, emphatic, and unwelcome suggestions to the hospital staff as to how things should be run.

Rainard Robbins of TIAA, as director of the first joint AAUP-AAC study of academic retirement policies, reported in 1950 on 1,500 questionnaire replies received from a survey of college administrative officers, AAUP chapters, and TIAA annuitants.[13] The pensioners provided the "most extensive and thoughtful replies" on such "unsettled issues" as retirement age, "tapering off," and size of retirement benefits. Robbins found that generally "the pensioner replies were buoyant," but that more than half had some kind of employment in retirement, and that even these annuitants believed current benefits were inadequate.

---

[13]Robbins, "Issues in Retirement: A Collection of Views," *Association of American Colleges Bulletin* 36 (December 1950), pp. 534–51.

The next effort to get people to think ahead about retirement was a 1951 TIAA *Bulletin* that I wrote, titled "What'll I Do with Those Fifteen Years?" It pointed out that many people give a good deal of attention to career decisions but very little to what they will do in retirement. It tried to get people to ask themselves the right questions, and then figure out the right answers *for them*.

In more recent years, TIAA's studies on adjustment to retirement have been done under the rapidly changing environment of federal legislation doing away with fixed retirement ages. The full impact of the law has not yet hit the colleges but will in 1994. Meanwhile, many states have already uncapped mandatory retirement.

My Purpose Holds. This joint venture with Mark Ingraham, published in 1974, was titled *My Purpose Holds: Reactions and Experiences in Retirement of TIAA-CREF Annuitants*.[14] Once again, the college world wrote most of the book; Ingraham and collaborator James Mulanaphy of TIAA selected choice comments from upwards of 1,200 annuitant replies. Delightful, poignant, irritated, happy, frustrated, contented remarks appear in profusion throughout the study.

Its 14 chapters cover such topics as when to retire; where to live; financial status, problems, and advice; aging and health; activities during retirement; and the unhappy side of retirement. And finally is a chapter titled "And They Give Advice," a distillation of the lifetime wisdom of thoughtful, articulate, productive people: I should have put more of my tennis years into golf; reduce the cocktail hour to a quarter hour; burn all credit cards; say no to all committees, etc.; don't retire; accept retirement with faith in God, with gratitude, with courage, and also with a sense of humor.

Ingraham and Mulanaphy scanned the variety of points of view. Only a few teasers can be quoted here:

> We began retirement planning 20 years before the event and are most happy with the results.
>
> I think I am enjoying retirement more than any other period in my life. Of course I cannot but miss the moments of ecstasy that are far rarer now than in my youth. On the other hand, I have discovered that, as I find myself face to face with the realization that my life on this earth is actually finite, that I have only a very limited number of years to spend here, every aspect of existence acquires a deeper meaning, greater value, a new brilliance; the sun shines brighter, the

---

[14]Mark H. Ingraham, with the collaboration of James M. Mulanaphy, *My Purpose Holds: Reactions and Experiences in Retirement of TIAA-CREF Annuitants* (New York: TIAA-CREF, 1974).

autumn leaves on the maples are more golden, on the oaks more piercingly red, every human contact is a little more meaningful, and, best of all, friends are dearer. In other words I am learning the glory of the transitory.

Don't expect retirement to be great or not great. Just let it happen.

I've known a few teachers who wanted to go on teaching until they dropped dead, and long after their students wished they would.

I usually work in the morning and retire in the afternoon—I'm semi-retired.

The unscheduled life, denied me for so many years, is such a sheer joy to me (even after two years) that I really revel in it! For there is time at last to watch the flowers grow.

I can remember very well my deep resentment when I was forced to enter TIAA at the age of 30 and how silly I thought it was. Now it is the very fine frosting on my cake.

I wanted to live a little before I died a lot.

Do what you have wanted to do; if it's lawful. If it's just loafing, do so and don't feel guilty. Never mind about leaving your children anything. This can foul up your using your money as you like. We save between trips; then blow it in a short time.

Retirement Preparation in Higher Education. Mulanaphy's 1978 study reported on counseling and information programs on college campuses and revealed a sparsity of good programs. Many colleges had excellent educational counseling for students, personnel counseling and training for staff members, and graduate and professional training, but little or nothing for retiring faculty or staff. Sponsored by the Lilly Endowment, the study *Retirement Preparation in Higher Education,* helped lead to TIAA's communitywide retirement counseling seminars.

To help with planning for retirement, TIAA-CREF commenced a major effort in the 1970s with publication of booklets, campus visits, and correspondence. In 1980, TIAA sent the publication *From Now to Retirement* to 165,000 participants over age 55. TIAA-CREF expanded its on-campus retirement planning seminars "designed to make the transition to retirement more successful, financially and psychologically."

Plans and expectations. Forty-one percent of TIAA-CREF participants between ages 59 to 69 were "looking forward to retiring," according to another Mulanaphy attitude study, published in 1981.[15] Twenty-two percent indicated they disliked the idea of retiring, 24 percent stated they were neutral, and 12 percent were not certain how they felt about it.

---

[15]James M. Mulanaphy, *Plans and Expectations for Retirement of TIAA-CREF Participants* (New York: TIAA-CREF, 1981).

This study was updated in 1988, with essentially the same findings.[16] Both surveys underscore the significant influence of adequate retirement income in the decision to retire. The studies also confirm that the decision *when* to retire is essentially a personal decision for most policyholders.

Voices of Experience. *Voices of Experience, 1,500 Retired People Talk about Retirement,* a 1983 TIAA-CREF study by Mario A. Milletti, was written in a very different economic environment from Ingraham in 1972 or Robbins in the late 1940s. But Milletti found equal concern among retired TIAA-CREF annuitants about inflation, about living with or caring for aged parents, about living in retirement communities, and other persistent issues. There seems to be a universality over time of the retirement experience.[17]

The same 1983 TIAA-CREF study delved deeply into finances, housing, activities, health, and other aspects of TIAA-CREF annuitants' retirement experiences.[18] As to satisfaction with retirement, 51 percent of TIAA-CREF annuitants reported they were very satisfied and an additional 41 percent said they were reasonably satisfied. Just 5 percent indicated they were not satisfied and the remaining 3 percent were not certain or did not answer. Satisfaction with retirement is highly correlated with level of retirement income, whether retirement was compulsory or voluntary, and with marriage, and health, as might be expected. But there were wide variances within the groups studied.

Brainpower a'Wasting

One of the persistent hopes in meeting the retirement challenge is for better utilization of the talents of retired professors. A number of efforts have been made, of which several are reported on below.

Dr. James A. Perkins of the Carnegie Corporation asked TIAA in 1955 to study "the possibility of a scheme whereby some of our less well known colleges and universities would be able to bring to their campuses for a period of one or two semesters some of our distinguished but retired professors."[19] He mentioned the John H. Whitney

[16]Kevin Gray, *Retirement Plans and Expectations of TIAA-CREF Policyholders* (New York: TIAA-CREF, 1988).

[17]Mario A. Milletti, *Voices of Experience: 1,500 Retired People Talk about Retirement* (New York: TIAA-CREF, 1984, 1986, 1987).

[18]James M. Mulanaphy, *Lessons on Retirement: A Statistical Report of the 1982–83 Survey of Retired TIAA-CREF Annuitants* (New York: TIAA-CREF, 1984).

[19]Perkins to McAllister Lloyd, March 11, 1955, Carnegie Corporation Archives, TIAA file.

Foundation, which was soon to wind down its program of sponsoring such campus visits.

Retired Professors Registry. At the meeting of the American Council on Education in October 1955, Mac Lloyd and I talked with Dr. Ralph Fuchs, general secretary of the AAUP, as to whether the AAUP would be willing to sponsor a registry of retired professors. We suggested TIAA would establish such a registry, pending its being taken over by the AAUP or the Association of American Colleges or both.

By November 1957, everything was in place and the establishment of the Retired Professors Registry was announced jointly by Dr. Theodore A. Distler, executive director of the Association of American Colleges, and Dr. Robert K. Carr, general secretary of the American Association of University Professors. TIAA had obtained a significant grant to the sponsoring organizations from the Ford Foundation. Dr. Louis D. Corson, dean of men at the University of Alabama, was appointed director. The Retired Professors Registry was off to a good start. The number of registrants grew at a satisfactory pace, as did the number of available jobs. An interesting development occurred; the registry arranged with General Electric to list its qualified retirees and also with the U.S. Army for its officers, who generally retired at young ages.

Encouraged by the good start, in September 1959, I drafted an article, but never published it, called, "Brainpower a'Wasting." It emphasized the substantial reservoir of talent represented by professors retiring under the then-fixed retirement ages of many colleges throughout the United States. It recommended greater diversity and experimentation, including use of flexible retirement ages, recall of retired professors for particular research or teaching assignments, tapering off, and employing retired professors from other institutions. Each of these methods was in use at several or many colleges.

At the Registry, the number of referrals rose spectacularly during the first part of the 1960s to approximately 3,500 in 1967. But it then began declining rapidly to 1,974 in 1968, 1,432 in 1969, and to about 400 in early 1970. Problems were surfacing. Most of the placements turned out to be for a semester or an academic year to replace someone on sabbatical, a late temporary appointment just before a new academic year commenced, or other short-term appointments. The AAUP tracked only referrals, not appointments, so it was impossible to determine actual experience. It was clearly, however, a high-cost operation.

A major problem developed that may plague future efforts. As faculty shortages in the 1940s and 1950s turned into surpluses, a sparse registry list turned into an oversupply of enrollees. The older continuing staff members on college campuses were already standing in the way of younger colleagues and were not warmly welcomed at new campuses when they sought employment after retirement.

In 1970, the Retired Professors Registry was disbanded and the listing service part of it was turned over to the AAUP.

National Committee on the Emeriti. The Registry was not the only failure in what seemed to be such a promising way to use experience and intellect and offer productive scholarly lives to many people. Constantine Panunzio of the University of California at Los Angeles established the National Committee on the Emeriti, Inc., in the 1950s. Dr. Panunzio publicized his venture vigorously and emotionally, raising expectations of retired professors, especially the older ones, that they would soon have lucrative jobs. His thesis that the world owed the retired professor continuing college employment did not seem to work out. The Panunzio effort dwindled in the 1960s.

Academy of Independent Scholars. Still another noble effort was the Academy of Independent Scholars. It was established in 1979, with the help of grants from Carnegie Corporation and the Andrew W. Mellon Foundation, by the noted economists Kenneth E. Boulding and Lawrence Senesh, professors emeriti of the University of Colorado. Their approach was to try to provide funds for research, travel, lecturing, and public service for interested senior scholars. They recognized that severance from institutional support diminished the intellectual efforts of academic scholars. At its height, the academy enrolled over 400 scholars. But little additional foundation and corporate financial support was forthcoming. The academy was disbanded in 1987.

Among the moving epitaphs for the academy was one by Harlan Cleveland of the University of Minnesota:

> The Academy of Independent Scholars was such a good idea that it will shortly have to be reinvented. . . . Nearly all the policy about the elderly has been focused on the 15 to 20 percent who are unable to cope without massive support systems—hospitals, nursing homes, special transportation, home-delivered meals, or whatever. Without neglecting the compassionate end of the scale, we (as a society) need to devote much more time, attention, and imagination to the 80-plus percent of the elderly and coping. The academy . . . has been a rare and precious improvisation on this theme.[20]

These were the major efforts to use retired academic talent and to offer interesting assignments to older scholars. Someday, someone or something will tap the pool of creativity, wisdom, and vision of older

---

[20]Quoted in *Academy Notes* 7 (August 1987), p. 1.

college faculty members skilled in working at the outer edges of knowledge and turn it into a vital force for themselves and society. It could be that the voluntary sector of the economy offers more possibilities than those yet mined.

COMMUNICATIONS

College Advisory Services

The heart of TIAA-CREF's personal contact with institutions on their designing of benefit plans is the college service group. In the very early days, TIAA President Pritchett would visit individual cooperating institutions, talking with the president, the top business officer, and perhaps a faculty committee concerning the installation of a retirement plan. When I arrived in 1941, one of my early assignments was to share in college and university visits, then handled mostly by President Henry James and Vice President Rainard Robbins. I found this a most rewarding responsibility—much travel, but contact with people I liked and respected.

At the end of World War II, TIAA formalized the institutional counseling service and placed it under William H. Cobb, formerly vice president for finance of the University of Iowa. I followed Cobb and in turn was succeeded by Tom Edwards. Robert E. Fisher developed broad contacts with private colleges and educational associations; George R. Harrison, having been a bank trust officer, became the technical expert on all phases of pension plan design; and we gave Joseph W. Kifner a mandate to organize a major effort to extend TIAA-CREF services within the public college and university sector.

Over the years, the counseling and development activities became far larger and more sophisticated. Subsequent heads of the effort were Donald S. Willard, Francis A. Loewald, and John J. McCormack. In addition to leading the college counseling effort, John McCormack is a principal representative of TIAA-CREF in Washington.

Extension of Social Security coverage, development of major medical, disability, and group life insurance, and a number of other products, such as supplemental retirement annuities, retirement transition benefit, and cost of living insurance, increased the demands both on TIAA-CREF's staff and on college personnel and business operations. As mentioned elsewhere, colleges and TIAA-CREF have to deal with ever more complex governmental regulations. Many college officers have served higher education with distinction in handling these developments. TIAA-CREF has developed a diverse and highly professional staff to handle the increasingly complex aspects of benefit plan counseling. This includes effective development of college retirement plan provisions, compliance with complicated federal and state laws and regulations, and tax matters.

Institutes. One of the effective, efficient, face-to-face communications methods developed in the 1950s was nationwide college institutes. A major challenge for TIAA has always been to communicate effectively with the college world while keeping its costs low. When Social Security was finally extended to the private colleges as of January 1951, TIAA's small staff faced the problem of talking with the entire college world, working with colleges and universities in adjusting their TIAA retirement plans to coordinate with Social Security, and informing college staff members about their new Social Security coverage.

Much of this communication was accomplished by a series of institutes at which top TIAA officers met with college officers and faculty members. This method provided a useful interchange of ideas and assured that material being discussed was pertinent to questions being asked. This same communications method was used to explain CREF in 1952; Social Security to public institutions when it was extended to them in 1955; and major medical and disability insurance when TIAA introduced them in 1956. From 1956 to 1978, institutes were a regular feature of TIAA-CREF communications. They were then superseded by branch offices and extended individual contact.

Branch offices. With TIAA-CREF's rapid growth in number of cooperating educational institutions and participants, it became more efficient and effective to establish regional offices, to work closely with the growing number of plan administrators and the developing network of experts, and to visit campuses and meet with groups of staff members. The first branch offices were established in Atlanta and San Francisco in November 1982. Now, TIAA-CREF has many officers and highly professional specialists working directly with the colleges, regionally or from New York, and maintains branch offices in Atlanta, Boston, Chicago, Dallas, Denver, Detroit, New York, Philadelphia, San Francisco, and Washington, D.C.

Individuals. A major challenge for TIAA-CREF has always been to communicate with large numbers of individuals, now over a million participants, on complex concepts. Over the years, leaflets, bulletins, pamphlets, booklets, and books have been developed to meet the informational needs. For example, the *Participant* newsletter, initiated in 1972, provides an overview of important developments and issues for TIAA-CREF policyholders, while the quarterly transaction reports and the annual annuity benefit reports give policyholders specific information about their own accounts. One of the most interesting series was designed to counsel people approaching retirement. The availability of computers and instantaneous access to financial and individual data have vastly increased the scope of individual information provided by letter, telephone, and other personal communication devices. Because TIAA and CREF have no soliciting agents, most communications are written, giving a challenge to staff members to prepare readable, accurate and informative material and a challenge to policyholders to read with care and attention material about what is, in most cases, their largest source of savings.

A document of major importance to policyholders is the annual report of TIAA-CREF. Many life insurance companies count on their agents to keep policyholders informed and send out only minimal annual reports. For TIAA-CREF's participants, its annual report is the comprehensive communication covering stewardship during the previous year, financial information, investment experience, and important governmental and tax actions affecting benefit arrangements. Many other matters—investment policy and performance, fiduciary responsibilities, new products or services—receive full reporting in the annual report.

Just ask us, we can now tell you. Computers and communication advances have offered vast increases in the quantity and speed of information available to TIAA policyholders. TIAA's first remittances in 1918 no doubt were prepared by green-eyeshaded quill penners from the colleges transcribed by green-eyeshaded quill penners at TIAA. Electronic accounting machines "revolutionized" these clerical operations with punch-card operations and were in turn made obsolete by IBM 1401 machines in the early 1960s, IBM 360s later in the decade, and then, revolution on top of revolution.

Substantial direct computer-to-computer conversation with the educational institutions now takes place. Forty years ago, by employing rows of skilled computers (people were the "computers" then) TIAA could send out the 55,000 "blue slip" premium reports and projections to its participants by the first of April. Now, once all the input has been recorded, personalized reports of premiums received, interest credited, and benefits purchased and projected can be sent out to a million participants a day or two after the computers are let loose.

Concurrently, a battery of terminals at desks of TIAA-CREF specialists provide the information for toll-free telephone calls or transaction activities. In 1989, there were over 500,000 toll-free calls to TIAA-CREF's participant information and benefit payment centers; the automated telephone service processed some 13,250 calls per month. Within five days of the end of each quarter, TIAA mails out over 1 million reports of accumulation status.

These technological developments have provided order-of-magnitude increases in the capacity of TIAA-CREF and other financial institutions to serve participants with current, comprehensive information and complex data.

TIAA-CREF Informational Material

TIAA-CREF sends to colleges and policyholders a constant stream of informational material relating to decisions facing participants. This includes publications on supplemental retirement annuities; continuing participation in Social Security; choices for receiving benefits; allocating premiums between TIAA and CREF; and tax questions for annuitants.

In 1977, "Reflections for Tomorrow," TIAA's first corporate film, presented a broad overview of the TIAA-CREF retirement program and how it works. A video production group was established in the mid-1980s, and is responsible for producing a wide variety of training and informational videos. And personal computer software disks are available from TIAA-CREF for individuals wanting to turn out their own computations.

NEW VENTURES

TIAA frequently has worked with foundations and other educational organizations to study, initiate, and strengthen organizations designed to serve the college world and meet needs of its people. The Retired Professors Registry and the Faculty Children's Tuition Exchange were mentioned earlier in this chapter. Other organizations such as the Common Fund and the Investor Responsibility Research Center deserve mention here.

The Common Fund

Few organizations have been planned quite as far ahead as the Common Fund for Nonprofit Organizations. Chartered at TIAA's instigation by a special act of the New York legislature in 1955, the Common Fund was a direct outgrowth of CREF. It was designed to help educational institutions increase the productivity of their endowments. For reasons given below, the Common Fund did not become operational until 1971.

Upon receiving the New York State Charter establishing the Common Fund for Nonprofit Organizations, TIAA proposed to work with Ford Foundation financial support toward its implementation. Several factors intervened to push it to a back burner. One was that the Ford Motor Company made "too much" money in 1955 and paid out very large dividends to stockholders, including the Ford Foundation. The foundation had to disburse a massive amount of funds in compliance with the Internal Revenue Code. It decided on its stunning $500 million set of grants to colleges and universities and hospitals. But it also decided not to risk the chance that the colleges would suddenly dump $100 to $200 million on a fledgling Common Fund, so it with-held its financial support.

Not until 1966 did the Ford Foundation regain interest. McGeorge Bundy, then president, had concluded college endowments in general were poorly managed and so stated vigorously in the foundation's an-nual report. I called Dr. Bundy to tell him about the plans we had developed and about the charter for a Common Fund for Nonprofit Organizations that we had obtained from the New York legislature. He was interested. I offered the charter and TIAA's expertise; Bundy of-fered financial support to get the fund going and expense subventions for the first few years; we agreed that TIAA would organize, promote, and establish the new fund as an independent organization.

Eight days after the charter for the Common Fund was activated in June 1969, nine educational institutions had agreed to be its first institutional members and to form its first operational board. These were: the Association of American Colleges, California Institute of Technology, Collegiate School (New York), Dartmouth College, Maca-lester College, Mercer University, University of Michigan, Princeton University, and Shaw University.

William Slater, then TIAA's director of research, headed the orga-nizational efforts. John Meck, the highly regarded treasurer of Dart-mouth and a CREF trustee, was elected chairman of the new board. Working with TIAA and with this newly constituted board of trust-ees, Ford made grants of $2.8 million during the first three years of operation of the fund plus enough to reimburse TIAA for expenses incurred in the fund's organization and for continuing work with the fund's trustees.

The new fund was especially fortunate in its choice of president and staff director. George F. Keane, a former TIAA-CREF officer, has provided distinguished leadership as president from the fund's incep-tion. The Common Fund commenced operations July 1, 1971, with more than 70 colleges, universities, and independent schools partici-pating as charter members. By 1988, it had become a set of funds to-taling over $7 billion in assets and with nearly 1,000 participating member institutions.

A crucial early policy decision was to use outside investment managers. The initial operating board selected three equity managers after a nationwide search for its first investment fund, a common stock fund. By 1988, the Common Fund offered nine funds ranging from equities to bond to international funds to a "South Africa Free Fund" and short-term funds and asset allocation arrangements. It uses about 40 investment managers, each with distinct management expertise and style.

But this is not a history of the Common Fund. TIAA-CREF and the Common Fund have shared objectives, officers, trustees, and an abiding effort to serve higher education. We are pleased to have played a significant role in establishment of the Common Fund and have watched with pride as it earned an enviable reputation for service to the college world.

Investor Responsibility Research Center

When social issues on corporate proxies began to arise, colleges and universities, and TIAA-CREF, foundations and other endowed institutions, and pension funds found themselves making overlapping visits to the same companies and to South Africa on fact-finding missions. As discussed in Chapter 13, informal discussions among a number of officers from these institutions ultimately led in 1972 to establishment of the Investor Responsibility Research Center (IRRC). TIAA-CREF has been represented on the center's board since its inception.

Student Loan Discount Fund

In the spring of 1958, TIAA decided to do something about student loan funds. The first formal step toward implementation was a meeting attended by Messrs. Devereux C. Josephs of the New York Life Insurance Company and former TIAA president; Charles G. Stradella of General Motors Acceptance Corporation; Cloyd Laporte of Dewey Ballantine, TIAA counsel; and R. McAllister Lloyd, William C. Greenough, and Francis P. King of TIAA.

The group considered the need for loan funds and the chances of changing the negative American viewpoint toward borrowing for higher education expenses. We met with Ivy League presidents, Beardsley Ruml (a well-known businessman and political counselor), foundation executives, and many others. In view of the subsequent history of noncollection of student loans, it is interesting to note one of the earliest conclusions of the TIAA-sponsored committee: "It was agreed that the fund should be made available to all colleges, but that it was up to the Student Loan Discount Fund to examine the credit risk involved and, further, to help educate business officers on credit selection."[21]

TIAA made much progress with the idea during the summer. Meanwhile, Congress was becoming vitally interested. The National Defense Education Act of 1958 provided substantial sums for a federal loan program. The committee "decided to suspend its operations for the time being" and turn over its studies to the government. The federal program filled the gap in student loan fund needs so fully that TIAA did not return to the subject.

---

[21]Frank P. King, "Summary Record of Meeting March 18, 1958", WCG files.

Related Activities

By its very nature, TIAA-CREF has attracted the interest and service on its board and committees of many of America's outstanding educators. In like manner, TIAA-CREF's officers have been interested in many other organizations in higher education. They helped to organize such institutions as the Overseas Education Service and the ones mentioned above. They have served on committees too numerous to mention of the ACE, AAUP, AAC, and others. This mutual activity has been useful.

Over the years, TIAA-CREF's chairmen, presidents, and other officers have also served as trustees on a variety of other *pro bono* boards. Only a sample can be given here: the Agricultural Development Council, the American Academy in Rome, the American Geographical Society, the Asia Society, the Aspen Institute for Humanistic Studies, various Carnegie boards, the Committee for Economic Development, the Devereux Foundation, the Huntington Library and Art Gallery, the Metropolitan Museum of Art, the New York Public Library, the New York Historical Society, the Overseas Development Council, the Rockefeller Foundation, the Rockefeller Institute for Medical Research, and the Russell Sage Foundation.

PART SIX

Security Achieved, Mostly Loyal Opposition, Future Agenda

CHAPTER 24

Security Achieved

College staff members entered the 1980s at a high point in financial security. Virtually all colleges had retirement plans, and the benefits available from TIAA-CREF and other pension systems, supplementing Social Security, had reached a solid level of adequacy scarcely contemplated over the decades. The colleges had installed plans to protect against the financial problems of total disability and large medical expenses and had added good group life insurance benefits to supplement the life insurance staff members carried on their own.

By 1980, 3,400 nonprofit educational institutions had joined in an immense cooperative venture in portable pension plans. More than 700,000 persons were participating in the retirement plans alone. Total assets of TIAA-CREF reached $14.7 billion by the start of 1980, and assets were more than doubling every four years. Total assets reached $35.1 billion by 1984 because of strong CREF performance and were up to $60 billion by 1988; they hit $70 billion by the end of that year. And TIAA-CREF became the largest pension fund, as shown in Table 24–1.

Strong investment experience over the decades accounted for much of the advancement toward security. In 1980, TIAA annuitants were receiving 15 to 30 percent more dollar annuity income than when they retired 10 to 15 years previously on what they thought would be fixed-dollar annuities.

Common stock prices, and therefore the values of participants' CREF accounts, were nearly twice as high in 1980 as at the low on the Dow index of 578 in December 1974 and nearly five times as high in 1987. For those who look only at the highs, stock prices were essentially flat for a dozen years; they had risen to a high of 985 on the

TABLE 24–1 Top 10 Pension Funds

Rank	Pension Fund Sponsor	Assets in Millions
1	TIAA-CREF	$67,141
2	California Public Employees	45,940
3	New York State/Local	37,918
4	General Motors	37,600
5	N.Y.C. Retirement Systems	35,537
6	AT&T	35,143
7	General Electric	25,300
8	California State Teachers	24,721
9	New York State Teachers	22,779
10	IBM	21,761

SOURCE: From a list of the top 200 pension funds/sponsors in *Pensions & Investment Age*, January 23, 1989. Reprinted with the permission of *Pensions & Investment Age*, Copyright Crain Communications, 1989.

popular Dow index in December 1968, to another high of 1,052 in January 1973, and to 1,015 in September 1976.

For CREF's steady participants in the retirement plans, the 1970s were a period of remarkable opportunity. If $100 a month was invested in a CREF deferred annuity from January 1970 to December 1979, a total of $12,000 would have been invested. With no further premiums, the CREF accumulation, after all expenses, would have been valued at $15,724 on January 1, 1980; five years later, it would have been $31,302; and on December 31, 1988, the initial $12,000 would have grown to $62,470. A pleasant reward for the so-called disappointing common stock period of the 1970s! The 1980s became the enjoyable period of rising and high common stock performance for both contributing and retired CREF participants.

During the 1970s, Social Security was making major strides in the level of social benefits provided for Americans. The 1974 law increased benefits and provided that all future benefits would rise automatically with increases in the cost of living.

But benefit increases in the 1970s outran Social Security's financial base. This was corrected by 1983 legislation. I was involved in recommending some of the changes through my membership on the President's Commission on Pension Planning and as chairman of the Committee for Economic Development Subcommittee on Reforming Retirement Policies.

Social Security, plus TIAA, plus CREF, plus strong investment earnings, plus strong college and individual contributions to annuities, plus other benefit plans had provided the great majority of college staff members with a reasonable level of economic security in retirement or in preretirement adversity.

TIAA and CREF had reached a solid level of accomplishment by 1980. It had met many challenges; many were to come. One unsolved problem was the painfully divisive issue of whether equal monthly benefits or equal lifetime benefits were the fairer system for both men and women, an issue not fully resolved by the courts, as discussed in Chapter 21. It was an issue that for the first time divided the college world significantly on a benefit matter.

CHANGING OF THE GUARD

Greenough Graduates

Since TIAA-CREF is expected to last hundreds of years, and I may not be that durable, the time for me to retire as CEO came August 1, 1979. I had joined the staff of a small, well-thought-of pension plan for college members in 1941. Only two of us, McAllister Lloyd and I, had headed the operation for the entire period after World War II. I could look back with satisfaction to the period of exponential growth and service of TIAA. I could remember with pleasure working with many fine people in the college world and TIAA-CREF's trustees, officers, and staff. I could contemplate with special pleasure the success of CREF. I could watch from the sidelines as unsolved or new challenges were met. It was my wife's and my turn to say, "It's my retirement money—take good care of it."

Tom Edwards Elected Chairman

Tom Edwards, elected chairman and CEO by the board to take office August 1, 1979, had already given long service to TIAA-CREF, its policyholders, and its cooperating institutions. A Phi Beta Kappa graduate of the University of North Carolina, Edwards served in the Army for four years and then for two years with the Northwestern Mutual Life Insurance Company before joining TIAA in 1948. He was in charge of TIAA's college and individual counseling services for many years. He was elected president in 1967.

In addition to his management responsibilities, Edwards' clear writing style had enriched much of the explanatory material for policyholders and participating institutions. He had served on a number of pro bono boards of trustees and of national pension study groups. Edwards was a key figure in the postwar period and would now preside over turbulent times in the history of financial institutions and of TIAA-CREF itself.

FORCES FOR CHANGE

Many inside and outside factors made the 1980s a time ripe for rapid change at TIAA-CREF. The following developments had profound ef-

INTO THE 1980s
MATURITY

Thomas C. Edwards
President, 1967–79
Chairman and CEO, 1979–84
Service, 1947–84
(Bachrach)

James G. MacDonald, 1957–87
President, 1979–84
Chairman and CEO, 1984–87
Service, 1957–87

fects on savings and investment in the United States and direct or indirect effects on TIAA-CREF.

Demographic Changes

Powerful forces include the aging of the professorial staffs, the emergence of two-earner and two-pension-owner families, the movement of the baby-boom generation through the school system and now through the working years, increasing life expectancy, and the elimination of fixed retirement ages.

Deregulation within the Financial World

Deregulation freed the banks, securities firms, and savings institutions to offer competitive products at competitive interest rates. This

Walter G. Ehlers
President, 1984–88
Service, 1969–88
(Bachrach)

led to extended competition and overlapping functions among banks, brokerages, savings institutions, life insurance companies, mutual funds, and pension funds.

Deregulation of savings institutions occurred in the middle of volatile interest rates. A major change occurred when federal agencies discarded Regulation Q, which had for decades mandated low enough interest rates on deposits to assure profitability of nearly all banking institutions, no matter how ineffectively they were managed. There followed a dangerously large number of massively bad investment practices, leading to colossal federal bailouts.

On May 1, 1975, high, fixed commission rates on stock exchange transactions were eliminated. This was a sort of deregulation. It provided substantial reductions in costs for CREF and released opportunities for additional computerization of the investment search process. The college world's needs had some effect on the decision through my being a public member of the New York Stock Exchange Board of Directors.

Federal Influence on Pensions

Federal regulation was being heaped on pensions as fast as it was being removed from other financial institutions. It brought financial scrutiny, fiduciary responsibility, and adequate funding to the management of employer pension plans. It brought major improvements in provisions under private pension plans such as early vesting and assured ownership rights that had always been part of the college world pensions.

But it also brought intrusive regulating of ordinary operations and mandating of many of the terms of employment involved in private retirement planning, raising the costs and hackles of pension administrators. It is difficult for regulations designed for all types of pension plans to adjust appropriately to diverse employment situations such as college professors, airline pilots, miners, and retail workers. It dampens diversity and innovation. And much of this is inappropriate because the government already controls all the rules for over half of the economic security provision through the Social Security system.

Public tax policy during the 1970s encouraged savings for retirement. The mechanisms stemmed from the part of the Technical Amendments Act obtained by TIAA-CREF for the college world in 1958. This was then extended to public schoolteachers and some other public employees and later to all workers through Keogh plans, self-employment retirement savings plans, and ESOPs (employee stock ownership plans). These devices fostered a burst of public interest in retirement savings before tax, intense competition for savers' dollars, and heightened retirement security.

Federal interest continued during the 1980s. The 1981 Tax Act introduced a variety of new opportunities for tax-favored savings, in addition to the favorable tax treatment available to educators through their institution's tax deferred annuity plan. Congress introduced all savers certificates and IRAs through qualified voluntary employee contributions (QVECs). But then the 1986 tax act set complicated and lower limits on some of the tax-encouraged savings arrangements. Congress also eliminated age 70 mandatory retirement for other than tenured staff members and eliminated it for those on tenure after December 31, 1993.

Congress also caused the first breach in full vesting of TIAA-CREF college plans by mandating coverage under retirement plans at young ages. As reported in the 1988 chairman's report of TIAA-CREF, "On the cost containment front, we responded to institutional requests for delayed vesting for faculty at younger ages, so as to minimize employer expenses during the high-turnover years." This was another example of an unintended result of narrowly based social legislation.

Changing Financial Arena

Except for TIAA-CREF, the Equitable, the Metropolitan, Prudential, the Phoenix Mutual, and a few others, life insurance companies were largely out of the annuity business before the 1950s. But with the advent of CREF and the subsequent separate accounts for pension funds, life insurance companies entered the corporate pension arena with vigor, and they began to emphasize individual annuities. TIAA-CREF has always had aggressive competitors but until recently largely unsuccessful ones. There is nothing proprietary, or protected by patent or copyright, in any of TIAA-CREF's methods of operation or offerings. In the academic tradition, it has always made all of its information, contract provisions, and operations available for study and adoption.

Commercial life insurance companies can and at times have copied contracts almost verbatim. HERAA (Higher Education Retirement Annuity Association, a for-profit subsidiary of Integrated Resources, New York) was set up in November 1987 to compete specifically for TIAA-CREF's market.

The 1980s have seen an explosion of new mutual funds. Mutual funds can not write lifetime annuities, but they can provide tax-sheltered savings arrangements. This occurred first through ERISA and then through liberalization in later years. This encouraged mutual funds to compete vigorously for retirement business on the college campuses. The New York Times and The Wall Street Journal report daily on large families of funds; there are more than 1,600 funds in operation. They cover all kinds of investments, from common stock growth, income, international, specific industry, and many other specialized stock funds to bond funds, money market obligations, and real estate through real estate investment trusts (REITs).

Technological Change

Computerization led within TIAA to a revolution every three or four years in the efficiency with which the hundreds of millions of precise financial transactions can be carried out, in the ready availability of information that can be offered participants, and especially in investment analysis and transactions.

The communications revolution provided new opportunities for effective communications with participants. TIAA-CREF participants can now find the value of their annuity accumulations at any time, 24 hours a day, seven days a week, through an automated telephone service, and they can transfer funds among certain TIAA-CREF funds from 8 A.M. to 8 P.M. weekdays. This does not mean participants should continually shift back and forth among funds. But it does offer a remarkable contrast to the early decades of CREF when the idea was that participants should make long-term decisions as to allocations between TIAA and CREF and stick with them for strong long-term investment experience.

Size

TIAA-CREF's massive growth in assets during the post-World War II period to $70 billion in 1988 brought it to the leading edge of America's financial institutions and to the head of the list in pensions. But being the largest is not always comfortable, as AT&T, General Motors, New York City, and other behemoths know. As TIAA-CREF became huge, with a vast spread of investments and broad coverage in the educational world, it began to suffer the same fate as so many other successful, dominant organizations—it became an attractive target.

TIAA-CREF's longtime strategy of "quiet exclusivity" had brought it incredible growth and increasing prominence. But there is no place for a $25 billion or a $70 billion giant to hide. New strategies were called for.

GRADED BENEFIT PAYMENT METHOD

Meanwhile, a noteworthy product was introduced to participants. On January 1, 1982, TIAA announced yet another of its inflation-protection devices. TIAA made available its graded benefit payment method to allow individuals to take a lower annuity benefit in the initial years in return for a probably much larger annuity as they grow older. This system works in tandem with CREF to allow annuitants to plow forward some of their lifetime annuity income to provide further protection against inflation. (The graded benefit is discussed in Chapter 16.) The graded benefit joined the other three TIAA inflation-induced developments—CREF in 1952, the disability income inflation escalator in 1967, and the cost-of-living life insurance provision in 1973.

CLIMATE FOR CHANGE

The 1980s brought progress, growth, and conflict to the college pension system. The most fundamental of the issues concerned college and staff member savings under the regular operation of the basic college retirement plan. Cashability, transferability, flexibility—the "bility" issues—became prominent. In the first seven decades of TIAA-CREF, one of the central strengths of the college system was the noncashability and nontransferability of annuity savings before retirement. This protected the individual against depleting his or her retirement savings by spending them before retirement for routine living expenses, emergencies, poor investments, or lack of foresight.

Retirement means loss of earned income, unemployment, at a time of life when much greater medical expenses are likely to be incurred. The college has always had a basic, overriding interest in all

this—it installs a retirement plan so it can part in a socially acceptable manner at an appropriate point with its superannuated staff
members. The oft-repeated past experience of some non-TIAA-CREF
plans has been devastatingly convincing that cash, loan, or lump-sum
values did militate against security in retirement.

But a question arises: Has the very success of TIAA-CREF in recent decades changed the situation? TIAA-CREF benefits arising from
the regular operation of college retirement plans, with the strong additions for investment earnings, give far more leeway than before.
Furthermore, in 1988, for workers retiring at age 65, Social Security
provided a replacement rate of 71 percent at the lower levels of earnings; 41 percent for average earnings; and 23 percent at the maximum
wage base used in Social Security, $45,000.

Retired people have one risk parameter if they are just barely going to make it financially and quite another if, as a remarkable number now attest, they have more to live on than they did while
employed.

The achievement of reasonable income adequacy and the revolution occurring in financial services brought challenging questions.
Should changes be made in TIAA-CREF governance, in the financial
counseling it offered, in its descriptive materials? What would be the
effect of changes in the financial world on TIAA-CREF and the college world's benefit plans?

A basic set of fundamental pension principles, "paternalistic"
and "inflexible" some called them, had served the college world well
during the developmental 60 years. Was it time for more flexibility,
more individual choice and responsibility, more chance to opt for
alternative financing vehicles than TIAA-CREF then provided? But
if such flexibility were offered, would it deteriorate into cash withdrawals at changes of employment and at retirement, frustrating the
purposes of the retirement system?

TIAA and CREF, perhaps because they gave participants more
flexibility than almost any other pension fund, began to receive requests for still greater flexibility. Several colleges, individuals, and
educational associations led this effort. Unfortunately, the requests
were met at TIAA-CREF in the early 1980s with, "We like it as it is"
and "If it ain't broke. . . . " Undoubtedly, for the great majority of institutions and individuals, this was an acceptable response, but not
for some. In their essay in the *TIAA-CREF 1982 Annual Report*, Tom
Edwards, chairman, and James G. MacDonald, president, responded
to what was shortly to escalate into a major issue:

Whose Concern Is It Anyway?

On some campuses the traditional view of pension concerns and responsibilities has been replaced by one that shifts them from the em-

ployer to each plan participant. After all, goes the argument, as long as these pension contributions are visibly and fully vested in the individual, "Whose concern is it anyway?" So at some institutions the customary protective aspects of pension plans have given way to a hands-off, multiple-choice, sink-or-swim freedom as to how future pension funds will be invested and ultimately paid out. To each person is given the decision of where to send current pension plan contributions, whether to TIAA-CREF or to other financial media. . . .

Employers and employees alike have a stake in the provisions and the end results of their pension plan. . . . We believe a pension plan has the best chance of fulfilling [its] objective if its investment focus is long term, and its provisions are geared to producing an income that will last as long as the retired staff member lives. . . .

In short, we are not planning to enter the banking business, to merge with or take over other types of financial organizations, or to try to emulate the many emerging fund cafeterias. . . . We do intend to keep developing and implementing those changes and new services that seem both in step with the times and appropriate for this pension system.

Edwards addressed the 1982 meeting of the National Association of College and University Business Officers in Los Angeles on July 26. He included a discussion of adequacy of retirement benefits and the investment moves TIAA and CREF were taking to combat the inflation of the late 1970s. He emphasized the "variety of financial goodies being marketed for the everyday consumer—TDAs, IRAs, QVECs, money market funds, bank CDs, silver, gold, gems, and oil wells."

Edwards then spoke strongly in favor of limiting options:

I think the institution's most important question here is whether giving multiple options will defeat the essential purpose of its pension plan: that is, systematically accumulating enough during the working years to assure both the employer and the employee that the parting at retirement will be orderly and that the retired worker will have an income from the plan that can't be outlived. . . .

Can you retain enough control to keep your plan on course, or will it be all sail and no rudder? If there's a push for multiple choice on your campus, you may want to go for it. But first satisfy yourself that you'll still have a pension plan by limiting alternatives, specifying the provisions and getting the support services you need. . . . And lest it go unsaid, if your present plan is meeting reasonable objectives by normal retirement age . . . there's a lot to be said today for staying with something that works.

In the same month, the first of a two-part report by the National Association of College and University Business Officers (NACUBO) was published in the form of an interview with four senior officers of TIAA-CREF: Tom Edwards, Walter G. Ehlers, James S. Martin, and

John J. McCormack.[1] The questions covered availability of options and investment experience and demonstrated the focusing of interest on TIAA-CREF.

TIAA-CREF's then leaders were defending the fundamental ideas, philosophies, and innovations that had carried it to a pinnacle of success in the pension world. They were describing the policies and products that had built the most successful multi-employer pension system ever. They were trying to counteract the attacks of competitors offering cashable, nonpension products as substitutes for retirement income policies. But they attacked reasonable suggestions for new services with a vigor equal to that reflected in their attack on unhelpful suggestions.

The top management was perceived by both friend and critic to be saying there was no room for improvement. Suggestions for new funds and new options were attacked as being merely imitative and that they would establish a financial mobile, tinkling in the variable wind. This resulted during the mid-1980s in TIAA-CREF leadership developing a reputation for stubborn resistance to change and evolution.

Since the start in 1918, TIAA and then TIAA-CREF and the college world had been vigorous, stimulating colleagues. Much of the innovativeness had been encouraged by the imagination and receptivity of the educational enterprise. For decades, the constructive, vigorous discussions and actions on mutual challenges had enriched the relationships among the college world and TIAA-CREF, its servant. It was severely damaging when this mutual problem-solving approach started to erode.

---

[1]"NACUBO Report: TIAA-CREF," *Business Officer,* July 1982, pp. 11–13.

CHAPTER 25

Mostly Loyal Opposition

Many studies of college benefit plans and of TIAA-CREF services to the colleges have been conducted over the years. The early Carnegie studies, the statements of principles of the AAUP-AAC, the analyses by TIAA-CREF, and the discussions surrounding them have been especially powerful in determining the provisions and options of benefit plans.

The period from 1983 to 1987 saw a different series of examinations of TIAA and CREF. It became a period of analysis, criticism, and controversy. Most were constructive, fair, useful, and led to needed changes. Some were destructive, incorrect, and unfair. Some were in the form of newspaper articles, speeches, comments. Some were in the form of individual attacks on the system. Some were in the form of long, expensive commission studies and publications. As top management's defensiveness increased and as delays on the long-promised money market annuity turned from months into years, the decibels of the criticism increased. By failing to anticipate, or to react effectively to the early requests for moderate change, the stage was set for later dramatic action.

It would be scholarly, but repetitious, to present here an analysis of each of the reports and its conclusions and to indicate how the changes that were to take place in TIAA-CREF were affected by each recommendation and each report. It would be attention-getting to describe the vehemence and intensity of some of the criticism. But these studies run to hundreds of pages and are currently available. Here we will give a short overview of each study and some of the reactions, give references, and then present the changes made in TIAA and in CREF toward the end of the decade.

Robert L. Jacobson of the *Chronicle of Higher Education* wrote several articles about TIAA-CREF, the first of which was published November 24, 1982. Jacobson stated, "Over the years, since the establishment of TIAA in 1918 and CREF in 1952, the companies have built a mostly favorable reputation in academe." But TIAA-CREF officers felt that was the last thing good he had to say about the companies for the next several articles. He discussed flexibilities, options, investment experience, and defections from the TIAA-CREF fold.

> Reports from a small but growing number of colleges and universities point to similar disenchantment among academic employees across the country, raising the possibility that TIAA-CREF plans may soon face a major wave of competition from mutual funds.

He then reported that Johns Hopkins University was opening three new investment options for its faculty and senior staff. The University of Rochester opened such a choice in 1981, and Stanford University was studying alternatives. He listed four others currently considering alternatives out of the then 3,600 participating institutions.

Jacobson added:

> Some of the recent complaints against TIAA and CREF have focused on their policies of barring participants from freely shifting their previously invested premiums between regular and variable annuities as they may see fit, and prohibiting them from "cashing out"—or withdrawing—more than 10 percent of their pension funds in a lump sum at retirement.

A January 13, 1983, letter from David Z. Robinson, vice president of Carnegie Corporation of New York, to Tom Edwards, said:

> Recently, a number of events have occurred that make me feel profound changes will take place in TIAA's national role. Some of these changes may be beneficial to the policyholders. I will welcome them even if they are detrimental to TIAA. Some of these changes will be bad for the institutions and policyholders and TIAA.

Dr. Robinson subsequently wrote a long memorandum asking many questions about retirement ages, contribution levels, voluntary or compulsory participation, income options after retirement, whether to provide cash at retirement (lump-sum option), and whether improvements in Social Security have made private pensions unnecessary for small colleges. He then sponsored what became the Commission on College Retirement, chaired by Oscar Ruebhausen, and discussed further below.

The May 1983 issue of NACUBO's *Business Officer* carried a long article by Roy A. Schotland, professor of law at Georgetown University, criticizing TIAA-CREF for "its lack of flexibility for participants." This had to do with what he called the locked-in retirement accounts, available only as a retirement benefit. Schotland called for a number of changes, including colleges offering alternatives to TIAA-CREF, more consistent reporting of investment results, changes in governance, and hiring some outside investment managers for CREF. Coupled with what some considered ineffective response to its critics by TIAA-CREF, Schotland's attacks fueled the escalating demands for change.

The discussion turned into controversy and spread to other publications. The *Chronicle of Higher Education, Institutional Investor,* and *Higher Education Daily* all quoted TIAA-CREF Chairman Edwards as firmly rebutting Schotland's demands. As Edwards said in the July 1983 *Institutional Investor:* "At the present time, we're not considering multiple funds. We don't have much doubt but that would basically alter our whole purpose. . . . We're planning to remain a pension system. Let me put it that way." *The Wall Street Journal* of September 14, 1983, and *Barron's* of November 5, 1984, published critical articles about these previously low-profile pension plans.

In 1983, plans to study TIAA-CREF in depth were separately announced by three organizations: Carnegie Corporation of New York, with its proposed Commission on College Retirement; the National Association of College and University Business Officers Ad Hoc Committee on TIAA-CREF; and TIAA-CREF's own Trustees Ad Hoc Committee on Goals and Objectives.

In this arena of discussion, each study benefited from the ones that had preceded it, and, at its best, each provided new information and perspectives. At times it was difficult to discern the light from the heat. And despite the heat, there was little fusion of ideas.

MACDONALD SUCCEEDS EDWARDS

Tom Edwards retired as chairman and CEO of TIAA-CREF February 1, 1984, and was succeeded by James G. MacDonald. Edwards had joined TIAA in 1948 to develop its life insurance offerings for college staff members. During his 36 years, he was successively responsible for life insurance, individual counseling, and subsequently the advisory division in charge of communications and plan development with the college world. He became president in 1967 and succeeded me as chairman in August 1979. He was a central figure in the growth of benefit plans for the colleges for over a third of a century. The

Annual Report included a fitting acknowledgment of Edwards's "dedicated and able service . . . and . . . the importance of his dynamic leadership during a period of historic economic, social, and legal changes."

James G. MacDonald, the new chairman and CEO, had, as mentioned in Chapter 17, joined TIAA in 1956 to organize its new group insurance division to provide disability income and major medical insurance under the Ford Foundation $5 million grant. He became president in August 1979 and chairman on the retirement of Edwards in 1984. Walter G. Ehlers, who had joined TIAA in 1969 as a securities investment officer, was made president, succeeding MacDonald. James S. Martin, executive vice president since 1979, at the same time was promoted to chairman of the CREF finance committee and member of the CREF board of trustees. He had joined the CREF investment office as vice president and investment manager in 1974.

In his chairman's report for 1985, MacDonald stated:

> We continue to believe that a pension plan should provide retirement benefits only in the form of a lifetime income. However, for those institutions that believe [their] pension plan needs . . . would be better served by a plan which provides a lump-sum cash option . . . last year we made available the Group Retirement Annuity (GRA).

PERSPECTIVE—THE GOOD NEWS

By 1984, it was clear that TIAA-CREF's critics were articulate and determined. What was not so clear, however, was how widely dissatisfaction—or satisfaction, for that matter—was felt by TIAA-CREF policyholders. Therefore, TIAA-CREF commissioned the Roper Organization to conduct a survey of TIAA-CREF's image among both active TIAA-CREF participants and administrators. A total of 1,500 telephone interviews were conducted using a sample size typical of a nationwide Gallup or Harris opinion poll.

The Roper "Image" study's overall findings, published in July 1984, showed that 57 percent of active participants were very satisfied with TIAA-CREF and an additional 35 percent were somewhat satisfied, for a total of 92 percent. Less than one half of 1 percent of participants were not at all satisfied, and the remaining 8 percent answered "not too satisfied" or "don't know." With administrators, the figures were 70 percent very satisfied and 27 percent somewhat satisfied for a total of 97 percent in the top two categories.

Some perspective is useful when considering such figures. A 1984 poll by the National Opinion Research Center found only one institution—medicine—in which a majority, 51 percent, of those surveyed had a "great deal of confidence."[1] A 1988 Harris Poll reported that only 15 percent of the public gave Congress a high confidence rating.[2] Only 19 percent of those surveyed gave a vote of high confidence for leaders of American business, and only 13 percent for those in law firms.

In 1987, Roper again surveyed TIAA-CREF participants and administrators in a detailed set of studies conducted jointly for the Washington Higher Education Secretariat's Pension Issues Committee[3] and TIAA-CREF.[4]

The primary purpose of the Pension Issues Study was to determine what individuals and institutional officers want and expect from a pension plan. Questions covered areas such as current level of satisfaction, knowledge of the plan, views on choices and flexibilities available, and needs and desires for change. Sixty percent of surveyed participants indicated they were very satisfied with TIAA-CREF, and more than 70 percent of participants wanted few or no changes in TIAA-CREF products and services. Institutional officers were asked to rate TIAA-CREF on eight service and performance aspects. Majorities of 70 percent or more rated TIAA-CREF as excellent or good on six of the eight. Two somewhat lower marks, 48 percent to 68 percent excellent or good, were given to TIAA-CREF's responsiveness to changing institutional and changing employee needs. A majority of institutional officers saw the need for changes in products and services.

These were powerful votes of confidence in TIAA-CREF and its work with educators over the decades. They were strong confirmations of the basic benefit programs and products. But they were not mandates for no change—for everything OK as is. They were clearly a call for new options, products, and services.

NACUBO REPORT

A NACUBO ad hoc committee on TIAA-CREF published the first in a series of critical reports in August 1984 in its *Business Officer*

---

[1]"National Opinion Research Center, General Social Surveys—Confidence in Institutions Trend," Public Opinion Archive, The Roper Center, University of Connecticut, Storrs.

[2]The Harris Poll, news release, May 8, 1988, Public Opinion Archive.

[3]The Washington Higher Education Secretariat, convened and coordinated by the American Council on Education, is comprised of the chief executive officers of over 30 national higher educational associations. The Secretariat's Pension Issues Committee was appointed in December 1985 to meet with TIAA-CREF "to consider jointly those matters related to the objectives of colleges and universities in offering pension plan coverage for their faculty and staff members."

[4]*Report of the Pension Issues Study Conducted for the Washington Higher Education Secretariat and TIAA-CREF* (New York: The Roper Organization, October 1987). The 329-page report is summarized in a separate "Executive Summary." The February 1988 TIAA-CREF *Participant* includes a summary of the report's highlights.

magazine.[5] The committee criticized the companies for not creating new funds. It recommended "a range of investment alternatives," including external rollover opportunities, a family of investment funds within TIAA-CREF, payout options under certain conditions, and further study of flexibility for "old" versus "new" money.

This report was one of the first to center on what NACUBO called TIAA-CREF's "reluctance to increase flexibility for 'old money,' that is, the over $15 billion already invested in TIAA and the $15 billion already invested in CREF."

This attacked the basic philosophy of the first fully vested and portable plan to be developed, that is, that the college contribution is paid to an annuity contract owned by the individual, but only available as a lifetime annuity or death benefit. This assures the college the funds it contributed for a particular purpose will be used for that purpose. As one college president said:

> Vesting, that superbly virtuous characteristic of TIAA-CREF, seems to me to be the principal reason the distinction between a pension fund and a savings account is so often ignored. The "old money" was contributed under a fixed and clear set of understandings.

COMMITTEE ON GOALS AND OBJECTIVES

TIAA-CREF's Ad Hoc Committee on Goals and Objectives was formed in early 1984 "to study and define the goals and purposes of TIAA-CREF for the remainder of this decade."[6] Composed of current and past trustees, the committee carefully reconsidered the fundamental philosophies of college benefit plans, including a review of the recommendations of the successive joint AAUP-AAC statement of principles. It found them sound, viable, and crucial.

The committee considered extensive information and documentation, including actuarial, investment, and financial data, material provided by NACUBO, the Consortium for the Financing of Higher Education, and the Employee Benefit Research Institute. Among its major conclusions and recommendations, the ad hoc committee agreed that an "interest only" option should be provided (available January 1, 1989) and affirmed the plans for introduction of a money market annuity.

---

[5]See the following articles in *Business Officer:* "NACUBO Report: TIAA-CREF User Issues," August 1984, pp. 15–23; "TIAA-CREF Responds to NACUBO Report," September 1984, pp. 11–12; "NACUBO and TIAA-CREF Reports: How They Compare," April 1985, p. 9; "NACUBO Subcommittee Concerned over TIAA-CREF Projection Statements," May 1985, p. 8; "NACUBO Report: Committee on TIAA-CREF Issues Final Report; Focus Is on Flexibility," October 1985, pp. 31–35.

[6]*Report of the TIAA-CREF Ad Hoc Committee on Goals and Objectives to the Joint Boards of Trustees of TIAA-CREF, December 31, 1984* (New York: TIAA-CREF, 1984).

The ad hoc committee's final report, submitted to the boards December 31, 1984, ran 224 pages. Copies of the report went to 3,700 cooperating educational institutions and associations, and a summary was sent to all participants.

For investment options, the ad hoc committee recommended a long-term marked-to-market bond fund as a third CREF fund. Unlike NACUBO, the ad hoc committee took a much more cautious view of other possible new funds: It opposed the so-called low-risk, high-risk, and balanced funds and suggested further study be given to an equity real estate fund. The committee also rejected any *retroactive* rollover or cashout options, that is, any relaxation of rules pertaining to "old money" accumulated in individual annuities over the years. The committee recommended the group retirement annuity for institutions wishing to provide cash or transfer options at the time of employment termination or retirement.

COMMISSION ON COLLEGE RETIREMENT

Carnegie Corporation of New York voted $750,000 in 1983, and the Ford Foundation, the William and Flora Hewlett Foundation, and the Andrew W. Mellon Foundation added smaller amounts for a total of $1.5 million to revisit provisions of retirement plans in light of changes in recent years. Carnegie added $500,000 in 1986 for distribution and follow up on the reports and to study long-term care for catastrophic illnesses.[7] The study covered the effect on college retirement ages of ADEA's change in mandatory age, the effect of other governmental actions such as ERISA, the lessening of distinctions among financial institutions such as banks, pension funds, and brokerage houses, and new options for investment and benefits.

The commission began issuing reports in January 1986. The subjects ranged from retirement age policy to long-term health care. Other commission recommendations included a call for wider use of partial indexing methods to offset inflation, such as the TIAA graded benefit annuity; increased availability of financial information and planning services; and a proposed plan for long-term health care insurance.

Two of the reports discussed the issue of transferability. The commission's policy statement recommended the adoption of alternatives

---

[7]*Retirement Ages for College and University Personnel* (New York: Commission on College Retirement, January 1986); *Transferability of Funds Being Accumulated by TIAA-CREF for the Benefit of College and University Personnel* (May 1986); *A Pension Program for College and University Personnel* (May 1986); *Implementing Financial Planning, Information, and Administrative Services: Discussion Draft* (July 1986); *A Plan to Create Comprehensive Group Long-Term Care Insurance for College and University Personnel* (July 1986); *Transferability of Funds Invested with TIAA-CREF: The Legal Issues* (May 1987).

to TIAA-CREF and, within prescribed procedures, full transferability of accumulated TIAA-CREF assets held for individuals ("old money") to alternate vendors.

This report concluded TIAA-CREF might be required under New York State law, at the joint request of an employer and employee, to transfer previously accumulated funds to other pension vehicles. This statement in the commission report was quickly attacked by the Washington Pension Issues Committee as being "irresponsible," "destructive," and litigious.[8] TIAA-CREF asked the law firm of Dewey Ballantine to analyze the contracts and the state and federal insurance and pension laws applicable to TIAA-CREF pension plans. Dewey Ballantine's conclusions differed markedly from those of the commission, which it concluded were in error.[9]

MONEY MARKET FUND

In April 1982, a task force under the direction of Jim MacDonald, president, was appointed to design and implement a money market account and to take cognizance of the hurdles of Internal Revenue and the SEC. This proved to be a massive and complicated job, requiring restructuring to place participant records on a daily basis and long confrontations with competitors and some educators in connection with registration with the SEC. The money market account did not become operative until April 1, 1988. This six-year delay became a focal point of criticism of TIAA-CREF for presumed foot-dragging and unresponsiveness.

Demand for a money market account arose in the late 1970s and early 1980s when inflation in American soared to double-digit levels. This drove all interest rates to the highest points ever reached in peacetime America. Commercial paper rates reached a nearly 17 percent annual rate of total return for 1981 and were much higher at times during the year. This was an inversion of historical interest rates; short-term rates exceeded long-term rates by about 2 or 3 percent. The inversion lasted about 18 months.

Eighteen months is a short time when investing pension savings. But it was the third time in a decade that short-term rates had exceeded long-term rates, leading some to conclude that inversions might become a more frequent phenomenon in the future. This produced a sustained demand for a money market fund at TIAA-CREF by some of the study committees, colleges, and individuals in the early 1980s.

---

[8]Quoted in *Chronicle of Higher Education*, May 28, 1986.

[9]The legal opinion papers are included in the commission's second report on *Transferability*, May 1987.

Over the long run, stocks have provided substantially larger total return for savers than other investments, but they are more volatile. Long-term bonds and mortgages tend to outrun money market-type investments by a substantial margin during periods of level or declining interest rates. But interest rates rose so steadily and at times rapidly throughout much of the 1950s, 60s, and 70s that money market investments toward the end of the period became more than usually competitive with longer maturity portfolio holdings.

First Money Market Fund

Money market funds have been an enormously successful financial innovation. A former TIAA securities department head, Henry B. R. Brown, established the first fund in the early 1970s, leading to a $300 billion industry. (He wistfully commented to me recently that he would be fabulously wealthy except "you can't patent an idea." I told him it was ever thus—it was the same with CREF.) Brown was with TIAA from 1963 to 1968. He and Bruce Bent, also a former TIAA securities officer, filed for SEC registration of the Reserve Fund, a money market fund, in February 1970. Their new fund started selling to the public January 1, 1973.

Money market funds cannot issue lifetime annuities, so they do not directly meet pension needs. A number of life insurance companies established money market variable annuity plans starting in 1982 to fill this market.

Economic Research

Comparative performance of various kinds of investments have been widely studied over the last dozen years. The Ibbotson-Sinquefield studies, published first in 1976 in the *Journal of Business*, have provided a comprehensive comparison of performance of various financial instruments over time. The latest study, for 1926 to 1988, showed common stocks provided a total return of 10 percent a year, but with high volatility. Total return on long-term corporate bonds happened to be just half that for stocks, 5 percent, with far less volatility. U.S. Treasury bills provided total return of only 3.5 percent annually, but with low volatility. This was the same conclusion reached in my study for CREF, *A New Approach to Retirement Income*, covering 1880 to 1950, that over any of the periods approaching 30 years in length, common stocks had performed better than any of the alternatives.

Dr. Zvi Bodie, then associate professor of finance at Boston University and a research associate of the National Bureau of Economic

Research, published in the *Journal of Portfolio Management* in 1980 an article concluding that in the short term, and year by year, money market obligations track inflation more closely than either stocks or bonds. They generally would not provide as much total income as a common stock fund, but they would track year-by-year cost of living changes more closely.

Dr. Steven Weisbart, now second vice president, headed TIAA's economic research work for the money market fund. One of his most important conclusions was that if a money market fund had been in operation from 1952 to 1988, its annual performance would not have differed much from that of TIAA, although variations during short periods would have been substantial. During the entire period, CREF stock performance would have materially exceeded both of the other funds, but with much greater year-by-year variability.

In designing a money market account for TIAA-CREF, the task force decided all of the main aspects of the existing college pension arrangements would be kept in place. This meant TIAA-CREF eligibility rules would be the same for the new account; accounting, advisory, and other services to the colleges would be extended to accommodate the new account; and the same income options available from TIAA and CREF during retirement would be provided for participants.

Administration

Most of the operational departments of TIAA-CREF faced extensive planning work for the new money market fund. Over 1 million new riders to CREF certificates would be issued; actuarial calculations and projections were necessary; the existing explanatory material for participants and college officers would be rewritten and much new material written; and increases in skilled staff were planned for. But by far the biggest job was shifting all of the existing CREF common stock fund, not just the new fund, to daily accounting, to confirm to the SEC's requirements for mutual funds.

The SEC's requirement for daily accounting and valuation necessitated multiple new accounting, annuity, and investment systems; extensive changes in existing computer programs; and a major increase in capacity to handle processing and changes in allocations by a million participants. The effort, headed mainly by John A. Putney, Jr., executive vice president, took several years and involved many TIAA-CREF staff members. Such extraordinary realigning of multiple systems occurs rarely. It took a long time to accomplish, accounting for some of the delay in introducing the money market account. But when the switch was thrown April 1, 1988, everything went smoothly.

Corporate Organization

By far the most portentous early decision in connection with the money market account was to make it a separate CREF fund account. An option was to place it in TIAA, but the new fund would then have had to provide guarantees under state insurance laws. This would require reserves and compliance with other not-too-relevant aspects of insurance law and regulations. The option of establishing a separate mutual fund would not provide the essential element of a life annuity for participants. A third option, establishing a separate corporation, such as CREF, under Trustees of T.I.A.A. Stock, was also discarded, perhaps without enough serious consideration, in view of what happened later.

The final choice was to make the new fund a part of a series fund structure in CREF. This decision then drove many subsequent crucial decisions and was a factor in the delays before the money market account became operative April 1, 1988. The next chapter will conclude the discussion of the money market fund introduction and will also cover the difficult negotiations leading to SEC registration of CREF.

CHAPTER 26

Future Agenda

MANAGEMENT CHANGES

Dr. Clifton R. Wharton, Jr., Becomes Chairman

TIAA-CREF crossed the $50 billion mark by the end of 1986, became the largest private pension plan in the world, and elected a new chief executive officer to preside over the next $50 billion surge.

This significant change in command at TIAA-CREF was effective February 1, 1987. The boards of trustees elected Clifton R. Wharton, Jr., chairman and chief executive officer following the decision of James G. MacDonald to take early retirement after a 31-year career with the companies. Before becoming head of TIAA-CREF, Dr. Wharton was chancellor of the State University of New York, America's largest university system, from 1978 to 1987. Before heading SUNY, Dr. Wharton was president of Michigan State University from 1970 to 1978 and an officer of the Agricultural Development Council from 1957 to 1969. He is a specialist in economic development and U.S. foreign policy. As head of TIAA-CREF, Dr. Wharton became the only black to lead a Fortune 500 service company.

When he joined TIAA-CREF, Dr. Wharton was chairman of the Rockefeller Foundation and director of such corporations as Ford Motor Co. and Time Inc. He holds a B.A. in history from Harvard, an M.A. from Johns Hopkins University, and an M.A. and Ph.D. in economics from the University of Chicago.

Dr. Wharton moved on several fronts to address the climate of criticism. He set about energizing the major changes that are to ensue in TIAA-CREF's pension offerings and approach. This included implementation of the money market fund and its concomitant

1987–
FUTURE AGENDA

Clifton R. Wharton, Jr. *Chairman and CEO, 1987–*	*John H. Biggs* *President, 1989–* *(Bachrach)*

registration of CREF with the SEC. It included other new products and funds, new attitudes toward "old money," and other new products and services that were to come. He established an ombudsman system, perhaps the only formally designated ombudsman for customers of a U.S. financial service organization. Dr. Wharton appointed the Future Agenda Committee, whose recommendations are now being implemented.

Top Management Changes

James G. MacDonald, who stepped down as chairman of TIAA-CREF on February 1, 1987, was president from 1979 to 1984 and chairman for the ensuing three years. The boards expressed their appreciation for MacDonald's services as trustee and chairman and before that as president and longtime officer:

[His] emphasis on thorough and balanced consideration of complex issues, his willingness to respect an individual's views, and the sound and steady judgment he has brought to bear in making unusually difficult strategic decisions, have done much to guide TIAA-CREF through a period of fundamental change for the organization.

Walter G. Ehlers, who joined TIAA-CREF as investment officer in the TIAA securities department in 1969, was president from 1984 until his retirement in 1988. James S. Martin continued as executive vice president of TIAA-CREF and chairman of the finance committee of CREF. Both are mentioned at greater length in the investment sections of this study.

John H. Biggs was elected president of TIAA-CREF at the annual board meeting in November 1988, effective February 1, 1989. Biggs, a CREF trustee since 1983, was chief executive officer of the Centerre Trust Company of St. Louis. Previously, he had been vice chancellor for financial affairs of Washington University in St. Louis. He served on various advisory groups for educational and financial institutions and is the author of actuarial articles on pensions. A fellow of the Society of Actuaries, he early became interested in variable annuities. His 1969 article titled "Alternatives in Variable Annuity Benefit Design" was used for a decade in the Society of Actuaries courses.[1] He received a bachelor's degree from Harvard and a Ph.D. in economics from Washington University. Biggs brings to his responsibilities at TIAA-CREF a combination of executive and administrative experience in the educational and financial world relevant to TIAA-CREF management.

MONEY MARKET FUND

CREF's new fund, a money market variable annuity, as reported in the previous chapter, became available to participants April 1, 1988. The money market account is invested in U.S. government obligations, bank obligations, commercial paper, repurchase agreements, and corporate debt securities such as bonds having a remaining maturity of less than two years.

The investment objective of CREF's money market account, as stated in published material, "is to realize high current income to the extent consistent with liquidity and preservation of capital." The "high current income" sought is what is available from investing in high-quality money market instruments maturing generally in one year or less. The "capital preservation" derives from short-term dol-

---

[1]John H. Biggs, "Alternatives in Variable Annuity Benefit Design," *Transactions of the Society of Actuaries* 21 (November 1969), pp. 495–528.

lar valuation of the savings fund, insulated from potential capital gains and losses provided by equities and long-term bonds.

The money market account was introduced to provide additional diversification of savings for retirement and flexibility to shift funds back and forth from stocks to fixed-dollar assets.

The new fund got off to a fast start; by the end of its first three months of operation in June 30, 1988, its assets totaled $362 million and by the end of 1989, had reached $2 billion.

SECURITIES AND EXCHANGE COMMISSION

During 1987 and 1988, two developments that were to have major consequences for the TIAA-CREF of the future moved along more or less concurrently. One was the progress of CREF's registration with the Securities and Exchange Commission; the other was the formulation and approval of a special trustee report and recommendations, *TIAA-CREF: The Future Agenda*.

To a significant extent, particularly with respect to the subjects of transferability and cashability, the two proceedings were interrelated. Certain recommendations contained in *The Future Agenda* actually preceded the results of the SEC action, but they could not be implemented until completion of the SEC matter, into which they became incorporated.

In preparation for the introduction of the money market fund, CREF had formally filed its registration statement with the SEC on September 26, 1985.

It was accompanied by a request for exemptive relief from certain requirements of the Investment Company Act of 1940 primarily in order to continue as a pension system. In particular, relief was sought from the requirement that accumulated CREF funds be available for cash-out on seven days notice and from the act's procedures on election of trustees. As indicated in Chapter 9, CREF previously had been exempt from SEC registration as a 501(c) (3) nonprofit organization.

The SEC registration, however, had ramifications that went well beyond what initially had been seen as a more-or-less routine filing. But this was not known in July 1987 when the SEC, by a vote of 3–0, conditionally approved CREF's application for exemptive relief. Encouraged by this affirmative indication, TIAA-CREF set October 1 for the introduction of the money market fund.

As part of the approval process, the SEC allowed interested parties until August 4 to file requests for a hearing. By the time that date rolled around, some formidable parties had intervened. These included the American Council on Education together with the American Association of University Professors, the National Education

Association, Stanford University, and the Investment Company Institute, representing the mutual fund industry. All wanted an opportunity to express their views on changes CREF might be making.

Another issue that came more sharply into focus as a result of the new developments was CREF's governance. Traditionally, the 20 members of the CREF operating Board of Trustees were formally elected by the Members of CREF, with four of them selected by policyholders through the Policyholder Nominating Committee. Under the Investment Company Act, however, all trustees would be required to be elected by the "shareholders," that is, the participants. CREF had sought an exemption to be able to continue its long-standing practice that had worked so well.

Faced with the prospect of a full-scale SEC proceeding, which could culminate in a formal hearing, TIAA-CREF had no immediate recourse but to postpone introduction of the money market fund. In October, it filed an application for temporary relief so the money market fund could become effective pending the outcome of the overall process.

The temporary relief was granted January 21, 1988. At the same time, the SEC administrative law judge set March 16 for a hearing for the application of permanent relief. CREF then prepared materials for an April 1 money market launch.

At the March prehearing conference, the SEC administrative law judge set a formal hearing date for June 6, but he strongly urged the parties to negotiate a settlement and avoid the lengthy and costly process. The parties accepted, and a series of hearing postponements was granted to encourage the process.

From May through December 1988, TIAA-CREF representatives, headed by John McCormack, executive vice president for Pension and Annuity Services, and Peter Clapman, senior vice president and associate general counsel, held extensive discussions with attorneys for the intervenors in Washington.

Coincident with the maneuvering, *The Future Agenda* was following its own track. Released in November 1987, it included a recommendation providing for the transferability of CREF "new money" and called for a study of the possibility of "old money" transfers. On April 28, 1988, following completion of this study, the trustees formally approved an "old money" transfer model. These actions helped reduce the distance between the parties in the SEC negotiations, but long hours were spent in hammering out the details. To help speed the process, CREF removed its request for exemption on the governance issue.

The agreement finally was reached December 21, 1988, with all the major intervenors adding their signatures. Essentially, it provided that new transferability and cashability options would go into effect within six months of the date the SEC issued its final order accepting the settlement. CREF decided it would use the occasion to also offer institutions two new CREF investment funds, recommended in *The Future Agenda*, for their pension plans.

On August 22, 1989, the final SEC order was issued, approving the terms of the settlement and ending four years of strenuous endeavor.

The agreement provided for unprecedented flexibility for policyholders to transfer their funds between various investment alternatives or to receive lump-sum payments on termination of employment, subject to their employer's approval. And it provided for direct election of CREF trustees.

The major provisions of the revolutionary agreement were:

- To the extent permitted by the employer's pension plan, employees will have the option of transferring CREF accumulations to alternate funding vehicles approved in the college's plan.
- As a separate option, lump-sum distributions of CREF accumulations can be made at the termination of employment to the extent permitted by the college's pension plan.
- CREF funds accumulated under a prior employer's plan can be transferred if provided for under the prior employer's plan. If not, they can be transferred if the prior employer gives consent.
- CREF will fully inform employers of the lump-sum option details and election procedure but will have the right to advise employers that it has historically recommended against lump-sum distributions.
- CREF must adopt and implement voting procedures in compliance with the provisions of the Investment Company Act of 1940, under which all CREF trustees will be elected by participants.

THE FUTURE AGENDA

By far the most significant of all the studies and reports is the 1987 one titled *TIAA-CREF: The Future Agenda*.[2]

The various committees on college pension funds during the 1980s had distinguished themselves from earlier TIAA-CREF,

---

[2]*TIAA-CREF: The Future Agenda. Report of the Special Trustee Joint Committee, November 18, 1987* (New York: TIAA-CREF, 1987). See also the "Executive Summary."

Carnegie, AAUP, AAC, and other surveys by their contentiousness—either vigorous criticism or vigorous defense or both. The "thesis" and the "antithesis" led to the "synthesis." Dr. Wharton appointed a special trustee joint committee on *The Future Agenda*. The committee was given two charges: first, "to study TIAA-CREF management recommendations on prospective pension planning policy . . . and to consider appropriate pension plan objectives and plan administration." And second, "to review recommendations made in recent years by various educational associations and by pension-oriented study groups." With the advent of this effort, the climate returned to a positive, program-building endeavor.

The committee produced a draft report in just four months from June to September 1987. The draft of the agenda was distributed widely, to presidents, business officers, and faculty committees for comment. Representatives from TIAA-CREF's Institutional Counseling Service met with college and university administrators around the country. All told, the committee drew on hundreds of responses—letters, telephone calls, group and one-on-one discussions. Positive and encouraging comments were in abundance, as were repeated calls for TIAA-CREF to seek transferability of "old money." But thoughtful caution was also expressed about new funds—who should bear the responsibility for their cost and the amount of information and counseling needed for participants to make intelligent decisions.

The final result was a set of 26 recommendations covering much of TIAA-CREF's service to the college world.

At the start of 1990, the 12 policyholder services recommendations had been implemented or were in progress. Planning for 8 of the 14 recommendations regarding new product and governance recommendations was also complete, 2 others were in progress, and 4 were pending.

The committee's recommendation of five new CREF funds and one new TIAA fund was designed to provide new options to the continuing main TIAA and CREF funds. They would be in addition to the recently added CREF money market fund. The new TIAA II fixed-dollar fund would permit greater transferability among funds.

The call for new funds was responsive to the many requests for options to the existing TIAA-CREF funds. Individuals could design their own mix of investment funds supporting their retirement. The recommended addition of new funds did not raise particularly difficult philosophical questions. It did raise practical problems.

As indicated in the Roper reports, a large majority of TIAA-CREF participants are satisfied with the choices they already have, and many do not consider themselves sophisticated in investment matters, nor do they want to get involved in sorting among additional options. So it was vitally important to continue the long-standing basic funds.

In view of the changes in the 1980s, the time had clearly arrived to give greater choice to those who wanted it. Even if they were, as some said, mainly economists and finance professors, with an occasional mathematician or physicist or philosopher, perhaps it was their turn. And the time also had come to reassure participants that the "classic" TIAA and CREF equity funds continued available for their use without material change.

The first two new funds to be offered (effective March 1, 1990) were the CREF Bond Market Account and the CREF Social Choice Account. The latter was in recognition of a relatively small but persistent demand over many years for policyholders who wanted a "socially responsible" fund.

The new product flexibilities also are useful additions to the TIAA-CREF system. The loan value option and the "interest only" option both were made possible recently by changes in the federal rules applicable to 403(b) annuities.

Now for the explosive proposal.[3] As the Agenda Committee stated it: "Explore overcoming the obstacles to transferability of regular retirement annuity accumulations; studying the feasibility of CREF transfers first; and then the best method of providing TIAA transferability." This "old money" subject refers to accumulations in TIAA and CREF derived from premiums already paid to, and accumulating

---

[3]Since I am writing this history, I owe it to the reader to give some idea of my reaction to as significant a document as *The Future Agenda.* During my retirement in the last 10 years, I have refrained from making any comments not specifically requested, but comments were so requested in this case. My own seven-page memorandum commented favorably on the report in general and with special enthusiasm for new funds suggested and the extensions of policyholder services. "Such flexibility should be provided for individual savings."

I did have one fundamental reservation. I took major exception to the recommendation that the decision as to whether to allow lump-sum distributions and transfers of "old" as well as new money should be returned to each institution. I believe this to be a system-wide decision in a multi-employer arrangement such as TIAA-CREF, not one to be made by each institution. "It would be a calamity to change (TIAA-CREF) from a nationwide system to essentially a set of single-employer plans by making each employer make decisions that should be made by the system as a whole." And I commented: "It is fun to beat TIAA-CREF over the head for their 'paternalism.' But the preservation of retirement benefits provision is not TIAA-CREF's, it was in the original Carnegie study setting up TIAA; it has been in every AAUP-AAC report on good retirement practices; it is in the thoughtful writing on the subject; it has served well in practice; and it is an essential ingredient of true portability. . . . Once the genie of cash and transferability of old and new funds for all institutions is out of the bottle, it can't be stuffed back in." From now on it will be the colleges that are "paternalistic" if they are not "flexible" in allowing wide transfers of existing funds and choice among outside funds and lump-sum payments. But perhaps the time has come for even this fundamental provision to change. And it has been changed.

in, existing TIAA and CREF annuity contracts under the college retirement plans.

The issue is not whether there should be freedom for the individual to manage his or her own personal savings, as distinct from the amounts set aside under the regular operation of the college retirement plan. This choice and freedom was extended by TIAA-CREF in 1973 when the cashable TIAA-CREF supplemental retirement annuity contracts were introduced. They have been used widely since, mostly in connection with the tax-deferred savings arrangements approved by Congress.

This most basic of the recommended changes is the relaxation of inviolability of pension savings at TIAA-CREF, and therefore at the colleges. For 70 years, the no-cash-value philosophy has prevailed in the basic retirement plan. The strong philosophy was that security of educators in retirement, and their right to have full and immediate vesting and ownership of all employer contributions, rested on noncashability. Now, under the pressure of outside criticism, recommendations of external committees, and accommodations to SEC agreements, this decision is to be given to the individual colleges to make, instead of by all the participating institutions acting through the system itself, TIAA-CREF. This places the college at the pressure point of paternalism, a difficult position for it to occupy.

Will it work? It is a very big step.

Service to Participants

The Future Agenda committee made 12 recommendations as to addition and extension of services for policyholders. It emphasized the importance of information at the individual policyholder level. It recommended the establishment of a policyholder ombudsman. Dr. Wharton appointed Louis Garcia, longtime corporate secretary, to the new post of ombudsman. He also established the TIAA-CREF "At Your Service" system.

The agenda committee suggested changing the corporate name of the top boards to more clearly reflect their primary duties as "overseers and electors." It also suggested a new committee on products and services to concentrate board attention on these two functions.

TIAA-CREF moved rapidly to implement the recommendations, including those that were fundamental changes in the venerable and successful system. Dr. Wharton's chairman's report to the board stated in November 1989:

> In years to come, the date August 22, 1989, may be thought of as just another hot, summer day. But, for the current generation of

TIAA-CREF trustees, employees, institutions, and policyholders, it marks the formal end of one exciting era and the beginning of another.

That was the date the Securities and Exchange Commission issued its order ending a legal process that began in 1985 when CREF first moved to register under the Investment Company Act of 1940. The August signing of the order also started the clock moving on implementation of a wide array of new options—new CREF investment funds, transferability, cashability, services—and other major modifications of the traditional TIAA-CREF way of doing business. . . .

With transferability and cashability we are moving into uncharted waters. Each of these has the potential to do damage to the basic retirement and pension philosophy pioneered by TIAA-CREF over the past 71 years. And, for the first time, institutions are having to make very basic decisions on the options they will permit their employees to select. We plan to work very closely with staff benefit administrators and with policyholders to objectively set forth the pros and cons of these new opportunities.

Classic TIAA-CREF Going Well

Change makes more gripping reading than the story of continuing successful management of TIAA-CREF in all of its divisions. During the 1980s, as reported in the chapters on TIAA and on CREF investments, continued progress was made in the move toward financial security in retirement. Communications with 4,300 colleges and 1 million participants entailed millions of reports, newsletters, announcements, acknowledgments, and telephone contacts. Educational research during the 1980s emphasized attitudinal research, especially with retired people. TIAA-CREF received many millions of premium payments and credited them to participants' accounts. And all of the regular legal, actuarial, accounting, administrative, and other policyholder service activities continued on schedule.

Estimated January 1, 1990

Institutions participating in TIAA-CREF System	4,325
Policyholders accumulating annuity benefits	1,070,000
Policyholders receiving annuity income	215,000
Individuals covered by TIAA group insurance plans	550,000
Benefits during 1989	$2,000,000,000

These advances toward economic security of college people can be summarized in one exponential sequence, the growth of TIAA until 1952 and the subsequent growth of TIAA-CREF:

TIAA-CREF Assets

$1,000,000	1918
10,000,000	1927
100,000,000	1939
1,000,000,000	1961
10,000,000,000	1977
83,000,000,000	1989
100,000,000,000	199?

Future History

TIAA starts out its second 70 years and CREF its second generation under new rules. The SEC agreement and the many other changes represent fundamental shifts in the college world's approach to retirement planning. For its first 70 years, TIAA plans contained the protection to all employers in the system that transferring faculty and other staff members would have appropriate vested savings for the years worked for prior employers.

As America moves toward reliance on individuals to make intelligent choices, so moves the college world. CREF's and TIAA's governance will be different. Change is risky; to make no change is usually riskier. As Robert H. Atwell, president of the American Council on Education and a CREF trustee, said regarding the SEC registration and other changes, "This is certainly a landmark settlement—it brings to the academic community important protections and new opportunities, which will enhance the retirement programs of our institution and their staffs."

How will TIAA-CREF weather the coming intense competition for college and individual benefit plans? The October 19, 1988, *Chronicle of Higher Education* put it this way:

> A battle for the multibillion dollar college pension market is under way. . . . In one corner, with more than $60 billion in assets, 70 years of pension experience, and nearly a million policyholders at 4,000 universities and other nonprofit educational organizations, would be higher education's largest and oldest pension companies: the Teachers Insurance and Annuity Association and College Retirement Equities Fund. . . . In the other corner, the challengers: a pack of investment companies, insurance companies, and other financial competitors hungrily eyeing a lucrative market that shows promising signs of opening up.

TIAA-CREF can be expected to lose some ground as the competition scrambles onto the college campuses. But will TIAA-CREF in the long run gain because of the changes? Will exclusivity continue to be significant? If TIAA-CREF doubles in size every four years as in recent decades where will it find suitable investments? How worldwide will its already worldwide reach extend? The truly important thing is whether the college world and those who choose careers in it will be more secure.

"Till Life Do Us Part"

Life insurance and private pensions aim at the ultimate in social good. They are a remarkable mechanism in a democratic society. They are voluntary private-sector enterprises, without government subsidy. Their objective is to transfer funds from those who need them less to those who need them more; from those who live to the survivors of those who die; from the well to the sick; from "myself when young" to "myself when old."

TIAA-CREF welcomes new annuitants to the fold by saying, in the transmittal letter, that this new contract establishes a lifelong relationship between the participant and TIAA-CREF. This relationship may last a few years or 70 years. As a contract, it endures longer than almost any other.

Over the decades, the pension world has moved philosophically far toward the college world's approach to pensions. Now the colleges have moved again, toward a world of individual responsibility.

Will TIAA-CREF philosophies continue to make a difference in higher education? In the broader pension world?

Unquestionably.

Will TIAA-CREF continue its charter function "to aid and strengthen higher education"?

Of course.

Presidents and Chairmen TIAA, 1918–89, and CREF, 1952–89

	President	Chairman and CEO
Henry S. Pritchett	1918–30	
James W. Glover	1930–32	
Henry James	1932–43	1932–47
Devereux C. Josephs	1943–45	
R. McAllister Lloyd	1945–57	1947–63
William C. Greenough	1957–67	1963–79
Thomas C. Edwards	1967–79	1979–84
James G. MacDonald	1979–84	1984–87
Walter G. Ehlers	1984–88	
Clifton R. Wharton, Jr.		1987–
John H. Biggs	1989–	

Frank A. Vanderlip was nonofficer chairman of the board of TIAA from 1918–32.

Trustees, 1918–89

Trustees of T.I.A.A. Stock, 1938–89, and Members of CREF, 1952–89

Name of Trustee	Term
Anderson, Robert O. Atlantic Richfield Company	1971–78
Atwell, Robert H. American Council on Education	1987–89
Bell, Elliott V. McGraw-Hill Publishing Company	1952–66
Bell, Laird Bell, Boyd, Marshall & Lloyd	1938–52
Bowen, Howard R. Claremont Graduate School	1973–83
Conklin, George T., Jr. Guardian Life Insurance Company of America	1982–89
Davis, John William Davis, Polk, Wardwell, Gardiner & Reed	1938–45
Douglas, Lewis W. Ambassador to the Court of St. James'	1938–47
Edwards, Thomas C. TIAA-CREF	1979–84
Foster, Luther H. Tuskegee University	1983–87
Friday, William C. University of North Carolina	1986–
Gardner, John W. Common Cause	1968–71
Garvin, Clifton C., Jr. Exxon Corporation	1978–82
Gifford, Walter S. American Telephone & Telegraph Company	1943–50
Gray, Hanna Holborn University of Chicago	1978–85
Greenough, William C. TIAA-CREF	1962–79
Hadley, Morris Milbank, Tweed, Hope & Hadley	1945–49

Adler, Frederick R. 1977–
  Reavis & McGrath
Alexander, David 1970–
  Pomona College
Alexander, James S. 1948–66
  Associated Universities, Inc.
Alexis, Marcus* 1986–
  University of Illinois at Chicago
Amon, A. Howard, Jr. 1987–
  J. C. Penney Company
Aydelotte, Frank* 1923–27
  Swarthmore College
Babbage, Richard G. 1933–34
  U. S. Realty and Improvement Company
Baldwin, George J. 1918–21
  American International Corporation
Bates, Grace E.* 1965–69
  Mount Holyoke College
Baxter, James P. III* 1955–59
  Williams College
Beebe, Howard F. 1923–26
  Harris, Forbes & Co.
Belknap, Waldron P. 1935–43
  Bankers Trust Company
Bell, Carolyn Shaw* 1977–85
  Wellesley College
Bevan, David C. 1969–70
  Penn Central Company
Biggs, John H. 1989–
  TIAA-CREF
Bliss, Gilbert Ames* 1930–34
  University of Chicago
Blunt, Albert C. III 1962–87
  The Hanover Shoe, Inc.
Bonbright, James C.* 1941–45
  Columbia University
Bowman, (Anderson) Mary Jean* 1972–76
  University of Chicago
Boyer, Ernest L. 1975–77
  State University of New York
Boyle, John B. 1948–52
  W. T. Grant Company
Bramson, Leon* 1973–78
  Swarthmore College
Brown, James Douglas* 1939–43
  Princeton University
Buck, Paul H.* 1954–58
  Harvard University
Campbell, Joseph 1950–55
  Columbia University
Carleton, Willard T. 1984–
  University of Arizona
Carmichael, Oliver C.* 1939–44
  Vanderbilt University
Cartter, Allan M.* 1967–71
  New York University
Clark, Robert C.* 1988–
  Harvard University
Cole, Charles Woolsey* 1950–54
  Amherst College

Comstock, (Notestein) Ada M.*   1940–44
  Radcliffe College
Conklin, George T., Jr.   1956–84
  Guardian Life Insurance Company of America
Crawford, Morris D., Jr.   1965–85
  Bowery Savings Bank
Day, Edmund E.*   1932–41
  Cornell University
Distler, Theodore A,   1962–66
  Association of American Colleges
Edwards, Flora Mancuso   1989–
  Middlesex County College
Edwards, Thomas C.   1966–84
  TIAA-CREF
Ehlers, Walter G.   1983–88
  TIAA-CREF
Elchlepp, Jane G., M.D.*   1982–86
  Duke University
Fairchild, Henry Pratt*   1945–49
  New York University
Ferry, Frederick C.   1918–20
  Hamilton College
Fishbein, Estelle A.*   1987–
  Johns Hopkins University
Fisher, Joseph L.   1965–74
  Resources for the Future, Inc.
Forbes, Allen B.   1918–23
  Harris, Forbes & Co.
Ford, Frederick R.   1983–
  Purdue University
Foster, Luther H.*   1957–61
  Tuskegee Institute
Franks, Robert A.   1918–35
  Carnegie Corporation of New York
Friday, William C.   1970–74
  University of North Carolina
Garrison, Lloyd K.*   1937–39
  University of Wisconsin
Gauss, Christian*   1929–39
  Princeton University
Glover, James W.*   1918–32
  University of Michigan; TIAA
Goetze, Frederick A.   1918–50
  Columbia University
Gould, Samuel B.   1968–76
  State University of New York
Greenough, William C.   1955–84
  TIAA-CREF
Griswold, Erwin N.*   1942–46
  Harvard University
Guthmann, Harry G.*   1947–51
  Northwestern University
Guttentag, Jack M.*   1978–82
  University of Pennsylvania
Hall, J. Parker   1963–70
  University of Chicago
Hall, Samuel S.   1918–36
  Mutual Life Insurance Company of New York
Hamada, Robert S.*   1984–88
  University of Chicago

Hamilton, Ruth Simms	1989–
Michigan State University	
Hayes, Henry R.	1922–52
Stone & Webster, Inc.	
Henderson, Robert	1934–41
Equitable Life Assurance Society	
Henderson, Vivian W.*	1971–75
Clark College	
Himstead, Ralph E.*	1951–55
American Association of University Professors	
Hurd, Richard M.	1952–60
Hurd & Co., Inc.	
Ingraham, Mark H.*	1949–53
University of Wisconsin	
Innis, Harold A.*	1943–47
University of Toronto	
Jackson, J. Hugh*	1946–50
Stanford University	
James, Henry	1932–47
TIAA	
Jay, Pierre	1932–45
Fiduciary Trust Company of New York	
Jenkins, Wilmer A.	1962–71
TIAA-CREF	
Josephs, Devereux C.	1943–48
TIAA	
Kane, Edward J.*	1975–87
Ohio State University	
Kelly, Dorothy Ann, O.S.U.	1987–
College of New Rochelle	
Kirkpatrick, John I.	1951–63
University of Chicago	
Knowler, Lloyd A.*	1958–62
State University of Iowa	
Knox, R. Baylor	1934–48
City Bank Farmers Trust Company	
Kreps, Juanita M.*	1968–72
Duke University	
Lamont, Thomas W.	1918–20
J. P. Morgan & Co.	
Laporte, Cloyd	1948–62
Dewey, Ballantine, Bushby, Palmer & Wood	
Lester, Richard A.*	1959–63
Princeton University	
Lewis, Ben W.*	1964–68
Ford Foundation	
Lindquist, Warren T.	1975–81
SCETAM, Inc.	
Lindsay, Samuel McCune*	1921–25
Columbia University	
Lloyd, R. McAllister	1945–68
TIAA-CREF	
MacDonald, James G.	1979–
TIAA-CREF	
MacDonald, Milton T.	1951–65
T. B. O'Toole, Inc.	
Mackenzie, Michael A.	1918–37
University of Toronto	
MacKenzie, Norman A. M.	1948–63
University of British Columbia	

Maclean, Joseph B.   1937–59
   Mutual Life Insurance Company
Mahlstedt, Walter   1970–79
   TIAA-CREF
Mason, Edward S.*   1956–60
   Harvard University
McCahan, David*   1944–48*
   University of Pennsylvania
McDonald, George C.   1935–48
   McDonald, Currie & Company
Meck, John F.   1965–67
   Dartmouth College
Miller, William O.*   1927–31
   University of Pennsylvania
Mitchell, Charles E.   1919–33
   National City Bank
Moulton, Harold G.*   1935–39
   Brookings Institution
Munro, William B.*   1934–38
   California Institute of Technology
Newcomer, Mabel*   1948–52
   Vassar College
Nicely, James M.   1946–64
   Ford Foundation
Nicolson, Frank W.   1918–20
   Wesleyan University
Ogburn, William F.*   1936–40
   University of Chicago
Odegaard, Charles E.   1963–70
   University of Washington
Oliver, William T.   1922–32
   Bank of Montreal
Olson, (Spieckerman) Josephine E.*   1974–86
   University of Pittsburgh
Pannell, (Taylor) Anne Thomas Gary*   1963–64
   Sweet Briar College
Perkins, James A.   1957–65
   Cornell University
Plimpton, Francis T. P.   1946–68
   Debevoise, Plimpton, Lyons & Gates
Pritchett, Henry S.   1918–34
   TIAA
Reed, Alfred Z.   1918–23
   Carnegie Foundation for the Advancement of Teaching
Reinhardt, Uwe E.*   1978–
   Princeton University
Rich, Charles V.   1918–21
   National City Bank
Richardson, R. G. D.*   1926–35
   Brown University
Richter, Otto C.   1959–62
   American Telephone and Telegraph Company
Rietz, Henry L.*   1933–37
   State University of Iowa
Robbins, Rainard B.   1945–51
   TIAA
Robichek, Alexander A.*   1976–78
   Stanford University
Root, Elihu, Jr.   1920–46
   Root, Clark, Buckner & Ballantine

Sauvain, Harry C.*   1966–76
  Indiana University
Scanlon, John J.   1971–79
  American Telephone and Telegraph Company
Scholes, Myron S.*   1979–83
  University of Chicago
Schwulst, Earl Bryan   1943–65
  Bowery Savings Bank
Seager, Henry R.*   1925–29
  Columbia University
Shalala, Donna E.*   1985–89
  University of Wisconsin, Madison
Shaw, Edward S.*   1963–67
  Stanford University
Shaw, Walter B.   1980–
  Turner Corporation
Simon, Leonard S.*   1981–
  Rochester Community Savings Bank
Sinclair, John S.   1939–48
  New York Life Insurance Company
Slater, Joseph E.*   1970–82
  Aspen Institute for Humanistic Studies
Slichter, Sumner H.*   1952–56
  Harvard University
Smith, Shirley W.   1939–51
  University of Michigan
Smith, Sidney E.*   1938–42
  University of Manitoba
Spencer, William I.   1968–74
  First National City Bank
Surrey, Stanley S.*   1972–78
  Harvard University
Taylor, Jacob B.   1959–62
  General Telephone & Electronics Corporation
Thompson, Earle S.   1948–59
  West Penn Electric Company
Thorne, Landon K.   1939–44
  New York, N.Y.
Tobin, James*   1969–72
  Yale University
Tregurtha, Paul R.   1981–
  Mormac Marine Group, Inc.
Turner, Howard S.   1970–80
  Turner Construction Company
Tuttle, Franklin B.   1952–70
  Atlantic Mutual Insurance Company
Umbeck, Sharvy G.   1966–73
  Knox College
Urstadt, Charles J.   1985–
  Urstadt Property Company, Inc.
Vanderlip, Frank A.   1918–32
  American International Corporation
Vaughan, Walter   1918–21
  McGill University
Wallace, Phyllis A.*   1980–89
  Massachusetts Institute of Technology
Waltrip, William H.   1980–
  IU International Corporation
Warner, Leslie H.   1965–81
  General Telephone & Electronics Corporation

Warren, Francis B.	1961–69
Turner Construction Company	
Wharton, Clifton R., Jr.	1986–
TIAA-CREF	
Whitney, George	1920–39
J. P. Morgan & Company	
Whittlesey, Charles R.*	1962–66
University of Pennsylvania	
Wilcox, Clair*	1960–63
Swarthmore College	
Willits, Joseph Henry	1941–57
Rockefeller Foundation	
Wilson, Charles Z., Jr.	1976–81
University of California, Los Angeles	
Wilson, O. Meredith*	1961–65
University of Minnesota	

Trustees of CREF, 1952–89

Name of Trustee	Term
Ackerman, Laurence J.	1954–62
University of Connecticut	
Adelman, Irma*	1984–88
University of California at Berkeley	
Adams, Roger*	1953–57
University of Illinois	
Atwell, Robert H.	1989–
American Council on Education	
Bailey, Elizabeth E.*	1986–
Carnegie Mellon University	
Benston, George J.*	1977–81
University of Rochester	
Bernstein, Peter L.	1977–88
Peter L. Bernstein, Inc.	
Bevan, William*	1972–
John D. and Catherine T. MacArthur Foundation	
Biggs, John H.	1983–
TIAA-CREF	
Biggs, William R.	1952–55
Bank of New York	
Blanding, Sarah G.*	1956–60
Vassar College	
Blum, Walter J.*	1970–82
University of Chicago	
Boulding, Kenneth E.*	1958–62
University of Michigan	
Bowen, Howard R.*	1960–64
Claremont Graduate School	1966–70
Bramson, Leon	1978–79
Swarthmore College	
Brimmer, Andrew F.	1984–
Brimmer & Company, Inc.	
Brinkerhoff, James F.	1981–
University of Michigan	
Brown, Fred E.	1960–81
J. & W. Seligman & Co.	

*Policyholder-selected trustee

Bunting, (Smith) Mary I.   1971–78
   Radcliffe College
Carleton, Willard T.*   1980–84
   University of North Carolina at Chapel Hill
Claflin, William H., III   1964–72
   Tucker, Anthony & R. L. Day
Cole, Charles W.*   1952–54
   Amherst College
Conway, Jill Ker   1977–85
   Smith College
Daum, F. Arnold   1972–78
   Cahill Gordon & Reindel
Davis, Shelby Cullom   1952–71
   United States Ambassador to Switzerland
Dorsett, Burt N.   1969–77
   CREF
Dougall, Herbert E.*   1955–59
   Stanford University
Dunckel, Wallis B.   1952–67
   Bankers Trust Company
Durland, Lewis H.   1952–56
   Cornell University
Edwards, Thomas C.   1967–84
   TIAA-CREF
Edwards, William F.*   1959–63
   University of Utah
Ehlers, Walter G.   1983–88
   TIAA-CREF
Foster, Luther H.   1963–83
   Tuskegee Institute
Fowler, Harry W.   1958–78
   Fiduciary Trust Company of New York
Friedman, Benjamin M.*   1978–82
   Harvard University
Friedman, Milton*   1964–68
   University of Chicago
Gage, Charles S.   1959–67
   Yale University
Gilbert, Edes P.   1989–
   The Spence School
Greenough, William C.   1954–84
   TIAA-CREF
Hall, Alan V.   1978–
   Shell International Petroleum Company
Hardin, Clifford M.   1963–66
   University of Nebraska
Heller, Walter W.*   1968–72
   University of Minnesota
Himstead, Ralph E.*   1952–55
   American Association of University Professors
Hoagland, Warren E.   1952–63
   Standard Oil Company (New Jersey)
Ingraham, Mark H.*   1952–53
   University of Wisconsin
Isaacs, Kenneth L.   1952–64
   Massachusetts Investors Trust
Jackson, J. Hugh   1952–59
   Stanford University
Jacob, (Fotheringham) Nancy L.*   1979–
   University of Washington

Kanter, Rosabeth Moss*   1985–89
   Harvard University
Kaufman, George G.*   1982–86
   Loyola University of Chicago
Keeton, Robert E.*   1965–69
   Harvard University
Kirby, Robert G.   1980–
   Capital Guardian Trust Company
Knowles, Marjorie Fine*   1983–
   Georgia State University
Kozmetsky, George   1972–76
   University of Texas
Kreps, Juanita M.   1972–77
   Duke University
Laporte, Cloyd   1952–62
   Dewey, Ballantine, Bushby, Palmer & Wood
Light, Jay O.*   1987–
   Harvard University
Litchfield, Edward H.*   1961–65
   University of Pittsburgh
Lloyd, R. McAllister   1952–68
   TIAA-CREF
Lovell, Robert M., Jr.   1977–
   First Quadrant Corp.
Lumiansky, Robert M.   1966–74
   University of Pennsylvania
MacDonald, James G.   1978–87
   TIAA-CREF
Machlup, Fritz*   1963–67
   Princeton University
Maclean, Joseph B.   1952–57
   Mutual Life Insurance Company
Malkiel, Burton G.*   1969–73
   Princeton University
Mansfield, Richard H.   1953–64
   Lazard Frères & Co.
Martin, James S.   1983–
   TIAA-CREF
McCahan, David   1952–54
   University of Pennsylvania
McRae, Roderick   1955–60
   Bank of New York
Meck, John F.   1967–78
   Dartmouth College
Merton, Robert C.*   1988–
   Harvard University
Milbank, Samuel R.   1952–72
   Wood, Struthers & Winthrop, Inc.
Miller, Paul F., Jr.   1973–80
   Miller, Anderson & Sherrerd
Murray, Roger F.   1956–72
   Columbia University; TIAA-CREF
Newcomer, Mabel*   1952–53
   Vassar College
Parks, W. Robert   1971–83
   Iowa State University
Parsons, Richard D.   1989–
   Dime Savings Bank of New York
Pierpont, Wilbur K.   1957–81
   University of Michigan

Pollock, Thomas C.   1962–70
  New York University
Pynchon, David M.*   1973–77
  Deerfield Academy
Randolph, Francis F.   1952–58
  J. & W. Seligman & Co.
Ross, Stephen A.*   1981–
  Yale University
Samuelson, Paul A.*   1974–85
  Massachusetts Institute of Technology
Sharpe, William F.*   1975–83
  Stanford University
Sneed, Joseph T.*   1967–71
  Duke University
Slichter, Sumner H.*   1952–56
  Harvard University
Spindler, Harry K.   1985–
  State University of New York
Sullivan, Richard H.*   1962–66
  Reed College
Truman, David B.   1982–86
  Mount Holyoke College
Wallis, W. Allen*   1957–61
  University of Chicago
Wells, Herman B   1952–72
  Indiana University
West, Richard R.*   1976–80
  Dartmouth College
Wharton, Clifton R., Jr.   1986–
  TIAA-CREF
Wild, Payson*   1954–58
  Northwestern University
Williams, Dave H.   1981–
  Alliance Capital Management Corporation
Wilson, Charles Z., Jr.*   1971–75
  University of California, Los Angeles
Woolley, Samuel H.   1964–77
  Bank of New York

Balloting for Policyholder-Selected Trustees, 1968–88

TIAA Balloting

Year	Total Votes	Winner	Winner's Discipline
1968	76,777	Juanita M. Kreps	Economics
1969	78,646	James Tobin	Economics
1970	80,202	Joseph E. Slater	History
1971	86,337	Vivian W. Henderson	Economics
1972	85,447	Mary Jean Bowman	Economics
1973	87,294	Leon Bramson	Sociology
1974	89,728	Josephine E. Olson	Economics
1975	92,556	Edward J. Kane	Economics
1976	74,931	Alexander A. Robichek	Finance
1977	110,065	Carolyn Shaw Bell	Economics
1978	116,310	Jack M. Guttentag	Finance
1979	116,273	Myron S. Scholes	Finance
1980	129,236	Phyllis A. Wallace	Economics
1981	129,465	Leonard S. Simon	Business Administration
1982	143,985	Jane G. Elchlepp, M.D.	Medicine
1983	134,447	Henry J. Aaron	Economics
1984	149,228	Robert S. Hamada	Finance
1985	154,890	Donna E. Shalala	Political Science
1986	134,157	Marcus Alexis	Economics
1987	126,505	Estelle A. Fishbein	Law
1988	75,834	Robert C. Clark	Law

CREF Balloting

Year	Total Votes	Winner	Winner's Discipline
1968	56,608	Walter W. Heller	Economics
1969	56,354	Burton G. Malkiel	Economics
1970	61,372	Walter J. Blum	Law
1971	68,822	Charles Z. Wilson, Jr.	Economics
1972	69,450	William Bevan	Psychology
1973	71,998	David M. Pynchon	English
1974	75,832	Paul A. Samuelson	Economics
1975	76,091	William F. Sharpe	Finance
1976	61,412	Richard R. West	Finance
1977	88,987	George J. Benston	Accounting and Finance
1978	93,677	Benjamin M. Friedman	Economics
1979	92,217	Nancy L. Jacob	Finance
1980	100,732	Willard T. Carleton	Finance
1981	99,657	Stephen A. Ross	Economics
1982	115,121	George G. Kaufman	Finance
1983	128,087	Marjorie F. Knowles	Law
1984	114,349	Irma Adelman	Economics
1985	116,237	Rosabeth Moss Kanter	Sociology
1986	107,365	Elizabeth E. Bailey	Economics
1987	99,577	Jay O. Light	Business Administration
1988	63,137	Robert C. Merton	Finance

Name Index

Subject Index

A

AAC; *see* Association of American Colleges

AAUP; *see* American Association of University Professors

ACE; *see* American Council on Education

Active/passive investing, 153–54

Academy of Independent Scholars, 325

Accumulation unit value, CREF
defined, 102
historical values, 160

Actuarial assumptions; *see also* Annuities; Annuity contracts; *and* Mortality tables
CREF units, 98–103
TIAA annuity rates, 31–32, 68–73

Actuarial Society of America, 31

ADEA; *see* Age Discrimination in Employment Act

Age Discrimination in Employment Act of 1967 (ADEA) and amendments, 207–8, 352

American Association of University Professors (AAUP), 19, 23, 116, 187, 213, 316–17, 319–20, 324–25, 360–61; *see also* Statement of Principles, AAUP-AAC
committees on TIAA and CREF
1918, 29–30
1941, 72
1972–73, 226, 275–78, 294–95
and women, fair annuity benefits issue, 294–95

American Council on Education (ACE), 116, 213, 274, 295, 301, 324, 360–61

American Experience Table of Mortality, 40

American Express Company, 4

American Institute of Actuaries, 31

Annuities; *see also* Private pension plans
actuarial difficulties in writing, 31–32, 40, 68–70
and life insurance companies, 41, 68, 72, 132–33, 341

Annuity contracts; *see also* Retirement transition benefit *and* Supplemental retirement annuity
CREF
essential features, 98–103
original restrictions, 104–6
sex-neutral benefits, 302–3
TIAA
Carnegie grant for pre-1936 business losses, 73–74
essential features, 24–26, 28, 68–73
expense loading, 71
graded benefit payment method, 228–30
guaranteed interest rate, 31–32, 69–73
mortality tables, 31–32, 69–73, 303
1941 contract, 71–72
rate changes, 70–72
sex-neutral benefits, 302–3

Annuity unit value, CREF
defined, 102–3
historical values, 161

Arizona Governing Committee case; *see* Norris case

Armstrong investigation, 26–27, 112

Association of American Colleges (AAC), 23, 64, 211, 213, 243, 324; *see also* Statement of Principles, AAUP-AAC